A Time of Change:

Questioning the 'Collapse' of Anuradhapura, Sri Lanka

Keir Magalie Strickland

Archaeopress Archaeology

ARCHAEOPRESS PUBLISHING LTD
Gordon House
276 Banbury Road
Oxford OX2 7ED

www.archaeopress.com

ISBN 978 1 78491 632 9
ISBN 978 1 78491 633 6 (e-Pdf)

© Archaeopress and K M Strickland 2017

All rights reserved. No part of this book may be reproduced, in any form or
by any means, electronic, mechanical, photocopying or otherwise,
without the prior written permission of the copyright owners.

Printed in England by Holywell Press, Oxford
This book is available direct from Archaeopress or from our website www.archaeopress.com

Contents

Preface vii

Chapter 1: Introduction 1
    1.1 Introduction 1
    1.2 Aims 1
    1.3 Significance of the study 2
    1.4 Structure 3

Chapter 2: Anuradhapura: Geography, Environment and History of Research 5
    2.1 Introduction 5
    2.2 The Geographical Context 5
        2.2.1: Geology 5
        2.2.2: Topography 5
        2.2.3: Climate 6
        2.2.4: The Palaeoenvironment 7
    2.3 A History of Research at Anuradhapura 8
        2.3.1: Historical Topography 9
        2.3.2: Research driven archaeology 12
    2.4 Conclusion 13

Chapter 3: Collapse 17
    3.1 Introduction 17
    3.2 What is collapse & what collapses? 17
        3.2.1: What is collapse? 17
        The Collapse 17
        The Aftermath 18
        Diachronic Aspects 18
        3.2.2: What Collapses? 18
    3.3 Collapse Theory 19
    3.4 Collapse Theory in South Asia 20
    3.5 Sri Lankan Collapse Studies 21
    3.5 The "Collapse" of Anuradhapura 22
        3.5.1: The Invasion Model 22
        3.5.2: The Malarial Model 24
        3.5.3: The Imperial Model 26
    3.6 Conclusion 28

Chapter 4: Methodology 29
    4.1 Introduction 29
    4.2: The Datasets 29
        4.2.1: Defining the Citadel 29
        4.2.1.1: The Citadel Dataset 30
        4.2.2: Defining the Sacred City 30
        4.2.3: Defining the Hinterland 31
        4.2.4: The Pali chronicles 33
    4.3 The chronological sequence 33
        4.3.1: The Architectural Sequence 33
        4.3.2: Ceramics as Chronological Indicators 36
        4.3.3: Other Chronological Indicators 36
    4.4 Methodological Approaches to Cultural Change 36
        4.4.1: The Anuradhapura Ceramics 37
    4.5 Population Estimations 39
    4.6 Archaeologically characterising the models 39
        4.6.1: The Invasion Model 40

Chapter 5: The Citadel 57
5.1 Introduction 57
5.2 Population & Monumental Construction 57
5.2.1: The Structural Sequence 57
5.3: Traditional elite 67
5.3.2: Luxury goods 69
5.3.3: Summary 70
5.4: New Elite 70
5.4.1: Violence 70
5.5: Long distance trade, craft specialisation & manufacturing 74
5.5.1: Glazed ceramics 75
5.5.2: Metalworking 79
5.5.3: Glass artefacts (excluding beads) 80
5.5.4: Glass beads 81
5.5.5: Worked and precious stone artefacts 83
5.5.6: Summary 86
5.6: Conclusion 86

Chapter 6: The Sacred City 98
6.1 Introduction 98
6.2: Population & monumental construction 98
6.2.1: The Structural Sequence of the Sacred City 99
6.2.1.1: Period F 99
6.2.1.2: Periods C,D&E 100
6.3: Traditional elite 104
6.3.1: The Padhanaghara Parivena and the rise of Asceticism 105
6.3.2: The Pabbata Vihara & the rise of Mahayanism 105
6.4: New elite 106
6.4.1: Violence 106
6.4.2: A South Indian Influence? 107
6.5: Long distance trade, craft specialisation & manufacturing 108
6.5.1: Imported Artefacts 108
6.5.2: Manufacturing 110
6.6: Conclusion 112

Chapter 7: The Hinterland 124
7.1 Introduction 124
7.2 Population 124
7.3: Traditional Elite 128
7.3.1: Late monastic construction 129
7.4: New Elite 131
7.4.1: South Indian Influence 131
7.4.2: After Collapse 132
7.5: Monumental Construction 132
7.5.1: Monumental monastic architecture within the hinterland 132
7.5.2: The Hydraulic Landscape 132
7.6: Trade and Manufacturing 137
7.6.1: Long Distance Trade 137
7.6.2: Craft Specialisation 137
7.7: Conclusion 137

Chapter 8: The Discussion **147**
    8.1: Introduction 147
    8.2 Does Anuradhapura Collapse? 147
        During Collapse 147
        After Collapse 148
    8.3 Testing the Invasion Model 150
        8.3.1: The Invasion Model – The Citadel 150
        8.3.2: The Invasion Model – The Sacred City 151
        8.3.3: The Invasion Model – The hinterland 152
        8.3.4: The Invasion Model – Summary 153
    8.4 Testing the Malarial Model 153
        8.4.1: The Malarial Model – The Citadel 153
        8.4.2: The Malarial Model – The Sacred City 154
        8.4.3: The Malarial Model – The hinterland 154
        8.4.4: The Malarial Model – Summary 155
    8.5 Testing the Imperial Model 155
        8.5.1: The Imperial Model – The Citadel 155
        8.5.2: The Imperial Model – The Sacred City 156
        8.5.3: The Imperial Model – The hinterland 157
        8.5.4: The Imperial Model – Summary 158
    8.6: The Wider Early Mediaeval Milieu 158
        8.6.1: Mantai 158
        8.6.2: North and East of Sri Lanka 159
        8.6.3: Polonnaruva 160
        8.6.4: Indian Ocean Region 161
    8.7 Anuradhapura's Collapse 161
        8.7.1: The Economic Power of the Sangha 162
        8.7.2: Royal power and legitimation 163
        8.7.3: Theoretical Perspectives 164
        8.7.4: Choosing to Collapse 164
    8.7: Conclusion 165

Chapter 9: Conclusion **175**
    9.1 Introduction 175
    9.2: The Expanded Imperial Model 175
    9.3 Future Directions 176
    9.4 Problems encountered 178
    9.5 Significance of research 178

References **179**

Websites Accessed: **197**

Figures

1.01: The ruins of Jetavana Vihara, Anuradhapura, 1896 (after Cave 1897: Pl.XXXIII) 4

2.01: Sri Lanka within the Indian Ocean (after Coningham et al. 2006: 3) 14

2.02: Topographic map of Sri Lanka (after Coningham et al. 1999: 13) 15

2.03: Schematic diagram of Anuradhapura soilscape with associated land-use and archaeological features (after Simpson et al. 2008b: 30) 16

2.04: H.C.P. Bell at Polonarruva (after Karunaratne 1990: 34) 16

4.01: Plan of Anuradhapura showing Citadel and three primary Buddhist fraternities (after Coningham et al. 1999: 29) 49

4.02: ASW2 plan of the Citadel (after Coningham et al. 1999: 32) 50

4.03: Diagrammatic plan of Anuradhapura (after Coningham et al. 1999: 30) 51

4.04: Anuradhapura hinterland survey area 52

4.05: Anuradhapura Hinterland survey results by site type (after Coningham and Gunawardhana 2013) ... 53

4.06: Diagrammatic layout of pabbata viharas (after Bandaranayake 1974: 68) 54

4.07: Diagrammatic layout of pancayatana parivena (after Bandaranayake 1974: 87) 55

4.08: Example of double-platform site (after Wijesuriya 1998: 59) 56

5.01: Southern section of ASW2 trench, with strata of structural periods displayed along the left axis (after Coningham et al. 1999: 87) 88

5.02: Plan of structural period F (after Coningham 1999: 111) 89

5.03: Elevation of Period F pillared hall (after Coningham 1999: 113) 90

5.04: Plan of structural phase D&E of ASW2 (after Coningham 1999: 116) 91

5.05: Plan of Building A (after Paranavitana 1936: 07) 92

5.06: Plan of Gedige (after Bandaranayake 1974: 204) 93

5.07: Plan of Structural Phase B1 (after Coningham et al. 1999: 119) 94

5.08: Plan of Structural Phase B3 (after Coningham et al. 1999: 120) 95

5.09: Plan of period B street (after Ayrton 1924: 51) 96

5.10: ASW2 Faunal Assemblage by Class (after Young et al. 2006) 96

5.11: ASW2 metal artefacts by type (after Coningham & Harrison 2006: 27-76) 97

6.01: The Sacred City, Anuradhapura (after Wijesuriya 1998: 172 & Bandaranayake 1974: 34) 114

6.02: ASW2 structural periods and Abhayagiri Vihara Project typological periods 115

6.03: Anuradhapura's Hydraulic Network (after Nicholas 1960; Seneviratna 1989: 94) 116

6.04: Example of double-platform monastery from the Western Monasteries (after Wijesuriya 1998: 56) 117

6.05: Example of a decorated urinal stone from the Western Monasteries (after Bell 1914d: Plates IV & V) 118

6.06: Site plan of Puliyankulama (after Wijesuriya 1998: 54) 119

6.07: Bronze of Indra recovered from Puliyankulama (after Bell 1914c: Plate DD) 120

6.08: 10th century Durga statue from Anuradhapura (ex situ) 121

6.09: Stucco heads from Building 21, Pankuliya & Building 11 of the "Hindu Ruins" (after Bell 1914a: Plates XXIX, XXX; Bell 1914b: Plate XXXV) 121

6.10: 10th century Sri Lankan bronze seated Buddha, found in Thailand (image ref. von Schroeder 1990: 206) 122

6.11: 9th and 10th century Sacred City ornamental pillar capitals (after Bandaranayake 1974: 349) 123

6.12: Evolution of balustrades and guardstones (after Bandaranayake 1974: 335) 123

7.01: Map of Hinterland sites discussed in Chapter 7 (image by author) 139

7.02: Site B009 showing postholes of single structural phase (image by Anuradhapura Hinterland project) 140

7.03: Depth of cultural material at F102 140

7.04: SF1647 Polonnaruva style appliqué ware (image from Anuradhapura Hinterland project) 141

7.05: Trench at A155 (Veheragala) showing structural sequence (image from Anuradhapura Hinterland project) .. 142

7.06: Map of padhanaghara pariveṇa sites (after Wijesuriya 1998: 171) 143

7.07: Section showing tile collapse in moat of C112 (image from Anuradhapura Hinterland project) 144

7.08: Thirappane cascade system (after Jayatilaka et al. 2001: 02) 145

7.09: Site Plan of Ritagala (after Wijesuriya 1998: 192) 146

8.01: Distribution of Epigraphia Zeylanica inscriptions (image ref: author) 170

8.02: Distribution of Epigraphia Zeylanica inscriptions (image ref: author) 171

8.03: Positive feedback loop of alienation of Royal power 172

8.04: Graphic visualisation of exchange between monarchy and sangha 172

8.05: The marginal product of increasing complexity in Greek agriculture (image ref. Tainter 1988: 97) 172

8.06: Parenthetical flow chart of Anuradhapura's collapse (after Phillips 1979; Renfrew 1987; Tainter 1988; Mortazavi 2004) 173

8.07: Mobility of Sri Lanka's Capitals (Image by author) 174

Tables

4.02: Anuradhapura Hinterland transect survey sites 32
4.03: Late chronologically significant ASW2 coarseware forms 36
4.04: Functions of diagnostic ceramic types from ethnographic parallels found in modern Anuradhapura District, Sri Lanka (after Davis 2008: 35) 38
4.05: Coarse-wares ceramic types by function (after Davis 2008: 36) 39
4.06: The Invasion Model's Archaeological Signature 46
4.07: The Malarial Model's Archaeological Signature 47
4.08: The Imperial Model's Archaeological Signature 48
5.01: ASW2 Faunal Assemblage (after Young et al. 2006: 592) 63
5.02: Major exploited species (after Young et al. 2006: 592) 64
5.03: Other species identified in periods B through F (after Young et al. 2006: 593-595) 65
5.04: The functional groups of coarsewares at ASW2 by Structural Period (after Coningham et al. 2006) 68
5.05: Total weight and sherd count of coarsewares at ASW2 by period 69
5.07: ASW2 Metal artefacts by type (after Coningham & Harrison 2006: 27-76) 70
5.08: Human Remains at ASW2 (after Knusel et al. 2006) 71
5.09: Appliqué ware sherds from Alahana Parivena, Polonnaruva 73
5.10: Appliqué ware sherds from ASW2, Anuradhapura 73
5.11: Origin of glazed ceramics at ASW2 by period (after Seely et al. 2006) 75
5.12: West Asian glazed wares at ASW2 (after Seely et al. 2006) 76
5.13: East Asian glazed wares at ASW2 (after Seely et al. 2006) 78
5.14: Evidence of late metalworking at ASW2 (after McDonnell et al. 2006) 79
5.15: Glass Artefacts recovered from ASW2 80
5.16: Geographical source of ASW2 glass vessel fragments (after Coningham 2006: 333-376) 81
5.17: ASW2 glass bead assemblage (after Coningham 2006) 82
5.19: Geographic source of ASW2 stone artefacts (after Coningham et al. 2006) 83
5.20: Stone artefact forms at ASW2 (after Coningham et al. 2006) 84
5.21: ASW2 stone types (after Coningham et al. 2006) 85
6.01: The Bhojanasalas of Anuradhapura (after Bandaranayake 1974: 297) 101
6.02: The Major Urban Tanks of Anuradhapura (modern state) 103
6.03: Clay "bullets" from Abhayagiri Vihara Project site one (after Wikramagamage 1984: 10) 107
6.04: Abhayagiri Vihara Project glazed ceramics (after Bouzek et al. 1993: 87) 109
6.05: Jetavanaramaya Project Bead Assemblage (after Ratnayake 1984: 115-116) 111
6.06: The Sacred City's Archaeological Signature 113
7.01: Anuradhapura Hinterland Survey Ceramic Scatters 125
7.02: Size and sherd density of Transect Survey Ceramic Scatter sites 126
7.03: Late chronologically significant ASW2 coarseware forms 127
7.04: Monastic Sites identified on transect survey 128
7.05: Yoda-elas of the North Central Province (after Seneviratna 1989: 92) 136
7.06: The Hinterland's Archaeological Signature 138
8.01: Anuradhapura's Archaeological Signature 166
8.02: The Invasion Model's Archaeological Signature 167
8.03: The Malarial Model's Archaeological Signature 168
8.04: The Imperial Model's Archaeological Signature 169

Preface

This book represents the publication of my doctoral thesis and while I have edited, nipped and tucked, and expanded some sections, I have resisted the urge to extensively rewrite. Consequently, the structure of the original thesis remains, with its data heavy chapters and a focus upon methodology. However, I believe this "showing of my workings" has value, as I have written before (Strickland 2011) regarding the methodological challenges that archaeologists face in studying societal transformation and "collapse".

The text reassesses the Early Mediaeval "collapse" of Anuradhapura, Sri Lanka, through explicit reference to the archaeological record. The study of Anuradhapura's terminal period has been dominated by a reliance upon textual sources, resulting in a monocausal and politically charged narrative depicting an eleventh century invasion by the South Indian Cholas as resulting directly in the collapse of Anuradhapura (Codrington 1960), bringing to an end over a millennium of rule from Sri Lanka's first capital. Such is the dominance of this collapse narrative, few alternative explanations for the abandonment of Anuradhapura have been posited, and just two alternative collapse models, a "malarial" model (Nicholls 1921; Still 1930) and an "imperial" model (Spencer 1983; Indrapala 2005), have been propounded. This book thus aims to test whether Anuradhapura truly "collapses", and to test the established model for this apparent collapse.

After archaeologically defining collapse, the three collapse models are synthesised and translated into archaeological signatures (archaeologically visible characteristics and sequences). This book then presents and analyses data from over a century of archaeological investigations at Anuradhapura, focussing upon the datasets of the ASW2 excavations within its Citadel (Coningham et al. 1999 & 2006) and the recent Anuradhapura Hinterland Project (Coningham & Gunawardana 2013) survey of the hinterland. The data is summarised and presented graphically, facilitating comparison with the theoretical archaeological signatures of the three collapse models. The presence or absence of the archaeological characteristics of collapse are identified in each zone, testing whether Anuradhapura actually collapsed. The archaeological signatures of collapse for each of the three zones are then compared with the anticipated signatures developed from the three collapse models, before, finally, the archaeological "collapse" of Anuradhapura is related to collapse theory in an attempt to best understand the underlying dynamic processes

Chapter 1: Introduction

"Anuradhapura is emphatically a city of the dead. Scarce a step can be taken, but they eye falls upon some memorial of the past. The mounds one carelessly passes are the sepulchres of Kings; the bricks that the foot strikes the remains of palaces... Amidst a silence as profound as that of the grave, rise the colossal remains of a city whose walls were 64 miles in circumference, once echoed with the merry voices of children, while processions of kings and priests wound along the broad pavements of the now deserted courts..."

(Liesching 1869: 193)

1.1 Introduction

The ancient city of Anuradhapura was the capital of Sri Lanka for over a millennium; its massive stupas rising over the jungle, its gigantic reservoirs turning an arid land green and its Kings and Queens ruling over the island of Sri Lanka. Pilgrims came all the way from China (Hulagalle 2005: 14), envoys were sent to Emperor Claudius in Rome (ibid.: 2), traders from all across the Indian Ocean and the Near East (Coningham 1999 & 2006), and on several occasions rival kingdoms sent soldiers to sack the city (Mvs; Cvs). After its 11th century collapse, Anuradhapura lay undisturbed for nearly a thousand years in ruins, drowning beneath the roots and leaves of the jungle tide, until the nineteenth century when the British began the active re-colonisation of the island's dry-zone and initiated more than a century of archaeological research on Anuradhapura.

If the past truly is another country, then nowhere, and nowhen, attracts as many visitors as the "lost" or "dead" civilisations of the past; Ancient Rome, the Khmer, the Maya, the Indus, Mesopotamia, Ancient Egypt, Mycenae... These are names that resonate through the ages, conjuring images of huge cities, majestic monuments, and breathtaking feats of engineering and architecture that still inspire us today.

Certainly in Sri Lanka the halcyonised era of Anuradhapura has remained very much a part of the public consciousness (see Coningham & Lewer 1999 for a full discussion); appearing on stamps, bank-notes as well as being a major centre of international Buddhist pilgrimage and a UNESCO World Heritage Site.

In May 2009 the Sri Lankan government declared victory over the Liberation Tigers of Tamil Eelam (LTTE), bringing to an end a civil insurgency lasting three decades. However, while this insurgency officially started in the 1980s, factions upon either side of the conflict have long used archaeology to root this ethnic conflict in the events of the first millennium AD (Tambiah 1986; Coningham & Lewer 1999 & 2000), and a key aspect of this politically charged narrative is the eleventh century collapse of Sri Lanka's first capital, Anuradhapura, recorded in the great Pali chronicles of Sri Lanka (Mvs; Cvs; Geiger 1928 & 1934).

The capital of Sri Lanka for over a millennium, Anuradhapura was a major Indian Ocean centre. Broadly divided into a fortified Citadel, a surrounding monastic zone (the Sacred City) and hinterland, it remains highly politicised and idealised today (ibid.). A key element of this public consciousness is the widely accepted explanation for the city's Early Mediaeval collapse, recorded in the Culavamsa, one of the great Pali chronicles of Sri Lanka (Geiger 1929 & 1934). This describes an eleventh-century sacking by an invading Cola army, leaving Anuradhapura "violently destroyed" (Cvs.lv.21), bringing to an end nearly 1500 years of Buddhist rule from Anuradhapura, and leaving the city in ruins (see Fig. 1.01).

This "sacking" has been integrated into the narrative of the civil conflict, portrayed as a clash of religions and ethnicities; the Saivite Tamils invading and destroying the golden age of the Sinhalese Buddhists (Coningham & Lewer 1999 & 2000). As an anonymous Tamil historian wrote recently; "Archaeology has always been political in Sri Lanka" (cited in Page 2010), and it is sadly impossible for the archaeologist to control how their findings are used, or who they are used by.

However, the "collapse" of Anuradhapura has never been archaeologically investigated, let alone verified, indeed this "collapse" could conceivably be argued to be a transformation or transition resulting in a religious and geographical shift (this, and other alternatives to "collapse" will be discussed in greater detail in Chapter Three). Instead the Pali chronicles have been awarded great credibility within Sri Lankan archaeology and history, in the words of one excavator; "to study the history of Ancient Anuradhapura, the data available in the Pali chronicles is invaluable" (Ratnayake 2008: 158). Although they are undoubtedly valuable resources, the over-reliance and unquestioning acceptance of the vamsas has had a huge, and arguably stultifying, effect on the study of the "demise" of the Anuradhapura period.

1.2 Aims

The two core aims of this volume are to establish whether or not Anuradhapura can actually be said to have "collapsed", and to test the propounded explanations for this apparent collapse against the archaeological record. These aims will be achieved through analysing the archaeological data produced by over a century of research at Anuradhapura, and utilising this data to test the three existing models for Anuradhapura's collapse. These are the monocausal Invasion Model of the vamsas, as advocated for example by Geiger (1929) or Codrington (1960), the Malarial Model advocated by Nicholls (1921) and Still (1930), and the synthetic Imperial Model as advocated by Spencer (1976 & 1983) and Indrapala (2005). All three of these models are based primarily upon textual studies of the vamsas and epigraphic data, and all three models identify the Cola invasion as the primary cause for the initial collapse of Anuradhapura. They are thus representative of the general consensus view that the eleventh century Cola invasion ended "the golden era of Sri Lankan history" (Dias 1990: 151).

1.3 Significance of the study

Geographically and culturally, Sri Lanka is a distinct regional unit within South Asian archaeology, and one that has been studied and investigated for over a century. However, the collapse of Anuradhapura itself has typically been confined to a postscript or footnote within the island's history. This is even more notable within the archaeological literature, with almost all of the focus formerly placed upon identifying sites mentioned in the Pali chronicles (or vamsas) of the Island (Ayrton 1924; Hocart 1924; Paranavitana 1936), and latterly upon the origins (Coningham 1999) or fluorescence of Anuradhapura (Deraniyagala 1957; Deraniyagala 1972, 1986; Coningham et al. 2007). Consequently, analysis of Anuradhapura's final phase has been confined to brief descriptive accounts of "squatter occupation" in the city's final structural phases; "ephemeral mud structures in the foundations of which fragments of the older buildings were freely used" (Paranavitana 1936: 03), none of which were recorded in detail.

The study of Anuradhapura's collapse has, therefore, been dominated by historians, in turn leading to explanations that are founded upon the vamsas. Such explanations do not all presuppose the complete accuracy of the great Pali chronicles, but they are guided by their dependency upon the vamsas and their lack of alternative data sources. This has resulted in a research environment where the most detailed examinations of Early Mediaeval Sri Lanka are to be found in studies of Cola warfare (Spencer 1976 & 1983) or Tamil ethnic identity (Indrapala 2005), works written by scholars whose primary research interests are external to Anuradhapura.

However, while these works are of good quality, it is a reflection on the field that the most detailed accounts of Anuradhapura's collapse are within works focussed externally, where the collapse is almost incidental. This same lack of research focus can be seen in other examples of hegemonic decline and urban collapse in Early Mediaeval South Asia, such as the thirteenth century collapse of the Colas (Heitzman 1987) or the fourteenth century collapse of Polonnaruva (Seneviratna 1998).

The few studies that have paid attention to Anuradhapura's collapse were primarily carried out before the outbreak of violence (e.g. Nicholls 1921; Still 1930; Codrington 1960; Spencer 1976 & 1983) and in the subsequent years the disciplines of archaeology and collapse studies have made great advances in both theory and practice (e.g. scientific dating, geoarchaeology, geophysics etc.). Furthermore, a huge quantity of new archaeological data has been generated for Anuradhapura's hinterland by the Anuradhapura Hinterland survey (Coningham & Gunawardhana 2013) within which I carried out five seasons of transect- survey and excavation, as well as for the Citadel by the ASW2 excavations (Coningham 1999 & 2006). Consequently, an archaeological re-evaluation of Anuradhapura's collapse has the potential to be extremely rewarding, not to mention timely. Such a study would be of significance to historians and archaeologists in Sri Lanka, and indeed South Asia as a whole.

However, such a study has greater potential than simply casting new light upon Anuradhapura's collapse, it could also greatly contribute to the archaeological study of collapse, and the formulation of archaeological collapse theory. Scholars have discussed collapse for millennia, unfortunately however, archaeology has arguably never fully engaged with the subject, and archaeological collapse studies have become increasingly marginalised over the past 50 years. Almost as if, as archaeologists, we have become so trained in the reconstruction of ruins and the reading of debris that we now focus automatically upon the mature form of any subject we study. This has left the archaeological world focussed upon the emergences, developments and golden-ages of civilisations and their cities. For example, one recent reprint of an archaeological textbook, Patterns in Prehistory (Wenke 2006), devoted over 350 pages to the origins and emergence of complex societies all over the world, over a period of nearly 10,000 years, but less than 10 pages to the theme of collapse. Fagan's People of the Earth (Fagan 2007) was little better and throughout excavation reports, books on any past civilisation, city or people; the focus seems again and again to be on emergences, rather than endings.

Despite this imbalance of focus, there is still a credible body of collapse theory examining how and why civilisations collapsed but within archaeology it is restricted to specific examples of societal collapse, predominantly that of the Maya (e.g. Culbert 1973; Sabloff 1973; Hammond 1977; Phillips 1979; Gill 2000; Lucero 2002; Webster 2002; Haug et al. 2003). In turn, the study of universal collapse theories has become dominated by academics from disciplines such as ecology, history, anthropology or sociology (e.g. Turchin 2003 or Diamond 2005, both primarily ecologists). During my master's thesis, back in 2005, I attempted to test several global the collapse models of Tainter (1988), Turchin (2003), and Diamond (2005) through explicit reference to the archaeological record of six sites from three world civilisations (Strickland 2011).

However, despite all being comprehensively examined, excavated, and indeed published, there was simply insufficient archaeological data from the periods in question. In the conclusion I highlighted the need for archaeological data generation for collapse theory (Strickland 2011: 137). It is not enough to consider the issue as an afterthought when writing up the site report. The question must be there at the beginning of any such project and must be incorporated into the research design. This volume thus has the potential to act as an exemplar for archaeological collapse studies, integrating high level collapse theory (e.g. Tainter 1988) with the archaeological record, thus enabling the formation of archaeological collapse theory.

1.4 Structure

Having thus introduced the aims, content and significance of the study, Chapter Two will now lay the academic foundations for this volume by placing Anuradhapura into an environmental, geographical and academic context. Chapter Three will then define "collapse" as well as establishing "what" collapses, before setting out the history of collapse studies in South Asia, and finally examining the three models propounded for Anuradhapura's collapse; Chapter Four will set out the methodology to be used in testing the three models against the archaeological record of Anuradhapura, before Chapters Five, Six and Seven present the archaeological data from Anuradhapura's Citadel, Sacred City, and hinterland respectively. Having presented the data, Chapter Eight will attempt to answer the twin aims of the thesis, first establishing whether or not Anuradhapura collapses, before comparing the data with each of the three models, as set out in Chapter Four. Finally, Chapter Nine will conclude the volume by relating the collapse of Anuradhapura to collapse theory, and suggesting future research directions.

Fig.1.01: The ruins of Jetavana Vihara, Anuradhapura, 1896
(after Bell 1914a: Pl.V.a)

Chapter 2: Anuradhapura: Geography, Environment and History of Research

2.1 Introduction

It should be noted that the North Central Province is an area defined by modern political boundaries, and thus is a somewhat artificial construct to impose upon the geography of Early Mediaeval Sri Lanka. However, for the purposes of this background it is a more precise and functional area than the more ephemeral "kingdom", especially as the geographical limits of political rule and influence were rarely fixed, and indeed shifted greatly over the Anuradhapura period (Cartman 1957: 23 – 40).

2.2 The Geographical Context

The tropical Indian Ocean island of Sri Lanka has been strategically important for almost two millennia due to its central location within the Indian Ocean (Deraniyagala 1992 vol.II: 484), providing access to trade networks stretching to the Persian Gulf in the West and Southeast Asia to the East (Basham 1973: 14; Tampoe 1995: 160),. As a result, it has attracted a number of colonial European powers, and from 1505 to 1948 the island was ruled successively by the Portuguese (1505-1658), the Dutch (1658-1795), and finally the British (1795-1948), before achieving independence in 1948 (Cartman 1957: 41 - 60). Today, the island is divided into nine administrative provinces, of which North Central Province (NCP) is one. Each province is further subdivided into districts, in the case of the NCP Anuradhapura District and Polonnaruva District. The NCP covers a total of 10,531km^2, with 7,128km^2 in the Anuradhapura District and 3,403km^2 in the Polonnaruva District. NCP effectively corresponds to the kingdom of Rajarata, centred as it is around the ancient cities of Anuradhapura and Polonnaruva. The modern city of Anuradhapura, lying on the banks of the Malvatu Oya, is located immediately southeast of the archaeological ruins of ancient Anuradhapura. Although it is now estimated to have a population of over 800,000 (http://www.statistics.gov.lk/PopHouSat), the area was near abandoned when the British first arrived with an "urban" population of just 702 in 1871 (Christie 1891: 38).

2.2.1: Geology

As seen in figure 2.01, the island lies just 50km off the south coast of India (Deraniyagala 1992 vol.II: 481) and geologically speaking is a southern continuation of the Indian Deccan Massif (Peiris 1977: 4), separated from the subcontinent by the Palk Strait (de Silva 1977: 2) across which a chain of small islands known as Adam's Bridge stretch. It is thought that the narrow strip of sea that now divides Sri Lanka from India formed during the Miocene around 12 million years ago (Coningham 1999: 7).

The geology of the island is dominated by crystalline Precambrian rocks and can broadly be divided into two geological zones, the Highland and Vijayan Series (Peiris 1977: 4). The Highland Series consist of highly metamorphosed sedimentary rocks and form a spine 50 to 100 miles wide running from the southwest of the island, through the centre of the island, and up to the northeastern coast. On either side of this "spine" are found the younger Vijayan Series, formed by the granitisation and migmatisation of rocks from the Highland Series and consisting of various granites, gneisses and migmatites (*ibid.*: 5).

Sri Lanka's crystalline rocks are ideally suitable for structural use, possessing both durability and strength (Cooray 1984: 231-232). Marbles, particularly the dolomitic marbles of the Western Vijayan Complex and the Highland Series, have been used extensively due to their attractive appearance and the ease with which they are worked (Coningham 1999: 8). Granite, quartzite and garnetiferous gneiss have all also been used in construction (*ibid.*). It is generally accepted that dolomite limestones were utilised structurally and artistically before granite and garnetiferous gneiss came into use (*ibid.*), something seen at both Sigiriya (Bandaranayake 1984: 15) and Anuradhapura (Coningham 1999: 8). It has been argued that this is because limestone would have been easier to work, while the harder rocks could only be worked once new tools and techniques had been developed (Wijesekera 1962: 179).

Sri Lanka is also a rich source of gemstones, with corundum (ruby and sapphire), beryl (aquamarine), chrysoberyl (alexandrite and cat's eye), spinel, topaz, tourmaline, garnet, zircon, quartz (amethyst and citrine) and feldspar (moonstone) all found in the southwestern gemfields (Cooray 1984: 241-249). All of these were used during the Anuradhapura Period, with varied examples being found at Polonnaruva, Sigiriya, Tissamaharama, the Sacred City of Anuradhapura, and almost all being found archaeologically within the ASW2 excavations in Anuradhapura's Citadel (Coningham 1999: 8).

2.2.2: Topography

The geological assemblages described above have been folded, ruptured, faulted, and weathered over millions of years, forming Sri Lanka's diverse surface morphology. The south-central zone of the island is dominated by a roughly triangular area of mountains, the Central Highlands, which taper off towards the northeastern coast through a series of low ridges (Peiris 1977: 8).

Anuradhapura lies in the north-central lowlands of the island (shown in figure 2.02). These lowland plains are less than 30m above sea level (ASL) and stretching across to the western coast (Cooray 1984: 49), are transversed by a series of rivers that rise in the foothills of the Central Highlands and run out to the coast in the northwest as can be seen in figure 2.02. Most of these rivers do not run to any significant length, though the Malvatu Oya, rising in the higher ground northwest of Sigiriya, runs northwest for 332km, ending in the lagoons below Mantai (Wright 1999: 154). This river, along with the Kala Oya and Modaragam Aru, dominates the drainage system of the Anuradhapura region, with the ancient city of Anuradhapura lying on the western bank of the Malvatu Oya.

While the plains are relatively even, Anuradhapura's hinterland is characterised by a gently undulating topography that rises from west to east, with isolated granite erosion remnants or inselbergs forming dramatic hills in places. Mihintale (309m ASL) and Ritagala (766m ASL) being well known examples (Coningham 1999: 7). As well as these dramatic outcrops there are also a large number of smaller granite outcrops running roughly parallel in a north-south alignment across the landscape. These outcrops are numerous and although the majority are low, often no more than exposed rock at ground level, there are a considerable number of larger outcrops. This undulating riverine landscape is schematically illustrated in figure 2.03.

2.2.3: Climate

Despite Sri Lanka's relatively small size, the island can be divided into two distinct zones: a Dry Zone and a Wet Zone (Coningham & Strickland 2007). The Wet Zone is characterised by an average annual rainfall of over 1900mm and incorporates the southwest and the centre of the island (*ibid.*). The Dry Zone covers the remaining two-thirds of the island and is characterised by low level dry plains that stretch from the far north of the island, down the east coast and to the far south (*ibid.*). This zone has sometimes been further subdivided through the addition of a third area, the Arid Zone (Cook 1932; Bailey 1952). This term is applied to areas with an average annual rainfall of less than 1250mm the Arid Zone, thus incorporating the northwest coast and the far southeast (Tennakoon 1980). The climate of Sri Lanka is influenced by its proximity to the Indian sub-continent, its insularity, and the presence of a central mountain mass within the island (Peiris 1977: 12). As a result of these factors the island has an oceanic climate that is nevertheless heavily influenced by both the South-West Monsoon (SWM) and North-East Monsoon (NEM) (Coningham 1999: 9). These monsoon periods last over half the year and neatly divide the climatic year into four, with two dry seasons and two wet seasons. Although the dates of the seasons vary somewhat across Sri Lanka, the northern Dry Zone sees the SWM wet season run from around March – May, and the NEM wet season from around October – December (Simpson et al. 2008b). It is important to stress that this data is taken from recent readings, and are merely representative of the island's climate; palaeoenvironmental research has shown that there have been fluctuations and shifts in climate within the past two millennia (e.g. Agnihotri et al. 2002; Yadava et al. 2004; Sinha et al. 2005; Caner et al. 2006; Maher & Hu 2006; Gunnell et al. 2007). As such, modern rainfall figures are only an indication of levels of magnitude, and as a guide to the underpinnings of the island's climate. The palaeoenvironment is discussed in greater detail shortly in section **2.2.4**.

The average annual rainfall for the Dry Zone as a whole is around 1900mm but falls as low as 750mm in the coastal strip between Mannar and Puttalam (Somasekaram 1988), which is the lowest (driest) in the country. Recent meteorological data from the Maha Illuppallamma Agricultural Research Station (located within Anuradhapura's hinterland) recorded an average annual rainfall of ca. 1490mm with an average annual evapotranspiration of ca. 2453mm (Jayatilaka et al. 2001: 3), an evapotranspiration rate exceeding the average monthly precipitation throughout the year except for during the main wet-season of the NEM (October – December) (Jayatilaka et al. 2003; Shaw & Sutcliffe 2003). Additionally the underlying crystalline rocks have a low porosity, and are close to the surface, leading to an extremely high run-off of around 38% of all water falling in the Dry Zone (Cooray 1984: 256). Furthermore, of the rivers in the Dry Zone only the Mahaveli Ganga has a perennial flow (Coningham 1999: 9).

All of these factors combine to create an environment in which the planned management of water is vital to the support of any sedentary population, particularly of an urban nature. Because rainfall is limited to specific "wet" seasons, with quite severe water deficits for the rest of the year, water storage (natural or artificial) is of the utmost importance. There are a variety of manners in which water is stored naturally, ranging from aquifers and 'rock cisterns' to natural pools known as *villus* (Cooray 1984). However, aquifers and similar geological structures are limited in Sri Lanka and it is estimated that only 10% of rainfall within the Dry Zone is stored within aquifers, where it can be reached through the construction of wells ranging in depth between 3-12m (*ibid.*). Such wells are relatively uncommon though within the dry zone as many of these aquifers do not store water year round, drying up in the dry seasons. In the area around Anuradhapura there are discrete bands of fractured rock which act as localised aquifers, but they are far from common (Coningham 1999: 9), and exploitation of such aquifers is uncommon, with most wells instead located below village tank and bunds, or alongside irrigation canals where they can tap into water draining from these hydraulic systems (Cooray 1984: 257). Rainfall is also sometimes stored naturally in natural "cisterns" located on the granite outcrops and boulders that mark the landscape, but these are very limited in size, and again do not store water throughout the year (Coningham & Allchin 1995). Finally rainwater is sometimes found stored in natural clay-lined pools (*villus*) in the west of the Anuradhapura region but again there are relatively few of these (Deraniyagala 1992: 372) and they are generally small in size (Parker 1909: 360).

2.2.4: The Palaeoenvironment

As will be seen in Chapter Three, a common model for collapse is that of the "environmental model" – usually invoking some catastrophic environmental event or shift as a prime mover. However, this has never been proposed in Sri Lanka, even after over fifty years of such models being applied to South Asian collapse studies (e.g. Sahni 1956; Raikes 1964; Dales 1966; Raikes 1967; Raikes 1968; Rafique Mughal 1992; Dales et al. 1997). This is presumably in part due to the paucity of any palaeoenvironmental research carried out in Sri Lanka, though there is currently no reason to invoke environmental factors. This book will be utilising new data from geoarchaeological investigations carried out as part of the Anuradhapura Hinterland survey (Coningham & Gunawardhana 2013), though this research has focussed upon issues of land usage and management rather than those of climate change, the first such work to be carried out in Sri Lanka. Indeed, though more work has been done on Sri Lanka's palaeoclimate than on human management of the landscape, it has been recognised that there is practically "*no tradition of studying Late Quaternary vegetation and climate history*" (Premathilake & Risberg 2003: 1525). A current project investigating high-resolution speleothem study of monsoon variability in the Holocene of Sri Lanka has recently been started by Dr. Kathleen Johnson of the University of California, Irvine, and offers the potential for an extremely fine resolution mapping of rainfall fluctuations over the past 2000 years (Johnson 2008 *pers. comm.*), but unfortunately, no preliminary results are available at this time.

From the studies that have been carried out, it is possible make some limited statements regarding Sri Lanka's palaeoenvironment. A preliminary palynological examination of sediments from the Potana cave at Sigiriya indicated that around 3700 BC a slightly more humid climate would have prevailed (Premathilake & Caratini 1994: 10). More recently (in Sri Lanka's environmental history) a limited and somewhat brief investigation into fluvial sediments from Ratnapura (in the south central area of Sri Lanka within the "wet" zone) suggested that *Syzygium* spp (a genus of flowering shrubs and evergreen trees belonging to the myrtle family) dominated the forests of the middle Pleistocene (Mittre & Robert 1965), while research at a lagoon on the south west coast produced a 5m long sediment core covering approximately the last 800 years, that indicated the area was dominated by mangrove forests during the early mediaeval period (Thanikaomoni 1985: 75). However, all of these studies have worked within broad chronological frameworks, as well as in the main focussing upon much older periods than the period of interest here. Thanikaomoni's findings (1985) are of the right period, but of no real significance.

One of the more recent studies that has attempted to describe Late Quaternary climate changes within a tighter chronological framework was a palynological study of the Horton Plains (Premathilake & Risberg 2003; Premathilake 2006). This consisted of a single 6m core retrieved from the Horton Plains (c.2200m ASL) in the central hill country area of Sri Lanka (Premathilake & Risberg 2003: 1525). This is admittedly a distinctly different climatic zone from Anuradhapura, but due to the shallow nature of sediments in the dry zones, and steep geomorphology of much of the rest of the island, the Horton Plains are one of the few areas suitable for stratigraphic palynological investigations (Premathilake & Risberg 2003: 1526).

The study was able to identify climate changes over the course of approximately the last 24,000 years. Broadly speaking the results suggested that the period from 24,000 – 18,500 BP was characterised by a semi-arid climate, followed by increasing humidity (rain fall), peaking around 13,000 BP before decreasing from the beginning of the tenth millennium BC until the middle of the fourth, resulting in a semi arid environment once again (*ibid.*: 1536). This was followed by an increase in rain fall again across the first and second millennia BC, before again falling off to a relatively dry last 2000 years, marked only by two episodes of significantly high rainfall, both of which fall well after the Anuradhapura period and are associated with the onset of the industrial revolution and the Mediaeval Warm Period (*ibid.*: 1538). However, the chronological framework of this study was formed around fourteen bulk samples from the peat, dated by radiocarbon age determination (ibid.: 1527) and it should be noted that such dates are not always reliable and are open to contamination leading to dates that are too young (Olsson 1974; Possnert 1990) or too old (Nilsson et al. 2001). Additionally, around 3000 BP, several of Premathilake and Risberg's calibrated dates are inverted (i.e. earlier dates are found stratigraphically above later dates and vice versa) (Premathilake and Risberg 2003: 1529). This, added to a highly variable rate of accumulation (*ibid.*) results in a very unstable chronological framework, and greatly weakens any conclusions drawn from the study.

These findings have been mirrored by studies in southern India (e.g. Caner et al. 2006), but the resolution of such studies is extremely poor, and all that can be said is that throughout the Early Mediaeval period; "*the South West*

Monsoon was relatively weak" (Premathilake & Risberg 2003: 1538), and that there was an event around the fourteenth century AD marked by strong rainfall and corresponding with the shift from the Mediaeval Warm Period (Morrill et al. 2003: 472), normally dated to between 900 – 1300 AD (Karlén et al. 1999a & 1999b; Jones et al. 2001; Gunnarsson & Linderholm 2002), to what is commonly referred to as the "Little Ice Age" (Morrill et al. 2003: 472). However, such terms are far from helpful due to the temporal and spatial inconsistency displayed in climate change, with records from these periods displaying immense variation in both the timing of these climatic events, and their actual climatic effect (Grove 1988; Bradley & Jones 1993; Hughes & Diaz 1994; Mann et al. 1999; Crowley & Lowery 2000; Morrill et al. 2003).

Palaeoclimatic research from the wider area of South Asia (e.g. Yadava et al. 2004; Yadava & Ramesh 2005; Caner et al. 2006; Gunnell et al. 2007), the Middle East (e.g. Fleitmann et al. 2003), East Asia (e.g. Gasse et al. 1991; Liu et al. 2004; Maher & Hu 2006) and North Africa (e.g. de Menocal et al. 2000) has established that, as highlighted in the Horton Plains palynological core (Premathilake & Risberg 2003; Premathilake 2006) there was a significant and abrupt shift in the SWM across both South and South-East Asia during the fourteenth century (Morrill et al. 2003: 469-472). However, this change was spatially heterogeneous, in that rainfall dramatically increased in some areas (e.g. Sri Lanka and east-central China) while dramatically decreasing in others (e.g. Tibet, the Arabian Sea, north-east China and Taiwan) (*ibid.*: 469). This variation in rainfall change clearly demonstrates how complicated the transposition of palaeoclimatic change from other regions to Sri Lanka is.

Despite these issues, a small number of studies of Holocene monsoon variation in southern India offer not only a far greater chronological resolution, but are also from the same climatic region as Sri Lanka's North Central Province, and these studies have great potential for illuminating climate change in Sri Lanka due to the huge influence the South-West (SWM) and North-East (NEM) Monsoons have on the regions climate. One such recent study of interest (Gunnell et al. 2007) attempts to link climate change to socioeconomic change in southeast India during the Holocene. While such theories have been well documented and established around the North Atlantic (typically linked to the Mediaeval Warm Period or Little Ice Age, e.g. Grove 1988), they are still relatively new to the Tropics, and have typically been modelled in the form of catastrophic events such as societal collapse (e.g. Haug et al. 2003; Diamond 2005; Fletcher et al. 2008). Gunnell et al. (2007) specifically investigate the effects of monsoon variability upon the development of the hydraulic landscape of southeast India, and argue that increases in both the SWM and NEM between the eleventh and thirteenth centuries saw a corresponding increase in the development of its artificial hydraulic landscape (*ibid.*: 213).

Summarising the palaeoenvironmental studies of the South Asian and Sri Lankan palaeoclimate, it can clearly be seen that although it is possible to identify broad changes in climate at a low diachronic resolution, it is currently impossible to conclusively identify either a precise scale of Early Mediaeval climate change, or indeed precisely when these changes occur. As such, until such diachronic precision is available it is impossible to firmly link any such climate changes to Anuradhapura's collapse.

2.3 A History of Research at Anuradhapura

Given the emphasis placed upon the Pali chronicles in the study of Sri Lankan archaeology, particularly in the case of Anuradhapura's collapse, it is important to understand not only *what* archaeological research has taken place at Anuradhapura, but also the theoretical environment within which this research has been conducted. This not only forms the archaeological record available to interpret, but also informs our understanding of that record.

From a nineteenth century, Euro-centric, perspective the city of Anuradhapura was "lost" for over 800 years after its eleventh century collapse (de Silva 1999: 244), and was only "rediscovered" by the British in the nineteenth century. In reality the city's archaeological sequence clearly shows continued activity and occupation at Anuradhapura until around the thirteenth century (Coningham 1999: 15), while the *Culavamsa* records King Vijayabahu IV (r. 1270-1272) completing restorations to the city (*Cvs*.xxxviii.83). Shortly after this Vijayabahu IV placed the city under the protection of the Vanni rulers (*Cvs*.xxxviii.89), suggesting the Sinhala Kings were no longer powerful enough or too distant to defend the region.

The earliest European referent to the ruins comes from the British sailor Robert Knox who was held captive in Sri Lanka for 19 years in the seventeenth century (Knox 1681). Upon his escape, and return to Great Britain, he wrote an account of his experiences in Sri Lanka, entitled *An Historical Relation of the Island of Ceylon*, a book that has since become a valuable insight into seventeenth century Sri Lanka. Held captive in the Kandyan Kingdom, his escape route took him through an area called "*Anarodgburro*", a rendering of the Tamil name for Anuradhapura (Indrapala 2005: 276). This lingual difference demonstrates how much had changed at Anuradhapura, with Knox reporting that the locals did not speak Sinhala, and were "Malabars" (Knox 1681: 159). This ethnic shift was also noted by British colonial offices in the nineteenth century, reporting that

"As Anuradhapura and Polonnaruva were abandoned forever, a thick belt of jungle separated the Tamil north from the Sinhalese south" (cited in Indrapala 2005: 276). Although the city had clearly gone, the Kandyan name for the settlement, Nuvaravanniya or 'Vanni of the City', displays knowledge of the site's history (Dewaraja 1988: 237). This is further supported by Knox's description of the settlement of Anuradhapura as being low density in nature; *"not so much a particular single town, as a territory... a vast great plain ... in the midst whereof is a lake, which may be a mile over, not natural, but made by art"* (Knox 1681: 159). However he also described *"a world of hewn Stone Pillars, standing upright, and other heaps of hewn stones, which I suppose formerly were buildings"* (*ibid.*).

Interest in Sri Lanka's ancient history increased dramatically after the first English translation of the *Mahavamsa* (Turnour 1837), giving the British an "historical" framework in which to interpret the ruins, prompting the publication of a number of "histories" (e.g. Forbes 1841; Knighton 1845; Knighton 1854; Barrow 1857; Tennent 1860). Although Turnour's work (and later Geiger's definitive translations (Geiger 1929 & 1934)) played a huge role in kick-starting Sri Lankan archaeology, it has also had a stultifying effect in the continued reliance upon the Pali chronicles, and an unwillingness to challenge the framework they provide.

2.3.1: Historical Topography

Early research at Anuradhapura was characterised by the mapping of events and locations from the Pali chronicles onto the extant archaeological features of Anuradhapura; the massive stupas, gigantic tanks and pillared halls. Early interest was also shown in the island's inscriptions, predominantly found on pillars and rock outcrops (e.g. Chetty 1848; Brodie 1853; Lee 1871; Rhys Davids 1871) and this quickly became a systematic survey (e.g. de Zoysa 1873; Muller 1880 & 1883; Gunasekera 1882). In 1904 Part One of the first volume of the Epigraphia Zeylanica was published (collated in Wickremasinghe 1912), and over the next 30 years this would be supplemented by a further three volumes (Wickremasinghe 1928; Wickremasinghe & Codrington 1933; Codrington & Paranvitana 1934), forming a comprehensive catalogue of the inscriptions of Sri Lanka, as well as greatly supplementing the proto-historical records of the Pali chronicles.

The first limited archaeological excavations at Anuradhapura were carried out in 1884 (Burrows 1886; Burrows 1887; Karunaratne 1990: 3), focussing upon the clearing and restoration of significant architectural features, such as the "stone canopy" near the "stone canoe" (Burrows 1887: 2). Minimal attention was paid to archaeological artefacts, for example the large number of glazed tiles discovered in an irrigation channel were recorded (*ibid.*: 8), but these excavations were clearly more treasure hunting than they were archaeology; *"It may be doubted whether there is anything much more exciting than the finding of a really fine archaeological treasure which has lain hid for many centuries."* (Burrows 1887: 1), and there is no recording of more mundane artefacts such as ceramics.

The creation of the Archaeological Survey of Ceylon (ASC), and appointment of H.C.P. Bell (shown in figure 2.04) as the first Archaeological Commissioner, in 1890 (Wijesekera 1990: xviii) saw archaeological research on the island develop rapidly, with Anuradhapura quickly becoming the primary focus of the work carried out by the fledgling ASC. Bell quickly set about systematically clearing and surveying the extant ruins of Anuradhapura, to better enable the *"excavation of likely sites"* (Karunaratne 1990: 6). The jungle covering these areas was cleared and burned, exposing the extant remains such as the "stone canoe" (Mahapali) and "brick building" (Gedige) that Burrows had identified a decade earlier, as well as identifying, for the first time, a large number of pillared and walled structures, the stone bridges north-west of Jetavana, and indeed much of the extant remains of the archaeological reserve of Anuradhapura (Bell 1892, 1893, 1904a, Bell 1904b, Bell1904c & Bell 1904d).

At this early point, the Pali chronicles were already at the core of archaeological research, and the mapping of events and sites mentioned within the Pali chronicles onto the archaeological remains was the primary method of archaeological interpretation. The latter was assisted by the continued veneration of several monuments, including the sacred Bodhi tree (Coningham 1999: 16), and the sizable volume of translated inscriptions (Muller 1883). Other sites, such as the large tanks, were quickly identified through their size and topographical descriptions in the *Mahavamsa*. For example, Parker identified Basavakkulam (then dry) as King Pandukabhaya's Abhaya tank through a reference in the *Mahavamsa*, describing the tank as lying to the east of the city (*Mvs*.x.84), combined with the discovery of a tenth century inscription by the side of the tank prohibiting fishing in a tank of that name (Parker 1909: 360). Similarly, the Tissaveva was identified as the large dry tank lying south of Anuradhapura's ruins in similar fashion from a reference in the *Mahavamsa* to the ancient tank of that name lying southwest of the Mirisavati stupa (*Mvs*.xxvi). Not all such identifications were accurate, and many were quickly refuted (Coningham 1999: 16). The most dramatic misidentification wrongly led to the Abhayagiri vihara being identified as the Jetavana vihara (and vice versa), though this was rectified in 1924 (Hocart 1924: 10-14). In many cases, these identifications were undoubtedly valuable, and for the time no more theoretically limited than in comparable areas of archaeological research. However, this reliance upon the Pali chronicles laid the foundations for archaeological interpretation in Sri Lanka for the next century, and have resulted in Sri Lankan archaeology becoming indistinguishably intertwined with the Pali chronicles, leaving many archaeologists to answer archaeological questions, such as that of Anuradhapura's collapse, through explicit reference to purely textual sources.

Among the first sites to be excavated under the ASC were the "Buddhist Railing" at Jetavana (Bell 1904a: 7) and a mound near the "Gal-ge" which revealed foundations including eight brick elephants, resembling the elephant revetment around Ruanvelisaya (Karunaratne 1990: 12). Soon afterwards, excavations began at the "Hindu Ruins" (Bell 1904c: 5; Bell 1904d: 4 – 5) and over the following years a large number of sites were excavated by the ASC, exposing as much of the ancient city as possible. Although these excavations were crude by modern standards, with only rudimentary recording and the sole aim of exposing extant architecture, they were nevertheless invaluable both in terms of establishing a methodical archaeological framework for the recording and conserving of the archaeological remains of Anuradhapura, and also for the consistently thorough publishing of these mappings and excavations by the ASC. Although there were some limitations, as while conclusions and inferences were published, the data typically was not. Thus, for the excavation of the Jetavana "Buddhist Railings" all that is published is their postulated dimensions, form and layout, along with an inference as to the cause of their fragmentary nature;

"The indescribable confusion in which the fragments were found heaped upon one another, and the almost entire wreck of the railing, leave little room for doubt that this unique relic of Ceylon Buddhist architecture must have perished under the ruthless destruction of those invaders from South India at whose door lies the mutilation and ruin of the best works of sculptor's art in Anuradhapura" (Bell 1904a: 7).

Around this time the circuit work (surveying of sites and inscriptions within the North Central Province) of the ASC began. Although the major focus of the ASC was on the monumental sites; Anuradhapura, Polonnaruva, Sigiriya, and Mihintale, Bell also began extensive archaeological surveys of the surrounding landscapes (Karunaratne 1990: 13). This survey was carried out in an entirely non-probabilistic fashion, typically by asking villagers of nearby ruins or inscriptions, and while valuable for the recording and protection of a number of larger sites (such as Ritagala or Hathttikuchchi) such surveys were typically carried out in only a few days, and the recording of sites was limited to the existence of an ancient vihara or inscription (Karunaratne 1990: 13). After 1894 the work of the ASC began to increase in scale and quantity, as Bell set about excavating the Citadel, Thuparama, Jetavana, Abhayagiri, and some nine further clusters of "ruins" within Anuradhapura (Karunaratne 1990: 17-27). At the same time excavation and recording began at Polonnaruva and Sigiriya and circuit work continued throughout; focused upon the North Central Province, but covering the entire island in scope (*ibid.*).

This early work of the ASC was also characterised by the restorations carried out at Anuradhapura and it is predominantly these "restored ruins" that are visible today. One criticism levelled at these restorations (Marcus Fernando 1990: 94) was the clear desire that the visitor be unaware that any restoration has been undertaken. This approach led to a "beautification" of many ruins and makes it difficult to distinguish restoration, repair and extant remains. This repair work can be viewed in retrospect as something of a two-edged blade. It is likely that without conservation many such features would have been destroyed entirely over the past century, whether by weathering and bioturbation, agricultural and urban development, or simply by looting. However, it is also true that the restoration of many sites has rendered any further archaeological investigations impossible, as the archaeological remains have been irreversibly destroyed, augmented or replaced. These same issues are seen across the world and are far from a localised issue.

Adding to the complexity of this issue, the dual nature of many of the remains, as both archaeological and religious monuments, was the cause of conflict, greatly exacerbated by rising ethnic and religious tensions and a growing desire for independence. In particular, this manifested in an extremely poor relationship between the Department of Archaeology and the Atamasthana Committee (an Anuradhapura based Buddhist organisation). Bell in particular felt that there was no reason for the Atamasthana Committee to be granted money for the maintenance of the major stupas at Anuradhapura (Bell 1911b: 563), and labelled their 1890 restorations of Mirisavati carried out with prison labour at the expense of a Thai prince as being, "*on wrong lines, incomplete, and... scientifically unprofitable*", while their restorations at Abhayagiri were "*only partially successful, proving insecure and pro-tanto futile, as borne out by the total collapse of the west face*" (cited in Hettiaratchi 1990: 45). This relationship was further strained by the continued construction of numerous new Buddhist structures shrines among the archaeological ruins (Hettiaratchi 1990: 46), despite the Atamasthana Committee publicly stating that such construction was to be halted (*ibid.*), resulting in a strained relationship between the archaeologists and the local *sangha*. This came to a head in 1914 with a dispute between the Department of Archaeology and the Mihintale Buddhist Society over the ownership of the Mihintale monuments, only resolved when the Colonial Secretary decided in favour of the Department (*ibid.*).

This led to the creation of the "Register of Ruins in Ceylon" and a concerted effort by the Department of Archaeology to create and maintain archaeological reserves to "*better preserve and protect the archaeological heritage of Sri Lanka*" (*ibid.*: 45). Without doubt, the crowning achievement of this was the protection of ancient Anuradhapura from the sprawling urban growth of 20th century development. This was not without its challenges, and in 1927 the ASC annual report records that it had not yet been "*possible to settle the details of new boundaries in Anuradhapura*" (Hocart 1928b: 5). Describing Anuradhapura at this time Marcus Fernando writes that;

"*Its main street ran very close to the Sri Maha Bodhi Tree. Slum dwellings came close to the Sri Maha Bodhi tree on more than one side. Lines of shop buildings skirted a wide network of roads. Scattered all over were the houses of the townsfolk. The government hospital, the Post Office, other government offices and quarters for government servants. There came up the church, the mosque and the Hindu temple. All these buildings rose over the buried Buddhist ruins of old. The Archaeological Commissioner was once constrained to say that "It is not impossible that the Medical Officer of Anuradhapura sleeps over the ashes of Elara""* (Marcus Fernando 1990: 94).

However, even the formation of the Anuradhapura Archaeological Reserve did not stop the destruction of archaeological remains, as people used stones from the archaeological sites as construction materials for new buildings, and pilgrims unwittingly using sculptures to make fire-places (ibid: 95), a scene repeated at many other archaeological reserves with many examples of pilgrims and "laymen" damaging monuments at sites across Sri Lanka (Hocart 1928b: 5). However, the creation of these Archaeological Reserves, along with the posting of guards at larger sites such as Sigiriya, Mihintale, Yapahuwa, and Anuradhapura (Hettiaratchi 1990: 89) and the management of vegetation at sites (Hettiaratchi 1990: 51) greatly reduced such damage.

Throughout this time archaeological investigations remained primarily focused upon the North-Central province (Hettiaratchi 1990: 51) and excavations continued at Anuradhapura during this period (1912-1930), including Ayrton's excavation of the Ratnaprasada which finally led to the correction of the misidentification of the Abhayagiri and Jetavana stupas (Ayrton 1924: 1-18). Although excavation still focussed upon identifying structures referred to within the Pali chronicles, and as such no strict attention was paid to assessing the terminal periods of Anuradhapura's occupation, an important aspect of Ayrton's excavations was the explicit attention he paid to the dating of structures, writing that, "*the number of buildings to which dates can be assigned, even approximately, is so small, that it is very satisfactory that we are able to even suggest possible dates for all the buildings excavated during the past fifteen months*" (cited in Hettiaratchi 1990: 55).

The outbreak and aftermath of the second World War halted archaeological research at Anuradhapura, and the only discoveries made during this period occurred during the restoration of Buddhist monuments. For example, the discovery of caskets containing "*gold and crystal reliquaries*" within earlier structures whilst digging the foundations of the new elephant wall at Ruanvelisaya in 1946 (Marcus Fernando 1990: 98). Unfortunately, such "discoveries" were made in the absence of archaeologists, and no records were kept for such finds, nor were the structures investigated further for fear of delaying restoration work (*ibid.*).

Throughout the subsequent decades the Department of Archaeology continued to excavate, clear, and conserve as before – with no research aim beyond the exposing of architectural remains, and relatively little publishing of findings (Wijayapala 1990: 134-135). This included excavations at Anuradhapura's Mahavihara, along with a number of other sites. In 1960, the southern gate of the Citadel was excavated in a project including the investigation of both the gatehouse, Citadel wall and the street that run northwards from this gate (Godakumbura 1961), while the eastern gate of the Citadel was excavated in 1975 by Silva (Coningham 1993b, 1994a).

Archaeological activity at Anuradhapura accelerated rapidly in the 1980s, with the inception of several major archaeological projects and the formation of a new institution, funded by the Central Cultural Fund (CCF), and charged with; "*developing, restoring, and preserving cultural and religious monuments in Sri Lanka and the development of religious and cultural activities in Sri Lanka and abroad*" (Uduwara 1990: 153), popularly referred to as the Cultural Triangle due to the geographical location of the three main sites; Anuradhapura, Sigiriya and Polonnaruva. However, despite the stated aims of the CCF, its excavations within the Sacred City lacked clear research aims, and were not strikingly distinct from the antiquarian clearing and restoring of the ASC. One of the first major actions of the Cultural Triangle was the initiation of excavations within Anuradhapura's Sacred City at the Abhayagiri Vihara (Wikramagamage et al. 1983; Wikramagamage 1984; Wikramagamage et al. 1984; Bouzek et al. 1986; Wikramagamage 1992; Bouzek 1993) and Jetavana Vihara (Ratnayake 1984). It is these excavations that will provide the core data for the analysis and evaluation of the terminal periods of the Sacred City within this volume (Chapter 6). Unfortunately, final excavation reports for these excavations have never been produced, and in the case of Ratnayake's Jetavana excavations produced just a single preliminary report after one season (*ibid.*).

2.3.2: Research driven archaeology

'Writing in 1972, Siran Deraniyagala remarked that while the island's prehistory had been studied more intensively than any other South Asian country's, Sri Lanka's historic archaeology had been overly dominated by epigraphy and history (Deraniyagala 1972: 52). While this critique still holds true today, it was even more apt at the time, and it was shortly afterwards that the focus of archaeological research on the island changed. The earlier reactive approach was replaced by a more proactive research, with research questions posed, and the fieldwork tailored to address those questions.

Arguably the first such excavation was Paranavitana's excavations at the Daldage within the Citadel, at that time the most comprehensively published excavations carried out at Anuradhapura (Paranavitana 1936). These were notable for the comparative level of attention paid to context and stratigraphy, and the intent to develop an archaeological sequence. Although basic by modern standards, Paranavitana's use and publication of stratum and comparative dating renders these excavations open to re-interpretation in the light of further data. However, although Paranavitana's excavations were more rigorous in both their execution and publication, they were unfortunately less rigorous in their treatment of the terminal deposits at Anuradhapura. For example the final phase of structures revealed at the excavations between the Mahapali and Gedige were not planned, and were dismissively described as "*ephemeral mud structures in the foundations of which fragments of the older buildings were used*" (Paranavitana 1936: 3). This in itself is sadly an improvement upon earlier excavations that typically failed to mention these structural phases at all.

This was followed by the sondages of P.E.P. Deraniyagala (1957) and Sesteri (1958). These focussed upon the Gedige area of the Citadel, and collaboratively aimed to address the depth and antiquity of cultural occupation at Anuradhapura (Coningham 1999: 16), specifically through the comparative typological analyses of ceramics (Wijayapala 1990: 135). One of the key differences between the excavations of Sesteri and Deraniyagala, and Paranavitana's 24 years earlier, was their focus on depth. Thus when Sesteri or Deraniyagala reached a floor, old land surface or major structure they cut through it, recording everything, to reach the archaeological deposits below. In comparison, earlier excavations had reached a structural layer and stopped – cleaning and conserving to that level (Coningham 1999: 17). The excavations of Deraniyagala and Sesteri were followed in 1969 by a second phase of deep sondages aimed at reaching bedrock, and providing a long temporal sequence for the Citadel (Codrington 1969; Deraniyagala 1972). Four sondages were placed in the base of P.E.P. Deraniyagala and Sesteri's trench, and excavated contextually down to a depth of 7.6m creating, for the first time, a cultural sequence stretching over more than a millennium of urban occupation at Anuradhapura (Deraniyagala 1972). A decade later this research question was expanded upon by Siran Deraniyagala, who directed the Anuradhapura Citadel Archaeological Project (ACAP), excavating fourteen sondages at various locations across the Citadel in order to trace the development of the site over time (Coningham 1999: 17). However, such sondages were unlikely to provide an adequate artefactual or structural sequence a sub-project aimed at excavating a 100m^2 trench, ASW2, in the centre of the site, adjacent to sondage ASW1.

In the introduction to the first volume of the ASW2 excavation report Coningham (Coningham 1999: 3) prefaces the report by citing Cunliffe's warning that; "*...no excavation report, however detailed, can hope to be more than an interim summary of a site. To suggest more would be naive or arrogant. A data-set of this kind... will continue to be reworked by students for the foreseeable future asking new and increasingly sophisticated questions. These reports merely advertise what is available and offer some general approximations to the truth which may help those interested in these matters to design new and more penetrating analyses*" (Cunliffe 1984: viii). In the context that Coningham quotes this, the warning reflects the fact that any interpretations and conclusions made within the report are effectively transitory – and will undoubtedly be adapted, supplemented, and challenged as new analyses are carried out, new interpretations are made, and new comparisons are made with other sites and sources.

However, the key is that these further analyses and interpretations are only possible because of the quality and scope of the data published, because *everything* (the full artefact catalogue, context register, scientific dates etc.) is published (Coningham 1999 & 2006). Unfortunately, all of the above excavations have one common failing, that of the publishing of the final excavation reports, or indeed the lack of any such publications. A number of preliminary reports were published, however over the following decades no further publications have been forthcoming. In some cases, the reports are apparently still being worked upon, however given the period that has elapsed, the continued absence of any such final reports is disappointing. Sadly, this same criticism can be levelled at the island's first major archaeological settlement survey, the Sigiriya-Dambulla survey of the late 1980s (Bandaranayake et al. 1990), which again published a preliminary report at the time, but nothing since.

Thankfully, as already referred to, one of these archaeological projects, the Sri Lankan-British excavations at Salgha Watta, Anuradhapura (ASW2), has been fully published – both in a series of preliminary reports (Coningham 1991, 1992, 1993b, 1994a; Coningham & Allchin 1992), and in a two volume excavation report (Coningham 1999 & 2006). These excavations not only provided an artefactual sequence covering the entirety of the Anuradhapura period, but critically provided a *published* artefactual sequence (Coningham 1999 & 2006). This then, for the first time, enabled comparative analysis of material, and thus sites, from across Sri Lanka, and even the Indian Ocean. Furthermore, this material was tied into a relatively tight diachronic framework, formed by a combination of relative and absolute dating (Coningham & Batt 1999: 125), something that is vital for the interpretation of cultural and societal change – especially in the case of societal or urban collapse. It is these excavation reports, and perhaps, most importantly, this cultural and artefactual sequence, that will effectively form the data-spine of this volume. Without the quality and level of detail of the published material from ASW2, many of the earlier excavations mentioned in this chapter would be rendered little more than anecdotal in their utility, it is the scope and chronological precision of the artefactual sequence formed by the ASW2 excavations that facilitates ready comparison of materials from other sites and excavations across Anuradhapura, and indeed Sri Lanka and beyond.

The second phase of the Sri Lankan-British Anuradhapura project, that began with the ASW2 excavations, focussed upon the hinterland of Anuradhapura, as, although the city (both sacred and secular), has been intensively studied for over a century the hinterland has been largely ignored. Started in 2005, the *Anuradhapura Hinterland Project* (Coningham & Gunawardhana 2013), systematically surveyed the hinterland of Anuradhapura over five seasons with the aim of modelling the networks between urban and non-urban communities and the environment within the plain of Anuradhapura over the course of two millennia (*ibid.*). This project utilised probabilistic transects to survey the hinterland to a radial distance of 50km from the Citadel, allowing the generation of a predictive settlement pattern for the hinterland of ancient Anuradhapura. The project also carried out a non-probabilistic survey of the Malvatu Oya river, as well as several ancient canals, in order to better understand the routes of communication and trade during the Anuradhapura period. A sample of the archaeological sites found were targeted for further investigation through auger coring, geophysical survey and small scale excavations in order to better understand the nature, period and usage of such sites. Running alongside the settlement survey and excavations, pedological and geomorphological investigations were carried out at selected settlement, agricultural, and hydraulic sites to gain further information about ancient landscape management and exploitation.

2.4 Conclusion

Sri Lanka, while influenced by the Indian subcontinent, has remained environmentally, culturally and historically distinct. The island's location in the Indian Ocean has given it huge significance in maritime trade for over two millennia, and the rich natural resources of the island have attracted both traders and invasions. However, despite the rich natural resources of the island, the North-Central Province, ancient heartland of the Anuradhapura Kingdom, is only able to support high density population with a carefully managed and maintained monumental hydraulic landscape.

This chapter has established that over a century of archaeological research has been carried out on the island, the majority of which has focussed upon the monumental urban centres. However, despite this level of focus Sri Lankan archaeology has long been handicapped by a dependency upon the Pali chronicles which has severely hindered the development of research driven scientific archaeology within the island. Thankfully, over the past three decades, such an archaeological research paradigm has begun to be created by a series of international collaborative projects (e.g. Prematilleke 1982a, 1982b, 1982c, 1985, 1987, 1989; Bouzek 1993; Coningham 1999, 2006).

Having set out the environmental and academic context, the next chapter will now establish the *theoretical* background for this volume, examining concepts of collapse, a brief history of collapse theory, and the three established models for Anuradhapura's collapse that are to be tested.

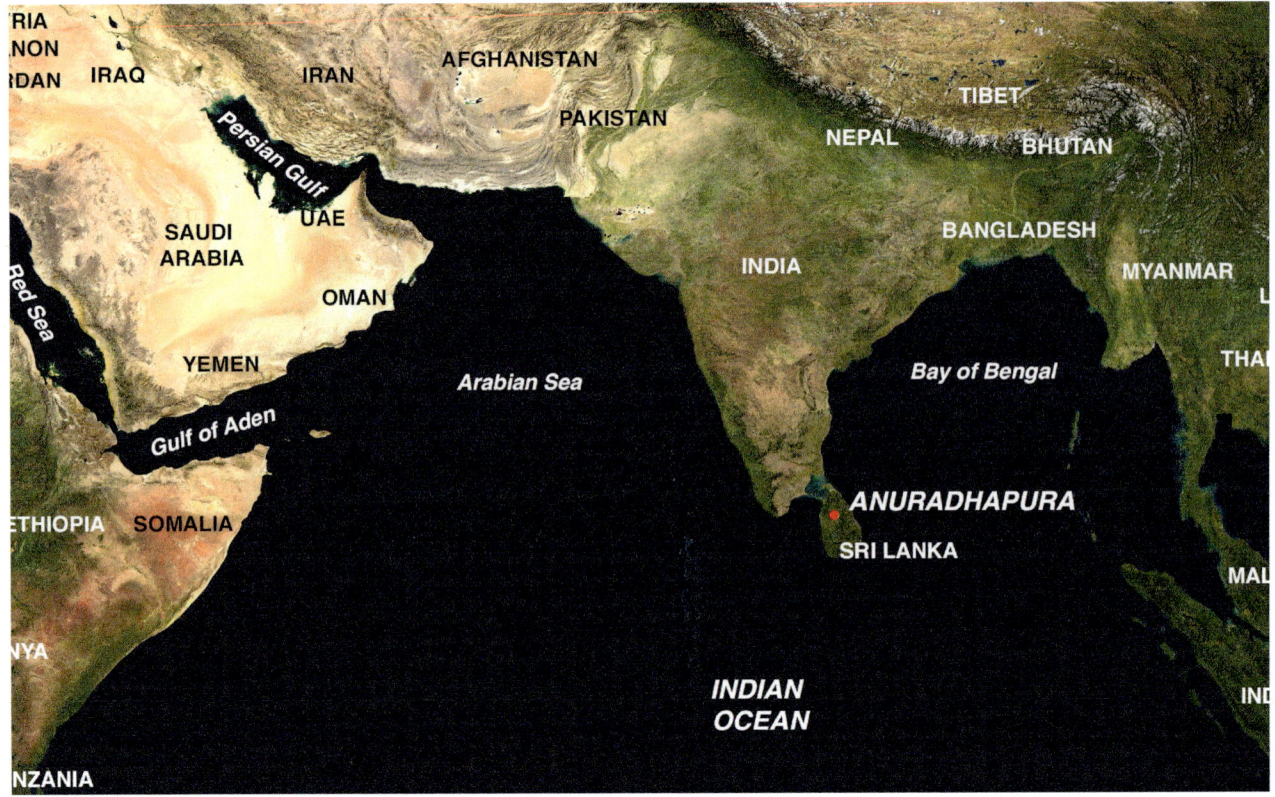

Figure 2.01: Sri Lanka within the Indian Ocean
(Image by Author)

CHAPTER 2: ANURADHAPURA: GEOGRAPHY, ENVIRONMENT AND HISTORY OF RESEARCH

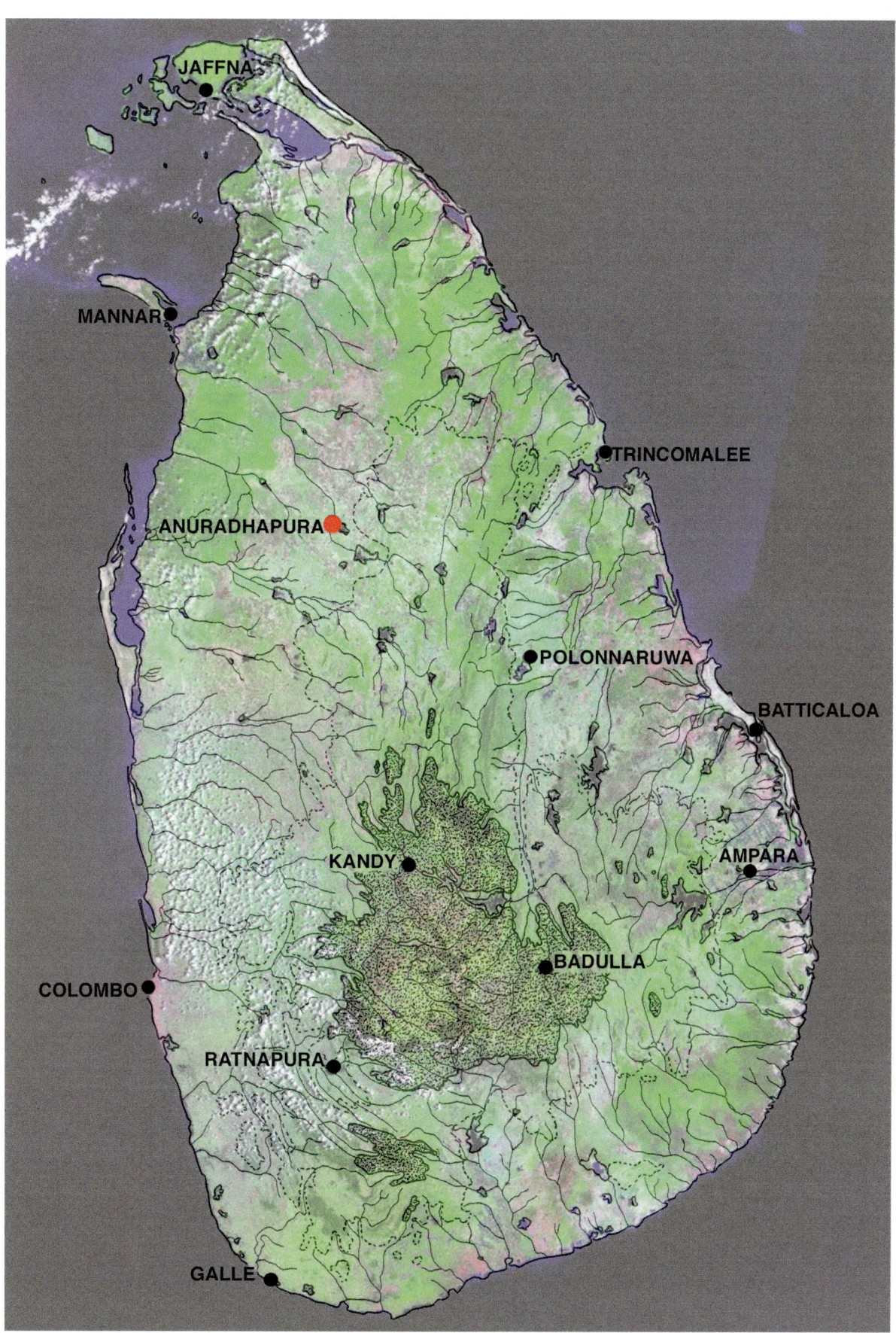

FIGURE 2.02: TOPOGRAPHIC MAP OF SRI LANKA
(AFTER CONINGHAM ET AL. 1999: 13)

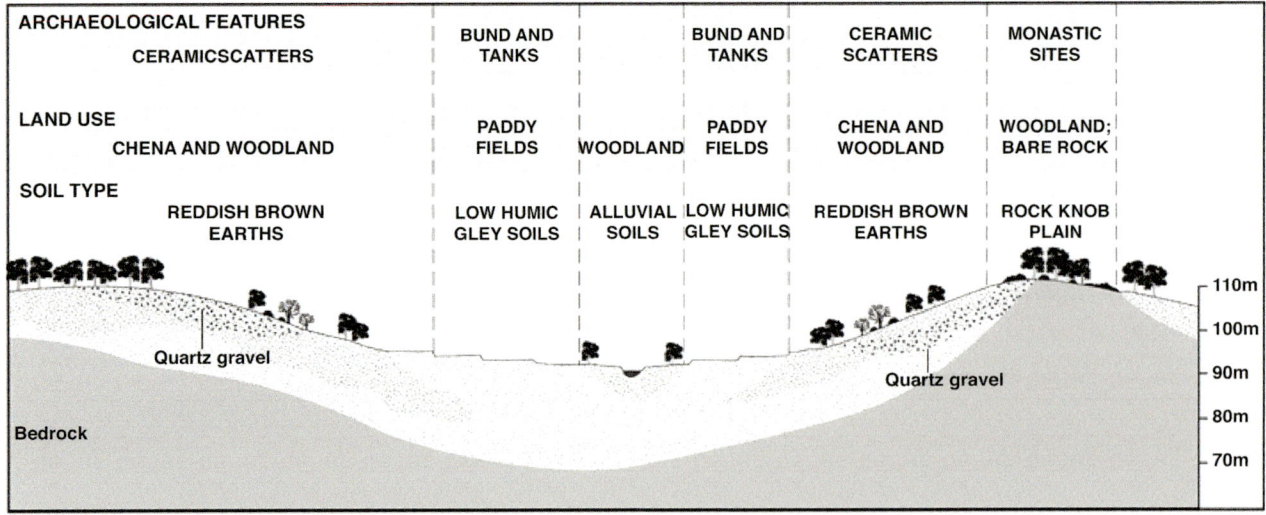

Figure 2.03: Schematic diagram of Anuradhapura soilscape with associated land-use and archaeological features (after Simpson et al. 2008b: 30)

Figure 2.04: H.C.P. Bell at Polonnaruva (after Karunaratne 1990: 34)

Chapter 3: Collapse

3.1 Introduction

Chapter Two set out Anuradhapura's environmental, geographical, climatic and archaeological background, summarising over a hundred years of archaeological and historical research, and outlining the datasets available for use within this volume. Chapter Three will synthesise and critically examine the three primary models for the apparent "collapse" of Anuradhapura (Invasion, Malarial and Imperial). However, before this can be completed, the term "collapse" must be clearly defined, along with *what* it is that collapses, and what the primary alternatives to collapse are.

3.2 What is collapse & what collapses?

3.2.1: What is collapse?

It is dangerous to refer to "collapse" repeatedly without defining it precisely, and setting out and defining alternative societal transformations to "collapse". The word "collapse" conjures up dramatic images of ruined cities, but collapse is not a static object, it is a complex dynamic process that is continuously variable, and it is crucial that this is remembered when studying collapse. The collapse of a complex society is not, as evocative or romantic as it may seem, the *death* of that society, and Sorokin in particular has repeatedly criticised such language, arguing that there is almost always some cultural continuity between the society that has "died", and the subsequent society that emerges in its place (Sorokin 1950 & 1957). The collapse of any complex society must be considered to be a rapid loss of the very complexity that defines it, though this does not mean a complete loss of any particular set of cultural traits. For example, in the collapse of the Western Roman Civilisation, almost all cities continued to be occupied and there was no change in the languages spoken or the peoples living in those cities (Liebeschuetz 2001: 29-104). Instead, there was a reduction in the level of *social complexity*; a reduction in monumental construction (Foss 1979: 70 & 80), a reduction in craft specialist skills (Arthur & Patterson 1994: 409-440), a reduction in coinage stamped (Liebeschuetz 2001: 23), and a reduction in written proclamations (Mrozek 1973: 355-368). In essence a reduction in the characteristics that defined that complex society (Childe 1950), but not a complete loss and by no means a "death".

One key factor appears to be the rate at which these characteristics are lost, and this is reflected in several definitions of "collapse", as well as differentiating collapse from a slower, more gradual, decline. For example, Tainter defined collapse as a *"rapid, substantial decline in an established level of complexity"* (Tainter 1988: 38), while Diamond produced a similar, although more specific, definition, describing collapse as; *"a drastic decrease in human population size and/or political /economic/social complexity, over a considerable area, for an extended time"* (Diamond 2005: 03). However, these definitions are vague and all encompassing, and thus difficult to apply critically. Renfrew (1984: 367-370) gives a more detailed set of characteristics that he argued defined systems collapse, and it is these that will be adopted within this volume. However, these characteristics cannot be considered an exhaustive checklist as there are a number that were never true of Anuradhapura in the first place (for example *"2.a: cessation of rich traditional burials"*) and still more that would be near impossible to identify archaeologically (for example *"1.b: Complete fragmentation or disappearance of military organisation into (at most) small, independent units"*). Renfrew split these characteristics into three groups; the Collapse, the Aftermath and Diachronic Aspects (inapplicable characteristics omitted) (Renfrew 1984: 367-370):

The Collapse

1. Collapse of central administrative organisation of the early state.
- Disappearance or reduction in number of levels of central place hierarchy.
- Abandonment of palaces and central storage facilities
- Eclipse of temples as major religious centres (often with their survival, modified, as local shrines).
- Effective loss of literacy for secular and religious purposes
- Abandonment of public building works.

2. Disappearance of the traditional elite class.
- Abandonment of rich residences, or their re-use in impoverished style by "squatters".
- Cessation in the use of costly assemblages of luxury goods, although individual items may survive.

3. Collapse of centralised economy.
- Cessation of large-scale redistribution or market exchange.
- Coinage (where applicable) no longer issued or exchanged commercially.
- External trade very markedly reduced, and traditional trade routes disappear.
- Volume of internal exchange markedly reduced.
- Cessation of craft-specialist manufacture.
- Cessation of specialised or organised agricultural production. With agriculture instead based upon a local 'homestead' basis with diversified crop spectrum and mixed farming.

4. Settlement shift and population decline.
- Abandonment of many settlements.
- Marked reduction in population density.

The Aftermath

5. Development of romantic Dark Age myth.
- Tendency among early chroniclers to personalise historical explanations, so that change is assigned to individual deeds, battles, and invasions, and often to attribute the decline to hostile powers outside the state.
- Paucity of archaeological evidence after collapse compared with that for preceding period (arising from loss of literacy and abandonment or diminution of urban areas).
- Tendency among historians to accept as evidence traditional narratives first set down in writing some centuries after the collapse.
- Slow development of Dark Age archaeology, hampered both by the preceding item and by focus on the larger and more obvious central place sites of the vanished state.

Diachronic Aspects

6. The collapse may take around 100 years for completion (Renfrew 1984: 369).
7. Dislocations are evident in the earlier part of that period, the underlying factors finding expression in human conflicts.

3.2.2: What Collapses?

As mentioned above, a number of Renfrew's characteristics are simply not applicable in the case of Anuradhapura, this is after all not the collapse of an entire society, but of an urban centre and its economic hinterland. Fortunately the two are not only comparable, but have frequently overlapped academically, with scholars seemingly using "urban" and "civilisation" almost interchangeably.

The seminal archaeological work on defining "civilisation" is Childe's 1950 paper *"The Urban Revolution"*. Childe laid out ten criteria for defining "urbanisation", which was, as defined by Childe (Childe 1950), unique to "civilisation" and, vice versa, all civilisations have been essentially urban (Bairoch 1988: 01-70). This again is problematic because "urbanisation" is, like "civilisation" a word with certain assumptions based upon the classical, Hellenistic, concept of a city: a model completely at odds with the primarily ritually focussed low-density urban forms of the Maya (Thompson 1970), East Asia (Cressey 1955: 15), Ancient Egypt (Wilson 1960; Abu-Lughod 1969: 164) and arguably most of South Asia.

However, setting aside the issue of preconceptions, it is this close relationship between "civilisation" (and thus complex societies) and "urbanisation" that allows the application of collapse theory to Anuradhapura's "collapse". Childe's list of traits has been implicitly adopted by archaeology as a field of study, although the efficacy of such a check-list approach has been challenged (Trigger 2003: 43). Trigger argues that Childe clearly believed that these traits had *"evolved in a co-evolutionary fashion and were all present in any social system that had reached a certain level of complexity"* (Trigger 2003: 43). Trigger goes on to compare Childe's trait list to the trait lists used by culture historians to identify cultures in the first half of the twentieth century and the lists of traits used by evolutionary anthropologists to delineate stages of cultural development. One of the main problems with such an approach is that it relies on implicit understandings and definitions. Childe defined terms like "city", "monumental architecture", "exact sciences" and "systems of recording" in the loosest possible terms. Thus even small disagreements on how one defines or interprets each criterion will affect which societies are called civilisations, consequently archaeologists using very precise definitions of "urbanism" have argued that civilisations such as the Maya (Thompson 1970) or Ancient Egypt (Wilson 1960) lacked them. Yet no one would argue that either of these were not "civilisations". Similarly the highly urbanised Yoruba have frequently been denied the status of civilisation, or even of having cities rather than towns, purely because they were non-literate (Sjoberg 1960).

Trigger propounded a definition of civilisation framed in terms of the *"general sorts of social, economic, and political institutions and the associated types of knowledge and beliefs"* (Trigger 2003: 44). However, this is extremely ephemeral, unwieldy, and near impossible to apply in presence/absence terms as required in the study of collapse. Consequently, Childe's checklist has been adopted, though often in expanded or adapted form.

Childe proposed that for a settlement to be called a "city" it needed:

1. Concentrations of a relatively large number of people in a restricted area.
2. Non-food producing workers, typically craft specialists, merchants, officials, and priests supported by the surpluses produced by farmers.
3. Production of an economic surplus and its appreciation by tithe or tax to a central authority.
4. Monumental public architecture as a display of social surplus. This includes such structures as temples, palaces, fortifications and tombs.
5. Developed social stratification featuring a ruling class exempt from manual labour.

6. Development of writing and numeric notation, originally to record economic surpluses, taxes and trade.
7. Exact and predictive sciences. Typically calendrical and mathematical, e.g. arithmetic, geometry and astronomy.
8. Figural, representative and monumental art.
9. Regular long distance trade of raw materials as both luxuries and industrial materials.
10. Residence-based group membership, in which people of all professions and classes could share in a sense of community.

Maisels (1999: 26) has since separated Childe's final point into three separate criteria:

11. Peasants, craftsmen and rulers form a community.
12. The social solidarity of the community is represented by the pre-eminence of temples and funerary cults.
13. State organisation is dominant and permanent.

Writing specifically about New World archaeology, Flannery (1994: 106-108) suggested the following amendments to the 10 criteria:

1. Population density – lower in both density and scale than suggested by Childe.
2. High variability in the ratio of farmers to non-food producers.
3. (no amendments)
4. Argues that the monumental buildings of "urban civilisation" are displays of the labour, or "manpower", at the disposal of the ruling elite.
5. Argues that the ruling elite are as much a product of ideology, genealogy and social form as they are a result of the concentration of surplus.
6. Argues against the importance of writing (or scripts) as a key criterion of civilisation.
7. (no amendments)
8. Redefines "natural or figural" artistic expression as "state art" involving an official style whose content was a form of propaganda.
9. Argues long distance trade was important long before urbanism.
10. Stresses the importance of kinship in the social order of New World cities, while accepting the increased importance of residence in the social order.

(Flannery 1994: 107-109)

Although Flannery was writing on New World societies, his general approach is the one that will be adopted here. Namely that Childe's checklist is a useful tool, but is neither exhaustive nor immutable, it is instead a framework that can be amended or adapted as needed. This will be done through reference to the archaeological sequence in Chapters Five, Six and Seven (for the Citadel, Sacred City and hinterland respectively) in comparison to the terminal period and period post-abandonment.

3.3 Collapse Theory

Collapse has been academically studied for centuries, from classical scholars such as Plato (1926), Aristotle (1984) and Polybius (1979), to 20th century heavyweights such as Spengler (1926) and Toynbee (1939), right up to more recent popular science authors such as Jared Diamond (2005). To critically summarise the theoretical models produced over these centuries of study they must be classified and grouped, this, however, is a subjective procedure, and has typically resulted in a polarised position with two opposing bodies of theory. For example, Sabloff (1973: 36) and Polybius (writing in the second century B.C.) both classified collapse theories by internal and external causes (Polybius 1979: 350) while a more recent trend has been to examine conflict vs. integration (Flannery 1972). Such a polarised approach to collapse theory can be seen throughout archaeology, particularly in classical areas of archaeology that received greater attention during the 19th century and early 20th century. The legacy of this culture historical period of work has cast a long shadow and some areas, such as South Asia, Mesoamerica and the Mediterranean, have only begun to emerge from this hangover recently. Indeed this polarised approach can be seen perfectly in the archaeology of the Indus Civilisation where there was a long debate over the cause of the Harappan collapse. However for a long time the debate was restricted to two basic explanations: the culture historical invasion model or the environmental prime mover model, no other explanations were considered and certainly no attempt was ever made to examine the unique characteristics of collapse at different sites. Instead there was simply a clash between culture historians who accepted the writings of the *Rigveda* (a set of ancient hymns that told of the coming of the Aryans to India) (Chanda 1926; Wheeler 1947 & 1950; Childe 1951; Piggot 1961) and archaeologists who supported environmental changes as the prime mover in the Harappan collapse (Marshall 1931; Stein 1931; Mackay 1937: 528; Sahni 1956; Raikes 1964, Raikes 1965, Dales 1966, Raikes 1967; Raikes 1968; Singh 1971; Singh *et al.* 1974; Rao 1979; Rafique Mughal 1992).

Perhaps a more utile approach is to follow Tainter's example (1988: 42), and classify collapse theories by causal theme, producing the following theoretical groups of collapse theory:

1. Resource depletion
2. New resource base
3. Catastrophe
4. Insufficient response to events
5. Other complex societies
6. Invasion
7. Class conflict
8. Social dysfunction
9. Mystical collapse
10. Chance concatenation of events
11. Economic factors

The majority of these theoretical groups are largely irrelevant here (for a detailed discussion see Tainter (1988: 39-90) or Strickland (2011: 20-29)), but it is important to be aware that a far wider range of theoretical models for collapse exist than those examined within this volume. The most clearly relevant of these collapse theories is perhaps the oldest, and possibly also the most common. Invasion and catastrophe have been invoked at some point as the cause for every civilisation's collapse to date (Tainter 1988: 63), and unsurprisingly so; barbarian invasion or catastrophic flooding provide a simple and explanation for an extremely complex question. However, while such events undoubtedly occur (see the barbarian incursions in the fall of the Western Roman Empire (Mazzarino 1966) or the catastrophic flooding of Lothal (Rao 1979)), this need to retreat to an external cause to explain complex cultural changes smacks of an unwillingness to engage with the problem. Furthermore this desire to explain away culture change by external influence harks back worryingly to the culture history approach of archaeologists like Kossinna (Kossinna 1911) or Childe (Childe 1925, 1926, 1928) who attributed changes in cultural form to invasions or migrations of peoples. This use of culture historical invasions was typically then used to legitimise the current elites, for example Wheeler's use of the Rigveda and Aryan invasion to establish Indian history as a series of Invasions, in which the British occupation was just the latest in a long series (Wheeler 1947, 1950), or the recent conflict in Sri Lanka, where ethnic identity and conflict is both fed by, and feeds into, the perceived conflicts of the past, specifically the sacking of Anuradhapura (Farmer 1963; Kemper 1991; Coningham & Lewer 1999; Coningham & Lewer 2000). Indeed in Sri Lanka there is a legitimate concern that current politics are creating an academic climate in which the aim is to validate or invalidate certain historical claims for the glorification or vilification of a political movement (Gunawardana 1994: 213).

Moreover such external explanations still fail to explain the collapse of these complex societies, yes, they provide a cause, but they fail to fully engage with the question. *How* is a dominant state overthrown by a weaker, tribally organised, people? No one disputes that cities are hit by earthquakes and floods yet the civilisations routinely withstand these catastrophes and continue (Tainter 1988: 53), as Adams pointed out; "accidents…happen to all societies at all stages of their history" (R.E.W. Adams 1983: 5).

As mentioned above (**3.2.1**), this period of culture-historical invasionist collapse theory was observed by Renfrew (1984: 367-370) and considered to be so common in societal collapse that he included it as a defining characteristic of societal collapse. Renfrew observed that, following collapse, romanticised "dark-age" myths were developed by new elites to legitimise themselves, leading to the creation of early chronicles, personalising events and blaming hostile external populations for the collapse (*ibid.*). Renfrew went on to suggest that historians would be inclined to accept these chronicles as truthful and that this acceptance would severely hinder our understanding of periods of collapse and the periods immediately subsequent (*ibid.*: 386-389). While it is unlikely that Renfrew had Sri Lanka in mind when he wrote those words, as will be seen in section 3.5, they can clearly be easily applied to Sri Lanka.

3.4 Collapse Theory in South Asia

Within South Asian archaeology only one "*collapse*" has received archaeological attention to date, that of the Harappan Civilisation at the beginning of the second millennium (e.g. Piggot 1961; Srivastava 1984). Leaving aside the question of whether or not the Harappan Civilisation can actually be said to have collapsed (see Shaffer 1992), it remains a case study of collapse that is frequently cited within collapse literature (e.g. Tainter 1988: 48).

It is interesting to compare the development of collapse theory for the Harappan Civilisation with that of Anuradhapura in Sri Lanka, as while the study of both began around the beginning of the twentieth century, the critical study of the Harappan collapse has continued over the past century, while the study of Anuradhapura's terminal period appears to have stagnated and stalled.

Critically, for the purposes of comparison, both the Harappan and Anuradhapura collapses appear to be described in proto-historical chronicles (as predicted by Renfrew (1984: 386-389)) both of which were first translated in the 1830s, the *Rigveda* by Rosen in 1830 and the *Mahavamsa* by Turnour in 1837. The *Rigveda* describes the coming of the Aryans, and in 1926 Chanda argued that the Aryan invasion of the *Rigveda* was directly responsible for the collapse of the Harappan Civilisation

(Chanda 1926: 5). Shortly after Wheeler connected the apparent "massacre" at Mohenjo-Daro with the *Rigveda*, again arguing that the Aryan invasion was responsible for the collapse of the Harappan Civilisation (Wheeler 1947 & 1950). This theory was initially supported by archaeologists such as Childe (Childe 1951) and Piggot (Piggot 1961). However, it was not long before it was challenged, first on the grounds of the age of the *Rigveda* (Pulsalker 1950), and then on the lack of archaeological evidence to support it, and the absence of archaeological evidence for such invasion or battles (Kane 1955). Since then many have argued against the Aryan invasion as the cause of the Harappan collapse, on the grounds of; the lack of evidence for an invasion or conflict (Dales 1964, Srivastava 1984, Dales 1987), the physical anthropology of skeletal remains (Walimbe 1993, Kennedy 1995), and linguistic studies (Leach 1995, Lal 1997).

It is at this juncture that the two collapses begin to differ, both in their characteristics and their study. Critically, although both the *Culavamsa* and *Rigveda* describe invasions, the section of the *Culavamsa* that describes the eleventh century Chola invasion is accepted to have been composed around the same period (Geiger 1960: 71), unlike the *Rigveda* which was composed several centuries after the "Aryan invasion", and not written down for several more centuries (Pulsalker 1950).

Consequently, while the Chola invasion remains the monolithic established cause of Anuradhapura's "collapse", the study of the Harappan Collapse progressed through several different classes of models. Firstly, remaining monocausal, catastrophic environmental models, citing flooding and shifts to river routes as prime movers for collapse (Mackay 1937; Sahni 1956; Raikes 1964, 1965, 1967 & 1968; Dales 1966; Rao 1979; Rafique Mughal 1992) were cited, but such a model was quickly challenged (Lambrick 1967; Ratnagar 2001: 140). Next, palynological studies suggesting climate change (Singh 1971, Singh *et al.* 1974), again quickly challenged (Misra 1984: 247). Other archaeologists suggested compatible economic models, arguing that the Harappans had over-exploited and worn out their landscape (Wheeler 1959: 113), leading to mass emigration and a shift to low-density dispersed settlement pattern (Fairservis Jr. 1967).

Finally, archaeologists began to combine causal factors, rejecting the simplistic monocausal models in favour of more complex explanations. Elements incorporated into such models included western trade disruption due to Sumerian political instability (McIntosh 2002: 188), malaria (Parpola 1994: 24), and the emergence of new crops – enabling the cultivation and settlement of previously uninhabitable lands (McIntosh 2002: 187). Thus a decrease in trade, flooding in some areas and a reduction in rainfall in others, the denudement of land around the larger cities and the introduction of new crops are all argued as combining to cause the abandonment of urban centres and the migration of the Harappan populace to new areas. Such polycausal models have been propounded recently by Shaffer (1993), Thapar (1993), Allchin (1990 & 1995), the Allchins (Allchin & Allchin 1997: 206-222), Kenoyer (1998) and most recently McIntosh (2002).

Although currently the most widely accepted explanation for the Harappan collapse, this polycausal model has still faced criticism. In particular, Possehl questions the aspect of long distance trade, pointing out the problem of the direction of causality (Possehl 2002: 241), i.e. did trade stop and result in the collapse of the Harappan Civilisation? Or did the collapse of the Harappan Civilisation result in the cessation of long distance trade?

This problem of direction of causality is one that sits at the core of collapse studies, as the loss of a defining characteristic (e.g. long distance trade, intensive agriculture, centralised economy etc.) is often considered to be a causal factor in collapse, yet collapse will inherently cause the loss of such defining characteristics. This has resulted in the placing of huge importance on temporal data and chronologies within collapse studies.

3.5 Sri Lankan Collapse Studies

Unfortunately, while the study of the Harappan Collapse started with a monocausal culture historical invasion model derived from proto-historical texts, and then progressed, the study of Anuradhapura's terminal period started there, and stopped. From the very beginning the archaeological data was interpreted within the framework of the Pali chronicles and epigraphic records, reducing the archaeological interpretation of Anuradhapura's late periods to, at best, basic description of artefacts, structural remains and deposits (e.g. Paranavitana 1936: 19 or Coningham 1999: 129-130), and at worst to verbatim repetition of the Pali chronicles regardless of the archaeological evidence. Examples of the latter can be seen in Paranavitana's excavations at the Mahapali (the alms hall) in 1933, where he describes the Mahapali's restoration by Mahinda IV "*after it had been burnt by the Chola army which invaded Ceylon*" (ibid: 24), or Seneviratna's 1994 guide to Anuradhapura, where he wrote that Anuradhapura: "*was sacked on at least four occasions before it was finally abandoned... The south Indian Cholas and Pandyans were responsible for these invasions, conquests and depredations... Even after Anuradhapura ceased to be the capital, the Kalinga invader, Magha... and Javanese invader Chandrabhanu... plundered and again destroyed the city*" (Seneviratna 1994: 34). Such acceptance of the Pali chronicles has left the "study" of Anuradhapura's terminal period confined to purely historical and epigraphic discussions, with archaeology ignoring the subject entirely.

Of course, it may be argued by many of the archaeologists who have "ignored" this question that history and archaeology are not mutually exclusive disciplines, and thus it is neither unusual nor counterproductive to utilise historical sources in such a fashion. As Sauer has pointed out, the fundamental questions asked by both archaeologists and historians are identical, and the sole difference between the two are the *"sources of information that are neglected in attempting to answer them"* (Sauer 2004: 17). However, Klejn has argued strongly for the distinction, writing that *"the fact it co-operates with history makes archaeology no more a kind of history... than contacts with me makes horses human, or vice versa"* (Klejn 2001: 39). It seems clear here that Sri Lankan archaeology, when tackling the question of Anuradhapura's terminal period, has abandoned anything resembling an archaeological approach – it has become the horse and neglected archaeological sources in attempting to answer the question of *why* Anuradhapura was abandoned.

3.5 The "Collapse" of Anuradhapura

The prevalent attitude to Anuradhapura's terminal period in Sri Lankan archaeology is exemplified by Coningham's summation (Coningham 1999: 15) that the city; *"was abandoned as a capital in AD 1017 by Mahinda V (r. 982 – 1029) in the face of increasing pressure from southern Indian polities"*. While there is certainly nothing conclusively incorrect or misleading with this explanation, it is representative in its brevity and lack of engagement with the collapse. In some cases this is because the research is focussed elsewhere, in the case of Coningham (1999) that focus being upon Anuradhapura's urban origins. However, in many cases it is simply because it is felt that the *Culavamsa* describes the events adequately (*Cvs*.lv) – so why waste time archaeologically questioning what we already know?

Spencer clearly recognised the limitations of such data sources, and stressed the need not only to study these sources, but to interpret, and even "decode" them (Spencer 1983: 04). Referring to claims of conquest and invasion in his introduction to *The Politics of Expansion*, Spencer argued that *"Such records often are not what they seem; they may say one thing but signify something else. Stated motives may not be real ones... they constitute idealized, and therefore incomplete, versions of events... we must make allowances for the ideological contexts within which these achievements were celebrated"* (Spencer 1983: 04).

However, this is sadly not representative, and the majority of studies of Anuradhapura's terminal period (e.g. Codrington 1960) have invariably examined it from the *a priori* assumption that the *Culavamsa*'s account is reliable enough to not only support such a study, but also provide the foundations and building blocks for that study. Indeed the only attempt to integrate observed data with the events described in the Pali chronicles was Still's (1930) correlation of malarial zones with the distribution of archaeological ruins and inscriptions, and this is discussed below.

Several academics (e.g. Codrington 1960; Spencer 1976; Spencer 1983; Indrapala 2005) have analysed the events (as described in the chronicles and inscriptions) that lead to the Chola invasion, the abandonment of Anuradhapura and the shift of power to Polonnaruva, though only Codrington had an archaeological background, and his "examination" of Anuradhapura's "collapse" is arguably effectively a simple summary of the *Culavamsa*. Both Spencer and Indrapala are historians, Spencer of the early Medieval South Indian kingdoms and Indrapala of Sri Lankan Tamils, and consequently their examinations of the collapse are derived from a combination of the chronicles and epigraphic data.

We now turn our attention to the three models for Anuradhapura's "collapse", the three models that will be tested here through reference to the archaeological record of Anuradhapura. It must be emphasised here that the three models presented here are not intended to be exhaustive of the possible explanations for Anuradhapura's apparent collapse – conjecturally one might add shifts in Indian Ocean trade routes, climactic or environmental change, or indeed any number of the classes of collapse theory discussed above in section **3.3**. Instead, these three models represent the only explanations that have (to date) *been actively propounded* for Anuradhapura's 11th century "collapse", hence their selection for testing. Potential further contributing causal factors will be introduced in Chapter Nine during the discussion of Anuradhapura's terminal period.

3.5.1: The Invasion Model

This, a simple surface reading of the *Culavamsa*'s description (*Cvs*.lv) of Anuradhapura's terminal period, is the most widely accepted explanation for Anuradhapura's terminal period, as well as the foundation upon which the other models are constructed. This monocausal external invasion model of collapse neatly assigns the cause of Anuradhapura's terminal period to the Cholas, invoking the complete destruction and abandonment of the city (both secular and sacred) and its surrounding hinterland. The model is summarised neatly by Codrington (1960), analysing little, questioning nothing, and in no significant fashion differing from the *Culavamsa*'s narrative – thus making it the perfect example of the established Invasion Model for Anuradhapura's terminal period.

The *Culavamsa* portrays the latter half of the first millennium AD as the fluorescence of the Anuradhapura period, with significant construction and repair throughout the Sacred City, Citadel and hinterland (*Cvs*.l-lii) and this view is widely accepted in Sri Lankan archaeology (e.g. Bandaranayake 1974; Seneviratna 1994). However, this period of prosperity is first interrupted in the mid ninth century AD, when a Pandyan invasion during the reign of King Sena I (r. 833 – 853) resulted in the sacking of Anuradhapura (*Cvs*.l.12-36), sparking a series of tit-for-tat conflicts with South Indian kingdoms (Codrington 1960: 94). However, while the Imperial Model attaches significance to this invasion (discussed below), the Invasion Model dismisses it as causing; "*no very great damage*" (*ibid.*). Instead, the Invasion Model ascribes the triggering of Anuradhapura's terminal period to the weak leadership of King Sena V (*r*. 972-982) and his general, Senapti Sena (*Cvs*.liv).

Codrington describes how Sena V "*murdered his general's brother with the result that the general rebelled, went to India, returned with an army, and though he allowed the king to retain his throne,* "made over the country to the Tamils", *that is the mercenaries. Anuradhapura was indeed so full of these... that Sena's successor Mahinda V found it difficult to govern; in his twelfth year the revenue being withheld he could not pay his hired troops, and on their rising fled to Ruhuna*" (Codrington 1960: 94).

Here, the *Culavamsa* appears to place blame on both Sena V and his general, Senapti Sena, for these events. While the execution of Mahamalla (Senapti Sena's brother) by the 12 year old monarch is excused (*Cvs.*liv.57), Senapti Sena is blamed for bringing a Tamil army of 95,000 into the country, whereupon he "*gave over the country to them*" (*Cvs*.liv.64), after which they "*plundered the whole country like devils and pillaging, seized the property of its inhabitants*" (*Cvs*.liv.66-67). Compounding this situation Sena V, who was allowed by Senapti Sena to return to power in at least name, is described as effectively drinking himself to death at just 22 years old; "*After taking intoxicating drinks he was like a wild beast gone mad. As he could no longer digest food the Ruler... died in the tenth year (of his reign)*" (Cvs.liv.185) after being misled by "*evil friends*" (Geiger 1929: 185).

Sena V was succeeded by his younger brother, Mahinda V (r. 982 - 1029 AD), the last king to rule from Anuradhapura (Coningham 1999: 157). Unfortunately, according to the *Culavamsa*, Mahinda V "*wandered from the path of statecraft and was of very weak character*" and as a result the "*peasants did not deliver him his share of the produce*" (*Cvs*.lv.3). By the tenth year of his reign, Mahinda V had "*entirely lost his fortune*" and was thus unable to pay his South Indian mercenaries (*Cvs.*lv.4). The mercenaries went on strike, laying siege to the royal palace and blocking food from entering to the king, crying "*So long as there is no pay he shall not eat*" (*Cvs*.lv.6). Mahinda V escaped through a hidden tunnel and fled southwards to Ruhuna (*Cvs*.lv.7-8), leaving Anuradhapura to be governed as the South Indian mercenaries saw fit (*Cvs*.lv.12-13).

The Chola King, Rajaraja I, hearing of the conditions in Sri Lanka from a horse-dealer returning from the island (*Cvs*.lv.13-14) invaded and in 1017 Rajaraja's successor, Rajendra I, completed the Chola invasion of Sri Lanka by taking Anuradhapura, capturing Mahinda V and the royal Sinhala regalia and sacking both the palaces and temples of Anuradhapura (*Cvs*.lv.16-22). The *Culavamsa* describes "*all the monasteries*" of Anuradhapura as being "*violently destroyed*" (*Cvs*.lv.21). Rajendra I then establishes a new capital at Polonnaruva from where the Cholas rule the majority of the island (Codrington 1960: 94).

The *Culavamsa* then skips the subsequent decades of Chola rule in Sri Lanka, focussing upon the internal disputes in the south of the island as Sri Lankan factions fight for power, before going on to describe the eventual victory of Vijayabahu I over the Chola forces, and his decision to rule from the Chola capital to Polonnaruva (Codrington 1960: 95). The description of the city as being "*utterly destroyed in every way by the Chola army*" (*Cvs*.lxxiv.1) has been taken as the reason for Vijayabahu's decision to shift the capital to Polonnaruva.

However, despite moving the capital, Vijayabahu I holds his royal consecration in the city (Codrington 1960: 95; *Cvs*.lix.8), as do a number of subsequent rulers, and orders fresh construction and repairs (*Cvs*.lix.2-3) to mark his coronation. Around 1100 AD he orders further repairs throughout the kingdom (*Cvs*.lx.48-51) and carries out repairs to the Bodhi Tree shrine and "the *vihara*" at Anuradhapura are repaired (*Cvs*.lx.62-63). While which monastery "the *vihara*" refers to is vague, it seems most likely this refers to the Mahavihara.

After this Anuradhapura goes unmentioned in the *Culavamsa* until the beginning of Parakramabahu's rule (r.1153-1186 AD), when the *Culavamsa* records his ordering wide scale restoration and repairs to the city of Anuradhapura; "*Which had been utterly destroyed in every way by the Chola army*" (*Cvs*.lxxiv.1). The *Culavamsa* describes how Parakramabahu "*...restored within a short time the large and the small walls, the streets, the pasadas and the gate towers. The charming bathing-ponds and the delightful gardens as they had been formerly; also the cetiyas of the three fraternities, the Mahacetiya and the others, as well as the numerous viharas such as the Lohapasada and the like, as well as the pasada serving him as a dwelling, with its gates, bastions, and towers, with its royal courtyard, and embellished with a charming moon chamber, and brought it about that the whole town furnished with these and other marvellous works was as aforetime. Thus he had the buildings set up by many former kings repaired in haste...*" (*Cvs*.lxxiv.8-14). This twelfth century attempt to restore Anuradhapura appears to have focussed predominantly upon the Buddhist fraternities, and the *Culavamsa* describes Parakramabahu's motivation in restoring Anuradhapura as being due to the city being; "*specially deserving of honour, since its soil was hallowed while he lived by the feet of the Master, distinguished by the wheel with its thousand spikes and its rim, and because it was the place where the southern branch of the Sacred Bodhi tree (was planted) and where a dona of relics was preserved*" (*Cvs*.lxxiv.2-4).

Clearly at this point, the *Culavamsa* considers Anuradhapura to be important for Buddhist reasons. As the authors of the *Culavamsa* were Buddhist monks this is perhaps unsurprising. Later on in his reign, Parakramabahu is attributed with renovating the Ruanvelisaya, Abhayagiri, Jetavana and Mirisavati stupas (*Cvs*.lxxviii.97-99), as well as clearing the courtyard of the *cetiya*, raising the 1600 pillars of the *Lohapasada* and restoring the structure to its former glory (*Cvs*.lxxviii.102-105), in addition to restoring a further 60 large *pasadas*, the "*boundary walls and numbers of parivenas*", restoring "*whatever was decayed or had fallen in*" at the Thuparama, and completely restoring the monasteries and stupas at Mihintale (*Cvs*. lxxviii.105-107). In total the renovations and repairs described by chapters lxxiv and lxxviii of the *Culavamsa* appear to amount to little less than a complete restoration of the Sacred City.

Approximately a century later, Vijayabahu IV (r.1270-72) is described as (once again) renovating the Ruanvelisaya stupa and Thuparama, around which a "*mighty forest – that was like a stronghold created by Mara*" had grown (*Cvs*.lxxxviii.80-85), suggesting the city had gone through another period of abandonment after the reign of Parakramabahu, certainly Anuradhapura is not mentioned within the Pali chronicles between the reigns of Parakramabahu and Vijayabahu IV. Following these final restorations by Vijayabahu IV, Anuradhapura vanishes from the Pali chronicles, with no further mention at all in the following five centuries of Sri Lankan "history". At this point the city and its hinterland were finished, abandoned, collapsed – the characteristics of Childe's checklist (Childe 1950) (with Maisel's additions (1999)) now absent from both the city its hinterland, and with Renfrew's characteristics of collapse (1984) all present.

As seen within the Invasion Model, there is no discussion of economics, population or settlement movements or dynamics, like much mediaeval history (both South Asian and European), change is seen as a product and result of the actions of rulers, of "leaders of men". Indeed this model is Tolstoy-esque in its reliance upon historical individuals, and fits almost perfectly with Klejn's analysis of the differing aims of archaeology and history as disciples; "*archaeology and history have different inspirations of knowledge; history strives to understand unique events and heroes, whereas archaeology is obsessed with generalisation*" (Klejn 2001: 35). Thus this model, with its heroic and villainous individuals, would seem a clear product of a purely historical approach. The *Culavamsa* presents us with an account of the collapse of Anuradhapura that could never be reached from a purely archaeological perspective. The high emphasis placed upon the actions of individuals such as Sena V, Mahinda V, Rajaraja I, Rajendra I, Vijayabahu I and Parakramabahu I, distinguish this account from any type of explanation for societal or urban collapse that could possibly be generated from archaeological data or by an archaeological approach.

3.5.2: The Malarial Model

This model is extremely basic, and again implicitly accepts the majority of *Culavamsa*'s narrative as described above (in section **3.5.1**). The difference comes in the manner in which the Malarial Model attempts to explain, not the initial abandonment of Anuradhapura (this is still ascribed to the Chola sacking of the city), but the failure of the Sinhalese to ever successfully restore or re-inhabit the city, arguing that epidemic levels of malaria would have made any such repopulation impossible. Thus, the initial abandonment and Chola destruction of the city and its hinterland are as described in the Invasion Model, with the model differing in the subsequent period.

Malaria, a disease that affects around 500 million people every year in tropical countries (WHO 1999), is caused by a single-celled parasite of the genus *Plasmodium*, and is transmitted from human to human by female mosquitoes of the genus *Anopheles* (Amerasinghe *et al.* 2001: 1), killing between one and three million people annually, and resulting in debility and lost economic productivity among survivors (Amerasinghe *et al.* 2001: 1). The larval stages of mosquitoes typically occur in fresh or brackish water, such as the "*watery habitats such as those found in irrigation systems*", as well as streams and rainwater pools (Amerasinghe et al. 2001: v), and has been associated (e.g. Oomen et al. 1990; Tiffen 1991; Birley 1991; Jobin 1999; Klinkenberg et al. 2004) with irrigation development such as that found in the Dry Zone of Sri Lanka. In addition to the malarial carrying *Anopheles*, other genii of mosquitoes occur in such habitats, and the females may transmit other diseases (e.g. *filariasis*, and arboviral infections such as Japanese encephalitis) (Amerasinghe 2001: 1).

Malaria has been a serious problem in the North Central Province of Sri Lanka since at least the eighteenth century, and was probably endemic in the area during Robert Knox's journey in the seventeenth century (Knox 1681). When the British administration first arrived in the North Central Province in 1833, Anuradhapura was thought to be the most "*unhealthy spot in the island during the rainy season*" (Knighton 1854: 140). The situation was so bad that the North Central Province headquarters were almost relocated, and were only kept in Anuradhapura due to the cost of moving and because *"Anuradhapura had been the seat of government of the ancient kings who had ruled the country for centuries ...it was also a sacred place to the Buddhists and the Sinhalese who regarded it with great veneration"* (Karunananda 2006: 15). However, the epidemic malaria was still such a problem that initially British staff stationed there were granted three months annual leave, from December to March (*ibid.*: 16). As an illustration of the scale of the problem, at around the same time (1870s/1880s) in nearby British ruled India, an expansion of the irrigation system resulted in the digging of 12,750 miles of canals, irrigating 6.3 million acres, – a vast project with huge potential for malarial expansion. It is difficult to accurately determine how many deaths were caused by malaria at this time in India, but the President of the India Officers Medical Board, Sir Joseph Fayrer, estimated that of the 4,975,042 registered deaths in India during the year of 1879, nearly 72% could be attributed to fevers (Fayrer 1882: 09), an epidemic comparable in scale to the Bubonic Plague in fourteenth century Europe (Webb 2009: 122).

Malaria was first linked to the abandonment of the Dry Zone urban centres by Lieutenant Fagan of the British Army in 1820 (Nicholls 1921: 1). Fagan, writing in the Ceylon Gazette, proposed that *"malaria was the primary cause which initiated the decay of these cities"* (cited in Nicholls 1921: 1). This argument was adopted a century later by Nicholls in a paper entitled *Malaria and the Lost Cities of Ceylon* (1921). Nicholls argued that it was clear that the ancient cities *"were not overwhelmed by a single great catastrophe. The energy of the people waned through many years and with it tanks were neglected, and cultivation disappeared from large areas, and decay slowly insinuated itself through the cities and the forests crept in"* (Nicholls 1921: 2). A decade later, Still argued along the same lines (although referring specifically to the urban collapse of Anuradhapura), following Nicholls' lead in drawing attention to the remarkable similarities between malarial levels and the distribution of ancient inscriptions throughout the island (Still 1930: 76), and the concentration of population in non-malarial zones by the time the Portuguese arrived (Nicholls 1921: 9). Nicholls' somewhat rudimentary argument ended here, with the assertion that *"the north-central areas of Ceylon could not have bred or supported the vast numbers of the active race that built and developed its ancient cities had malaria existed there at that time"* (Nicholls 1921: 10), continuing; *"once malaria was established the people and their culture would drift to the less malarious parts"* (*ibid.*: 11).

However, Nicholls did not connect the outbreak or spread of malaria with the Chola invasion, and it was Still who first argued that the invading Cholas were in fact directly responsible for unleashing malaria upon Anuradhapura, reasoning that, while the Sinhalese would have respected the monumental hydraulic landscape during internal conflicts, the Chola invaders; *"cared but to injure their opponents as quickly and as thoroughly as they could"* (Still 1930: 89). Still went on to argue that as the authors of the *Culavamsa* were monks they; *"knew little of the tactics of war and did not describe them"*, but it was possible to deduce from the lists of repairs that were implemented after the invasion (*Cvs.*lx.48-51) that the; *"tanks and channels suffered terrible damage in the war. Their bunds must have been cut as an ordinary tactic, or as reprisal... with disastrous results"* (Still 1930: 89).

More specifically, Still argued that the *"very life"* of ancient Anuradhapura was drawn from the water supply of Kalaveva tank, located some 53 miles south of the city, the water of which supplied not only the Citadel itself, but also the monasteries of the Sacred City and much of the hinterland. Thus by cutting this one channel; *"somewhere along its serpentine course of three-and-fifty miles... fields would be thrown out of cultivation, and standing crops ruined; clean running water, not only throughout the city but over wide areas, would dry rapidly under the tropical sun into a string of pools; millions of small fish would be left to perish of drought and millions more would be captured by birds where they still fought for life in water all too shallow for them; and mosquitoes would multiply at an appalling rate"* (*ibid.*: 90).

A similar picture was painted by a decade later by Brohier, who wrote that; *"...the wasted organizations could not repair the mighty artificial "tanks" and the canals of corresponding magnitude when they were wilfully damaged by the enemy or breached by the monsoon spates. Large morasses and stagnant waters which bred pestilence soon took their place"* (Brohier 1941: xvii).

This picture is devastating enough as it is, as established earlier artificial storage and transport of fresh water is absolutely necessary to the maintenance of a large population within the Dry Zone, and without it sustained agriculture was impossible. However, it was the mosquitoes that Still regarded as critical, writing that the; *"best way to combat malaria is to drain the pools where the larvae of the anopheles mosquitoes can live, and the second best way, where...the pools cannot be drained or filled in again, is to introduce small fish, who, multiplying quickly, feed upon the larvae and control them, preventing their increase"* (Still 1930: 90-91). The Chola invasion, and the destruction of the hydraulic landscape upon which Anuradhapura was so dependant, made both methods of managing malaria impossible and; *"we cannot doubt that was almost certainly followed by an epidemic of malaria. That is why the Sinhalese eventually became too enfeebled to keep up the mighty works their ancestors had built"* (*ibid.*).

In 1957 Murphey argued that; "*it seems almost out of the question that malaria could have caused the original abandonment*" (Murphey 1957: 198). Instead, Murphey argued that malaria arrived in the island around the fourteenth century AD (*ibid.*: 199). However, Murphey's rejection of malaria as a cause in Anuradhapura's abandonment relied entirely upon a single notation upon a sixteenth century Portuguese map of Sri Lanka, which notes that Ruhuna was depopulated by "sickness" three-hundred years earlier (Reimers 1929: v). While this "sickness" might well have been malaria there is no way to be sure, and more significantly, Ruhuna is in the far south of Sri Lanka, and it is quite possible that malaria was endemic in the Anuradhapura region long before it arrived in Ruhuna.

Self-evidently the primary difference between this model and the Invasion model, is in the emphasis placed upon malaria as the primary cause for the final abandonment of Anuradhapura, with the Malarial model envisioning a significant initial attempt at re-settlement of the city and its hinterland, only to be prevented by epidemic levels of malaria resulting in a relatively rapid decline.

3.5.3: *The Imperial Model*

This is the most recent and detailed of all explanations proposed for Anuradhapura's terminal period, and places the economic structure of Anuradhapura at the heart of its collapse. Despite the economic core of this model, it can also be described as polycausal in its invocation of several interwoven events and processes; economic stresses caused by inter polity conflict in the ninth and tenth centuries, the crystallization of economic structure, the Chola invasion, and religious and ethnic tensions (Spencer 1976 & 1983; Indrapala 2005: 231-232).

Before the details of this model are examined, there are two key factors that must be discussed in relation to the formation of this model. Firstly, it must be noted that the proponents of this model (Spencer and Indrapala) were explicitly writing about the Cholas (Spencer 1976 & 1983) and Tamils (Indrapala 2005) in Sri Lanka, rather than Anuradhapura itself. Despite this, these examinations of the collapse of Anuradhapura remain more detailed and critical than those that preceded them. Secondly, and as a result of the above point, this model is not set out explicitly by either Indrapala or Spencer. Instead the model, as used here, is derived synthetically from a number of separate discussions, arguments, and statements regarding the events before, during, and after the Chola invasion. In this respect the Imperial Model is a synthesis of peripheral discussions, rather than a clearly reasoned argument propounded by numerous academics.

As stated above the Imperial model invokes several different causal elements. However, that is not to say that this model actively contradicts the *Culavamsa*'s narrative, indeed the works of both Spencer (1976 & 1983) and Indrapala (2005) explore the *Culavamsa*'s account of the Chola invasions rather than actively arguing against it. Consequently, this model still sees Sena V and Mahinda V struggling as rulers (Spencer 1976: 410), still sees Senapti Sena rebelling with an army of South Indian mercenaries (*ibid.*), and still sees Rajaraja sacking Anuradhapura (*ibid.*: 411).

Effectively, the Imperial Model can be divided into two key elements; the initial collapse of Anuradhapura, and its subsequent abandonment by Vijayabahu I. Spencer, agreeing with earlier models, maintains that the city of Anuradhapura was devastated by the Chola invasion, quoting from the *Culavamsa*, Spencer writes (1976: 412) that; "*The Cholas seized the Mahesi, the jewels, the diadem that the King had inherited, the whole of the [royal] ornaments, the priceless diamond bracelet, a gift of the gods, the unbreakable sword and the relic of the torn strip of cloth... In the three fraternities and in all Lanka [breaking open] the relic chambers, [they carried away] many costly images of gold, etc., and while they violently destroyed here and there all the monasteries, like blood-sucking* yakkhas *they took all the treasures of Lanka for themselves*" (Cvs.lv.16-22 cited in Spencer 1976: 412). Spencer stresses that, even allowing for exaggeration by the chronicler of the *Culavamsa*, Anuradhapura has clearly been devastated – and that this is clearly a major factor in the initial abandonment of the city (Spencer 1986: 55). However, great significance is also attached to the earlier invasion by the Cholas around the middle of the tenth century, resulting in the end of "*the kingdom that had Anuradhapura as the power-centre*" (Indrapala 2005: 231). Indrapala goes on to argue that the Cholas were never interested in ruling Anuradhapura itself, and had "*in all probability already created elsewhere the necessary administrative structure necessary to them, namely the northern and eastern regions giving control of the major ports*" (*ibid.*).

Furthermore, the Cholas were Saivite and would have been understandably reluctant to occupy a centre of Theravada Buddhism, preferring instead to develop a new capital reflecting both Saivite Hinduism and Mahayana Buddhism in its architecture and temples (Indrapala 2005: 244-245 & 251), while ensuring the near elimination of the established Theravada *sangha*. This would have been necessary for the Cholas to take control of the economic surplus generated by the region, something Spencer argues was a prime motive for their invasion in the first place (1983: 64) as in the centuries prior to the Chola invasion the Buddhist monasteries had become pre-eminent economic institutions, and were critically involved in the economic administration of land and surplus (Liyanarachchi 2009: 109). Indeed, so involved were the *sangha* in the economy of Anuradhapura that their accounting and auditing practices were extremely sophisticated by the end of the tenth century (*ibid.*: 117).

Consequently, for the Cholas to re-direct economic surplus to their merchants, temples, and their homeland, they needed to remove the Buddhist *sangha* from the economic structure of Anuradhapura – resulting in the targeted destruction of not just the Citadel and Sacred City, but also of monastic sites within the hinterland of Anuradhapura as well.

But why then, when Vijayabahu reclaimed the throne of Sri Lanka from the Cholas, did he not return to Anuradhapura; the seat of royal power in the island for well over a millennium, the site of Buddha's visit to the island, the home of Sri Lanka's major monastic institutions and indeed one of the pre-eminent centres of Theravada teaching and learning in Asia? Surely, at a time when he was fighting to unify rival factions under his reign, such an opportunity to connect himself to over a millennium of Sinhala rule that came before him, and to the religious and spiritual heart of Sri Lanka, would be invaluable? Instead, Vijayabahu I chooses Polonnaruva as his capital – the former capital of the Cholas, and a city with a significant Saivite Hindu presence (Indrapala 2005: 250), marking the beginning of a new period of religious eclecticism in Sri Lanka in which the power of the Anuradhapura Buddhist fraternities is massively diminished (*ibid*.: 251).

Explaining Vijayabahu's decision to keep the capital at Polonnaruva, three major factors are stressed; firstly, the damage done to Anuradhapura by the Chola invasion (Spencer 1983: 54), secondly, the changes made to the administrative infrastructure of the island by the Cholas (Indrapala 2005: 251) including shifts in the long distance trade routes to bypass Anuradhapura (Spencer 1983: 59) and the removal of the *sangha* from the economic administration; and finally, a religious sea change within early Mediaeval Sri Lanka island (Indrapala 2005: 251).

Examining the first factor, the damage done to Anuradhapura by the Chola invasion, there appears little doubt within this model that the Cholas devastated the city, as has been described above with the Cholas even going so far as to smash the great stupas themselves (Spencer 1983: 54). However, similar destruction to Anuradhapura had been recorded in the Pali chronicles on at least four previous occasions during earlier Pandyan and Chola incursions (Seneviratna 1994: 34), and each time the city had been restored – palaces rebuilt, stupas re-clad, temples restored (*ibid*.). The Imperial model suggests two causes; firstly, that Vijayabahu I couldn't afford such major restorations and secondly, that the scale of the damage done was far higher than in previous sackings. Economic surplus had been flowing out of Sri Lanka (and into South India) for over half a century (Spencer 1983: 60), and the wealth of Anuradhapura had been, as has been discussed above, hugely diminished in the tenth century and subsequently plundered during the Chola conquest and occupation. Furthermore, just a century earlier during the reign of Mahinda V, the *Culavamsa* described how the young King had, by his tenth year as King, "entirely lost his fortune" (Cvs.lv.3), Anuradhapura was already in an economic depression before the Chola sacking. On top of this Vijayabahu I, even after driving the Cholas from island, was still far from secure on his new throne, and faced civil rebellion almost immediately after being crowned (Basham 1973: 21). This model thus argues that it is likely that such major restoration of the ruined city of Anuradhapura was simply too expensive at that time. Thus Vijayabahu I held his consecration at Anuradhapura for symbolic reasons, but for practical reasons ruled from Polonnaruva.

The second factor cited by this model as a cause of Anuradhapura's urban collapse is the alteration of the administrative infrastructure by the Cholas. Although Spencer sees the Chola invasion as utterly devastating to Anuradhapura as a city, he argues that the rural hinterland of the city would have been largely left untouched (Spencer 1976: 413). Pointing out that although the chronicles frequently glorified in the construction and repair of the hydraulic landscape, there is no mention whatsoever of any Chola damage to this irrigation system (Spencer 1983: 55), although he does suggest that the irrigation infrastructure might have suffered through negligence – due to either the inability to muster the necessary labour, or inexperience as to what is required (*ibid*.: 56). This is a key difference between the Imperial model and the Malarial and Invasion models, which both see the Cholas devastating the hydraulic landscape of the hinterland as an offensive tactic. In comparison, the Imperial model sees the devastation confined to the Citadel, Sacred City, and monastic sites of the hinterland. This is a point that both Spencer and Indrapala stress, arguing that the Chola administration was able to levy taxes on the rural population, on traders plying the main highways, on craftsmen and on merchants (Spencer 1983: 60), and that it is even possible that the existing local administrative structure was continued with a Chola "*superstructure*" replacing the previous elite (Indrapala 2005: 232). The damage to the wider rural population would have been deliberately minimal to ensure continued economic productivity, as it was this economic productivity that attracted the Chola invasion in the first place, in particular the maritime trade links to South East Asia from Sri Lanka (Spencer 1976: 414). The Chola invasion, argues Spencer, was not aimed at short term gain through plunder, but was an attempt to "*establish a forward military base and to institute a rudimentary tribute/tax system there, while undertaking occasional forays into more distant territories*" (Spencer 1976: 419).

However, while the rural landscape and populace were not intentionally damaged, the imposition of the Chola "superstructure" upon the administrative system of the island substantially weakened that system. The role of the Buddhist *sangha* in the administration of the rural landscape had grown greatly during the latter half of the millennium before the Chola invasion (Dias 1990: 151; Liyanarachchi 2009: 109), but economic importance within the kingdom was irrevocably damaged by the Chola invasion. The most obvious aspect of this damage was the sacking of the great Buddhist monasteries within the Sacred City of Anuradhapura, but arguably more damaging in the long run was the Chola reorganisation of the economic administration of the kingdom, that would likely have necessitated the destruction or eviction of monastic sites throughout the hinterland. Either way, when the Chola invaders removed the *sangha* from the summit of the Sri Lankan administrative system they effectively ended over a millennium of gradual accruement of land, of the rights to tithes and taxes from land, villages, tanks and canals, in short, of political and economic influence. Subsequently, when Vijayabahu I took the throne, he deliberately chose to maintain the economic administration set up by the imperial Cholas (Indrapala 2005: 251). This decision appears to be one of several steps taken by Vijayabahu to moderate the power and influence of the previously dominant Buddhist fraternities, though it would appear that the Cholas had already done much to weaken the *sangha*. As has been stated before Anuradhapura was one of the primary centres of Buddhist wisdom (primarily Theravada but to a lesser degree Mahayana) for the preceding thousand years, with three major Buddhist monasteries that had become powerful and influential political and economic factions within the Sri Lankan political landscape; thousands of monks called Anuradhapura home, and vast tracts of agricultural land were under the monastic ownership. Yet just a century later Vijayabahu I was forced to send to Myanmar for Buddhist monks in order to restore the *sangha* of Sri Lanka, such was its condition (*Cvs*.lx.4-6; Indrapala 2005: 239).

However, even after this influx of monks the religious balance of the Polonnaruva period was more eclectic, with "*a marked increase in mixed Buddhism, Brahmanical and Saiva practices at elite level*" (Indrapala 2005: 251). This was expressed in a number of manners, including royal patronage of Brahmanical rituals, royal matrimonial alliances with non-Buddhist Indian royal families, and eventually one monarch (Magha) openly choosing Saivism over Buddhism (ibid.: 254). It is thus argued that the power wielded by the three major Buddhist monasteries, the "three fraternities" (*Cvs*.lx.10) of the Mahavihara, Abhayagiri vihara and Jetavana vihara, would have been greatly weakened by their removal from the economic administration of Sri Lanka (Spencer 1983: 60), the movement of political primacy from Anuradhapura to Polonnaruva, and the loss of support of the ruling royal family (Indrapala 2005: 251-254). Anuradhapura was indelibly associated with both Buddhism and the "*three fraternities*", while the city of Polonnaruva now represented a harmonious coexistence of Buddhism and Saivism (Indrapala 2005: 252), one which also wielded far less political and economic weight. This shift in the religious and economic landscape of Sri Lanka and the Sri Lankan elite would have had a hugely detrimental effect on Anuradhapura's status within the island, leaving it a symbolic location for the Bodhi tree shrine and its stupas – but not a centre of political or economic power.

Consequently, the Imperial Model sees Anuradhapura's terminal period as three-fold; in the centuries leading up to the Chola invasion, the influence of South India (culturally and economically) upon Anuradhapura gradually increases along with contact and conflict between Anuradhapura and the South Indian polities. This may be seen as the groundwork or preparation for the "collapse". Subsequently, the Cholas invaded, sacking the city, attenuating the *sangha* and restructuring the island's economic infrastructure around Polonnaruva. This causes significant damage to the economic structure of Anuradhapura, including the shifting away of trade routes, the deterioration of the hydraulic infrastructure, and the loss of the administrative organisation (the sangha) that oversaw the economic collection and redistribution of surplus. Finally, when Vijayabahu came to power he chose to rule from Polonnaruva, transforming Anuradhapura into a symbolic site as religious power shifts away from an orthodox Buddhist hegemony to a more poly-religious climate in which Saivite Hinduism and Mahayanism were also openly and actively followed, sponsored and endorsed. The Citadel and Sacred City of Anuradhapura were now in ruins, and were only superficially restored or repaired – with no significant return of an elite presence within either the Citadel or Sacred City. Meanwhile the hinterland of Anuradhapura gradually deteriorated as the tank system was allowed to fall into disrepair and the population density fell due to the loss of the sangha.

3.6 Conclusion

This chapter laid out the theoretical background for this examination of Anuradhapura's "collapse", starting with an examination of the core issues of "civilisation" and "collapse", before summarising the development of collapse theory in South Asia and establishing the national collapse theory paradigm. Finally, the three models for Anuradhapura's terminal period were presented and modeled. The next chapter will now present and critically analyse the datasets that are to be used, identify archaeological chronological indicators, and archaeologically characterise each of the three models so that they may be tested against the data in Chapters Five, Six and Seven.

Chapter 4: Methodology

4.1 Introduction

The following chapter will present and critically analyse the three main datasets, as the differences between the datasets will alter what analyses are possible with each, and thus the methodology. Following this, key chronological indicators will be identified. As all three models see the collapse occur over approximately two centuries it is important that the archaeological data is as diachronically constrained as possible. Next, specific methodological approaches to determining cultural change at Anuradhapura sites will be discussed, focussing upon the analysis of material artefacts to identify changes in trade, religious activity and social status. Finally, the three collapse models will be characterised as archaeological signatures; archaeologically visible events and sequences. As the three models that are being tested are products of textual studies, this volume will take an explicitly archaeological perspective, focussing upon physical artefacts and structural remains.

However, before the above can be set out, it is necessary to examine the form and nature of Anuradhapura itself. As will be seen the tri-fold nature of Anuradhapura is reflected in the data-sets available and thus the methodological approaches to analysing each of those data sets.

4.2: The Datasets

Recent research (Coningham et al. 2007a) has highlighted the interactions, (economic, spiritual and political) between three distinct zones within the Buddhist temporality of Anuradhapura; the Citadel, the Sacred City, and the hinterland, schematically represented in figure 4.03. Due to the nature of archaeological research at Anuradhapura over the last century (see **2.3**) each of these zones has a distinct archaeological data-set; the Sacred City characterised by wide-area grid excavations of the major viharas (Ratnayake 1984; Wikragamage et al. 1983 and 1984; Wikragamage 1984 and 1992), the Citadel by the deep-sequence excavation of ASW2 (Coningham 1999 & 2006), and the hinterland by the recently completed multi-disciplinary British-Sri Lankan survey (Coningham et al. 2005, 2006a, 2006b, 2007 and 2007b). These data-sets are so different in form, scale and scope that they will require modified methodologies for the analysis of each one. It must be stressed that the "city" of Anuradhapura does not follow the Hellenistic, Mesopotamian or Mediaeval European models of urban form, and that within this world view the city is understood to be at the centre of the world – not simply in a geographical, political or economic sense, but as the centre of the cosmos and of order (Eck 1987: 04). As such, Anuradhapura was *"no casual cluster of buildings but a cosmography that reflected the universe"* (Wickremeratne 1987: 45), *"an ordered human habitation with... a 'self-image'"* (ibid.: 01). Thus while the Early Mediaeval city of Anuradhapura grew out of the Iron Age settlement identified in Period J of the ASW2 excavations (Coningham 1999: 73), it was clearly controlled in its growth, with careful planning at every phase of growth (Wickremeratne 1987: 48), developing outwards from its core – the Citadel.

4.2.1: Defining the Citadel

At the geographical centre of the city (as seen in figures 4.01 and 6.01), although not necessarily the symbolic centre of the city (arguably this was the Bodhi Tree (Wickremeratne 1987: 55)), was the fortified Citadel (figure 4.02), representing the seat of secular power in Anuradhapura (Wickremeratne 1987: 55). This was then surrounded by a far larger area of monumental monastic structures, monasteries and associated buildings termed the "Sacred City". Although the framing of the city in such a fashion leads to a clear distinction between the "secular" Citadel and the "monastic" Sacred City, it was likely more complex than such a simplistic distinction might suggest. Certainly, there were shrines, alms halls and other religious structures within the Citadel, and it is likely that there were a significant number of purely residential or industrial structures within the Sacred City. Furthermore, the Theravada Buddhist *sangha* and the "secular" monarchy were relatively synergetic, working together in a *"dialectical relationship, arising both from a necessary solidarity and a reciprocal control"* (Houtart 1977: 209; Wickremeratne 1987: 56). This will be discussed further in the discussion.

The Citadel (figure 4.02), also called the *Atu Nuvara* meaning Royal Enclosure or Palace Complex (Seneviratna 1994: 19), is a walled rectangular area measuring approximately 5km in circumference (Hocart 1924: 48). It appears to have followed a grid layout, with Hocart observing two arterial thoroughfares running north-south and east-west (Hocart 1928a: 151), and the Chinese pilgrim Faxian describing it as divided by four main streets running through the city from gates at each of the cardinal points (cited in Giles 1923: 69). Faxian described the city (believed to be referring explicitly to the Citadel rather than to the wider settlement) as;

"In this city there are many elders of the Buddhist laity; the dwellings of the head-merchants are very grand; and the side-streets and main thoroughfares are level and well kept. At all points where four roads meet there are chapels for preaching the Faith; and on the eighth, fourteenth and fifteenth of each month a lofty dais is arranged, where ecclesiastics and laymen come together from all quarters to hear the Faith expounded." (Giles 1923: 69-70).

In addition to the structural layout and form of the city being planned, the social layout is believed to have been carefully prescribed as well, with the *Mahavamsa* recording that when the city was founded as capital by King Pandukabhaya, he located four suburbs around the Citadel, one outside each of the four gates (*Mvs.* xx.88-90). Outside the Western Gate he established the common cemetery, the execution site, the house of the Great Sacrifice, the chapel of the Queens of the West, the banyan-tree of Vessavana and the Palmyra-tree of the Demon of the Maladies, and the quarters of the *yonas* or foreigners (*ibid.*). North-west of the common cemetery Pandukabhaya located a village for the 850 Candalas (the so called "outcaste" or unclean) that Pandukabhaya had set "*to the work of cleaning the* (streets of the) *town, ...cleaning the sewers, ...to bear the dead and ... be watchers in the cemetery*". Further north and east of the Candala village was built a second cemetery, called the Lower Cemetery, which was exclusively for the Candalas (*Mvs.*x.91-93). Thus we see urban planning not just in the form of laid out streets in a grid fashion, but also socially in the establishment of residential quarters and cemeteries for specific social groups. Unfortunately, these areas have not been identified, leaving our archaeological understanding of "secular" Anuradhapura primarily reliant upon the excavations carried out within the actual walled Citadel (Seneviratna 1994: 19), thus leaving the developed area surrounding the Citadel to be labelled as the Sacred City.

4.2.1.1: The Citadel Dataset

The research background of the ASW2 (Anuradhapura Salgaha Watta 2) sondage was described in Chapter Two (**2.3.2**), and the sequence created provides an exhaustive structural and artefactual sequence for the Citadel back to the settlement's Iron Age origins. However, it is not so much the ASW2 project's conclusions that will be utilized here, as the data itself thanks to their decision to publish *everything*; every artefact recovered published with context, structural phase and period as well as detailed descriptions. This enables a quantitative approach to artefactual analyses, for example comparing counts and weights of exotic ceramics in the periods leading up to, during, and after the collapse of Anuradhapura to assess fluctuations in long distance trade.

However, despite the exhaustive publishing and comprehensive artefactual sequence of the ASW2 project, there are some drawbacks to this dataset. The biggest is the spatial coverage offered by the ASW2 sondage, while the excavations covered two millennia of on-site occupation, it is a single 100m2 sample within the Citadel, an area of approximately 1,000,000m2. This may be partially overcome by incorporating the reports from earlier excavations within the Citadel, those of Bell (1893), Hocart (1924), Paranavitana (1936) and Deraniyagala (1972 & 1986). These reports are far more limited in their publishing of data, but their incorporation allows the examination of the Citadel's terminal period across a wider area, and avoids risks of inferring too much into a limited sample area.

The second problem with the Citadel data is one of chronological resolution. The latter periods of the ASW2 (Coningham 1999) and Gedige (Deraniyagala 1972 & 1986) sequences are extremely disturbed, with high levels of *ex-situ* artefacts and little in the way of intact structural remains. This has resulted in broad date ranges being attributed to these phases, for example periods C,D&E in the ASW2 sequence cover a period of almost 500 years (Coningham & Batt 1999: 129-130). This will be returned to later in the discussion of chronological indicators. Despite these broad date ranges, it is the ASW2 structural periods that will be used as the core chronology of this study, and applied to the Sacred City and Hinterland due to the scope and length of the ASW2 structural and artefactual sequence. This structural chronology and its approximate calendrical dates is presented below (table 4.01), although the sequence is presented and discussed in greater detail in chapters 5, 6 and 7.

Table 4.01: ASW2 structural periods

Period	Approximate date range (century AD)
F	c. 3rd – 7th
C, D & E	c. 6th – 10th
B	c. 11th – 12th

4.2.2: Defining the Sacred City

If the Citadel represented the seat of secular power within Anuradhapura (Wickremeratne 1987: 55), the larger area of monumental monastic shrines, viharas, and associated structures surrounding the Citadel represents a different, yet equally significant, heart of Anuradhapura. It is this outer monastic zone (shown in figures 4.01 and 6.01) that has been termed the "Sacred City".

As already stressed, the framing of the city in such a bipartite fashion leads to a simplified distinction between the "secular" (Citadel) and the "sacred" (Sacred City). Indeed, the aforementioned village of the Candalas, the quarters of the *yonas* and cemeteries described in the *Mahavamsa* (*Mvs.*x.91-93; *Mvs.*xx.88-90) would likely have lain within what is termed the "Sacred City", as the Sacred City is defined as much by its not being *within* the Citadel as it is by any "sacred" characteristics (for a full discussion see Silva 1979; Wickremeratne 1987 or Coningham 1993a). However, such a framing is both practicable and reflected by the archaeological datasets.

The Sacred City was dominated by the three major Buddhist fraternities clustered around the Citadel (Fig.4.01); the Mahavihara to the south, Jetavana vihara to the east, and Abhayagiri vihara to the north. The oldest of these, the Mahavihara, is believed to have been founded by Devanampiya Tissa (r. 250-210 BC) around 249 BC (*Mvs*.xv) and was the seat of orthodox Theravadism in Sri Lanka for over two millennia (Seneviratna 1994: 27). Abhayagiri Vihara was the next to be founded, around 89 BC (*Mvs*.xxxiii.83), shortly afterwards becoming the centre of the heterodox Mahayanists (*Mvs*.xxxiii.97; Seneviratna 1994: 27). The last of the great monastic complexes to be founded was Jetavana, under the rule of King Mahasena I (r. 274-301 AD) (Seneviratna 1994: 27). Although originally founded within the orthodox Mahavihara, Jetavana Vihara quickly seceded following a further rift within the Mahavihara (*Mvs*.xxxvii.32-39).

It is possible to sub-divide the Sacred City into three further zones; a core monastic zone formed by the major monasteries listed above, an agricultural zone surrounding this core including the major Anuradhapura tanks of Tissaveva, Nuvaraveva, Basavak Kulam and Bulan Kulam, and finally an outer ring of late Anuradhapura period monastic complexes, including Vessagiriya, Toluvila, Puliankulama, Vijayarama, Kiribat vihara, Pankuliya, Isurumuniya, Mullegala, Pacinatissapabbata and the so called 'Western Monasteries'.

4.2.2.1: The Sacred City Dataset

As described in Chapter Two, the early excavations within the Sacred City (Fig.6.01) were antiquarian and will primarily be used to compliment the records of the CCF excavations of the Abhayagiri and Jetavana viharas. In both cases the sites were divided into grids, with selected grid squares across the site excavated – sometimes down to natural, sometimes to what appears to be an arbitrary point (e.g. Ratnanayake 1984: 28). Unfortunately, as described in Chapter Two, no final reports have been published for either the Jetavanaramaya or Abhayagiri Vihara projects. The Abhayagiri excavations did produce four preliminary reports (two for the first season (Wikramagamage et al. 1983; Wikramagamage 1984) and two for the second (Wikramagamage et al. 1984; Wikramagamage 1992) in addition to two further preliminary publications from the project's Czech collaborators (Bouzek et al. 1986 & 1993).

However, the Jetavanaramaya Project, despite completing five seasons of excavation, produced only one preliminary report from their first season (Ratnayake 1984). Unfortunately, that single report is descriptive, lacking in clarity, and in places little more than a précis of the *Mahavamsa* with a meaningless description of pottery types by level (*ibid.*: 59). There is no interpretation, no structural sequence, no periodisation, and no clear aims, objectives, methodology or consistency. Indeed, there are conservation reports that are more informative. To underline the tragedy of this publishing (or lack thereof) a visit to the Jetavana museum demonstrates the wealth of artefacts recovered from these excavations – little to none of which have been published. Consequently, the bulk of the Sacred City dataset will be drawn from the Abhayagiri excavations which, while not perfect, are greater in both scale and quality than the single report from the Jetavanaramaya project.

4.2.3: Defining the Hinterland

The hinterland of Anuradhapura can be loosely defined as the tributary region surrounding and economically linked to the city (sacred and secular). However, such a definition does not lend itself to precise boundaries, and the adoption of the region defined by Coningham & Gunawardhana's hinterland survey (2013) will best allow the integration of this invaluable dataset. Within this survey the hinterland was delineated by a 25km radius (coincidentally the estimated distance an Ox-cart could travel in two days), later expanded to a 50km radius, centred upon the Citadel of Anuradhapura.

This landscape is made up of villages and paddy fields, the tanks and canals of the hydraulic landscape, the raw resources that are still exploited today (stone quarries, woodlands for timber and game, clay beds for bricks, terracotta and ceramics) and of course the temples, shrines and monasteries that made up the Buddhist temporality of Anuradhapura (Coningham et al. 2006a).

4.2.3.1: The hinterland dataset

The primary dataset for the hinterland is that of the Coningham and Gunawardhana hinterland survey (2013), which I worked upon for five seasons, leading teams of archaeologists on transect survey, excavation and post-excavation finds processing. Although multidisciplinary in its methodology, this project centred upon a probabilistic transect survey of the hinterland, designed to allow reliable general conclusions about the sample universe from the areas sampled. Twenty-four randomly generated transects of 20km were surveyed, covering a total area of 96 km². Allowing for the inaccessibility of the northern half of the survey universe (due to security concerns), this accounted for 2.44% of the survey universe, a semi-circle with a 50km radius and area of 3928.5 km².

Table 4.02: Anuradhapura Hinterland transect survey sites

Site Type	Number
Ceramic Scatters (all variations)	385
just ceramics	287
with brick	27
with tile	8
with brick & tile	12
with slag	49
with brick, tile & slag	2
Monastic Sites	98
lena (on outcrop)	39
stupa & lena (on outcrop)	9
stupa (on outcrop)	15
stupa (not on outcrop)	6
non-stupa site (on outcrop)	20
non-stupa site (not on outcrop)	8
Inscription	1
Undiagnostic site with pillars	48
Tanks	255
Stone bridges & annicuts	1
Quarrying sites	44
Conical holes	21
Canals, channels & hydraulic features	28
Possible Megalithic burials	7
Lithic scatters	3
Total	891

Archaeological sites were defined by a feature, find spot or scatter, and sites' locations were mapped by GPS, photographed it and sketched. Artefacts were recorded, collected and processed. In addition to the probabilistic transect survey non-probabilistic survey was carried out along the banks of the Malvatu Oya and of several ancient canals. The aim of these non-probabilistic surveys was to identify possible settlements and break of bulk points for transport along conduits linking the city with the coast. Selected sites were then subjected to further investigation through auger coring, geophysical survey by a team lead by Dr. Armin Schmidt, and/or excavation by a team lead by Professor Robin Coningham. Auger coring allowed identification of the depth and extent of sites, as well recording macro-stratigraphic details. Geophysical survey then defined site size and morphology. The geophysics and auger-core survey results were then utilised to decide which sites to sample by excavation, with four square metres excavated at selected sites. Cultural sediments were studied by a team from the University of Stirling lead by Professor Ian Simpson, using thin-section micromorphology and associated X-ray microprobe analytical techniques for further definition. Chronologies for the geomorphological survey element of the project were then established through combined AMS (accelerated mass spectrometry) radiocarbon dates and OSL (optically stimulated light) measurements.

In total 891 sites were identified on transect survey (Table 4.02), with a further 107 sites (94 archaeological, 5 quarrying and 27 ethnoarchaeological) identified during non-probabilistic River Survey, and 90 sites during non-probabilistic Canal Survey (15 tanks, 3 quarrying sites, 9 ethnoarchaeological sites and 65 archaeological sites). As seen above (Table 4.02), ceramic scatters were the most common site identified within the hinterland, with 385 sites or 43.2% of all recorded sites. These sites were primarily characterised by the presence of five or more ceramic sherds within one metre square. Ceramic scatters with slag, brick, or tile present were recorded as sub-categories of this site type. These were followed by tanks (ranging from small village to monumental) as the second major site class, with 28.6% of all sites. This is unsurprising given their size and visibility (even when disused and overgrown), and the importance of water storage and management within this eco-zone (Still 1931; Brohier 1934; Brohier 1941; Farmer 1954; Seneviratna 1989).

Monastic sites, (98 or 11% of sites recorded) were typically identified by the presence of either a stupa or *lena* (a rock shelter utilised by Buddhist monks), though other religious artefacts such as sri pada, Buddhist statues, *yantrigala* etc. were also used to identify such sites. Another category of sites, 'Undiagnostic site with pillars', were similar in nature to many monastic sites, but lacked any discernibly religious characteristics. Two such sites were excavated, revealing one to be monastic, while the other was revealed to be non-structural. It thus appears likely that many, if not the majority, of undiagnostic pillared sites would have been monastic in nature, though this is clearly conjectural. The other site types featured above were primarily characterised by a single characteristic; e.g. an inscription, canal, channel or annicut.

Clearly sites such as tanks or monastic sites on outcrops are more visible and thus likely to be identified and recorded, conversely artefact scatters and the like are more ephemeral and rendered near invisible in certain vegetation. For example, within elephant grass it is near impossible to identify surface scatters, while on a recently ploughed field such artefacts are highly visible and likely to have been brought to the surface through ploughing. As a result, while it is possible to simplistically multiple the number of sites by the percentage area of the hinterland surveyed (386 ceramic scatter sites and 98 monastic sites were identified within 2.44% of the hinterland area, therefore theoretically there could be as many as 15,820 ceramic scatters and

4,016 monastic sites within the full semi-circular 3928.5 km², and even 31,639 and 8,033 such sites within the full 7857 km2 hinterland), such extrapolations are clearly far too simplistic, especially as regards the latter, given that the vast majority of the area north of the Citadel was never surveyed.

The strength of this dataset is in its coverage of a large area around Anuradhapura, and, due to its probabilistic transects, its representivity of that hinterland. However, while this data is strong spatially, it is chronologically weak due to the surface identification of sites. However, it also offers a range of data forms, including OSL dates, geoarchaeological and targeted excavation data allowing both qualitative and quantitative analyses of the archaeological record.

4.2.4: The Pali chronicles

Given the importance placed upon, and reliance upon, the Pali chronicles in the study of the Anuradhapura period, and thus its collapse, it would be useful at this point to briefly examine the Pali chronicles or *vamsas*, of which there are three; the *Dipavamsa*, *Mahavamsa*, and *Culavamsa*. It should be noted that, although the *Mahavamsa* is a single chronicle in of itself, all three chronicles are also collectively referred to as the *Mahavamsa*, to avoid confusion this will not be done here.

Between the three chronicles over two millennia of Sri Lankan history is recorded in one of the longest unbroken historical accounts in the known world. The *Dipavamsa* is generally accepted to be the earliest, composed around the fourth – fifth century AD (Oldenberg 2006: 8-9), although it describes the same period and events as the *Mahavamsa*, starting with the arrival of Siddhartha Gautama on the island in the fifth century BC (Cousins 1996: 61). However, both the *Dipavamsa* and *Mahavamsa* are argued to have been composed several centuries *after* the events they describe, from an earlier chronicle, the *Mahavamsa Atthakatha*, which no longer exists (Geiger 2003: x). Despite this they differ in their length, style and sophistication, with the *Mahavamsa*, believed to have been written around the sixth century AD, being more detailed and sophisticated (Geiger 2003: xi). In addition, while the author of the *Dipavamsa* remains anonymous, the author of the *Mahavamsa* is believed to be the monk Mahanama (Geiger 2003: xi), though his role was that of a compiler – these are not events that were witnessed first or even second hand by the author. The *Culavamsa* too, though clearly written by multiple authors, appears to describe events from first or second hand reports (Geiger 1929: iv).

The *Culavamsa* covers the greatest period of the two millennia covered by the *vamsas*, starting where the *Mahavamsa* and *Dipavamsa* end (the fourth century AD) and finishing with the arrival of the British at the beginning of the nineteenth century AD. Despite covering a longer period, it is generally viewed as an addendum to the *Mahavamsa*, reflected in its name; the "*lesser* chronicle".

The bias of the chronicles' authors should be considered not only to affect the way in which events are described, but also which events are in fact recorded (Geiger 1929: v). Geiger highlights the example of Sigiriya, which is only mentioned four times in the *Culavamsa*, all passing references, and suggests that the account of Kassapa I might be different had the *Culavamsa* not been authored by Buddhist monks (*ibid.*), with Burrows arguing along similar lines (1887b: 54-55) in defence of Nissanka Malla (r.1187-1196 AD). This does not alter the significance of the chronicles, as all historical documents will be affected by similar biases. However, it is critical that this bias is borne in mind when using, challenging or interrogating the chronicles.

It is the *Culavamsa* that is most relevant to Anuradhapura's collapse; covering as it does the period under examination. Most critical are chapters LIII to LVIII which describe the century immediately preceding the Chola conquest of the Sri Lanka and Anuradhapura, the conquest, period of Chola rule, and the rise of Vijayabahu I (1055-1110). It is these chapters that have dictated how the collapse of Anuradhapura has been explained, and it is these chapters that have effectively repressed the analysis of this collapse.

4.3 The chronological sequence

As seen in all three of Anuradhapura's collapse models, the key events occur within less than two centuries, while the entire sequence from fluorescence to abandonment lasts little more than three centuries. It will thus be critical to diachronically constrain archaeological sites and events as tightly as possible. Where possible scientific dates will be used for this, but due to the number of excavations before the advent of scientific dating and the focus upon origins such dates are not available across the board, and are especially lacking for the Sacred City. As a result comparative dating will be used, though this will not allow the chronological resolution that luminescence and radiocarbon dating can offer.

4.3.1: The Architectural Sequence

One of the key forms of comparative dating applicable here is the structural and architectural forms used in the Royal and Monastic structures of the Anuradhapura period. The architecture of the rural populace is discussed in *Chapter 7: The* hinterland, but due its homogeneity over the past two millennia and the organic materials used it is unsuitable for use as chronological indicator. Bandaranayake (1974) developed four architectural periods for Anuradhapura, which can be summarised as follows:

4.3.1.1: Architectural Periods 1 & 2 (c.300 BC – c.450 AD)

These periods are significantly earlier than the period of interest here, but for the purposes of characterising the later periods it is useful to examine the form of the preceding phases. Bandaranayake describes the earliest phase of monastic architecture as; *"at best, only a grander version of the simple organic buildings of the country using mud, timber and thatch"* (Bandaranayake 1974: 23), serving the residential and ecclesiastical needs of the *sangha* (*ibid.*: 47). Consequently the only extant architectural remains from this period are the *lenas* found throughout the hinterland (*ibid.*: 23). Such *lenas*, rock shelters occupied by members of the *sangha*, are characterised by drip ledges and/or Early Brahmi Inscriptions (EBI) and are found in isolation, in concentrated clusters, and in conjunction with later monastic complexes upon outcrops.

Following this rudimentary initial phase is the initiation of formalised monastic architecture, characterised by the construction of *bodhigara* (or tree temples) (*ibid.*) and *uposathaghara* (a large structure in which the *sangha* would assemble to perform rituals (*ibid.*: 28)). These features formed the nuclei of the early organic monasteries, prior to the appearance of the stupa-centric monasteries around the first century BC (*ibid.*: 53). These early monastic complexes are seen in two forms, the first located upon hills or rocky outcrops and typically centred around *lenas*, better known examples being Mihintale and Vessagiriya, though such sites are found throughout the hinterland.

The second form is that of the viharas founded in the parks and groves surrounding the Citadel – such as the Mahavihara, Mirisavati vihara or Abhayagiri vihara, forming the Sacred City. The smaller stupas of the third century BC represent the earliest use of brick in such a substantial manner. Phase II is characterised by the monumental construction of stupas (with the construction of Ruanvelisaya, Mirisavati stupa and the Abhayagiri stupa (Bandaranayake 1974: 23)), as well as the first monumental tanks and canals, along with the emergence of stone sculpture, and the transition from the EBI of the preceding phase, to rock and slab inscriptions (*ibid.*). After the third century AD, the end of the "period of the stupa" Bandaranayake identifies the growth of the Buddhist image, image house, and the worship of the Tooth-Relic, along with the development of brick monastic structures (not stupas) such as the aforementioned image house (*ibid.*).

4.3.1.2: Architectural Period 3 (c.450 – c.680 AD)

This period is *"essentially a transitional phase"* (*ibid.*: 24), linking cultural changes to the development of architectural forms that, while rooted in the early centuries of the millennium, only reached their zenith in the final centuries of the millennium. The *pasada* and *patimaghara* of Period IV have their origins within this period, while the "organic monastery" continues to develop demonstrating a strong element of continuity. Period III sees the development of brick architecture to a greater level than seen earlier, although puddle mortar is still used for bonding. Stone is used extensively in steps, walls and paving, but there is a complete absence of stone pillars or mouldings (*ibid.*: 25), and the stone that is used is plainer in form than seen in Period IV. The stone of this period is typically a soft limestone, the same stone that was first used in Period II (*ibid.*).

4.3.1.3: Architectural Period 4 (c.680 – 1017 AD)

This is the maturation, fluorescence, and end of monastic architecture in the Anuradhapura Period, and Bandaranayake (1974: 25) splits this period into a formative (c.680 – c.750 AD) and consolidative (c.750 – 1017 AD) stage. This period is characterised by the introduction of stone pillars, replacing the timber of the preceding periods (although timber would still have been used for the superstructures) and the introduction of lime-mortar (replacing the puddle-mortar of earlier phases). The structural usage of stone increases throughout, where before stone was used sparingly from the seventh century onwards we see stone used throughout structures, in steps, stairs, base-mouldings, kerbs, pillars etc. (*ibid.*: 25). Additionally there is a shift from soft limestone to harder granite gneiss, more geologically common within the Anuradhapura hinterland, but also more difficult to work (*ibid.*). Although granite pillars and lime-mortar emerge around the beginning of the seventh century, they do not become widely established until the eighth century (*ibid.*).

Period IV also sees the establishment of several distinctive monastic forms that are exclusive to the latter centuries of the Anuradhapura period. These include the *pabbata vihara, the padhanaghara parivena* and the *pancayatana parivena* (*ibid.*: 25). Due to the importance of these monastic forms each will be briefly described.

The Pabbata Vihara: First identified as a distinct form by Hocart (1930: 10-12, 87-88), the term *pabbata vihara* ("mountain monastery") is found in the chronicles and though its origins appear to lie in the eighth century, this architectural form continues into the Polonnaruwa period (Bandaranayake 1974: 81). Despite the name, the *pabbata vihara* in its most formalised form is not found on terraced or elevated ground in any form different to the earlier "organic monasteries", though like many monasteries they are frequently found on hills or outcrops (*ibid.*: 69).

The defining characteristic of these sites is a homogenous layout, split along cardinal orientations with a large central sacred quadrangle containing a stupa, pasada, image house and bodhigara (Bandaranayake 1974: 73) (Fig.4.06). The dimensions of this quadrangle vary considerably, though Bandaranayake describes an average size of around 105m by 90m (1974: 73), but the layout of the four shrines within the central quadrangle follows regular patterns (*ibid.*). The remaining residential structures of the monastery are clustered into NW, NE, SW and SE zones and surrounded by a further wall and/or moat enclosing a large rectangular area around the central quadrangle and residential structures (*ibid.*: 58-85), (Fig.4.06).

The Pancayatana Parivena: While the *pabbata vihara* is primarily suburban, the *pancayatana parivena* is the typical late monastic form *within* the Sacred City (Bandaranayake 1974: 86). Characterised by an arrangement of five monastic structures (Fig.4.07), the *pancayatana parivena* typically sees four smaller cells (or *kuti*) clustered around a larger central *pasada*. The nature of this central structure has been contested, with early interpretations arguing in favour of a central vihara or shrine, rather than the residential *pasada* (*ibid.*: 91). Most striking however is the number of *pancayatana parivenas* found. For example, within Abhayagiri and the Mahavihara there appears to have existed as many as 36 such arrangements in each, while Jetavana and Mirisavati probably had half as many each. Due in part to this high frequency they are now interpreted as primarily residential monastic forms. In addition to the full *pancayatana parivena* there also exists two variations; the "semi- *pancayatana parivenas*", so called because they contain two, rather than four, *kutis* off the front corners of the pasada, and a more complex variant in which the number of *kutis* is multiplied rather than divided, although this variant is itself varied with no discernable standardised number (*ibid.*: 96). These variants do not appear to represent formative stages within the development of the *pancayatana parivena*.

The Padhanaghara Parivena: The *padhanaghara parivena*, or "double-platform" monastery (Bandaranayake 1974: 102) is quite unlike the *pabbata viharas* and *pancayatana parivenas,* and are predominantly situated in the western suburbs of the Sacred City (the so-called "Western Monasteries") and at Ritagala, some 35km south-east of Anuradhapura. The first "excavations" of such monasteries were carried out in the late nineteenth century at the Western Monasteries by Burrows (1886), though he erroneously interpreted them as royal "palaces" (*ibid.*: 1-3). Two decades later these sites were methodically investigated by Ayrton (1924), who identified the structures as monasteries as well as establishing the basic structural layout of the *padhanaghara parivenas*.

However, it is the work of Wijesuriya (1998) that has truly defined the *padhanaghara parivena*. These monastic sites are a distinct form, lacking the traditional ritual buildings (e.g. stupas, image houses, Bodhi shrines *etc*.) and instead centred around a moated double-platform with a central stone bridge connecting the platforms (Fig.4.07 above). Although these monasteries lack the monumental structures of the more common monastic forms, they still exhibit a high level of architectural perfection (Wijesuriya 1998: 3). They are typically located at least partially upon exposed bedrock (*ibid.*: 15), with the rear platform in particular being built directly upon such exposed rock (*ibid.*).

These monasteries are typical of Bandaranayake's final architectural period in that they display a great deal of stone within the structures, with the platforms constructed using massive stone blocks (*ibid.*: 18), the central bridge, mouldings, steps, balustrades, kerbs and pillars upon the rear platform – all were stone. The stone work was characteristically simple, with an "*almost total lack of surface carving*" (Bell 1911a: 52), indeed Hocart noted that the Western Monasteries were distinguished by the "*severity of their style, not an ornament beyond the mouldings, where ...there are any*" (Hocart 1924: 56). This is in contrast with the architectural remains of the same period within the great monasteries of the Sacred City (Wijesuriya 1998: 20). Reinforcing this asceticism, the only decorated features found at *padhanaghara parivenas* were the highly elaborate urinal stones, something Bandaranayake has interpreted as a symbolic rejection of such ornamentation and of conventional monasticism (Bandaranayake 1974: 133).

In addition to new monastic forms, this period sees the standardisation of established monastic structures such as the *pasada, cetiyaghara, bodhigara* and image-house (Bandaranayake 1974: 26), and a smaller number of new monastic structures, the most striking of which is the *gedige* – an image house constructed almost entirely from brick (*ibid.*). Although this structural form reaches its architectural pinnacle in the vaulted brick temples of Polonnaruwa (*ibid.*: 203), two examples have been found within the Citadel of Anuradhapura; 'Gedige' and 'Building A' (*ibid.*: 205). These structures (discussed in Chapter Five), are characterised by a wholly brick-built structure with a vaulted superstructure, architecturally unlike anything found in Sri Lanka prior to this period, although they bear similarities to the South Indian brick temples of the same era with a clear South Indian influence in the form of the Sri Lankan *gediges* (*ibid.*: 204).

4.3.2: Ceramics as Chronological Indicators

The ceramics of the Anuradhapura period can be divided into three primary groupings; coarsewares, finewares and glazed wares (Coningham 2006). These will be discussed in greater detail shortly, but for the purposes of comparative dating it is primarily the glazed wares that are of interest, as the coarsewares tend towards extremely long lived forms and wares, while the finewares are primarily early and comparatively rare.

Table 4.03: Late chronologically significant ASW2 coarseware forms

Period C,D&E and later	Period B and later
1/E/A/3	1/F/A/2
1/G/A/1	1/F/A/3
2/D/A/1	2/D/C/1
2/I/A/1	8/H/A/1
2/I/A/2	28/C/A/1
2/I/A/3	66/D/A/1
10/C/A/3	
23/B/A/1	
26/A/A/1	
62/D/A/1	

However, within the comprehensive ASW2 coarseware assemblage it is possible to identify ten coarseware forms that originate in Periods C,D&E, and a further seven coarseware forms that appear to originate after this period (shown in table 4.03 above), and thus after Anuradhapura's posited 11th century "collapse". These may thus be treated as chronological indicators of late activity, and the presence or absence of these late ceramic forms within the hinterland may provide at least some indication of non-elite human activity during and after Anuradhapura's terminal period.

4.3.3: Other Chronological Indicators

The remaining two key chronological indicators that will be used within this volume are both relatively simple and relate directly to the well established list of rulers (de Silva 1981: 565-570); coins and inscriptions. Coins have been in use in Sri Lanka since the latter half of the first millennium BC (de Silva 2000: 24). However, while significant symbols and elements of complex societies and centralised economies, a key importance of coins found in and around Anuradhapura is that of dating archaeological contexts. Due to the paucity of scientific dates from later Anuradhapura periods, coins offer one of the few ways of assigning dates to the structural and stratigraphic phases of Anuradhapura. While the presence of a coin within a context does not precisely locate that stratigraphic event in time (due to reuse and residuality) it can provide a definite *terminus post quem*.

In addition to temporal data, coins have been used archaeologically to improve understanding of contact between Sri Lanka and other coin franking polities, especially as indicators of long-distance trade routes (see Bopearachchi & Weerakkody 1998). The majority of these are of course South Indian, but a significant number of coins from further away have also been found (de Silva 2000: 05), including ancient Greek (Bopearachchi 1998: 133), early mediaeval Chinese (Codrington 1924: 166-169; Thierry 1998), Sassanid (de Silva 2000: 05), Islamic (Porter 1998) and Roman coins, with the latter found throughout Sri Lanka (for example Barrow 1857: 82-85; Bell 1891: 133-135; Ferguson 1905: 156-157; Still 1907: 161-190; Paranavitana 1950: 32; Goonetileke 1963: 200-203)). Thus the presence of such coins within the Citadel of Anuradhapura can act as indicators of contact and trade with differing regions and polities throughout the Early Mediaeval period.

Turning to inscriptions, because many inscriptions refer to historical individuals it is possible to ascribe dates to their inscription and thus associated archaeological contexts or structures. Unfortunately the number of epigraphic records in Anuradhapura post-tenth century AD is minimal. As has been already stated, the "historical" events described by these inscriptions will generally not be discussed in detail within this volume, such textual readings of Anuradhapura's collapse having already been carried out (e.g. Codrington 1960; Indrapala 1971a; Indrapala 2005) and indeed being the subject of this volume. However, where possible, broad trends visible in epigraphic records will be critically examined, as well as utilising them as chronological indicators.

4.4 Methodological Approaches to Cultural Change

The majority of the archaeological characteristics of collapse (examined in section **4.6**) are relatively straight forward to identify, for example the abandonment of sites, or the disappearance of long distance trade goods. Others can be examined quantitatively by comparing counts or weights of artefact types from different periods to determine changes in subsistence, trade, or industry. However, in some cases, specifically in the case of identifying changes to cultural activity, the methodological approach is somewhat more complex.

Chronological constraint aside, to support or reject any of the three models it will be necessary to identify changes in cultural activity at sites. Moving beyond the more superficial reading of the archaeological record, i.e. presence versus absence of culturally significant artefacts (for example Buddhist or Chola artefacts *etc.*) the coarsewares of Anuradhapura offer a valuable insight into the day to day activity on site.

4.4.1: The Anuradhapura Ceramics

Ceramics are perhaps the most ubiquitous of all archaeological artefacts, and this is certainly true in Sri Lanka (Gunasekera et al. 1971: 166). The reasons for this are many; their relative ease of manufacture, the difficulty in repairing broken ceramics, their utilitarian nature, and their survival within a range of environments. Within this volume the ceramics corpus of ASW2 will be analysed in an attempt to examine shifts in the social and economic conditions of the occupation within the Citadel as recorded by the ASW2 material sequence, primarily focussing upon shifts in long distance trade patterns and scale, changes to local manufacturing scale and techniques, as well as changes to the social status and form of human activity at ASW2.

4.4.1.1: The Classificatory System

For meaningful conclusions to be drawn from any corpus of ceramics it is necessary that they be formally classified into a typology that allows cross-site and cross-period comparison. Unfortunately, due to the numerous different manners in which ceramics may be classified (Velde & Druc 1999: 259), it is common for one region to have several different classificatory systems. The first classificatory system for Sri Lankan ceramics was that of Coomaraswamy (1906) who used ethnographic comparisons to develop a typology that, while acknowledging form, stressed function as the key factor. Unfortunately, this typology was not archaeologically effective (Deraniyagala 1984: 109) and it was not until the 1950s that Deraniyagala developed the first archaeological ceramic sequence (Deraniyagala 1957 & 1960) that focussed upon material form rather than function. However, in so doing it abandoned function as a typological element, undermining the efficaciousness of this approach. The typology of Gunasekera et al. (1971) was again of limited archaeological applicability due to its over-reliance upon museum exhibitions, though it did lay the groundwork for a classification based upon material form in conjunction with ethnographic analogy.

The first Sri Lankan typology to *successfully* combine the strands of form and function was developed by Deraniyagala's son during his excavations at Gedige (1972), and it is this system that has been adopted for the classification of coarse-wares within this volume, as well as by the ASW2 excavations (Coningham et al. 2006: 127) and the Anuradhapura Hinterland survey (Coningham and Gunawardhana 2013). It is this adoption by other projects and scholars that has made Deraniyagala's classification system so successful, as it encourages the comparison of material across sites and periods (Coningham et al. 2006: 127). Previously there was an inherent confusion in the different classificatory systems used, for example rouletted ware; termed Type 1 by Wheeler (1946), Form 1 by Begley (1981), Type 4 by Ragupathy (1987: 13) and Type 16 by Deraniyagala (1972: 77). Such an approach is counter-productive, and the adoption of a unifying coarseware typology is critical for Sri Lankan archaeology. That of Deraniyagala (1972) was selected because it incorporates form and function successfully into a single classificatory system.

In Deraniyagala's system, the form categories are classified into a hierarchical four tier system of *macro-* (1-84), *meso-* (A-S), *sub-* (A-F), and *variant-*form (1-4) (Coningham 2006: 175), thus labelling a specific type of bowl as, for example, Variant 1/B/A/1 (macro/meso/sub/variant). The macro-categories reflect functional forms developed through ethnographic study of modern Sri Lankan functional forms of coarse wares (Deraniyagala 1984), and it is these that will be primarily used here, as within the confines of this volume the meso-, sub-, and variant- forms are of little direct interest beyond serving to facilitate chronological distinctions between different forms (Coningham et al. 2006: 284). The meso-form refers to alterations in rim type, while the sub- and variant-forms are drawn from minor to medium changes in attributes of said ceramics (Deraniyagala, quoted in Coningham et al. 2006: 175).

4.4.1.2: Coarseware ceramics as indicators of social change

Ceramics are often used as indicators of social status, but such analyses have focussed upon what might be termed "luxury" ceramics; finewares or imported wares, with coarse wares typically overlooked as indicators of social status (Davis 2008: 26). However, the study of people and their society cannot be carried out in isolation from the material culture that they create and employ, "*pottery like any piece of material culture, is woven into the complex tapestry of people's lives*" (Skibo 1999: 1-2). Thus coarseware ceramics can be viewed as both characterising and defining different levels of society. Indeed Miller (1985: 11) has argued that material forms embody categorisation processes, and can be used in the study of categorisation itself, thus the variability of material forms is central to both the cultural formation and division of societies (Davis 2008: 26). This basic premise, that social differences are archaeologically visible within the ceramics corpus of a site, has underpinned numerous archaeological and ethnoarchaeological attempts to identify caste and social status spatially within settlements (for example Sinopoli 1999; Arthur 2006; Davis 2008). Here however the aim is not to identify different social strata across a single phase of occupation at ASW2, but to identify social and societal changes during Anuradhapura's terminal period. Such an approach has been successfully used on the earlier periods of the ASW2 sequence by Davis (2008: 31), though this study was aimed specifically at the identification of caste in antiquity.

Table 4.04: *Functions of diagnostic ceramic types from ethnographic parallels found in modern Anuradhapura District, Sri Lanka* (after Davis 2008: 35)

Name	Macro-form	Use
Lipa	72	Portable stove
Mudiya	(28),65,66, 67	Footless lid with basal rim folded inwards.
Nambiliya	1	Shallow bowls used for pre-cooking and food preparation. Some variants incised internally as a way of sifting sand and grit from rice before it is boiled.
Atili	2,3,4,17	Bowl with a mouth wider than its belly. Traditionally used for cooking.
Hali	5,6,7,8	Pot with mouth slightly smaller than width of its belly. Primarily used for cooking.
Kale	9,13	Jar with a long neck used for water storage.
Kotale	20	Jar used as a storage vessel.
Mutti	10,11,12,14,15,23	Jar with a mouth much smaller than its belly. Primarily used for cooking.
Mutti / Kale	18,22	Jar with a narrow mouth on a high neck with a thickened out-turned lip. Used for both cooking and storage.
Kemi	24	Jar with a spout used for drinking water but is also used in Buddhist rituals for washing hands and watering flowers.
Shallow bowl	36, 47	Bowl used as tableware.
Medium shallow bowl	37	Bowl used as tableware.
Deep bowl	19,38,40	Bowl used as tableware.
Cup	26,54	Consumption vessel for drinking.
Mati-koppe	21,(24),25,48,53,59,61	Non-carinated wide bowl used as tableware.
Patraya	56	Consumption vessel used by Buddhist monks/nuns as an alms-bowl for collecting alms from the laity.
Tali	16,28,29,30,31,44	Base of a flat dish with low walls. A form of tableware that is viewed as a prestige form.
Mati-koppe / Hali	60	Rimmed bowl similar in form to the diagnostic mati-koppe and hali.
Koppe / Mutti	27, 62	Bowl similar in form to the diagnostic mati-koppe and mutti, used as tableware
Pahan	51	Ceramic lamp

Deraniyagala's 84 diagnostic macro-forms can be grouped upon the basis of ethnographic study into 20 functional classes, and further grouped into five functional categories; Buddhist, food preparation, food production, food consumption, and storage (tables 4.04 and 4.05 above and below). These are broad groups, and give no allowance for the possibility that some ceramic forms might be used in more than one context, or serve more than one function. However, by classifying them in this manner it is possible to broadly assess the functional form of a coarse-ware ceramic assemblage, and thus gain an insight into the social status of the people who formed that ceramic assemblage. Unfortunately, due to the nature of the different datasets, this methodology may only be applied to the Citadel's dataset

Table 4.05: *Coarse-wares ceramic types by function* (after Davis 2008: 36)

Food Preparation	Food Production	Storage	Consumption	Buddhist	Other
nambiliya	atili	kale	mati-koppe	kemi	mudiya
-	hali	kotale	tali	patraya	pahan
-	mutti	mutti/kale	koppe-mutti	-	-
-	lipa	-	mati-koppe hali	-	-
-	-	-	Shallow bowl	-	-
-	-	-	Medium- shallow bowl	-	-
-	-	-	Deep bowl	-	-

4.5 Population Estimations

Archaeological population estimations have long been problematic (Kramer 1980 & 1982: 196-199; Erdosy 1995) and prone to wide ranging and often conflicting estimates and wide ranging methodologies that range from relatively simple site counts to extremely complex mathematical formulae involving artefact distributions, ethnoarchaeological examples and architectural forms (Kolb 1985: 582). The "wide ranging and conflicting" is particularly true of population estimates for ancient South Asian cities where literary sources remain the primary driver in such estimates (Lahiri 1998), with ethnographic observations and archaeological data tacked on as confirmation rather than being analysed (*ibid.*: 1). This can be seen at Anuradhapura, where population discussions have revolved around literary sources such as Faxian's fifth century description of over 10,000 monks and nuns alone living within the Sacred City (Bandaranayake 1974: 7, 92 & 288). That is not to dismiss this entire subsection of archaeological research as meaningless or fruitless, but it would appear clear that if we, as archaeologists, are to attempt to make valid population estimates, let alone fluctuations within a precise diachronic framework, comprehensive, secure, and diachronically constrained datasets are needed – ideally along with ethnoarchaeological comparatives.

However, as established in section 3.2, changes (specifically significant reductions) in population and/or population density are key in identifying or characterising "collapse". In light of the qualitative nature of much of the archaeological data for Anuradhapura's zones the focus within this study will be placed upon the *nature* of the occupation in each period, examining shifts in size, scale and form of occupation, but not attempting to attribute specific figures to the population of Anuradhapura's Citadel, Sacred City or Hinterland at any period of their occupation.

4.6 Archaeologically characterising the models

The previous chapter presented the three collapse models (Invasion, Malarial and Imperial) that have been propounded for Anuradhapura's collapse. However, to test these models they must be transformed into sequences of archaeologically visible events or processes, with emphasis placed upon the defining and distinctive characteristics of each model. As established (see section **3.5**) the models share similar events and processes, originating as they do from the same narrative. Consequently the *sequence* and *rate* at which these events and processes occur at is critical in distinguishing between the models.

This archaeological characterisation will primarily focus upon identifying a combination of Renfrew's characteristics of collapse (1984: 369), and the loss of Childe's urban characteristics (1950). These have been selected for archaeological visibility, their relevance to the societal form of Anuradhapura, and their applicability to the three zones of Anuradhapura. Thus, for example, Renfrew's "loss of socio-political integration", "loss of centralised economy" and "loss of political centralisation" will not be used as characteristics for each zone as they would only be visible across the whole of Anuradhapura. These broader characteristics will be examined in the discussion (Chapter Eight), but do not feature in the archaeological modelling of each collapse theory.

Instead the selected key characteristics will be:

1. Loss of traditional elite.
2. Rise of new elite.
3. Loss of population.
4. Cessation of monumental construction.
5. Cessation of Long distance trade.
6. Loss of craft specialisation.

The archaeological identification of these characteristics will also allow the fulfilment of one of the primary aims of this volume; establishing whether Anuradhapura does in fact collapse. The above characteristics will be used to characterise the archaeological signature of the dynamic collapse described by each of the models, and presented in tabular form (after collapse studies such as Mortazavi 2004 and Strickland 2011) for ease of comparison and summarisation of vast quantities of disparate archaeological datasets.

In addition to the graphical modelling of the collapse models, comparing the sequence and rate of the major collapse processes and events, key defining individual archaeological indicators will be identified for each of the three collapse theories. These are specific events or features unique to each collapse model, and thus cannot be incorporated into a comparative characterisation. Instead they will simply be examined in terms of presence/absence.

4.6.1: *The Invasion Model*

As presented in Chapter Three (section **3.5.1**) the core characteristic of this model is the Chola sacking of Anuradhapura in 1017 AD. The *Culavamsa* describes Anuradhapura as being "*violently destroyed*" (*Cvs*.lv.21), with all areas of the city and its hinterland abandoned at this point. This violent sacking is the trigger for all other collapse characteristics – the abandonment results directly in the failure of long distance trade, the disappearance of the traditional elite, the disappearance of luxury goods, the cessation of monumental construction and maintenance. It is a monolithic model that attributes the eleventh century collapse of Anuradhapura to the damage done by the invading Chola army. Unfortunately, due to the focus upon the elite, the Invasion Model is lacking in detail as regards events in the hinterland, though the assumption in works such as Codrington's (1960) is that there is a simultaneous abandonment of the hinterland along with the urban core.

The key events within this narrative can be chronologically summarised as follows, with the comparative archaeological characteristics following (**4.6.1.2**).

4.6.1.1: Chronological Narrative

- **c.833 – 853 AD:** Pandyan plundering of Anuradhapura. Description in *Culavamsa* (*Cvs*.l.33-36) is of theft of valuables rather than of physical destruction.
- **c.855 – 915 AD:** Numerous new constructions, restorations and repairs within the Sacred City (*Cvs*.l-lii).
- **c.924 – 935 AD:** During reign of Dapppula IV, Pandyan King seeks refuge at Anuradhapura, when rejected leaves behind Pandyan royal regalia in Anuradhapura (*Cvs*.liii.5-10; Codrington 1960: 94).
- **c.972 – 975 AD:** Sena V orders murder of his general's brother. This causes his general to rebel, bringing an army of Tamil mercenaries from India who then "*plundered the whole country like devils and pillaging, seized the properties of its inhabitants*" (*Cvs*.liv.66). Sena V rules for 10 years from Ruhuna, leaving Anuradhapura in the hands of the Tamil mercenaries (*Cvs*.liv.70-73).
- **c.995 AD:** Sena's successor, Mahinda V, struggles to govern due to being of "*very weak character*" and the large numbers of Tamil mercenaries still occupying Anuradhapura after Sena V's reign (*Cvs*.lv.2). By around his tenth/twelfth year of rule he has exhausted his coffers and is refused taxes by the peasant populace (*Cvs*.lv.3) leaving him unable to pay the mercenaries who revolt and lay siege to the Royal Palace (*Cvs*.lv.4-5). Although Mahinda V escapes word of Anuradhapura's plight reaches the Chola monarch Rajaraja I who takes advantage of the confusion in Anuradhapura and invades Sri Lanka.
- **c.1017 AD:** Rajaraja's son and successor Rajendra I completes the Chola invasion of Sri Lanka by taking Anuradhapura, capturing Mahinda V and the royal Sinhala regalia and sacking both the palaces and temples of Anuradhapura (*Cvs*.lv.16-22). The *Culavamsa* describes "*all the monasteries*" of Anuradhapura as being "*violently destroyed*" (*Cvs*.lv.21). Rajendra I then establishes a new capital at Polonnaruva from where the Cholas rule the majority of the island.
- **c.1073 AD:** Amid internal Chola conflict over their royal succession, Vijayabahu I drives the occupying Cholas from Anuradhapura and holds his coronation in the city (Codrington 1960: 95; *Cvs*.lix.8). In order to carry out his royal consecration at Anuradhapura a pasada is constructed and "*many other things... prepared*" (*Cvs*.lix.2-3) due to the destruction of the Chola invasion. However, despite retaking Anuradhapura Vijayabahu chooses to rule from Polonnaruva (Codrington 1960: 95).
- **c.1100 AD:** Vijayabahu I conducts major repairs and renovations to tanks throughout his kingdom (*Cvs*.lx.48-51), though no mention is made as to how they came to be in disrepair. Around the same time the Bodhi Tree shrine and "the *vihara*" at Anuradhapura are repaired (*Cvs*.lx.62-63). While which monastery "the *vihara*" refers to is vague it seems most likely this refers to the Mahavihara.

- **c.12-13th Cs AD:** Anuradhapura becomes peripheral in the chronicles, featuring only during the coronation of monarchs as a symbolic location, until wide scale repairs are carried out to the city's stupas, pasadas, walls, gates, temples and shrines during Parakramabahu's reign (r.1153-86 AD) (*Cvs*.lxxiv1-14; *Cvs*.lxxviii.97-107). A century later Vijayabahu IV (r.1270-72) carries out smaller scale restorations at the Thuparama and Ruanvelisaya (*Cvs*.lxxxviii.80-85).

- **c.14th C AD onwards:** Despite the repairs of the preceding century Anuradhapura never recovers its central position in the history of Sri Lanka (Codrington 1960: 96), and by the fourteenth century the city appears to be entirely abandoned.

4.6.1.2: Archaeological Characteristics

- **9th - mid 10thC AD: Fluorescence of Anuradhapura**
  i) High levels of long distance trade with both east and west.
  ii) High levels of craft specialisation.
  iii) High levels of elite construction, both royal and monastic.
  iv) High quantities of luxury goods found within Sacred City, Citadel and elite structures within hinterland.
  v) Population either stable or growing.

- **Late 10th C AD: Weak monarchy & misrule, Tamil mercenaries strike.**
  i) Decrease in construction and repair of monumental secular structures (Citadel).
  ii) Maintenance of monastic construction and maintenance.
  iii) Indications of low-scale conflict or unrest in Citadel.
  iv) Appearance of Tamil, Saivite or South Indian presence within Citadel, Sacred City and possibly hinterland.
  v) Long distance trade, luxury goods and craft specialisation all relatively stable.

- **c.1017 AD: Chola conquest of Anuradhapura.**
  i) Indications of violent conflict throughout Sacred City and Citadel, including fire damage, structural collapse, presence of weapons or violent death.
  ii) Artefactual indicators of Chola/South Indian military presence – for example coins, ceramic forms, inscriptions.
  iii) Wide scale and rapid abandonment of both the Citadel and Sacred City as well as rapid abandonment of Buddhist and high status sites within the hinterland. Remaining occupation to be both more piece-meal and of a poor structural quality.
  iv) Shrinkage/abandonment of major sites in the hinterland due to the movement of the political and economic centre to Polonnaruwa.
  v) Reduction in structural quality and cessation of monumental construction and/or repair. This includes a cessation of major tank and canal maintenance within the hinterland.
  vi) Significant reduction in Buddhist activity within both the Citadel and Sacred City.
  vii) Significant reduction/cessation in long distance trade.
  viii) Significant reduction in luxury goods (i.e. exotics and fine wares).

- **c.1073 AD: Coronation of Vijayabahu I at Anuradhapura.**
  i) Small scale repairs and/or new construction within the Sacred City and/or Citadel.
  ii) Potential re-occupation of Citadel and/or Sacred City on a significantly smaller and more sparse scale than pre-invasion.

- **c.1100 AD: Vijayabahu I conducts repairs throughout kingdom**
  i) Possible repair to major tanks in and around Anuradhapura. However, as none of the Anuradhapura tanks are mentioned by name in the *Culavamsa* this is speculative.
  ii) Repair/reconstruction within the Sacred City. Specifically, repair to Bodhi Tree shrine and "the *vihara*" at Anuradhapura (*Cvs*.lx.62-63). While which monastery "the *vihara*" refers to is unclear, it appears likely to refer to the Mahavihara.

- **c. 12thC – 13thC AD: Anuradhapura becomes peripheral**
  i) Continued ephemeral and patchwork settlement activity throughout the city.
  ii) Further small scale repairs to city's religious structures during Parakramabahu's (r.1153-86 AD) (*Cvs*.lxxiv1-14; *Cvs*.lxxviii.97-107) and Vijayabahu's reigns (r.1270-72) (*Cvs*.lxxxviii.80-85).

- **c.14thC AD onwards: Anuradhapura sinks beneath the "Jungle Tide"**
  i) Complete cessation of construction and settlement on the site of Anuradhapura.
  ii) hinterland almost entirely abandoned bar sparsely distributed small villages and small rain fed tanks.

As already discussed (section **4.6**), this information can now be summarised as seen in table 4.06, readily allowing comparison with the other models and the archaeological data presented in Chapters Five, Six and Seven.

4.6.2: The Malarial Model

The Malarial Model of Nicholls (1921) and Still (1930) (as set out in section **3.5.2**) is identical to the Invasion Model until the Chola invasion of 1017 AD. However, from this point on it posits, rather than an immediate collapse, a rapid decline due to the destruction of the hydraulic landscape and the malaria that follows.

The Malarial Model is characterised by its focus upon the tanks of Anuradhapura, and Still argued that the breaching of the tanks by the Cholas would lead quickly to the creation of malarial vectors throughout Anuradhapura (1930: 89-90). This should be archaeologically visible in the breaching of major tanks, especially those serving the Citadel and Sacred City. Still also suggested that damage to the tanks of Anuradhapura would cause a significant fall in the population of fish species living within them (*ibid*: 90), something that may be archaeologically visible in the economic package exploited by the inhabitants of Anuradhapura. The key events within the narrative sequence of this model can be summarised as follows, with the comparative archaeological characteristics of this model following (**4.6.2.2**).

4.6.2.1: Chronological Narrative

- **c.833 – 853 AD:** Pandyan plundering of Anuradhapura. Description in *Culavamsa* (*Cvs*.l.33-36) is of theft of valuables rather than of physical destruction.
- **c.855 – 915 AD:** Numerous new constructions, restorations and repairs within the Sacred City (*Cvs*.l-lii).
- **c.924 – 935 AD:** During reign of Dapppula IV, Pandyan King seeks refuge at Anuradhapura, when rejected leaves behind Pandyan royal regalia in Anuradhapura (*Cvs*.liii.5-10; Codrington 1960: 94).
- **c.972 – 975 AD:** Sena V orders murder of his general's brother. This causes his general to rebel, bringing an army of Tamil mercenaries from India who then *"plundered the whole country like devils and pillaging, seized the properties of its inhabitants"* (*Cvs*.liv.66). Sena V rules for 10 years from Ruhuna, leaving Anuradhapura in the hands of the Tamil mercenaries (*Cvs*.liv.70-73).
- **c.995 AD:** Sena's successor, Mahinda V, struggles to govern due to being of *"very weak character"* and the large numbers of Tamil mercenaries still occupying Anuradhapura after Sena V's reign (*Cvs*.lv.2). By around his tenth/twelfth year of rule he has exhausted his coffers and is refused taxes by the peasant populace (*Cvs*.lv.3) leaving him unable to pay the mercenaries who revolt and lay siege to the Royal Palace (Cvs.lv.4-5). Although Mahinda V escapes word of Anuradhapura's plight reaches the Chola monarch Rajaraja I who takes advantage of the confusion in Anuradhapura and invades Sri Lanka.
- **c.1017 AD:** Rajendra I sacks Anuradhapura, as in the Invasion Model, however in addition to the damage listed above, the Chola invasion also deliberately targets the tanks and canals of the Sacred City and Hinterland, cutting bunds in order to cause food shortages in and around Anuradhapura. The hydraulic infrastructure, already weakened by the weak kingship of Mahinda IV collapses providing ideal habitats for malarial vector mosquitoes.
- **c.1073 AD:** Although Vijayabahu returns to the city for his coronation the region is now a malarial hot-zone and uninhabitable (Still 1930: 91). This then causes Vijayabahu to rule from Polonnaruva (Codrington 1960: 95).
- **c.1100 AD:** Vijayabahu I conducts repairs and renovations to tanks (*Cvs*.lx.48-51) but due to the malaria epidemic in the Anuradhapura region such the repairs needed are impossible to effect (Still 1930: 91). Again despite low level repairs (the Bodhi Tree shrine and "the *vihara*" at Anuradhapura (*Cvs*.lx.62-63)) the region is now largely uninhabitable and capable only of supporting a token population.
- **c.13thC AD:** Malaria is by now endemic in the region (Still 1930: 91).
- **c.14thC AD onwards:** The region is now virtually uninhabitable and *"the jungle tide has risen and submerged that ancient kingdom so completely"* (ibid.).

4.6.2.2: Archaeological Characteristics

- **9th - mid 10thC AD: Fluorescence of Anuradhapura**
a) High levels of long distance trade with both east and west.
b) High levels of craft specialisation.
c) High levels of elite construction, both royal and monastic.
d) High quantities of luxury goods found within Sacred City, Citadel and elite structures within hinterland.
e) Population either stable or growing.
f) Hydraulic landscape well maintained; regular desilting and breaches repaired.

- **Late 10thC AD: Weak monarchy & misrule, Tamil mercenaries strike.**
a) Decrease in construction and repair of monumental secular structures (Citadel).
b) Maintenance of monastic construction and maintenance.
c) Indications of low-scale conflict or unrest in Citadel.
d) Appearance of Tamil, Saivite or South Indian presence within Citadel, Sacred City and possibly hinterland.
e) Long distance trade, luxury goods and craft specialisation all relatively stable.

- **c.1017 AD: Chola conquest of Anuradhapura.**
a) Wide spread damage to the tanks and canals of the Sacred City and hinterland and hinterland – including deliberate cutting of tank and canal bunds. Focus of this damage upon the major tanks/canals.
b) Indications of conflict throughout Sacred City, Citadel and hinterland including fire damage, structural collapse, presence of weapons or violent death.
c) Artefactual indicators of Chola/South Indian military presence – for example coins, ceramic forms, inscriptions.
d) Reduction in structural quality and cessation of monumental construction and/or repair. This includes a cessation of major tank and canal maintenance within the hinterland.
e) Sharp decline in Buddhist activity within both the Citadel and Sacred City.
f) Sharp decline in long distance trade.
g) Sharp decline in luxury goods (i.e. exotics and fine wares).

- **c.1073 AD: Vijayabahu coronation**
a) Spike in activity within the Citadel and Sacred City.
b) Piecemeal repairs to hydraulic landscape, tanks and canals silting.
c) Settlement activity in the hinterland rapidly declining compared to pre-Chola period, and largely limited to small villages with small rain-fed tanks.

- **c.1100 AD: Attempted repairs**
a) Small scale repairs within the Sacred City (the Bodhi Tree shrine and "the *vihara*" at Anuradhapura (*Cvs*.lx.62-63)).
b) Long distance trade, luxury goods and craft specialisation all now vastly reduced and declining.
c) Population of Sacred City, Citadel and hinterland greatly reduced and declining.

- **c.13thC AD: The Jungle Tide rises**
a) Tanks, channels and canals now almost completely abandoned with no evidence of de-silting or breach repair.
b) Monumental construction and repairs completely ceased, extremely limited and ephemeral occupation of the hinterland, Citadel and Sacred City.
c) Malaria is epidemic in remaining population.
d) Buddhist sites largely abandoned, absence of visible elite.
e) Complete absence of long distance trade, craft specialisation, or luxury goods.

- **c.14thC AD onwards: Anuradhapura sinks beneath the Jungle Tide**
a) Near total abandonment of sites throughout the hinterland, Sacred City and Citadel. Remaining settlement activity remaining is transient, ephemeral and reliant upon unconnected rainfed tanks.
b) Buddhist sites largely abandoned, absence of visible elite.
c) Complete absence of long distance trade, craft specialisation, or elite luxury goods.
d) Malaria remains endemic across Anuradhapura region.

This can be summarised as seen in table 4.07.

4.6.3: *The Imperial Model*

This model broadly accepts all of the individual events presented by the Invasion narrative (presented in section **B.1**), but through a critical reading of epigraphic records and the chronicles presents a more sophisticated model of Anuradhapura's collapse. It differs from the previous two models at an early stage, invoking the emergence South Indian influences within Anuradhapura from the 7th century onwards and portraying the 9th century as a far more troubled period, in which multiple conflicts with South Indian polities economically attenuates the royal rulers of Anuradhapura.

This model further differs after the Chola invasion of 1017 AD, implicitly dividing the hinterland in two; secular and sacred. The *sangha* are the economic administrators of the hinterland, and while the Cholas required an intact rural landscape and populace to continue production of economic surplus, taxes and tithes, they also required the removal of the traditional elite within that hinterland. Recent research (Coningham et al. 2007a; Liyanarachchi 2009) has demonstrated that not only were the Buddhist *sangha de jure* a part of the social elite, but that they were also heavily involved in the economic management of the rural hinterland, *de facto* if not *de jure* the rural administration. With the Cholas' need to remove the existing administration (Indrapala 2005: 232) the Imperial model sees an immediate collapse/abandonment of Buddhist monastic sites throughout the hinterland, followed by a gradual decline of the secular hinterland following the withdrawal of the imperial Cholas in the late eleventh century AD. Once again, a chronological narrative of events posited by the Imperial Model (**4.6.3.1**), followed by the comparative archaeological characteristics of this model (**4.6.3.2**) follows.

4.6.3.1: *Chronological Narrative*

- **c.7th – 10thCs AD:** Steady increase in Tamil influence in Sri Lanka through both trade and migration of Tamil Buddhists (Indrapala 2005: 193-196). This presence was concentrated in the north, around centres of long distance trade and Anuradhapura itself (*ibid*.: 200-204).
- **c.7th – 10thCs AD:** Rise in the influence of Mahayanism, coupled with increasing South Indian Mahayanist interactions and influence (Indrapala 2005: 189-190).
- **c.7th – 10thCs AD:** Steady increase in Saivite influence and presence within Sri Lanka, especially in the north of the island. This culminates in the 9th century conversion of Sena I (r.833-853) to Saivism.
- **c.7th – 9thCs AD:** Period of economic growth and wealth for Anuradhapura.
- **833 – 853 AD:** The first of a series of South Indian invasions, starting with plundering of Anuradhapura by Pandyan ruler Sri Malla Sri Vallabha (r.815-862) (Indrapala 2005: 188).
- **10thC AD:** Repairs and fresh construction throughout Sacred City, but secular wealth lower and less expenditure upon monumental secular construction.
- **c.950 AD:** Chola army invades Sri Lanka, defeating Udaya III, forcing him to abandon Anuradhapura and flee to Ruhuna (*Cvs*.liii.41-46; Indrapala 2005: 231).
- **c.972-1017 AD:** Severe and serious unrest and conflict within Anuradhapura. Economic shortfall following century of warfare.
- **c.1017-1073 AD:** The Cholas rule Sri Lanka as an imperial territory, directing economic surplus back to South India, and re-routing the valuable South-East Asian long-distance trade through Chola controlled ports and merchants (Spencer 1976: 61). The Buddhist hegemony is replaced by Saivite pre-eminence, with a large-scale depopulation of Buddhist clergy (Indrapala 2005: 239).
- **c.1073 AD:** Upon retaking Anuradhapura Vijayabahu holds his coronation there, a symbolic gesture at the former religious heart of the nation. However, due to the political instability in the South West of the island, and (critically) the shift in economic, political and spiritual power away from orthodox Theravada Buddhism, Vijayabahu chooses to rule from Polonnaruva (Indrapala 2005: 250).
- **c.1100 AD:** Vijayabahu I carries out repairs to the Bodhi Tree shrine and "the *vihara*" at Anuradhapura (*Cvs*.lx.62-63). Further repairs are carried out across the kingdom but these would have focussed upon the Polonnaruva region, with the repairs at Anuradhapura (to the Bodhi tree shrine and vihara) appearing to be symbolic rather than with any aim of restoring Anuradhapura.
- **c.13thC AD:** Anuradhapura remains marginalised as Parakramabahu embarks upon an ambitious and expensive program of construction and repairs around Polonnaruva. Anuradhapura remains a symbolic location for the coronation of monarchs but appears to have little importance beyond this historical legitimisation of monarchs. The tank system of Anuradhapura and its hinterland decays due to the absence of the administrative system that co-ordinated the maintenance of that system.
- **c.14thC AD onwards:** As Polonnaruva too collapses due to increased factionalism, civil conflict and an economic collapse, Anuradhapura is entirely abandoned.
- **4.6.3.2: Archaeological Characteristics**

- **c.7th – 10thCs AD: Rising Tamil, Mahayanist & Saivite influences**
a) Appearance of South Indian architectural forms, Tamil inscriptions, Saivite and/or Mahayanist religious artefacts and structures.

- **c.833–853 AD: Pandyan sacking of Anuradhapura.**
a) Indications of violent conflict especially throughout the Sacred City (Cvs.l.12-36), with focussed looting of Thuparama (Cvs.l.35) and Abhayagiri vihara (Cvs.l.34).

- **10thC AD: Weakening royal power**
a) Extensive fresh construction and repairs across Sacred City.
b) Evidence of conflict and civil unrest in Citadel.

- **c.1017 AD: Chola sacking of Anuradhapura.**
a) Evidence of Chola military presence in Anuradhapura.
b) Widespread and major damage to the Citadel and Sacred City.
c) Presence of Chola artefacts; coins, inscriptions, weapons etc.
d) Abandonment/collapse/destruction of Buddhist sites in hinterland.

- **c.1017-1073 AD: The Chola rule**
a) General abandonment of Citadel and Sacred City, visible in cessation of all construction and repairs, absence of long distance trade and luxury goods.
b) Any occupation of Citadel or Sacred City squatter in nature.
c) Dramatic reduction or even cessation of Buddhist activity within the Citadel and/or Sacred City.
d) Abandonment of monastic sites across hinterland.
e) Continued secular occupation of hinterland.
f) Cessation of long distance trade at Anuradhapura.
g) Cessation of craft specialisation at Anuradhapura.
h) Cessation of elite presence at Anuradhapura.
i) Re-organisation of economy around Polonnaruwa as capital (including long distance trade, craft specialisation, luxury goods, monumental construction, presence of visible elite etc.).

- **c.1073 AD: Vijayabahu coronation**
a) Small scale repairs, temporary structures erected within Sacred City and/or Citadel.
b) Continued absence of long distance trade, craft specialisation and luxury goods at Anuradhapura.
c) hinterland population declines.
d) Hydraulic landscape decays; channels and tanks silting up, breaches either not repaired or repaired poorly).

- **c.1100 AD: Attempted repairs**
a) Further small scale repairs within the Sacred City; the Bodhi Tree shrine and "the *vihara*" at Anuradhapura (*Cvs*.lx.62-63).
b) Continued "squatter" occupation within Citadel and/or Sacred City.
c) Continued absence of long distance trade items, luxury goods and Buddhist activities.
d) hinterland now largely abandoned.

- **c.13thC AD: Anuradhapura remains marginalised**
a) Continued sporadic activity and occupation of Anuradhapura.
b) Numbers of settlements within the hinterland dramatically reduced.
c) Buddhist activity within the hinterland dramatically reduced.
d) Hydraulic landscape continues to decay.

- **c.14thC AD onwards: Anuradhapura is fully abandoned**
a) The Sacred City, Citadel, and the hinterland are predominantly abandoned. Remaining occupation is sparse and ephemeral.

Once again, this can summarised as seen in table 4.08.

Table 4.06: *The Invasion Model's Archaeological Signature*

13th	12th	11th	10th	9th	Century AD	
Absent	←	Absent	→	→	Citadel	Population
Absent	←	Absent	→	→	Sacred City	
Absent	←	←	→	→	Hinterland	
Absent	←	Absent	→	→	Citadel	Monumental Construction
Absent	←	Absent	→	→	Sacred City	
Absent	←	Absent	→	→	Hinterland	
Absent	←	Absent	→	→	Citadel	Traditional Elite
Absent	←	Absent	→	→	Sacred City	
Absent	Absent	Absent	→	→	Hinterland	
Absent	Absent	→	Absent	Absent	Citadel	New Elite
Absent	Absent	→	Absent	Absent	Sacred City	
Absent	Absent	Absent	Absent	Absent	Hinterland	
Absent	Absent	Absent	→	→	Citadel	Long Distance Trade
Absent	Absent	Absent	→	→	Sacred City	
Absent	Absent	Absent	↓	↓	Hinterland	
Absent	←	Absent	→	→	Citadel	Craft Specialisation
Absent	←	Absent	→	→	Sacred City	
Absent	Absent	Absent	→	→	Hinterland	

KEY: ↑ High ↓ Low ↗ Rising ↘ Falling → Steady ✠ Absent

Table 4.07: *The Malarial Model's Archaeological Signature*

Century AD	9th	10th	11th	12th	13th	
Citadel	→	→	←	↙	✠	Population
Sacred City	→	→	←	↙	✠	
Hinterland	→	→	←	↙	✠	
Citadel	→	→	←	↙	✠	Monumental Construction
Sacred City	→	→	←	↙	✠	
Hinterland	→	→	←	↙	✠	
Citadel	→	→	↙	↙	✠	Traditional Elite
Sacred City	→	→	↙	↙	✠	
Hinterland	→	→	↙	↙	✠	
Citadel	✠	✠	→	✠	✠	New Elite
Sacred City	✠	✠	→	✠	✠	
Hinterland	✠	✠	→	✠	✠	
Citadel	→	→	↙	↙	✠	Long Distance Trade
Sacred City	→	→	↙	↙	✠	
Hinterland	↓	↓	↙	↙	✠	
Citadel	→	→	↙	↙	✠	Craft Specialisation
Sacred City	→	→	↙	↙	✠	
Hinterland	→	→	↙	↙	✠	

KEY: ↑ High ↓ Low ↗ Rising ↘ Falling → Steady ✠ Absent

A Time of Change: The "Collapse" of Anuradhapura, Sri Lanka

Table 4.08: *The Imperial Model's Archaeological Signature*

13th	12th	11th	10th	9th	Century AD	
✠	↙	←	↙	→	Citadel	Population
✠	↙	←	→	→	Sacred City	
✠	↙	↙	→	→	Hinterland	
✠	←	✠	↙	→	Citadel	Monumental Construction
✠	←	✠	→	→	Sacred City	
✠	↙	↙	→	→	Hinterland	
✠	←	✠	↙	→	Citadel	Traditional Elite
✠	←	✠	↘	→	Sacred City	
✠	✠	✠	↘	→	Hinterland	
✠	✠	✠	↘	←	Citadel	New Elite
✠	✠	✠	↘	←	Sacred City	
✠	✠	↘	↘	✠	Hinterland	
✠	✠	✠	→	→	Citadel	Long Distance Trade
✠	✠	✠	→	→	Sacred City	
✠	✠	✠	↓	↓	Hinterland	
✠	↙	↙	↙	→	Citadel	Craft Specialisation
✠	↙	↙	→	→	Sacred City	
✠	↙	↙	→	→	Hinterland	

KEY: ↑ High ↓ Low ↗ Rising ↘ Falling → Steady ✠ Absent

CHAPTER 4: METHODOLOGY

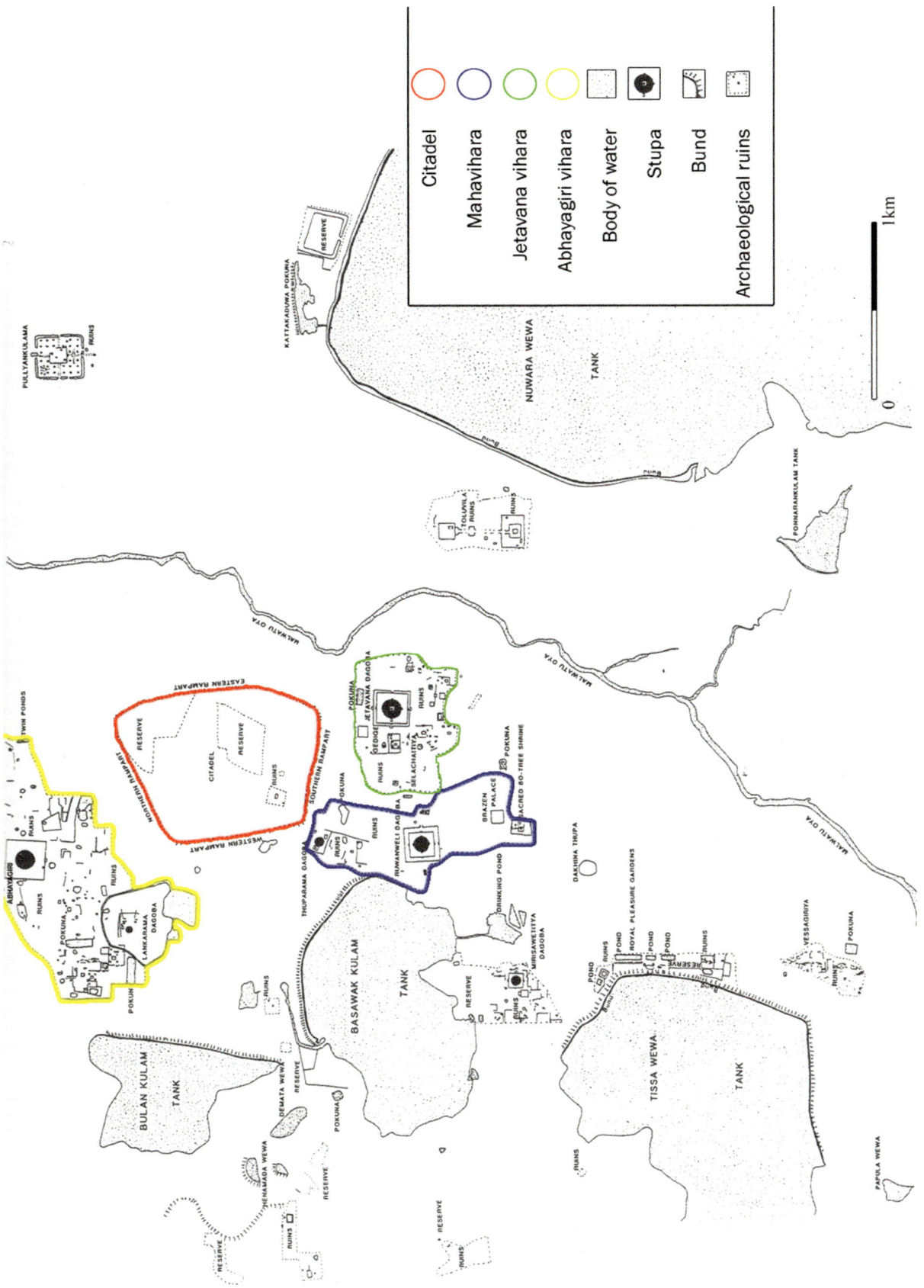

FIG.4.01: PLAN OF ANURADHAPURA SHOWING CITADEL AND THREE PRIMARY BUDDHIST FRATERNITIES
(AFTER CONINGHAM ET AL. 1999: 29)

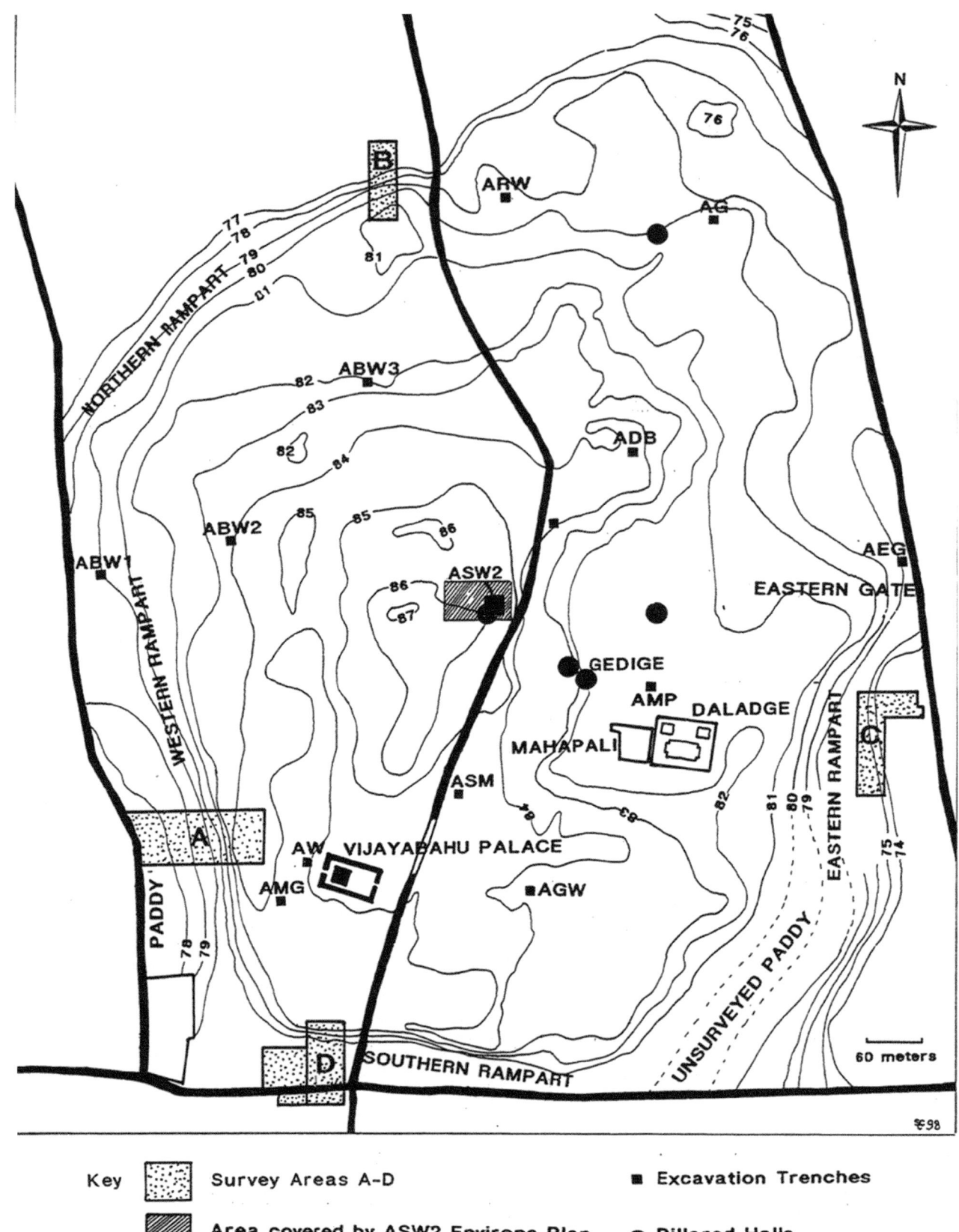

FIG.4.02: ASW2 PLAN OF THE CITADEL (AFTER CONINGHAM ET AL. 1999: 32)

CHAPTER 4: METHODOLOGY

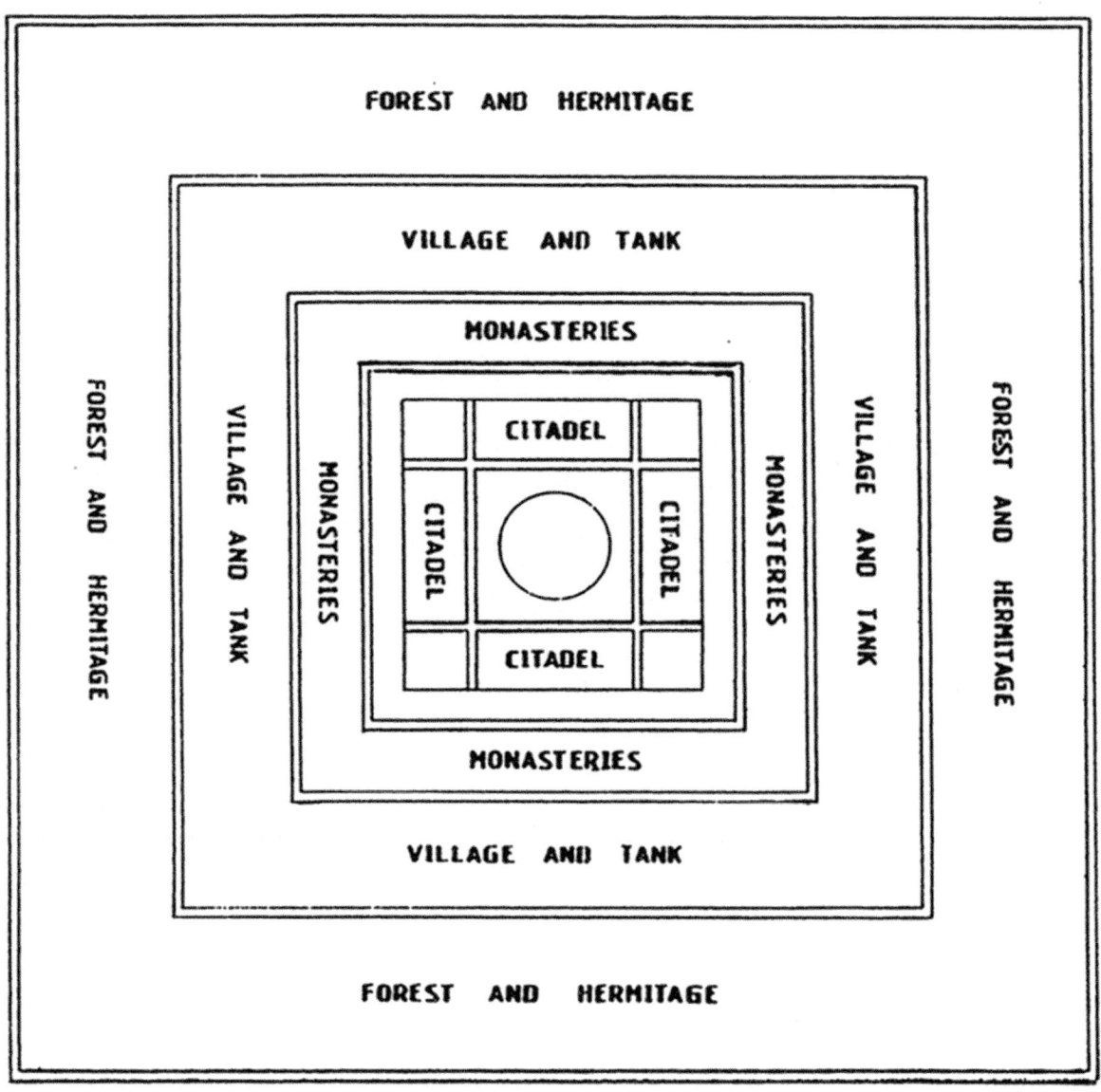

Fig.4.03: Diagrammatic plan of Anuradhapura (after Coningham et al. 1999: 30)

A Time of Change: The "Collapse" of Anuradhapura, Sri Lanka

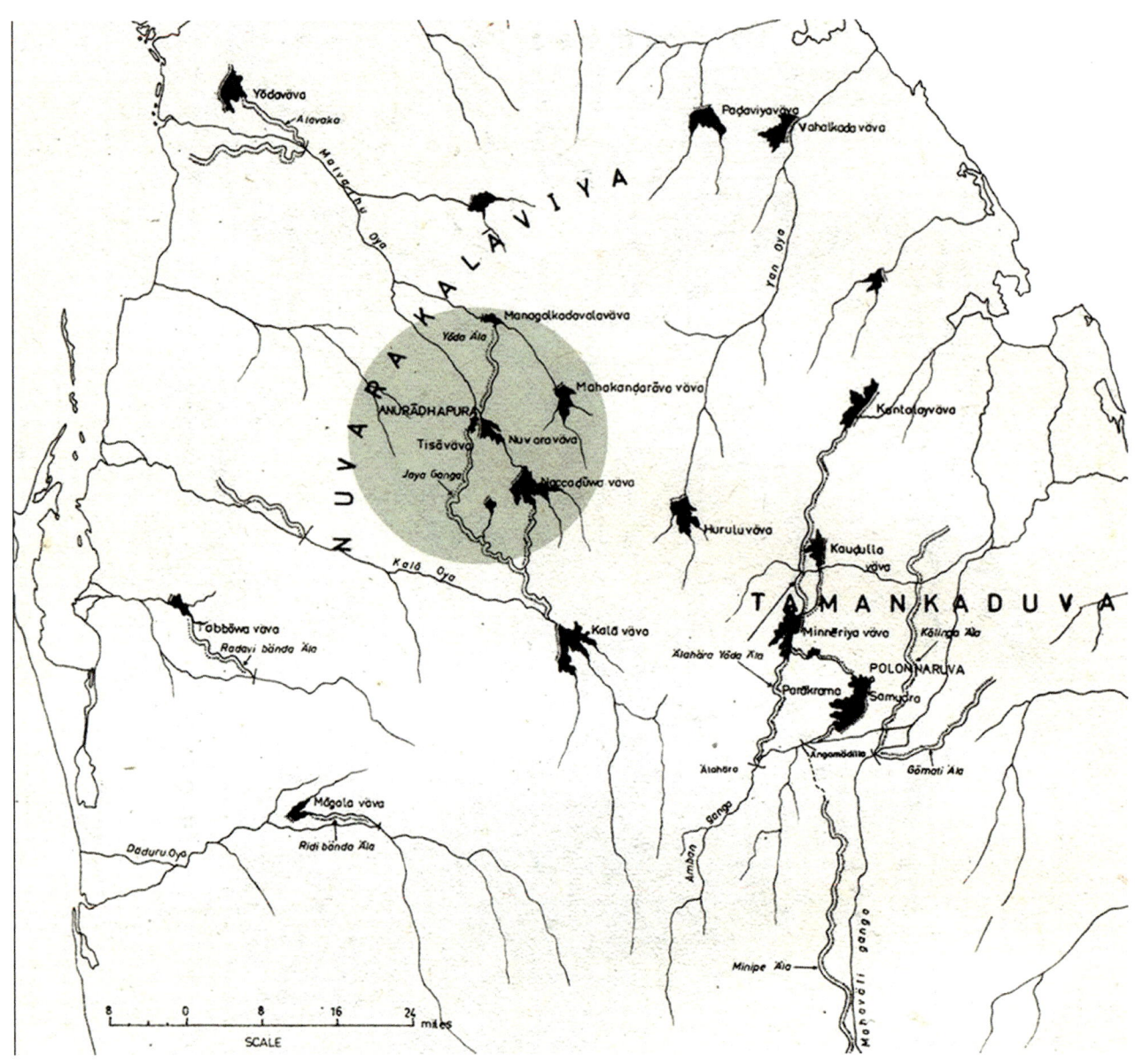

Fig.4.04: Anuradhapura hinterland survey area

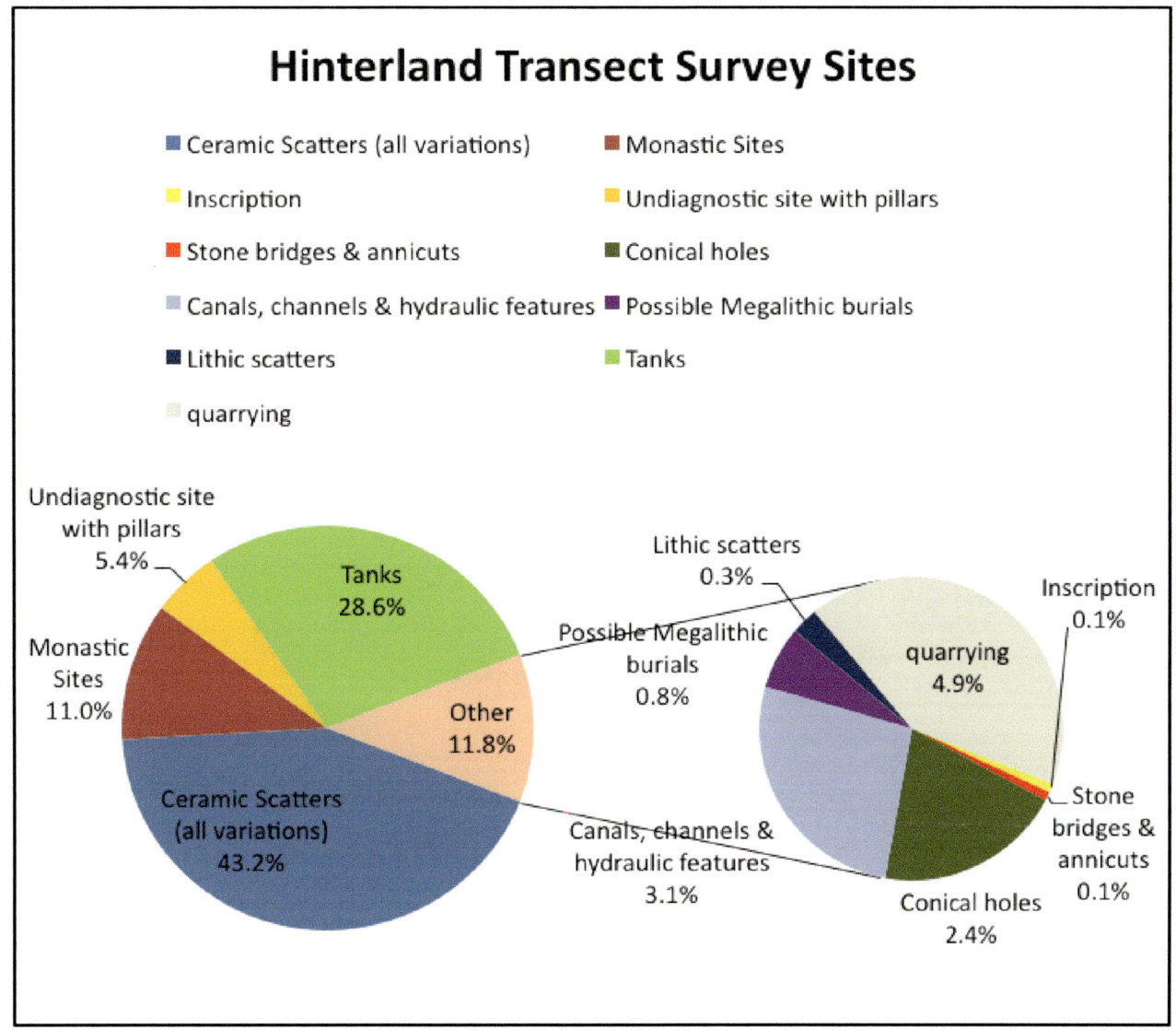

Fig.4.05: Anuradhapura Hinterland survey results by site type (after Coningham and Gunawardhana 2013)

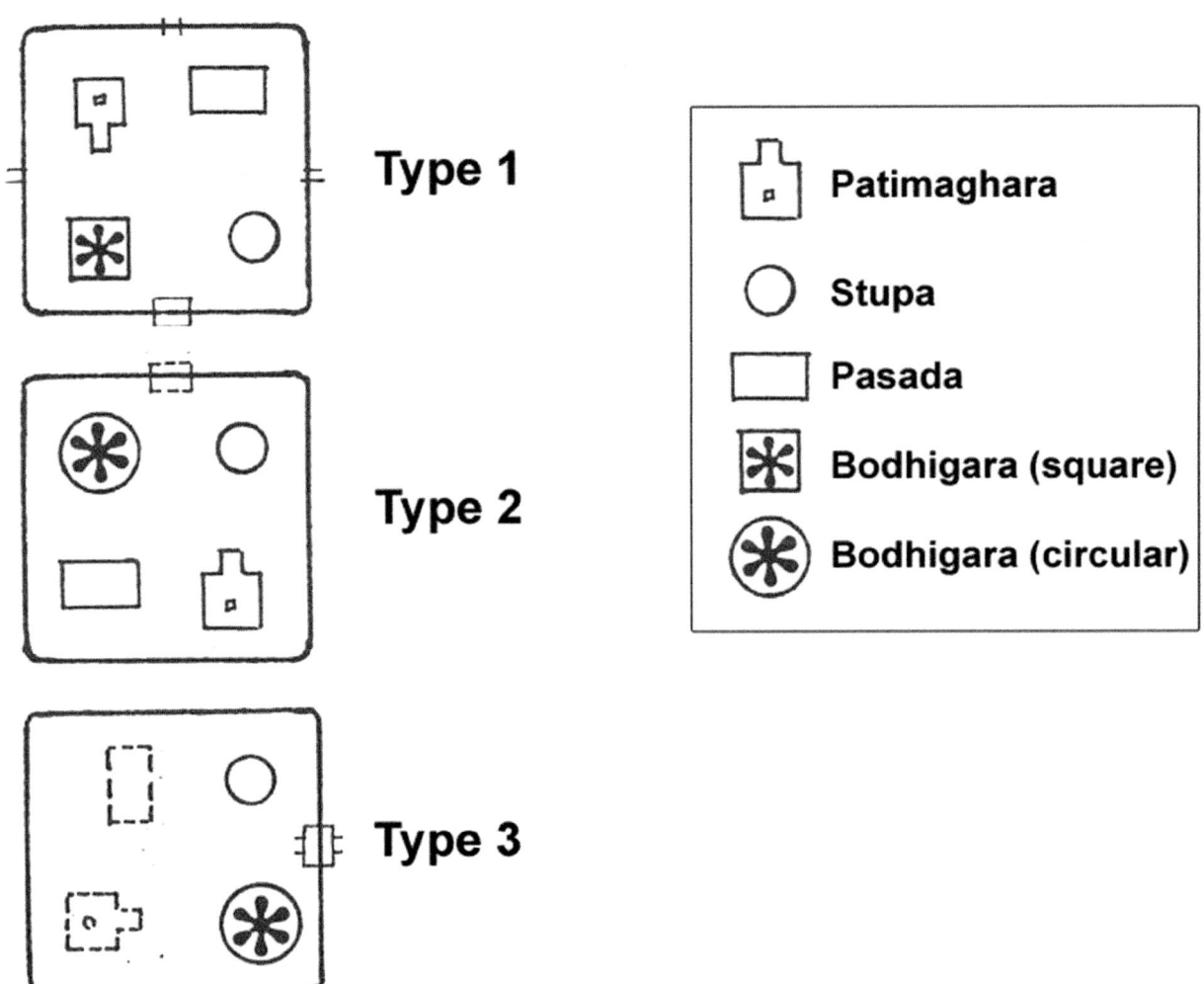

Fig.4.06: Diagrammatic layout of pabbata viharas (after Bandaranayake 1974: 68)

CHAPTER 4: METHODOLOGY

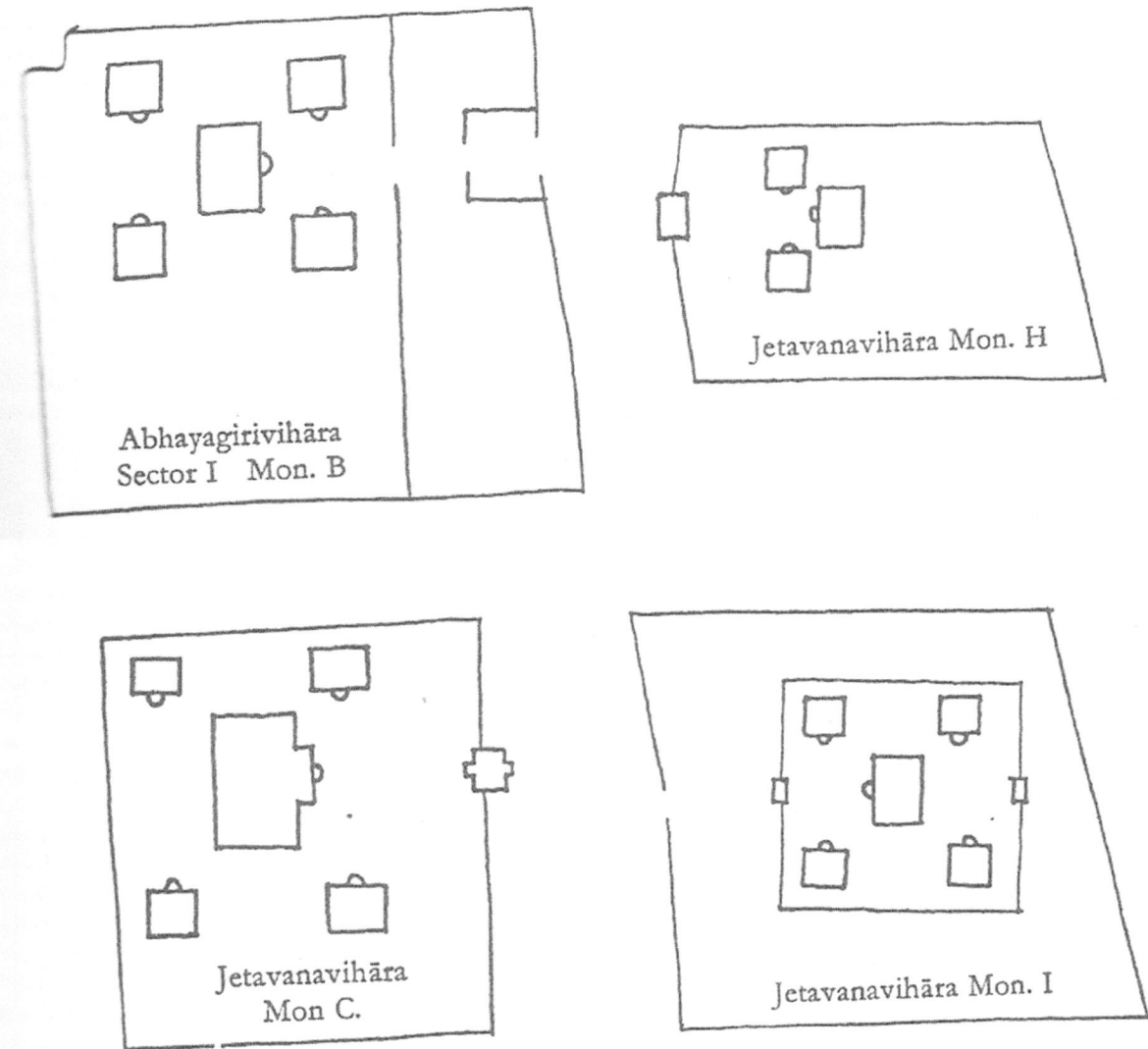

Fig.4.07: Diagrammatic layout of pancayatana parivena (after Bandaranayake 1974: 87)

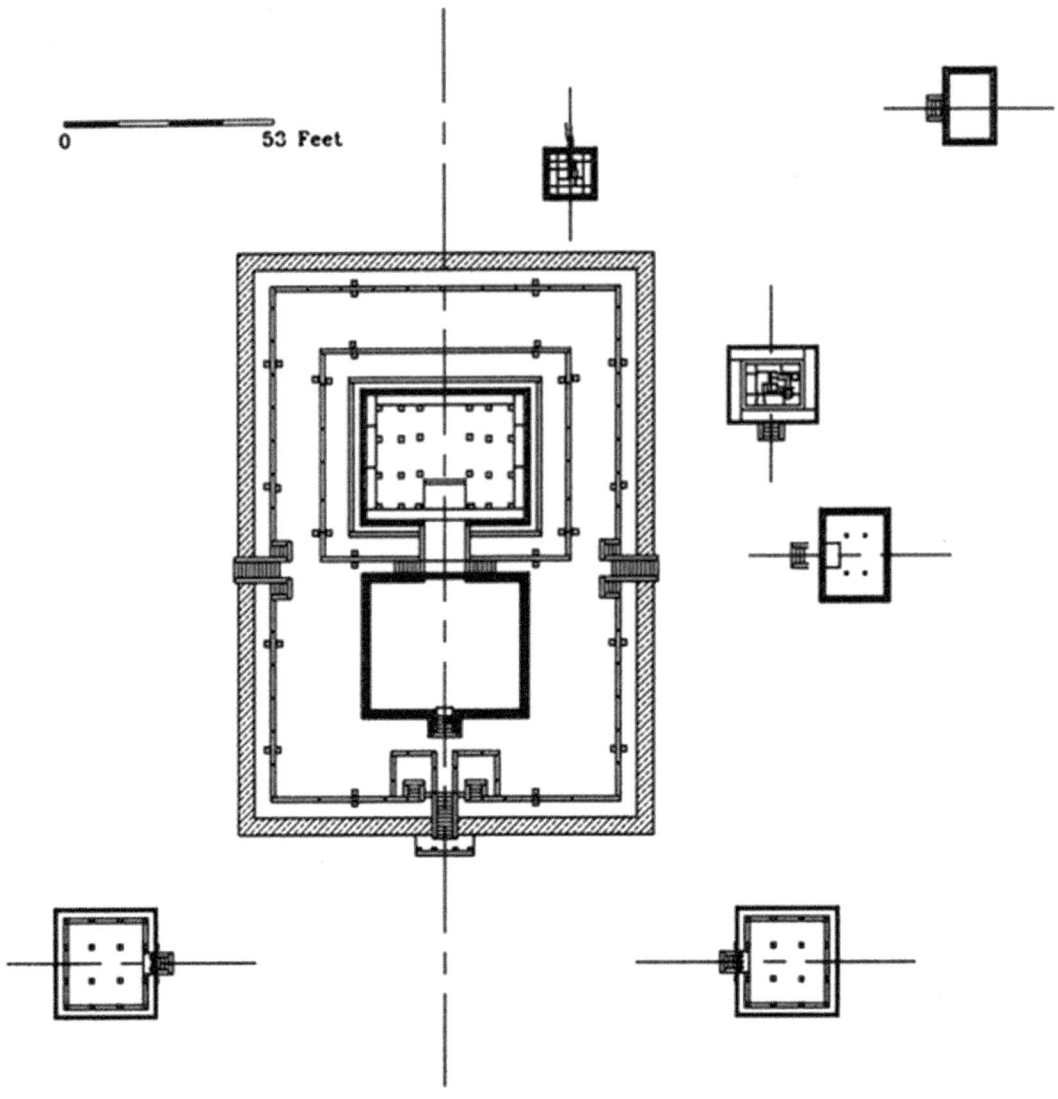

Fig.4.08: Example of double-platform site (after Wijesuriya 1998: 59)

Chapter 5:
The Citadel

"Anurádhapura was not one city, but two, one within the other, and that the royal residences and chief monastic edifices and dágabas were enclosed within walls of great strength"

(Smither 1894: i)

5.1 Introduction

Chapter Two set out the geographical and research background for this work and Chapter Three has synthesised the three collapse models that will be tested here; Invasion, Malarial and Imperial. Chapter Four then characterised these models archaeologically, focussing upon six key characteristics of complex societies and societal collapse; population levels and density, the traditional elite, the emergence of a new elite, monumental construction and maintenance, long distance trade, and craft specialisation and manufacturing.

Having set out the collapse models, and zonally archaeologically characterised them, the task is now to present the archaeological data for each of Anuradhapura's three zones. This will be done under the same six headings as the archaeological characterisations of the collapse models, namely Population, Traditional Elite, New Elite, monumental construction and maintenance, long distance trade and craft specialisation and manufacturing. Archaeologically it is the Citadel that effectively provides the master-sequence for the Anuradhapura period, formed by the ASW2 excavations and (critically) publications (Coningham et al. 1999 & 2006). Consequently, when presenting the archaeological data for Anuradhapura's terminal period, it is logical to start here.

5.2 Population & Monumental Construction

As discussed in section 4.5, population estimates (especially in South Asia) have long been problematic, and as a result the focus within the Citadel will lie upon the form of the structural sequence. Due to this focus upon the structural sequence, the examination of monumental construction will be included here, tied in as that is to the same structural sequence.

5.2.1: The Structural Sequence

The ASW2 excavations identified eleven structural periods (from earliest to latest K through A) (Coningham & Batt 1999: 125), corresponding well with those identified at Gedige (Deraniyagala 1972: 59) - though unfortunately Deraniyagala did not publish detailed records for the later periods. As the focus of this study is Anuradhapura's abandonment and the periods immediately preceding and succeeding this, only a small number of the structural periods at ASW2 are examined here, specifically periods B through F. Of these five structural periods, only periods B and F are characterised by the construction and/or occupation of structures, accordingly these periods will receive greater attention than periods C,D&E which are a macro period characterised by the cutting of robber pits to remove earlier structural materials (Coningham 1999: 80), grouped into a single, complex disturbed stratigraphic phase XCV (*ibid.*: 81). Further structural data, from other excavations and extant architecture, will be integrated following the examination of each of ASW2's structural periods.

5.2.1.1: *Structural Period F (c. third – seventh century AD)*

The earliest structural period to be examined within this volume, F is considerably earlier than the terminal phases of Anuradhapura. However, due to the disturbed nature of periods C,D&E (outlined below and displayed in figure 5.01) the diachronic window of study was extended back to period F to allow direct comparison between periods characterised by stable structural occupation, new construction, and securely *in situ* archaeological artefacts and remains.

Within the ASW2 sequence period F is represented by a large pillared hall orientated along cardinal axes (Coningham 1999: 79), and it is these stone pillars that so define this structural period (Bandaranayake 1974: 13). The pillared hall of ASW2 comprised at least five rows of five columns of ashlar pillars (see figure 5.02), with more potentially present under the trench baulks (Coningham 1999: 79). However, due to the subsequent periods of structural robbing, only 14 of these 25 pillars were extant when excavated (*ibid.*). Each of these pillars measured 4.6 metres long, 0.25 metres wide and 0.20 metres thick, although only the upper portion exposed above the brick pavement was dressed (*ibid.*).

Excavation revealed a clear structural sequence (partially displayed in figure 5.01) for the pillared hall that began with the hall's outline being delineated and the construction of the boundary walls. Construction was of a high quality, and where one corner of the boundary wall appears to have slumped, a small buttress was added to reinforce that section (*ibid.*). This was followed by the construction of the pillar foundations, which saw a cut made containing alternating courses of brick, mud-mortar and sand, on top of which was placed an ashlar saddlestone incised with two lines (one running north-south and one east-west) (*ibid.*). Coningham suggests two possible interpretations for these lines, the first being that they served as masons building lines for the laying out of the hall's groundplan, the second; that they serve as calculated lines of weakness, thus when the full weight of the roof was added to the pillars the saddlestone would fracture along predetermined lines, further anchoring the pillar in position (*ibid*.). Pillar (306), for example, did just this. Approximately 1.75 metres above the pillar foundations a brick pavement formed the floor of the pillared hall (*ibid*.), as can be seen in figure (5.03).

The plan of the hall (see figure 5.02) suggests a form of residential structure, a *kuti* or, in its larger form, *pasada* (Bandaranayake 1974: 251), described as "*a rectangular, walled edifice constructed on an elevated platform, with a regular series of columns ranged throughout the entire structure*" (*ibid*.). The internal space would thus have resembled a large hall, albeit one disrupted by numerous ashlar pillars. However, this space may have been compartmentalised using temporary or permanent partitions (Coningham 1999: 80). Although Bandaranayake describes such buildings as residential monastic buildings (Bandaranayake 1974: 251), this pillared hall was not necessarily monastic in function (Coningham 1999: 80), and it is reasonable to assume that secular elite residences would have had a similar form, using the same materials (Bandaranayake 1974: 384). Indeed, it is likely that many of the pillared structures within the Citadel represent secular residences modelled upon monastic structures, rather than monastic structures (Coningham 1999: 80).

The ASW2 period F pillared hall represents a classical form of Anuradhapura architecture, with load-bearing granite ashlar pillars supporting an upper storey, and a tiled roof upon a wood, brick and mud super structure (Bandaranayake 1974: 15), clearly representing a significant investment of labour and materials. Period F represents the earliest part of Bandaranayake's architectural *Phase IV* (as discussed in Chapter Four), as well as the early part of what Deraniyagala terms the 'Middle Historic Period', dating to 300-1250 AD, something corroborated by a radiocarbon sample (Beta-19624) from the foundations of a similar pillared hall adjacent to sondage APG (Deraniyagala 1990: 269) that provided a calibrated date of between 340 and 540 AD at a confidence of 68% (*ibid*.).

These dates are corroborated by the ASW2 Period F coin assemblage. 21 coins were recovered, the bulk (16 of the 21) of which were long-lived (third century BC – tenth century AD (Bopearachchi 2006: 7,10)) Punch-marked coins and Lakshmi Plaques. More useful was the single Late Roman Imperial Third Brass (SF677), dating to between the third and seventh centuries AD (Codrington 1924: 33). Codrington notes that direct trade with the Roman Empire ended with the fall of Alexandria in 638 AD (*ibid*.), and while Roman coins were hugely dominant within the coin assemblage recovered from Sigiriya, they were almost entirely absent from Polonnaruva,

whose emergence dates (according to the *Mahavamsa*) to the latter half of the seventh century (*ibid*.). The Late Roman Imperial Third Brass coin from period F was recovered from within the foundation cut of one of the pillars, suggesting that the construction of the pillared hall dates to between the third and seventh century AD. This date can be further constrained by the presence of a Maneless Lion type coin, dated third to fifth century AD and replaced as common currency by the Roman Third Brass (Codrington 1924: 25). The Maneless Lion coin was recovered from a foundation deposit below a layer of paving, stratigraphically earlier than the pillar foundation in which the Late Roman Imperial Third Brass was found (Bopearachchi 2006: 12), suggesting construction of the pillared hall occurred around the fifth century AD.

Other examples of period F architecture from across the Citadel (all of which can be termed monumental in scale and construction) include elements of the Mahapali alms hall, though this structure was later robbed and repaired extensively (Bandaranayake 1974: 288) resulting in extant remains that are not representative of this structural period in form or materials. This period can be structurally characterised by the introduction of stone pillars, replacing the wooden pillars of earlier periods (Bandaranayake 1974: 154, 255), structures that display clear evidence of planning, and with no evidence of reusing or "robbing" structural materials from earlier periods (Coningham 1999: 79).

5.2.1.2: *Structural Periods C,D&E (c. sixth – tenth century AD)*

Structural periods D and E (stratigraphic phase XCV) are represented by endemic levels of robbing activity rather than structures, seemingly focussed upon the recycling of construction materials. Period C meanwhile is a single *ex situ* fragment of lime-mortared wall lying within the fill of a period D&E robber pit (Coningham 1999: 80).

Turning first to the robber pits, at ASW2 this activity takes the form of a series of 17 intrusive robber pits cut from above, ranging in volume from 1.0 cubic metre in the case of the smallest, to 40.0 cubic metres in the case of the largest (*ibid*.). Consequently, periods D&E occupy the same physical strata as periods F and B, making it impossible to determine approximate age of later contexts within the Citadel by depth alone, a problem as some early excavations (e.g. Paranavitana 1936) recorded finds by depth below surface only.

These pits were then filled, in some cases by thin layers of silt and clay (suggesting the pits were gradually filled by erosion and aeolian deposits), while in others they contain single episode fills (Coningham 1999: 80). To further complicate the stratigraphy of this period, many pits and fills are subsequently cut by later pits (*ibid*.). Coningham argues that this is evidence that this robbing represents the excavation, removal, and reuse of stone blocks, bricks and other construction materials on a systematic level (*ibid.*). The pits are interpreted as robber pits, rather than rubbish pits or middens (although they clearly function as the latter once cut and abandoned), because they are cut with near vertical sides and are consistently located over the brick and stone foundations of ashlar pillars (Fig.5.04) (*ibid.*).

The pits cut through the Period F brick pavement to an average depth of 1.80 metres, just below the pillars' saddlestones or bases, allowing the 4.60 metre pillars to be rocked until toppled using the pillar's own weight, at which point the pillar could be hauled from the pit and transported to be reused, either in its entirety or broken up and reused (*ibid.*). This is the same method of pillar removal as practised by the archaeologists excavating ASW2, to allow them to continue excavating below the level of structural period F, taking some 14 men an average of 15 minutes, from start to finish, to remove a pillar measuring 4.6 x 0.25 x 0.20 metres (*ibid.*). The labour cost involved in retrieving dressed ashlar in this fashion is far smaller than would be involved in the quarrying, dressing and transporting of new ashlar pillars or blocks from quarries within the hinterland (Coningham 1999: 80).

This robbing activity was near universal across the Citadel, and almost certainly corresponds with the artefactually mixed "*rubbish heaps belonging to the upper stratum*" described by Paranavitana (1936: 11) during his excavations at Building A. Paranavitana also described similarly disturbed deposits present at the Mahapali excavations (*ibid.*: 26), where both the Daldage and Mahapali structures were severely damaged by such robbing (*ibid.*). Similar robber pits were identified in every one of Deraniyagala's 13 sondages (Coningham 1999: 80), and Deraniyagala's excavations at the Gedige, corresponding to his stratum 6, 8 and 9 (Deraniyagala 1972: 59) as well as stratum Ia (Deraniyagala 1986: 39). In all cases Deraniyagala describes "*structural detritus*" within extensive robber pits, as well as "*artefacts in random orientation*" (i.e. *ex situ*) (Deraniyagala 1972: 59). Such mixed deposits and intrusive cuts were also identified in the excavations at the southern ramparts of the Citadel (Ueyama & Nosaki 1993: 30), where the disturbed strata (Phase III) were described as consisting of "*largely disturbed and cut-pits containing many brickbats*" (*ibid.*).

There are records from structures across Anuradhapura of reused construction materials within many extant structures, for example Ayrton's 'Building under the Elephant Stables' (Ayrton 1924: 01), phase 6 of the ramparts (Coningham & Cheetham 1999: 54) or the Vijayabahu palace (Coningham 1999: 80), suggesting that the construction or repair of such structures may be responsible for this period of robbing. However, the spread of these robber pits across what appears to be the entirety of the Citadel, coupled with the apparently slow filling of these pits (Coningham 1999: 80) suggests that sizeable areas of the Citadel were effectively abandoned for a period, and used only as a source of structural materials for repairs elsewhere in the Citadel and Sacred City.

Turning to Period C, we see a structural period of monumental scale, though all that remains of this period in ASW2 is 21 courses of a 6.0 metre length of lime-mortared wall lying within the fill of a period D&E robber pit (Coningham 1999: 80). This brick wall was constructed on a foundation of six large (1.0 x 0.25 metres) ashlar blocks (Coningham 1999: 80). These blocks would most likely have been laid within a slot or partially clad in brickwork, as only the upper 20cm of each block were dressed, suggesting the lower portion was hidden from sight. Courses of bricks were then laid on top of these blocks using a lime mortar (*ibid.*). The bricks were uniform in size and shape, measuring 0.25 x 0.15 x 0.05 metres, and the construction is to a high standard both as regards materials and finish (*ibid.*).

Due to the *ex situ* location of this section of wall it is impossible to draw any strong inferences regarding the size, layout, function or significance of this structure, nor is it possible to determine where the fragment of wall originates from, certainly no other examples of lime mortared masonry were recorded within the ASW2 excavations, and the possibility remains that this fragment was moved some distance before deposition within the pit (*ibid.*). It is also difficult to fully integrate the structure that this section of wall originated from into the Anuradhapura Citadel's sequence, and it must thus be done stylistically rather than stratigraphically – linking it strongly to the Gedige and Building A (discussed shortly).

Throughout the ASW2 reports (Coningham 1999; Coningham 2006) periods C,D&E are grouped together as a single macro-stratigraphic phase. However, *architecturally* period C can be defined by the introduction of lime-mortared brick work, and represents the final monumental architectural period of Anuradhapura (Bandaranayake 1974: 25). Examples of similar construction can be seen within the Citadel at the Mahapali, Gedige and Building A, all of which lie just to the south-east of ASW2.

The final structural phase of the Mahapali, epigraphically dated to the reign of Mahinda IV (r.956-972 AD) is primarily stone, with relatively crude lime-mortared brickwork forming only the upper element of the walls (Paranavitana 1936: 26). Indeed this late re-construction (apparently after sacking by the 10th century Chola invasion) is described as "*crude and purely utilitarian*", and again features robbed structural material (Bandaranayake 1974: 289). In comparison, both

Building A and Gedige feature brick super-structures, sometimes described as of Polonnaruva style, and are likely very slightly earlier in date. Both Paranavitana (1936: 07) and Bandaranayake (1974: 205) both note that in plan Building A and the Gedige are virtually identical (figs. 5.05 and 5.06), although Building A is better preserved in plan and Gedige is preserved to a far greater height. Bandaranayake categorises these *gediges* as a late form of image-house (1974: 203), assigned to between the eighth and ninth centuries AD by Paranavitana (1936: 07), though this date is drawn from a stylistic assessment of some masons' marks within Building A, and is open to debate. It has also been noted that there is a similarity between contemporary South Indian architectural forms, Polonnaruva period architecture and Building A and Gedige at Anuradhapura. Indeed Burrows initially described Gedige as a *"large and lofty brick building which looks like a bit of Polonnaruva suddenly transplanted to this capital"* (Burrows 1886: 6).

Building A (Fig.5.05) was first exposed by open-area excavations between the Mahapali and Gedige in the 1930s, prior to which only a small portion of a stone pillar was visible above ground (Paranavitana 1936: 05). Excavations revealed a monumental brick structure with lime mortared brick walls surviving to a height of 2.44 metres from the original ground level (*ibid.*: 05). In plan both Building A and Gedige consist of a central chamber within which lies a large square stone platform (or *asana*) faced with moulded slabs of stone (*ibid.*: 06). This unusual platform has prompted Bandaranayake to suggest that Building A, Gedige, or indeed both structures, may have functioned as Tooth Relic temples (Bandaranayake 1974: 206).

Clearly, chronologically speaking, the pits of Periods D&E must have been cut after Period C at ASW2, for the wall fragment to then have fallen or been placed into it. Bandaranayake describes the vast majority of the extant architecture within the Citadel (and indeed Sacred City) as dating from this same period, ascribing such lime-mortared construction to around the ninth and tenth centuries (1974: 25). It thus seems likely that Period C represents the latter half of Bandaranayake's structural period IV (with F representing the earlier part), and thus the period in which the greater portion of extant architecture within the Citadel was constructed.

Subsequently, no earlier than the tenth century AD, construction and repairs were carried out using structural materials robbed from earlier periods. Unfortunately, due to the invasive nature of the robber pits, the mixed nature of the deposits within, and the apparent slow fill of the pits it is extremely difficult to apply dates to this period of robbing activity using comparative dating of artefacts. Thus although 31 coins were recovered from the pit fills of period D it is impossible to identify whether or not such coins are *in situ* or redeposited. This can be illustrated by the presence of two bull-marked Pandyan coins typically dated to between the ninth century AD (Chattopadhyaya 1977: 63; Bopearachchi 2006: 19) and the eleventh century AD (Pushparatnam 2002: 106) alongside three Late Roman Imperial Third Brass coins dated to between the third and seventh centuries AD (Codrington 1924: 33; Bopearachchi 2006: 18-19). Further artefacts support a *terminus post quem* for period D&E of around the ninth to tenth centuries AD, with the presence of a sizeable number of East and West Asian glazed wares, several of which are typically dated to the ninth-tenth centuries AD. (Seely et al. 2006), these are discussed below in section **5.6**.

5.2.1.3: *Structural Period B (c. eleventh – twelfth century AD)*

Succeeding a period of structural robbing and reuse (period D&E), Period B has been interpreted as a period of "squatter" occupation (Coningham & Batt 1999: 129), and is characterised by crudely constructed ephemeral structures that utilise a large quantity of robbed architectural material from earlier periods. In a sense this phase of occupation can be seen as a return to what is typically described as a traditional early Mediaeval Sinhalese village, described by Godakumbura as a group of huts positioned centrally within a network of fields, near a water source such as a river (Godakumbura 1963: 02).

Within the ASW2 sequence this period sees five successive structural phases (B1 through B5), of which the best preserved and most substantial is the first, B1 (Coningham 1999: 81). These structural phases sit upon a palaeosurface sealing the robbing activities Periods D&E, suggesting at least a brief hiatus between the end of the preceding period and the construction of the Period B structures. All five phases of the Period B structures follow a near identical plan, with a low building platform upon which a combination of re-used structural elements and perishable organic materials were combined, completely different to the "classical" Anuradhapura period stone pillars and blocks, fired brick and tile. It seems likely that two period F ashlar pillars, still standing *in situ*, would have been used to support both the roof and walls of the Period B structures, with wooden posts completing the roof supports (*ibid.*). If so, this would have given the structure a height of approximately 1.65 metres. The foundation deposits of the structure feature courses of re-used brickbat and fragments of ashlar, for example the foundation of structure B2 featured the base of a gneiss pillar within its foundations (*ibid.*), while the superstructure appears to have consisted of wattle and daub construction, as seen by the wattle and daub melt sealing phase B3, likely from the superstructure of structure B3 (*ibid.*).

Each of the structural phases were separated by further palaeosurfaces, again suggesting brief periods of abandonment and/or deliberate levelling between each phase, with structural elements from preceding Period B structures robbed and reused (*ibid.*). Indeed phases B2 and B3 were so badly robbed they exist only as incomplete groundplans (*ibid.*). A domestic fireplace was identified within phase B1, represented by an ash deposit, burnt brick fragments and finds of fragments of portable terracotta stoves or *lipa* (ibid.). In addition sets of post- or stake-holes interpreted as internal divides (a screen) were found within most of the phases, along with a shallow midden pit in phase B1 (*ibid.*). This strongly suggests that the occupation was domestic in nature, and the Period B structural form follows Godakumbura's description of the "*dwellings of the common man*" (1963: 27), which he describes as a "*structure with two roofs slanting on two sides. Wattle and daub walls... The building was rectangular about 20 feet by 10 feet, and divided in two. One part was converted into a room with walls on all four sides, ...a plain door to the front... generally on the east. The other part was walled only on three sides.*" (*ibid.*).

The end of structural Period B, and of occupation within the Citadel, is represented by a 0.50 metre deposit of windblown sedimentation building up over the site (*ibid.*: 82), with the next archaeological evidence of human activity on site dating to the early 20th century and ASW2 period A (*ibid.*). Unfortunately Period B, across the Citadel, was not usually recorded in such detail, and is typically either completely ignored, combined with surface deposits (for example Deraniyagala 1986), or described briefly in passing. An example of the latter is seen in Paranavitana's 1936 excavations at the Citadel, where he identified two separate structural periods, the latest of which lay just below the top-soil (Paranavitana 1936: 03). Unfortunately these structures were not planned, or indeed recorded in any detail, and the only documentation of these structures is Paranavitana's description of excavating through the "*vestiges of ephemeral mud structures in the foundations of which fragments of the older buildings were freely used*" (*ibid.*). Paranavitana did explain this lack of recording, writing that "*in this stratum there was not a single structure of which enough remained for a ground plan to be made*", before adding that "*these fragments of foundations had to be removed in order to lay bare the remains of more substantially built edifices of an earlier age*" (*ibid.*). This description of "*ephemeral mud structures*" close to the surface utilising robbed building materials within their foundations, clearly matches the structures recorded within period B at ASW2, with wattle and daub super-structures over brickbat and ashlar foundations (Coningham 1999: 81-82).

It would appear that during structural period B the inhabited area of the Citadel was reduced from 100ha in periods G and F to around 70ha, and fortunately an even earlier excavation within the Citadel did produce a detailed plan of six period B structures (fig.5.09 below) along what appears to be an ancient road (Ayrton 1924: 51). Ayrton excavated a large area to the west of the Gedige, exposing approximately six structures cardinally oriented along a road running north-south (*ibid.*). Only the lowest 0.30 metres, the foundations, of these structures survived and these were constructed using fragments of bricks and worked stone from earlier periods (Ayrton 1924: 51), as was the case in both ASW2 and Paranavitana's excavations. Once again the superstructure appears to have been comparable to what Ayrton describes as "modern peasant" houses with wattle and daub walls and cadjan leaf roofs, as very few bricks and no tiles were found (Ayrton 1924: 51).

However, despite the cruder construction materials and techniques displayed during this period, it is important to stress that the element of urban planning remained, with Ayrton (1924: 51) and Coningham (1999: 20) both highlighting the orientation of structures and streets along cardinal orientations. Unfortunately it is, again, extremely difficult to date Period B, due to the high number of artefacts from earlier periods that the robbing activity of period D&E brought to the surface. Thus although period B appears to post date the Chola sacking of the city (Coningham 1999: 20), and has a *terminus post quem* of around the tenth century AD (arrived at from the artefacts recovered from preceding structural periods and stratigraphic phases), the coins recovered from period B are typically regarded as early coin types – Lakshmi plaques, Punch-marked coins, Tree and Caitya type coins, all of which are regarded as having left common circulation by the second half of the first millennium AD (Codrington 1924; Bopearachchi 2006).

However, Paranavitana's excavations at the Gedige recovered a copper coin of Queen Lilavati (r. 1197 – 1200, 1209 – 1210 and 1211-1212) from the terminal structural phase (Paranavitana 1936: 03). This phase, characterised by "ephemeral mud structures" that utilised robbed architectural material from earlier buildings, can be judged to correspond with Period B as the terminal phase of construction and occupation within the Citadel. The presence of such a coin strongly suggests that period B, and settlement at Anuradhapura, must extend at least as late as the beginning of the thirteenth century AD., a date that corresponds well with the final references to Anuradhapura in the *Culavamsa* (*Cvs.* lxxxviii).

Frustratingly, the only monumental structure attributed to period B, the so called "Vijayabahu's palace", was completely excavated and restored between 1949 and 1950 with no excavation report ever published (Coningham 1999: 21). This structure, located in the southwest corner of the Citadel, has been interpreted as an eleventh century construction by Vijayabahu following his reclamation of the city around 1070AD, and has also been linked to Parakramabahu's apparent restorations at Anuradhapura (*Cvs.* xxiv.8-11) in the twelfth century AD (Coningham 1999: 21). Unfortunately such interpretations are heavily dependent upon the *Culavamsa*, and without published excavation reports, or indeed any archaeological data, it is very difficult to either validate or challenge these interpretations. However, this structure is architecturally very similar in form and orientation to the palace complexes at both Polonnaruva and Pandunuwara, though "Vijayabahu's Palace" is significantly smaller in scale (Coningham 1999: 21).

However, despite being "smaller" "Vijayabahu's Palace" is still monumental in scale, with the complete complex measuring some 200m x 200m externally, with a 10m x 10m gatehouse on the eastern side (possibly where the main thoroughfare lead). Internally an enclosure measuring 67m east-west and 40m north-south formed a large courtyard with a gallery measuring 5.8m wide running around all sides. The palace itself (22.5m x 20.4m) lay in the western half of the enclosure, while the eastern portion was apparently left open (*ibid.*). The similarity in form to the Polonnaruva and Pandunuwara palaces would certainly support the 11th century dating of the structure, though it is interesting to note that rather than the classic Anuradhapura period granite or even limestone pillars, Vijayabahu's Palace made extensive use of wooden pillars and featured almost no decorated or finely carved stonework – again this is at odds with the classic architecture of Periods F or C,D&E, but similar to structures at Polonnaruwa (Seneviratna 1994: 138).

5.2.1.4: *The Fortifications*

As has been mentioned on several occasions, the Citadel was a "walled" Citadel, surrounded, and indeed delineated, by a moat and banked earthworks capped with a wall and ramparts (Coningham & Cheetham 1999: 46). Excavations on the southern ramparts (Coningham 1993; Ueyama & Nosaki 1993) have shown a clear construction and alteration sequence that corresponds closely to the wider ASW2 structural sequence. By the end of period F (c. seventh century AD) the earthen ramparts of earlier periods had been capped with a brick wall (Coningham & Cheetham 1999: 53), raising the height of the ramparts to at least 4.40m (with a width of approximately 9m) and likely higher, though the subsequent phase of construction saw the capping brick wall ,levelled rendering the full period F height a mystery (*ibid.*: 52).

At some point over the next four to five centuries (corresponding *stratigraphically* and artefactually with periods C,D&E and B) the ramparts were expanded and widened, and increased in height to at least 7.9m, with an ashlar faced wall at the centre of the mound (ibid.: 53). Coningham cites the construction of this monumental ashlar wall as one of the primary causes for the extensive robbing activity within the Citadel during this period (*ibid.*: 54), though this period of rampart construction was itself also structurally looted (*ibid.*: 53). What appears to be a final phase of fortifications was identified above this period, in the presence of an uneven grit deposit including a shallow and ephemeral line of ashlar pillars that contained no diagnostic finds and did not correlate with any stratigraphic phases within the Citadel (*ibid.*). Coningham postulates that this might represent a late attempt to repair damaged fortifications post eleventh century AD (*ibid.*: 54), though he also suggests that it might represent spoil thrown up by Parker's irrigation ditch, which was cut along the line of the old moat in 1853 (*ibid.*).

Whatever the nature of the final rampart deposits, it is clear that late in the Anuradhapura period the ramparts were not just repaired, but were increased greatly in height, in addition to being fortified by a significant quantity of ashlar slabs – replacing the brickbat of the previous phase. This construction appears to have been at least partially responsible for the extensive robber pits within the Citadel, and strongly suggests that a significant emphases was being placed upon defensive fortifications, but also that insufficient resources were available (whether time, labour or money) to quarry and work new stone slabs, thus avoiding the damage to the very Citadel they were presumably protecting.

5.2.1.5: *Summary*

Monumental stone pillared structures emerge around the fifth century AD (period F), and the following three to four centuries see the architecture of the Citadel developing with clear continuity, typically featuring gneiss pillars, brick walls, multi-storey structures and tiled roofs (Bandaranayake 1974: 25). These structures are repaired and replaced with increasing complexity and sophistication, culminating around the eighth or ninth century with the construction of monumental Polonnaruva style brick super structures with lime-mortar bonding (period C).

However, shortly afterwards, around the 10th century AD, this structural period is subjected to sustained and widespread looting and robbing of structural materials (period D&E), with the robbed materials re-used in repairs around the Citadel and Sacred City, as well as greatly expanding the defensive ramparts. The period of structural robbing is clearly extended, and can be tentatively linked to the 10th century conflict and expenditure upon repairs identified by the Imperial Model (Indrapala 2005: 231; **4.6.3**). The final expansion and reinforcing of the fortifications can be tentatively dated to around the late 10th or early 11th century AD, which would correspond equally well with either the Chola invasion of 1017 AD or the Tamil mercenary revolt of 972 AD.

Following this period of endemic structural looting, the Citadel is occupied by punctuated phases of ephemeral structures incorporating robbed material from earlier structural periods and organic superstructures. This occupation, small in scale and grandeur, appears to have continued until around the thirteenth century before, finally, the Citadel is completely abandoned to the jungle tide, remaining so for over 500 years. This phase is strikingly different to those that preceded it, and appears to clearly represent post-collapse occupation. However, the potential 11th century construction of Vijayabahu's Palace can be linked to the 11th century restorations described in the *Culavamsa* and thus Invasion Model (*Cvs*.lix.2-3). However, the timber pillars and lack of decorated stonework in this structure suggest that this construction does not represent a concerted attempt to restore the Citadel, something borne out by the ephemeral nature of the wider occupation.

5.2.2: *Subsistence*

To maintain any urban population a rural hinterland must produce the food that necessary to support the urban non-food producing elite and craft specialists (Childe 1950). Even allowing for recent concepts of low-density urbanism (Fletcher 2009; Fletcher 2011) in which agricultural production occurs within the "city", there is no suggestion (or indeed sufficient space) for such to have occurred within the Citadel. The majority of the evidence for the agricultural productivity of the hinterland will be examined in Chapter Seven, however the extensive archaeozoological data from the ASW2 sequence is of interest in regards to the subsistence patterns of the Citadel's urban population.

5.2.2.1: *The ASW2 Faunal assemblage*

Unfortunately, the published quantities of faunal remains in the ASW2 report are contradictory, as seen in the difference in the totals given in the two tables below. However, as there is no way to determine the correct quantities, both tables will be given consideration, with the disclaimer that it appears likely that table 5.01 gives only preliminary results.

Table 5.01: *ASW2 Faunal Assemblage* (after Young et al. 2006: 592)

Group	Period B	Period C,D&E	Period F	Total
Domesticates	94 (235.7)	53 (190.2)	10 (89.0)	157 (514.9)
Hunted mammals	196 (330.1)	148 (384.9)	34 (245.0)	378 (960.0)
Exploited freshwater species	9 (73.0)	95 (398.0)	85 (476.0)	189 (947.0)
Exploited marine species	3 (9.0)	41 (182.0)	7 (21.0)	51 (212.0)
Non-exploited species	28 (162.1)	145 (407.1)	25 (109.0)	198 (678.2)
Unknown	0 (0.0)	6 (12.0)	9 (35.0)	15 (47.0)
Total:	330 (809.9)	488 (1574.2)	170 (975.0)	988 (3359.1)

However, period F represents centuries of urban occupation, at the heart of the wealthy and powerful capital, whilst period A represents centuries of abandonment, and K represents the earliest settled occupation at Anuradhapura around the beginning of the first millennium (Coningham & Batt 1999: 126). Going back to Young et al.'s suggested reasons for such changes in faunal assemblage, we can securely dismiss the possibility that periods A, F and K all featured similar population densities at the Citadel, furthermore it seems unlikely that around the third century AD Anuradhapura's population plummeted, only to rise again *after* the city was largely abandoned in period B.

It thus appears clear that during period F faunal detritus was removed from the area and disposed of elsewhere, indeed only ten fragments of the four primary exploited species were found in period F, with the majority of its assemblage formed by the "other species". We can see that despite containing more than twice as many faunal remains, the 'other species' of period F weigh less than a quarter of the comparable period B faunal remains (Young et al. 2006: 592).

Unfortunately, not only is the full species breakdown of those "other species" only *partially* published, but the ASW2 raw data that is published does not correspond to the overall figures published for ASW2 (table 5.02 previously). Whilst discussing the human remains recovered from period B at ASW2 a brief mention is made of 11,958g of faunal remains being recovered from period B, some ten times the published total. As a result it is extremely difficult to carry out anything resembling a comprehensive analysis of this part of the faunal assemblage, and entirely impossible to draw firm conclusions from it. However, some tentative observations can be made from the data presented in Table 5.03. Comparing periods B to F, in this data set at least, we see a dramatic decrease in the overall quantity and weight of faunal remains of "other species". Additionally we see a decrease in the number of genera present in that period, falling from 25 distinct genera in period F to 20 in Period B.

Table 5.02: Major exploited species (after Young et al. 2006: 592)

Major Species		Period B	Period C,D&E	Period F	Total
Axis axis ceylonesis	*number*	116	49	2	**167**
	weight (g)	68.2	47.6	20.0	**135.8**
Bos Taurus and indicus	*number*	81	28	1	**110**
	weight (g)	47.7	27.2	10.0	**84.9**
Parreysia corrugate	*number*	0	0	5	**5**
	weight (g)	0.0	0.0	50.0	**50.0**
Sus scrofa cristatus	*number*	56	26	2	**84**
	weight (g)	32.9	25.3	20.0	**78.2**
All other species	*number*	28	95	61	**188**
	weight (g)	1107.2	409.0	236.0	**1758.2**
Total	*number*	**281**	**198**	**71**	**564**
	weight (g)	**1256.0**	**500.1**	**336.0**	**2208.1**

Table 5.03: Other species identified in periods B through F (after Young et al. 2006: 593-595)

Species (common name)	Period B	Period C,D&E	Period F	Exploited for subsistence?
Mammals				
Bandicota (bandicoot)	1 (0.1)	3 (4.1)	0 (0.0)	No
Bubalus (buffalo)	5 (138.0)	5 (81.0)	3 (60.0)	Domestic
Canis (dog)	13 (132.0)	42 (222.0)	8 (75.0)	No
Capra (goat)	6 (43.0)	6 (33.0)	1 (6.0)	Domestic
Cervus (deer)	14 (151.0)	15 (105.0)	5 (112.0)	Hunted
Dugong (dugong)	0 (0.0)	0 (0.0)	0 (0.0)	Yes
Felis (cat)	6 (15.0)	11 (32.0)	0 (0.0)	No
Hystrix (porcupine)	0 (0.0)	1 (2.0)	0 (0.0)	No
Lepus (hare)	7 (65.0)	44 (130.0)	20 (79.0)	Hunted
Microchiroptera (bat)	0 (0.0)	0 (0.0)	2 (2.0)	No
Muntiacus (barking deer)	0 (0.0)	3 (19.0)	2 (8.0)	Hunted
Pteropus (flying fox)	0 (0.0)	1 (8.0)	1 (8.0)	No
Rattus (rat)	3 (6.0)	11 (18.0)	1 (1.0)	No
Tragulus (mouse-deer)	3 (13.0)	11 (58.0)	3 (6.0)	Hunted
Birds				
Aredaea (heron)	0 (0.0)	1 (1.0)	0 (0.0)	Unknown
Gallus (jungle/domestic fowl)	2 (7.0)	14 (49.0)	5 (13.0)	Domestic and / or hunted
Pavo (peafowl)	0 (0.0)	0 (0.0)	2 (16.0)	Unknown
(unidentified bird)	**0 (0.0)**	**5 (11.0)**	**7 (19.0)**	**Unknown**
Reptiles & Fish				
Crocodylus (crocodile)	2 (5.0)	6 (23.0)	0 (0.0)	No
Lissemys (turtle)	2 (6.0)	24 (106.0)	27 (173.0)	Hunted
Melanochelys (terrapin)	2 (33.0)	17 (115.0)	25 (193.0)	Hunted?
Monitor (monitor)	0 (0.0)	3 (13.0)	2 (7.0)	No
Mystus (catfish)	1 (1.0)	3 (3.0)	0 (0.0)	Hunted
Ophicephaloidea (snakehead fish)	1 (5.0)	4 (16.0)	0 (0.0)	Hunted
Serpentoid (snake)	1 (2.0)	3 (6.0)	0 (0.0)	No
Elasmobranchii (shark or ray)	1 (2.0)	4 (8.0)	1 (2.0)	Hunted
(unidentified fish)	**3 (28.0)**	**40 (148.0)**	**22 (52.0)**	**Hunted**
Bivalvia (marine bivalve)	0 (0.0)	12 (35.0)	0 (0.0)	Hunted
Cryptozona (land snail)	2 (2.0)	62 (74.0)	10 (12.0)	No
Cypraea (cowrie)	0 (0.0)	8 (26.0)	4 (8.0)	Hunted
Lamellaria (sea snail)	0 (0.0)	4 (5.0)	0 (0.0)	Hunted
Lamellidea (land snail)	0 (0.0)	2 (5.0)	1 (4.0)	No
Pila (freshwater snail)	0 (0.0)	5 (7.0)	1 (2.0)	Hunted
Strombus (conch)	0 (0.0)	3 (36.0)	1 (2.0)	Hunted
Thiara (freshwater snail)	0 (0.0)	2 (3.0)	5 (6.0)	Hunted
Turbinella (sea snail)	2 (7.0)	10 (72.0)	1 (9.0)	Hunted
Total	**77 (661.1)**	**385 (1474.1)**	**160 (875.0)**	**Total**
Number of genera	**20**	**33**	**25**	**36**

As demonstrated, period B is dominated by hunted, species, with freshwater species (such as *Lissemys*, *Thiara* or *Parreysia*) making up just 2.7%. In contrast the period F assemblage is dominated by freshwater species, making up 50% of the assemblage. Freshwater species such as freshwater snails (*Pila* and *Thiara*) which are entirely absent in period B, and freshwater turtles (*Lissemys*) and terrapins (*Melanochelys*) which form almost half of the period F assemblage with 366 grams of remains, compared to just 39 grams in period B. Although less dramatic, we also see a decrease in the number and weight of fish bones between F and B, falling from 22 bones (weighing 52 grams) in F to just five bones (weighing 34 grams) in period B.

Added to this we see a dramatic decrease in the freshwater corrugated clam, *Parreysia corrugata* after Period F. *Parreysia corrugata* not only makes up the vast majority of the shell assemblage, but also a sizeable percentage of the overall ASW2 faunal assemblage (Young et al. 2006: 550). Intriguingly this species is not present at all after period F, despite forming a major part of the faunal assemblage in all preceding periods - indeed this is the only species to be present in anything resembling significant quantities in period F (with five fragments weighing 50g) making its complete absence in periods C,D&E, B and A puzzling. Freshwater corrugated clam are easy to gather for food (Pearse et al. 1987: 347), and can live in either stagnant or running water (*ibid.*). The numerous rivers, canals, paddy fields and tanks in and around Anuradhapura and its hinterland would have provided a number of ideal habitats. Furthermore, because freshwater clams such as *Parreysia corrugata* are hermaphroditic and self-fertilising, they can not only rapidly colonise an area of water, but also easily maintain population levels, replenishing numbers when "farmed" (Young et al. 2006: 550), making them an ideal food source as they are both easy to collect and easy to maintain a high population. Which makes their complete absence in the later periods of the ASW2 sequence all the more curious, and strongly suggests that these habitats were lost or inaccessible, unless for a cultural reason the inhabitants of the Citadel ceased utilising this resource which appears unlikely.

This specific change might be explained in several ways; changes in waste disposal or species exploitation being the obvious ones, but one intriguing possibility is a that the dramatic decrease in freshwater species represents a change in local environment around Anuradhapura, resulting in the loss of suitable habitats for such species, specifically paddy fields. This would correspond well with the Malarial Model's suggestion of the deliberate destruction of the hydraulic landscape, though it appears to occur at least a century earlier than would be expected.

Marine species, while a minor component of the Anuradhapura faunal assemblage in all periods, are far lower in period B than any other period, falling from 8.4% in C,D&E and 4.1% in F, to just 0.9% in period B. One possible reason for such a fall could be reduced contact between the coastal regions of Sri Lanka and the city of Anuradhapura, which might be expected with the shift of trade routes away from Anuradhapura to Polonnaruva, a key element of the Imperial Model. Despite the low levels of marine species, the importance of fish (marine and freshwater) to the Anuradhapura period subsistence package should not be underestimated, indeed Deraniyagala described the Sri Lankan fish-curing industry as second in economic importance to that of agriculture alone over the last two thousand years (1933: 49), due to the taboo nature of beef. The fish was likely cured in a number of ways; drying, immersion in ghee, dry-salting, brine-curing, and smoking are all well established (Deraniyagala 1933: 53), but salting and drying are likely to have been the most common. Although there is no way of identifying such preservation archaeologically, we have fourteenth century historical records of fish curing in the Maldives from the Islamic traveller Ibn Batuta (cited in Deraniyagala 1933: 57), in addition to fish Dugong flesh (*ibid.*: 55) and turtle flesh and eggs (*ibid.*: 61) are (and likely were) also cured.

Overall the transition from Period F to B sees a decrease in both quantity and weight of "other species" faunal remains, there are several genera that buck this trend, including bandicoots (*Bandicota*), cats (*Felis*), dogs or jackals (*Canis*), rats (*Rattus*), deer and mouse-deer (*Cervus* and *Tragulus*), goats (*Capra*) and buffalo (*Bubalus*). Indeed both bandicoots and cats are entirely absent from period F, while both goats and rats are represented by just a single bone or tooth in period F. All of these species are either exploited for food and or traction (buffalo, goats, deer and mouse-deer) or are species that often live in or around human settlements, scavenging for food (rats, bandicoots, cats, dogs and/or jackals). In both cases the increase in their presence during period B can be interpreted as a reduction in the maintenance and cleanliness of the area, allowing increased numbers of scavengers and pests into the Citadel and not clearing rubbish from the area. Once again, this corresponds well with the period of unrest posited by the Imperial Model.

5.2.2.2: *Summary*

In summary, it would appear that during period F we see high levels of cleaning and waste disposal within the pillared hall, with relatively few faunal remains present in the archaeological record. The subsequent periods see a change in waste disposal and consequently have far larger faunal assemblages. This shift in waste disposal and cleaning of public residential areas is supported by the increase in scavenger species during period B. However, even allowing for this shift in waste disposal patterns, we see a huge drop in the exploitation of marine and freshwater species during period B. This could be attributed to a reduction in contact or trade with coastal regions, as well as potentially suggesting a loss of freshwater habitats around the Citadel, i.e. the canals, tanks and paddy fields of the Sacred City and hinterland. This strongly suggests that the tanks, and potentially paddy fields, of Anuradhapura were no longer functioning during Period B, i.e. post-tenth century AD. This fits well with the Malarial Model as propounded by Still (1930: 90).

5.3: Traditional elite

It is clear that long before the beginning of period F the Citadel was an elite zone, this seems beyond dispute and the Pali chronicles, inscriptions, structures and artefacts all clearly indicate this. The Pali chronicles are clear that the Citadel was the home to the ruling monarchs of the Anuradhapura kingdom, and this is widely accepted within Sri Lankan archaeology (Seneviratna 1994: 131-146), but at some point this elite status ended, and the question is when this change in the social status of the Citadel's inhabitants occurred.

Archaeological evidence for the presence of the elite will be found in diverse categories; in the presence/quantities of luxury goods (material wealth), the presence of exotic imported goods, the structural sequence (architectural forms), and epigraphic records. Imported goods are examined in section **5.6**, and the structural sequence has already been presented (section **5.2**). Consequently, the archaeological evidence to be examined here is the presence of locally manufactured luxury goods, and the functional forms of *coarseware*s – reflecting human activity on site.

5.3.1: *Coarseware forms as indicator of social status*

Using the methodology laid out in Chapter Four (section **4.4**), it is possible to examine the distribution of *coarseware* functional forms in succeeding structural periods at ASW2 in an attempt to identify changes in social activities occurring on site. When considering the data shown below (Table 5.04) it must be remembered that periods A and C,D&E consist of disturbed contexts, and are not archaeologically pristine, containing archaeological material that has been brought back into circulation by the robbing activity that characterized periods C,D&E within the Citadel.

Table 5.04: *The functional groups of coarsewares at ASW2 by Structural Period* (after Coningham et al. 2006)

Structural Period	Function	Sherds	Weight (g)	Percentage (by weight)
A	Buddhist	14	00560	00.61%
	Consumption	197	07845	08.49%
	Food Preparation	550	45540	49.31%
	Food Production	615	36835	39.89%
	Food Storage	11	00465	00.50%
	Other	38	01105	01.20%
B	Buddhist	18	00735	00.90%
	Consumption	132	04035	04.96%
	Food Preparation	455	47049	57.85%
	Food Production	451	28775	35.38%
	Food Storage	6	00270	00.33%
	Other	13	00470	00.58%
C,D&E	Buddhist	36	01346	00.98%
	Consumption	164	05178	03.78%
	Food Preparation	959	87854	64.09%
	Food Production	703	42160	30.76%
	Food Storage	3	00160	00.12%
	Other	12	00380	00.28%
F	Buddhist	8	00347	02.03%
	Consumption	156	05334	31.13%
	Food Preparation	30	02970	17.33%
	Food Production	142	07674	44.79%
	Food Storage	3	00165	00.96%
	Other	20	00645	03.76%

Comparing the two undisturbed periods of occupation (B and F) it is clear that there is a significant decrease in the quantity of coarse-wares associated with consumption of food (predominantly table-ware such as cups, bowls, *tali* or flat serving dishes), decreasing from 31.13% of the *coarseware* corpus in period F, to just 4.96% in period B. Indeed, compared even to the disturbed periods, the quantity of *consumption* related wares in period F are far greater than seen in any subsequent period. Conversely there is also a dramatic increase in the ratio of *nambiliya* (the only form associated with *food preparation*) after period F, rising from just 17.33% in period F to 57.85% in period B. Recent research (Davis 2008) has demonstrated that prior to period F there are no examples of *nambiliya* within the Citadel, strongly suggesting that rice preparation occurred outside of the Citadel prior to this point.

Again the functional makeup of the coarse-ware assemblages of periods A and C,D,& E largely mirror that of period B, with *nambiliya* dominating the functional groupings in all the disturbed periods. The categories of *food storage* and *other* are of negligible quantity in all periods and of no great significance within this context. We do see a distinct fall in the quantity of *Buddhist* coarse-ware forms subsequent to period F, however as the high of period F was just 2.03%, the subsequent drop to less than one percent in every subsequent period may not be significant, as a relatively small number of artefacts could easily distort the sample and cause such a shift. This is made even more likely by the relatively small assemblage from period F, in comparison to the coarseware assemblages of every other period, shown below (Table 5.05).

Table 5.05: Total weight and sherd count of coarsewares at ASW2 by period

Structural Period	Total Weight (kg)	Total Sherds
A	92.35	1425
B	81.33	1075
C,D&E	137.08	1877
F	17.14	359

(after Coningham et al. 2006)

In summary, there is a dramatic reduction in coarseware forms associated with consumption, and a dramatic increase in the frequency of *nambiliya* (food preparation) between period F and period B, or between Anuradhapura's fluorescence (c.400 – 700 AD) and a period of "squatter occupation" following the wide-scale abandonment of the Citadel. Coupled with the near disappearance of ceramic forms associated with Buddhist activities and we can infer a dramatic shift in the nature of the activities occurring within the Citadel; moving away from a high social status occupation with food prepared elsewhere and served to the residents of the Citadel, to a lower status occupation with food being prepared and consumed on site.

5.3.2: *Luxury goods*

In general we see a dramatic decrease in the quantity of luxury goods between Period F and period B. Six votive hoards were recovered from the foundations of the ASW2 Period F pillared hall, including one on the saddlestone of a pillar that contained 2300 glass beads, 21 ivory beads, and two alabaster beads, a miniature limestone stupa in conjunction with three glass bangles was recovered from the sand packing of another pillar. A bronze bowl was recovered from the rubble packing of one pillar (*ibid.*), while an earthenware vessel containing an iron nail, a conch-shaped green stone bead, a quartz bead blank, and a piece of molten glass were found on the saddlestone of a pillar that also featured carnelian, quartz amethyst and sapphire beads in its rubble packing. A similar vessel was found on the saddlestone of yet another pillar (*ibid.*). Unsurprisingly no such hoards were recovered from any of the ephemeral Period B structures.

The imported ceramics from the Far East and Middle East, glass artefacts and the like will be discussed below (**5.6**) as indicators of long distance trade. However, not all luxury goods were products of long distance trade, including precious metals, jewellery etc. Reflecting the coarseware assemblage that has been just discussed, we see a dramatic decrease in the quantities of metal artefacts between period F and B, including dramatic reductions in the quantities of copper and gold artefacts (Coningham & Harrison 2006: 27-76). Table 5.06 (below) shows the metal artefact assemblages for each structural period at ASW2, with period B (post-abandonment) containing very few metal artefacts of any kind.

Table 5.06: ASW2 Metal artefacts by metal (after Coningham & Harrison 2006: 27-76)

Period	Iron (g)	Copper Alloy (g)	Gold	Lead
B	30 (380.1)	6 (11.7)	1 (5.0)	0 (0.0)
C,D&E	72 (1726.6)	20 (38.0)	1 (5.0)	0 (0.0)
F	64 (1482.8)	24 (194.2)	4 (12.5)	0 (0.0)

Table 5.07 (below) and Fig.5.11 breaks down the metal artefacts by category, with gold considered a category because the majority of the gold artefacts were gold-leaf, their value clearly coming from the raw material rather than the form it had been worked into. Once again the material from periods C,D&E are of less interest due to the mixed nature of these deposits. Comparing Periods B and F, it is clear that there is a dramatic decrease across the range of metal artefact types, given that period B had a coarseware assemblage more than four times the size of that of period F, such a difference in metal assemblage is striking. While 112 metal artefacts were recovered from period F (weighing 1730.5 grams), only 44 metal artefacts were recovered from period B, weighing just 405.3 grams (Coningham & Harrison 2006). This decrease in metal artefacts is seen most prominently in the prestige categories of 'jewellery, vessels, and bells' and gold – of which none of the former were found in period B, and just one example of the latter was, although several such artefacts were recovered from the Mahapali excavations (Paranavitana 1936). These included two gold artefacts; a "gold or gold-plated spherical bead" from the upper contexts of period B (1936: 36), and a "tiny fragment of gold foil" from the earlier contexts of period B, at the Mahapali (*ibid.*: 35), along with a fragmented copper vessel, a copper ring from the earlier contexts of period B and a copper bell from the later contexts of period B (*ibid.*: 33). Back at ASW2, just four such artefacts were found in periods C, D and E – less than in period F. Of the seven 'jewellery, vessels, and bells' artefacts from period F, one was a fragment of a copper-alloy bell (sf1475), one was a copper-alloy stamp seal (sf676) that was part of a votive deposit, four were copper rings (sf2857, sf2850, sf2873 and sf2791) and one was a copper-alloy bowl measuring approximately 12cm in diameter. This last artefact was recovered in 64 pieces, one of which appears to have been a later patch, and was also located in a votive deposit beneath a stone pillar from the period F pillared hall (Coningham & Harrison 2006: 48). In addition to these ASW2 artefacts a copper ring was recovered from period F deposits at the Mahapali (Paranavitana 1936: 34).

Table 5.07: ASW2 Metal artefacts by type (after Coningham & Harrison 2006: 27-76)

Period	Metalworking (g)	Nails (g)	Pins, wire, sheets & miscellaneous (g)	Jewellery, vessels & bells (g)	Gold (g)	Coins (g)
A	9 (2431.3)	1 (30.3)	3 (57.6)	0 (0.0)	0 (0.0)	1 (2.2)
B	50 (6312.2)	18 (221.5)	18 (170.3)	0 (0.0)	1 (5.0)	7 (8.5)
C,D&E	102 (10587.1)	44 (754.4)	45 (1002.3)	3 (8.0)	1 (5.0)	33 (45.2)
F	21 (670.3)	40 (766.0)	41 (783.4)	7 (127.6)	4 (12.5)	20 (41.0)

In comparison to these prestigious artefacts, the artefacts of the first two categories, 'nails & nail-shafts' and 'bars, pins, wire, sheets & miscellaneous' are predominantly iron and are more structural or functional than prestige in nature, and it seems likely that these artefacts would have formed been part of larger items or structures. However, due to the fragmentary nature of many of these artefacts it is impossible to identify what these items or structures might have been (Coningham & Harrison 2006: 36). In particular it seems likely that many of the nails were associated with the use of terracotta roof tiles (Coningham & Harrison 2006: 39), certainly, as the period F structure was characterised by ashlar pillars and bricks, it seems likely that the super structure would have contained the only timber elements of the building (Bandaranayake 1974: 14), and thus that the iron nails recovered from this period represent structural remains from this very superstructure (Bandaranayake 1974: 363). This would also go some way to explaining the comparative scarcity of such artefacts in period B, where we see the larger, timber super-structured, pillared hall of period F replaced by ephemeral organic structures that feature neither timber nor terracotta roof tiles (Bandaranayake 1974: 14). Seven more nails (two copper and five iron) were recovered from the Mahapali excavations (Paranavitana 1936: 34), but without more detailed description of the contexts that these artefacts were recovered from, little significance can be attached to these artefacts.

Another interesting change in metal assemblages is the dramatic increase in metalworking residues after period F. This will be discussed in more detail in section 5.7 (manufacturing and craft specialisation), but is worth noting here that it may indicate either the movement of industrial activities into the Citadel, or a significant shift in cleaning and waste-disposal patterns within the Citadel. It is also worth highlighting the cautionary note that McDonnell et al. (2006: 85) raise regarding the residuality of slag, and the increased risk thus posed of re-distribution. This can only be exacerbated by the highly intrusive robbing pits of periods D&E.

5.3.3: *Summary*

Examining precious metals, votive hoards, architectural forms, and a functional reading of the coarseware assemblage there is a clear loss of elite between period F and period B. Where period F is characterised by the presence of indicators of wealth and high social status, period B is characterised by their absence. As will be seen in section **5.6** these results are mirrored by the ASW2 glass bead and glazed ceramics assemblage.

5.4: New Elite

As was established in Chapter Four, one of Renfrew's characteristics of collapse is the emergence of a new elite (1984: 369), and the Imperial Model stresses the growing influence of South Indian Tamils, Saivism and Mahayanism as critical in the changes that saw Anuradhapura abandoned (**4.6.3**). Furthermore all three of the collapse models for Anuradhapura see the primary cause of Anuradhapura's abandonment as the Chola sacking of the Citadel and Sacred City, with the Imperial Model also seeing the Cholas ruling the region for half a century afterwards, albeit from Polonnaruva (Spencer 1984). Consequently it is somewhat surprising to find no evidence of a Chola presence within the Citadel.

5.4.1: *Violence*

Looking first for evidence of a violent sacking, we see that no weapons were recovered from periods F through A, though axe heads, a spearhead, arrowheads and cleaver blades were recovered from earlier periods – demonstrating that such artefacts did exist and were preserved (McDonnell et al. 2006: 28 – 30). Nor is there any evidence of violent death or injuries, although human remains were recovered from periods F through A of the ASW2 sequence (Knusel et al. 2006). This was surprising, as both ancient and modern practices in South Asia forbid the depositing of human remains within areas designated as urban (or indeed settlement) (*ibid.*: 619). Typically the presence of human remains within a settlement is considered to be "polluting", and Early Historic texts state that not only should cremation grounds be well outside of the ideal city, but that the city itself should possess a gate which would be used only for the removal of corpses (*Arth*.2.36.31-33). Similar views are expressed in *The Laws of Manu*, where it is recorded that an individual that accidentally touches a human bone must be considered to be impure until they have performed set purification rituals (*Manudharmasastra* cited in Knusel et al. 2006: 622), while a later text (*the Manasara*) states that any land with exposed human bones is unsuitable for the laying out of a city (*Manasara* cited in Knusel et al. 2006: 622).

Shifting from prescribed behaviour to archaeological sites, there is a corresponding scarcity of human remains from South Asian archaeological sites. Knusel et al. (2006: 622) were able to identify just three such examples in India after a search through excavation reports from the Iron Age onwards; Rajghat in the Ganjetic valley (Narain & Roy 1978: 46), the megalithic site of Maski (Thapar 1957: 25) and Arikamedu (Wheeler 1946; Casal 1949). Although Arikamedu is a reasonable analogy with Anuradhapura (Knusel et al. 2006: 622) the human remains there were interpreted as intrusive (Wheller 1946: 26), clearly not the case in any of the ASW2 examples, although like the Arikamedu remains none can be considered to have been interned. Despite the presence of human remains in residential areas being proscribed, 93 fragments of human remains (ranging from individual teeth to long bones) were found within the ASW2 trench, in addition to a possible pit burial (*ibid.*). While the pit burial dates to an earlier phase of occupation at the Citadel, along with two fragments of human bone, 91 of the fragments originate from periods F through A (*ibid.*).

Table 5.08: *Human Remains at ASW2* (after Knusel et al. 2006)

	Period B	Period C,D&E	Period F	Total
Teeth	5 (9.0)	8 (21.0)	12 (13.0)	25 (53.0)
Bone fragments	14 (148.0)	48 (516.0)	4 (6.0)	66 (670.0)
Total	19 (157.0)	56 (537.0)	16 (19.0)	91 (723.0)

As can be seen in above (Table 5.08) both period B and periods C,D&E are dominated by bone fragments rather than teeth, while period F has just 4 fragments of human bone, weighing only 6.0 grams. Due to the size and condition of these artefacts it was not possible to gain any further information from these human remains. In contrast period C,D&E contained the greatest quantity of human remains, with 48 fragments, weighing 516.0 grams. These remains included long-bone fragments, a mandible, and 28 cranial fragments. Although clearly 48 fragments does not indicate 48 individuals, or even 48 complete bones, these bone fragments and teeth were recovered from sixteen different contexts, strongly arguing in favour of multiple individuals. However, it is also important to stress that these bones and teeth are almost certainly not from deliberate internments or individuals that died *en situ* as no evidence of articulation was found (Knusel et al. 2006: 619). Instead it seems likely that these bones were already fragmented and de-fleshed before being incorporated into pit-fills (in the case of period C,D&E) or packing levels (in the case of period B). The human remains from period B are again dominated by fragments of human bone, specifically eight cranial fragments from two contexts, along with long-bone and mandible fragments from different contexts (*ibid.*).

As has already been established, periods C,D&E and B are both characterised by greater quantities of refuse (that might normally be more carefully disposed of) being found, and this could go some way to explaining the presence of human remains in these contexts. Indeed one might even look to one of the tenth or eleventh century South Indian sackings of Anuradhapura as a potential provider of such human remains – especially if we are to interpret the structural looting of periods D&E as for repairs to the Citadel and Sacred City post-sacking. However, neither of these explanations would explain the presence of human remains in period F – a period that appears to be characterised by human occupation within a sizeable pillared hall. Another possible indicator of the sacking of Anuradhapura is the endemic structural looting and disturbance of structural period D&E. There is no doubt that the structural looting of earlier buildings, the extensive repairs, and the heavily disturbed strata suggest a chaotic period. However, there is no archaeological evidence to suggest that this was directly linked to the presence of a Chola army, indeed no artefacts that can be directly linked to the Cholas have been found within the Citadel (or elsewhere in Anuradhapura).

However, this is perhaps less surprising than might otherwise be thought. For example no Chola type coins were found at ASW2, (though two bronze Pandyan type coins were recovered both were recovered from robber pit fills from structural period D (Bopearachchi 2006: 13)), and while Chola coins have been identified in Sri Lanka, they are both rare and far less common than in quantity and variety than Pandyan type coins. At the National Museum, Colombo, there are 41 Pandyan coins in comparison to just three Chola coins (Krishnamurthy & Wickramasinghe 2005). There is a similar paucity of Chola inscriptions throughout Sri Lanka, though we know from the work of the ASI (Archaeological Survey of India) that Rajaraja and his son erected a large number of inscriptions across the Chola kingdom detailing their imperial victories (Rao & Rao 1987). The absence of Chola inscriptions in Anuradhapura might be attributable to deliberate destruction of said inscriptions after the expulsion of the Cholas by Vijayabahu, or potentially to the practice of both Rajaraja and his son Rajendra on making inscriptions on volumes of copper plates – greatly increasing the potential for metal recycling or reuse at a later date (Chhabra et al. 1953: 219). However, and regardless of the reason, despite over a century of archaeological excavation within the Citadel of Anuradhapura no direct evidence of a Chola presence has ever been found, unlike at Polonnaruwa as will be discussed in Chapter Eight.

5.4.2: *Appliqué wares* While no artefacts directly associated with the Cholas have been discovered in Anuradhapura, three coarse-ware sherds of a form previously identified only at Polonnaruva were identified in the ASW2 sequence, of interest due not only to their chronological significance, but also as potential indicators of religious change. This coarseware form, previously identified at the Alahana Parivena excavations (Prematilleke 1982a: 9 & 14; 1982b: 12; 1982c: 30 & 31; 1985: 60; 1988:40), and previously considered limited to Polonnaruva, is characterised by the presence of distinctive appliqué symbols such as *swastika*, *srivvatsa*, *vajra*, conch, frogs and *triratna* (Prematilleke 1982a: 10). The latter symbol has also been described at times as the Buddhist *vajra* (ibid.) and the Hindu *trisula* (Coningham 1999: 130). Prematilleke argues that, within the context of the other symbols used, it is most likely a *vajra*, one of the 'Eight Auspicious Symbols' of Buddhism (Prematilleke 1982a: 10). This argument is certainly reasonable, and a number of examples are clearly *vajra* (e.g. Fig.112a & 112b - Prematilleke 1982b; Pl.31 - Prematilleke 1988: 140).

However, there are also distinct trident shaped symbols (e.g. Fig.112c - Prematilleke 1982b, and Fig.39a - Prematilleke 1982c) that arguably bear a greater resemblance to the Buddhist *triratna* (Fig.112c - Prematilleke 1982b) than either the *vajra* or indeed the more Hindu *trisula* (Chandra 1996: 92). Of course it should also be noted that these symbols are extremely stylistically similar, and are used extensively in both Hinduism and Buddhism (Karunaratne 1979: 167; Chandra 1996: 90; Santiago 1999a: 37 & 39; Santiago 1999b: 46-47), as a result of this it is extremely difficult to distinguish between the Hindu *trisula* and the Buddhist *triratna* with any certainty, placing a huge emphasis upon context.

Table 5.09: Appliqué ware sherds from Alahana Parivena, Polonnaruva

Pit:	Symbol:	Vessel Type:	Diameter:	Date of layer:
E11.3.5(v)	Trisula (outcurving & facing outwards)	shallow dish w'broad rim	na	Post12th century (unsecure)
E9.8.6(ii)	Trisula (outcurving)	storage jar	na	13th century – Sahasa Malla coin E9.8.1
E7.7.8(ii)	Vajra (lengthways)	shallow dish w'broad rim	49cm	na
E8.9.9(iii)	Vajra (elongated) - lengthways	shallow dish w'broad rim	56cm	na
E6.3.4(ii)	Triratna (outcurving & facing outwards)	shallow dish w'broad rim	56cm	13th century – Lilavati coin in layer (ii), Sahasa Malla coin in layer (iii)
E6.8.6(iii)	Swastika	shallow dish w'medium rim	53cm	na
E6.S5.9.7 (baulk)	Srivvatsa?	storage jar	36cm	na
E6.S18.1.2(ii)	Svastika & trisula (outcurving & facing outwards)	shallow dish w'broad rim	64cm	Late 10th to Late 13th century – Sung Dynasty ceramics in layer (ii) (10: 40)
E6.S19.1.2(i)	Iguana rampant	shallow dish w'broad rim	65cm	na
E6.S4.1.2(ii)	hook with dot (vajra?)	shallow dish w'broad rim	62cm	13th century – Sahasa Malla coin in layer (ii)
E7.S8.3.3(iii)	Chowrie / camara	shallow dish w'broad rim	60cm	18th century – VOC coin in Layer (iii)
E8.S4.8.9(ii)	frog rampant	shallow dish w'broad rim	60cm	20th century – British coin found in layer (iii)
E11.S29.3.4(ii)	Trisula (outcurving and facing out)	shallow dish w'broad rim	na	13th century – 2 Sahasa Malla coins & 1 Lilavati coin found in same context
E9.S10.9.8(iii)	Vajra (diagonal)	shallow dish w'broad rim	55cm	13th century – Huge horde of Sahasa Malla coins found in layer (ii) of E8 (unsecure)

Table 5.10: Appliqué ware sherds from ASW2, Anuradhapura

SF#	Period	Symbol	Vessel Type	Diameter
00248	C,D,E	*trisula/triratna*	shallow dish w'broad rim	na
25169	F	*purna-ghata*	shallow dish w'broad rim	44cm
na	B1	*purna-ghata*	shallow dish w'broad rim	62cm

Given the context that these symbols appear in – alongside symbols that are both distinctly Buddhist (e.g. the *vajra*) and symbols that are distinctly Hindu (e.g. the *swastika*), from a city (Polonnaruva) prominently featuring both Hindu and Buddhist architecture and iconography (Indrapala 2005: 244-245), and (as discussed below) from a period that saw an unprecedented level of coexistence between Hinduism and Buddhism (Indrapala 2005: 247) it seems highly likely that the appliqué wares feature both a combination of Hindu and Buddhist symbols, along with others that are deliberately ambiguous and thus auspicious to members of both faiths. Such an interpretation is supported by the ASW appliqué ware sherds, two of which feature possible *purnaghata* (or vase of plenty) symbols. Again this symbol is considered auspicious in both Hinduism and Buddhism, although it is one of the eight auspicious symbols in both the Sinhalese and Tibetan Buddhist traditions and is arguably a Buddhist symbol (Harvey 1990: 74). One appliqué sherd with a similar symbol was identified at Polonnaruva (Prematilleke 1982c: 31), and although Prematilleke identified it as a possible *srivvatsa* (or endless knot) the symbol bears far greater similarity to the leaves and stem of the *purnaghata* (Harvey 1990: 74).

The first significance of finding this appliqué coarseware form within the Citadel of Anuradhapura is purely chronological, as this is clearly a late ceramic form belonging to the Polonnaruva period, thus post-dating the Anuradhapura period. Indeed if we examine the phases in which the 14 examples of appliqué ware were recovered from at Polonnaruva, we can see that they broadly date to the thirteenth century AD (1982a: 9 & 14; 1982b: 12; 1982c: 30 & 31; 1985: 60; 1988:40). The Alahana Parivena excavations were carried out following the grid system, excavated as pits which were excavated and recorded by layer, not context. It is thus possible to date layers both within a single pit as well as over a localised area, provided the bulk sections show continuity in the layers. All 14 appliqué sherds were recovered from different pits, of which it was possible to attribute dates to nine. Two of these were clearly from disturbed layers, as an 18th century Dutch coin was found in the same layer as one sherd (E7.S8.3.3(iii)), and a 20th century British coin was recovered from layer preceding another sherd (E8.S4.8.9(ii)) (Prematilleke 1982c: 30). Three further sherds can be dated through coins found in neighbouring pits, to post-twelfth century (E11.3.5(v)), and in two cases to the thirteenth century through Sahassa Malla (r. 1200 – 1202AD) coins (E9.8.6(ii) and E9.S10.9.8(iii)) (Prematilleke 1982a: 14 & 30; Prematilleke 1988: 40). Three sherds can be firmly dated to around the beginning of the thirteenth century AD by artefacts found within the same pit. The first, E11.S29.3.4(ii) being found in the same context as two Sahassa Mall and one Lilavati coins (Prematilleke 1985: 60 & 62). The second, E6.3.4(ii), was found in the same layer as a Lilavati coin, with a Sahassa Malla coin recovered from the layer below (Prematilleke 1982b: 12). The third being found in the same context as a Sahassa Malla coin (Prematilleke 1982c: 30). The final dateable appliqué ware sherd, E6.S18.1.2(ii), was found in the same context as sherds of Sung Dynasty ceramics – dated to between the late tenth and late thirteenth century AD (Prematilleke 1982c: 30).

The three appliqué sherds recovered from ASW2 all conform in style and form to the broad-rimmed shallow dish sherds recovered from the Alahana Parivena excavations at Polonnaruva. There are no examples of the appliqué decorated storage vessels seen at Polonnaruva. What is most striking about the ASW2 appliqué ware sherds is the presence of one sherd in the foundations of the Period F hall, dated earlier to between the fifth and seventh centuries AD, far earlier than would be expected for what was previously believed to have been a Polonnaruva period ceramic form. The presence of sherds in periods B and C,D&E is far less surprising and merely confirms that these structural periods are late in date. This early appearance in the foundation of the period F pillared hall is significant for the interpretation of the appliqué symbols themselves. Since these appliqué wares were initially confined both chronologically and geographically to Polonnaruva there was a strong argument to be made for the symbols adorning these wares to be Hindu in origin, or indeed deliberately unclear – representative of a period of Sri Lankan history in which Buddhism and Hinduisum successfully co-existed (Indrapala 2005: 247).

While these sherds of appliqué ware clearly do not represent a Chola presence, they may indicate a move away from the orthodox Theravada Buddhism of Anuradhapura, towards more Mahayana or even Saivite religious activity – as seen at Polonnaruva. This corresponds well with the rising influence of South Indian influences posited by the Imperial Model from the seventh century AD onwards, though this does require pushing the construction of the pillared hall to the upper limit of its date range.

5.5: Long distance trade, craft specialisation & manufacturing

Sri Lanka's location within the Indian Ocean places it, as discussed in Chapter Two, at the centre of the maritime Silk Route, lying as it does where the west and east Asian worlds meet (Seely et al. 2006: 91). This, in addition to an abundance of raw resources, its position as one of the foremost centres of Theravada Buddhist learning and teaching (ibid), and the economic surplus generated by the Anuradhapura hinterland, led to a burgeoning trade in imported luxuries (*ibid.*).

5.5.1: *Glazed ceramics*

Despite the discovery of locally manufactured glazed roof tiles (and even a manufacturing workshop of such glazed tiles (Wikramagamage et al. 1983: 347 & 364) there is no known indigenous tradition of glazed ceramics in Sri Lanka's early historic or early mediaeval periods (Hocart 1930: 90). In total 338 sherds of glazed ceramics were recovered from the ASW2 excavations, of which 325 were recovered from periods A-F, leaving just 13 sherds originating from the earlier periods. This is in stark contrast to both the *coarseware* and fineware ceramics, both of which peak around periods I and G. Indeed only four sherds of glazed ceramics were recovered from period F, displaying clearly that the importation of glazed ceramics to the Citadel at Anuradhapura was a late development.

The imported glazed ceramics of the early mediaeval period can be divided into two categories by source; those from West Asia and those from East Asia (Seely et al. 2006: 91). As can be seen below (Table 5.11) the majority (303 of the 325 sherds) of the glazed ceramics found at ASW2 originated from West Asia, predominantly the area of modern day Iran and Iraq, a trade route described as providing the "*largest revenue for the Sinhala Kings*" (DeZoysa 1988: 05). The East Asian ceramics all originate from China bar two sherds of coarse grey stoneware that may be from North Vietnam (Seely et al. 2006: 113).

Table 5.11: Origin of glazed ceramics at ASW2 by period (after Seely et al. 2006)

Structural Period	West Asian		East Asian		Europe	
B	81	849.9	5	63.0	0	0.0
C,D&E	203	2441.5	17	65.0	0	0.0
F	4	36.0	0	0.0	0	0.0

5.5.1.1: *The West Asian glazed wares*

As mentioned above, the West Asian glazed ceramics form the greater part of the glazed ceramics corpus at ASW2, ranging from the "*highly sophisticated*" Islamic lustre ware (Watson 2004: 38), to the "*common and abundant*" Sassanian-Islamic wares (Seely et al. 2006: 114). In all cases bar imitation lustre ware (of which only one sherd was found) the greatest quantities of all the West Asian glazed wares were recovered from the mixed deposits of periods C,D&E. This was seen in several other artefact categories (discussed elsewhere), and is unsurprising given the nature of these deposits. Of more interest is the relative scarcity of any glazed wares in period F, and the huge increase in period B, rising from just four sherds in period F to 81 in period B.

Table 5.12 (below) shows that there are two major West Asian glazed wares in the ASW2 sequence; Buff ware and Sassanian Islamic ware. By weight Buff ware is the most common "glazed" ware (although it is not in fact glazed (Seely et al.: 2006: 107)), while by sherd count Sassanian Islamic ware is the most common. Buff ware, dated to between the fifth and ninth centuries AD (Wijeyapala & Prickett 1986: 17), is an unglazed earthenware ranging in colour from red to a light tan, this ware is included in the glazed category due its imported nature and its characteristic interior (and occasionally exterior) black bituminous coating (Seely et al. 2006: 107). Buff ware ceramics were also identified within the Citadel during archaeological investigations at the southern rampart, where three sherds of Buff ware were recovered from Period A strata (Ueyama & Nosaki 1993: 46 & 47), and one sherd from a stratum corresponding to Period C,D&E (*ibid.*: 38), but due to the disturbed nature of these contexts no significance can be attached to these sherds.

Within the ASW2 sequence by far the greatest quantity of Buff ware was recovered from periods C,D&E, with 36 sherds weighing 1448 grams recovered from the disturbed strata. Additionally 15 sherds of Buff ware (weighing 374 grams) were recovered from period B. Although there is the potential for these sherds to be residual, due to the disturbances of the preceding periods, the number of sherds would argue against this. In addition to the sherds from the Citadel, a number of sherds of Buff ware were identified at Mantai (Wijeyapala & Prickett 1986: 17).

Table 5.12: West Asian glazed wares at ASW2 (after Seely et al. 2006)

Period	Ware	Date (typological)	Provenance	Sherds	Weight (g)
A	Buff ware	5th - 9th century	Iraq / Iran	8	410.0
A	Lead glazed ware	9th - 13th century	Iraq / Iran	1	28.0
A	Sassanian Islamic	2nd - 7th century	Iraq / Iran	3	37.0
A	undiagnostic	unknown	West Asia	1	4.0
A	White tin-glazed ware	9th - 10th century	Iraq / Iran	2	12.0
B	Buff ware	5th - 9th century	Iraq / Iran	15	374.0
B	Imitation lustre ware	9th - 10th century	Iran (Khurasan)	1	1.0
B	Lead glazed ware	9th - 13th century	Iraq / Iran	4	38.0
B	Lustre ware	9th - 10th century	Iraq	6	27.0
B	Sassanian Islamic	2nd – 7th century	Iraq / Iran	29	226.6
B	undiagnostic	9th - 13th century	Iraq / Iran	1	10.0
B	White tin-glazed ware	9th - 10th century	Iraq / Iran	25	169.3
C,D&E	Buff ware	5th - 9th century	Iraq / Iran	36	1448.0
C,D&E	Lead glazed ware	9th - 13th century	Iraq / Iran	6	96.5
C,D&E	Lustre ware	9th - 10th century	Iraq	28	58.4
C,D&E	Sassanian Islamic	2nd - 7th century	Iraq / Iran	76	460.5
C,D&E	undiagnostic	unknown	West Asia	6	35.3
C,D&E	White tin-glazed ware	9th - 10th century	Iraq / Iran	51	342.8
F	Sassanian Islamic	2nd - 7th century	Iraq / Iran	4	36.0

Sassanian-Islamic ware, sometimes called blue-glazed ware due to its blue alkaline-based copper glaze (Tampoe 1989: 11), was the second largest category of glazed ceramics found in the ASW2 sequence, and although not found in the same weight as Buff ware, a far higher number of Sassanian-Islamic sherds were recovered from the ASW2 excavations with 112 sherds (weighing 760.1 grams) recovered from periods A-F. This ware is also the first glazed ware to appear in the ASW2 sequence, with the earliest example found in period G. Like Buff ware, Sassanian-Islamic ware is an earthenware with a relatively coarse yellowish or greyish fabric that is characteristically coated with a turquoise glaze on the external surface and a cloudy, mottled glaze on the interior (Seely et al. 2006: 99). Where identifiable, the forms of the ASW2 Sassanian-Islamic wares appear to predominantly have been large storage jars (Seely et al. 2006: 99). It is difficult to assign a precise date to Sassanian-Islamic wares, with their date range covering the late Parthian to the early Islamic periods (Seely et al. 2006: 99), or approximately the second to seventh centuries AD. As was the case with Buff ware the greatest quantity of Sassanian-Islamic wares were recovered from periods C,D&E, however a sizeable number of sherds (29) were also recovered from period B, several centuries after this ware should have left circulation. Further sherds, albeit in much smaller quantities, were recovered from both period A (three sherds) and period F (four sherds) – indeed the Sassanian-Islamic ware sherds recovered from period F represent the only glazed ceramics from that period.

Similar finds were made during Deraniyagala's excavations in the Citadel at the Gedige (Deraniyagala 1992: 724 & 741), with Sassanian-Islamic sherds recovered from strata corresponding to Period F (*ibid.*) and this fits well with the distribution of Sassanian-Islamic ware sherds in the ASW2 sequence. In addition to the sherds recovered from the Citadel and Sacred City at Anuradhapura, Sassanian-Islamic wares have also been recovered from Mantai in the north of Sri Lanka (Carswell & Prickett 1984: 64), and the Gulf sites of Siraf, Iran (Whitehouse 1968: 14; Tampoe 1989: 31), and Sohar, Oman (Williamson 1974; Costa & Wilkinson 1987; Tampoe 1989: 106), Banbhore, Pakistan (Khan 1964: 54), the island of Kilwa Kisiwani off the coast of Tanzania (Chittick 1974: 302), the Indian Ocean sites of Manda, Shanga and Pate in the Lamu archipelago off the coast of Kenya (Horton 1986) and even as far away as the Red Sea site of Athar, in what is now Saudi Arabia (Zarins & Zahrani 1985: 75-83; Tampoe 1989: 110).

While both the Sassanian-Islamic and Buff wares are relatively early glazed wares, originating in the second and fifth centuries respectively, the remaining West Asian glazed ceramics are all much later developments, all originating after the ninth century AD. Both Lustre and White tin-glazed ware date from the ninth to tenth centuries AD, while Lead-glazed wares date from the ninth to thirteenth centuries AD. Lustre ware, a smooth yellow earthenware characterised by a white tin-glazed painted with a lustre over-glaze (Seely et al. 2006: 91), was produced by a small number of workshops around the area of Basra, Iraq (Watson 2004: 38). The ware is considered to be highly sophisticated in its decorative processes, and is widely considered a prestigious luxury good (*ibid.*: 46). However, despite being produced in such a limited area, the quantity produced and exported appears to have been extremely high (*ibid.*), with finds throughout the Middle East and South Asia, and even as far away as Spain (Caiger-Smith 1973).

Lustre ware sherds were only recovered from periods C,D,&E and period B, with 28 and six sherds respectively. Although it is not unusual for periods C,D&E to contain the largest quantity of a ware it is worth noting that, as there are no earlier examples of Lustre ware in the ASW2 sequence and as a large number of sherds were recovered, these sherds may be considered chronologically *in situ*. In addition to the "real" Lustre ware found at ASW2, one sherd of what has been termed 'Imitation' lustre ware (Wilkinson 1973: 181) was recovered (Seely et al. 2006: 93). This ware was produced in what is now the Khurasan region of Iran, and is best known from the site of Nishapur (*ibid.*). This particular sherd is deemed a failed imitation, as it lacks the metallic iridescence that characterises true Lustre ware, although it does appear to have belonged to the same type of vessel, a flared conical bowl. The most intriguing aspect of the discovery of a sherd of imitation lustre ware is its presence in Sri Lanka, as previously this ware was thought to be purely local to the Khurasan region, and was not believed to have been an export ware (*ibid.*). It is interesting to note that such is the prestige of lustre wares that forgeries and fakes are still produced today (see Norman 2004).

Closely related to the Lustre ware is White tin-glazed ware, ninth to tenth century AD, which originates from the area of modern day Iraq. This ware is characterised by a white tin glaze on a smooth yellow earthenware fabric, additionally some vessels are decorated with splashed green and cobalt in-glaze colouring (both identified at ASW2), in addition to turquoise, bichromatic and polychromatic colourations (Tampoe 1989: 35). Once again the largest quantity (51 sherds) of these sherds were recovered from periods C,D&E, with a further 25 sherds were recovered from period B (Seely et al. 2006: 94). In addition to the Citadel, this ware has been identified at Mantai (Carswell & Prickett 1984: 64), the Red Sea site of Athar (Zarins & Zahrani 1985: 75-83; Tampoe 1989: 110), Siraf (Whitehouse 1968: 15; Tampoe 1989: 33), Sohar, Oman (Williamson 1974; Costa & Wilkinson 1987; Tampoe 1989: 106), Banbhore, Pakistan (Khan 1963: 32-47; Tampoe 1989: 107), the island of Kilwa Kisiwani off the coast of Tanzania (Chittick 1974: 303) and the Indian Ocean sites of Manda, Shanga and Pate in the Lamu archipelago off the coast of Kenya (Horton 1986; Tampoe 1989: 111). Strikingly, Seely et al. (2006: 94) also note that although examples of this ware with cobalt decoration have been found at both ASW2 and Mantai, no examples of the closely related mid to late twelfth century tin-glazed frit-bodied ware have been found at either site, a clear indication of the cessation of long distance trade to the Citadel by this period.

Lead-glazed is the final West Asian glazed ware from the ASW2 sequence, and is also chronologically the latest West Asian glazed ware found at ASW2, dating to between the ninth and thirteenth centuries AD and originating from the area of Iran and Iraq (*ibid.*: 98). It is characterised by a clear yellowish glaze that is sometimes decorated with splashed copper derived green, and is sometimes entirely green (again copper derived (*ibid.*)). The stratigraphic and geographic distribution of Lead-glazed ware follows a similar pattern to that of White tin-glazed ware; restricted to periods C,D&E, B and A, with the greatest quantity of sherds, six, recovered from periods C,D&E and four sherds from period B (*ibid.*: 98). This ware has also, like the White tin-glazed ware, been found at Mantai (Carswell & Prickett 1984: 64; Wijeyapala & Prickett 1986: 18), Siraf (Tampoe 1989: 37), Sohar, Oman (Williamson 1974; Costa & Wilkinson 1987; Tampoe 1989: 106), Banbhore, Pakistan (Khan 1963: 32-47; Tampoe 1989: 107), the island of Kilwa Kisiwani off the coast of Tanzania (Chittick 1974: 303) and the Indian Ocean sites of Manda, Shanga and Pate in the Lamu archipelago off the coast of Kenya (Horton 1986; Tampoe 1989: 111).

5.5.1.2: *The East Asian glazed wares*

This category could just as well be named Chinese glazed ceramics, and is much smaller than that of the West Asian glazed wares, with only 22 sherds recovered from the ASW2 excavations (Seely et al. 2006). It should also be noted that within the ceramics assemblage of Siraf (and indeed other maritime trade sites of the Indian Ocean) Chinese glazed ceramics form only around 1% of said assemblages (Tampoe 1989: 47). All of the ASW2 East Asian glazed wares were restricted to periods C,D&E and period B (Seely et al. 2006: 111), with five sherds from the latter period and 17 from the mixed deposits of C,D&E. This corresponds well with what is known from documentary sources of trade relations between China and the Indian subcontinent, seeing trade flourish in the period between the seventh and thirteenth centuries AD (Ray 1987: 109; Tampoe 1989: 2; Krishna 2000: 121), this will be discussed in Chapter Eight.

Table 5.13: East Asian glazed wares at ASW2 (after Seely et al. 2006)

Period	Ware	Date (typological)	Provenance	Sherds	Weight (g)
B	Coarse grey stoneware	eighth - twelfth century	China / N. Vietnam	1	45.0
B	Xing ware	ninth – tenth century	Hebei, N. China	3	10.0
B	Yue green ware	ninth – tenth century	Zhejiang, S.E. China	1	4.0
C,D&E	Changsha painted stoneware	ninth century	Changsha, S.W. China	3	8.0
C,D&E	Coarse grey stoneware	eighth - twelfth century	China / N. Vietnam	1	13.0
C,D&E	Ding ware	ninth – tenth century	Hebei, N. China	1	11.0
C,D&E	Xing ware	ninth - tenth century	Hebei, N. China	7	18.1
C,D&E	Yue green ware	ninth – tenth century	Zhejiang, S.E. China	5	14.9

All of the East Asian glazed wares appear to be Chinese in origin, although two sherds of an unidentified coarse grey stoneware bearing an olive green glaze could originate from the region of North Vietnam (*ibid.*). Both sherds found here, one from period B and one from periods C,D&E, came from vessels in the form of storage jars (also known as *martavans* (*ibid.*)) and there is a possibility that these are in fact 'Dusun' stonewares (Harrison1965: 69). Similar sherds of Dusun *type* stonewares have been identified across the early Mediaeval Indian Ocean world, at Mantai to the north (Carswell & Prickett 1984: 64), as well as Siraf in the Gulf, Banbhore on the coast of Pakistan (Whitehouse 1968: 18; Tampoe 1989: 47), Sohar, Oman (Williamson 1974; Costa & Wilkinson 1987; Tampoe 1989: 106), Banbhore, Pakistan (Khan 1963: 32-47; Tampoe 1989: 107), and the Indian Ocean sites of Manda, Shanga and Pate in the Lamu archipelago off the coast of Kenya (Horton 1986 Tampoe 1989: 111).

The largest single group of East Asian glazed wares is the Xing wares, with ten sherds recovered, three from period B and seven from C,D&E (Seely et al. 2006: 112). This striking fine white porcelain ware, that likely originated from the Hebei province of Northern China (Wood 1999: 100)), belonged to the Tang dynasty and has been dated by Seely et al. (2006: 112) to between the ninth and tenth centuries AD, although dates as early as the late sixth century AD are possible (Wood 1999: 99). Xing wares were widely traded, often as a secondary cargo alongside silk, and have been found at Siraf (Seely et al. 2006: 112) Sohar, Oman (Williamson 1974; Costa & Wilkinson 1987; Tampoe 1989: 106) and Banbhore, Pakistan (Khan 1963: 32-47; Tampoe 1989: 107).

In addition to the Xing ware sherds, a single sherd of Ding ware was also tentatively identified at ASW2 from period C,D&E (Seely et al. 2006: 112). Ding ware, another high quality white porcelain from the Hebei province of Northern China, belonged to the later Song dynasty (Wood 1999: 100), and has been dated by Seely *at al.* to between the ninth and tenth centuries AD (2006: 112), although a later date range of the ninth – twelfth centuries AD has been suggested elsewhere (Wood 1999: 100). It is interesting to note that examples of Ding ware ceramics are extremely rare at Siraf (Tampoe 1989: 67).

The next largest group of East Asian glazed ceramics is that of Yue-green ware, of which six sherds were recovered – five from period D and one from period B (Seely *at al.* 2006: 112). This ware, predominantly found in the form of bowls (Tampoe 1989: 51) originates from the kilns of Zhejiang province, in S.E. China, and is a fine mid-grey stoneware bearing a thin olive coloured glaze (*ibid.*). Although the ware is a relatively long lived one (Wood 1999: 36), the examples identified in the ASW2 sequence have been dated to between the ninth and tenth centuries AD (Seely et al. 2006: 112). Further afield, sherds of Yue ware have been identified at the Red Sea site of Athar (Zarins & Zahrani 1985: 75-83; Tampoe 1989: 110), Siraf, where it was among the more common Chinese wares (Tampoe 1989: 51-54), Sohar (Williamson 1974; Costa & Wilkinson 1987; Tampoe 1989: 106), and Banbhore, Pakistan (Khan 1963: 32-47; Tampoe 1989: 107), as well as Mantai and Polonnaruva (Prickett 1990: 83) in Sri Lanka.

The final Chinese ware identified at ASW2 was that of Changsha painted stoneware, of which just three sherds were recovered, all found in the mixed deposits of period C,D&E (Seely et al. 2006: 111). This ware, also sometimes termed Tongguan ware (Wood 1999: 41), came from the Changsha region of Hunan in the S.E. of China during the Tang Dynasty, and can be dated to the between the ninth and tenth century (Seely et al. 2006: 111) at which time they were traded extensively outside of China, though they were do not appear to have ever been considered high status within China (Wood 1999:

41 & 43). This ware is characterised by a white slipped interior, at least a partial exterior slip, polychrome coloured lime-glazes and oxidised firings (*ibid.*). As with the previously examined Chinese glazed wares, this ware was traded extensively with the Middle East (*ibid.*: 43), and examples of Changsha painted stoneware have been identified at Siraf in the Gulf (Tampoe 1989: 54-56), Sohar, Oman (Williamson 1974; Costa & Wilkinson 1987; Tampoe 1989: 106), Manda, Shanga and Pate in the Lamu archipelago off the coast of Kenya (Horton 1986; Tampoe 1989: 111), Banbhore, Pakistan (Khan 1963: 32-47; Tampoe 1989: 107), as well as Mantai (Carswell & Prickett: 64) in Sri Lanka.

These tightly dated East Asian glazed wares clearly demonstrate that eastern trade was a very late development at Anuradhapura, starting around the eighth or ninth century Ads and ending around the tenth or eleventh century AD. Once again, this corresponds well with the eleventh century collapse of Anuradhapura, as well as supporting the Imperial Model's description of the Cholas taking control of the international trade routes. These imported ceramics also clearly demonstrate that, despite the mixed nature of the Period C,D&E deposits, there was still an established and wealthy elite present in the Citadel during this period.

5.5.2: *Metalworking*

By the beginning of period F there already existed an indigenous metalworking tradition dating back to at least the sixth century BC (Coningham & Batt 1999:126; McDonnell et al. 2006: 85). At the ASW2 excavations a variety of evidences of metalworking were identified, including fragments of crucible, ferrous slag, cinder and copper working residue – all of which are by-products of metalworking (McDonnell et al. 1999: 77). In addition a mould was recovered from period C,D&E, this is discussed shortly.

Table 5.14: Evidence of late metalworking at ASW2 (after McDonnell et al. 2006)

Period	Description	Quantity	Weight (g)
B	Copper working residue	2	33.5
B	Crucible Fragment	3	74.6
B	Ferrous slag	45	6204.1
C,D&E	Cinder	2	23.0
C,D&E	Copper working residue	3	85.6
C,D&E	Crucible Fragment	4	103.6
C,D&E	Ferrous slag	92	10239.9
C,D&E	Mould	1	135.0
F	Cinder	4	32.3
F	Copper working residue	1	28.9
F	Crucible Fragment	4	76.2
F	Ferrous slag	12	532.9

As can be seen in table 5.14, by far the greatest quantity of metalworking associated artefacts was found in period C,D&E, including 10.24 kg of ferrous slag, the largest quantity of ferrous slag found in any period in the ASW2 sequence. However this is problematic due to the mixed nature of the deposits from this period, and the high potential that slag possesses for residuality (due to its robust nature it does not degrade easily (Mc Donnell et al. 2006: 85). This can lead to reuse, with slag either intentionally used, or mixed up with over material, in the creation of packing deposits, foundation platforms etc. However, setting these issues to one side for the moment, it is interesting to note the huge increase in the quantity of ferrous slag recovered from period B (6.2kg in 45 fragments) compared to period F (0.5kg in 12 fragments). Bearing in mind the issue of residuality, it is thus possible to interpret this massive rise in ferrous slag in two distinct ways. Firstly, that there is an increase in iron-smithing on site during period B at ASW2, alternatively, this could represent a change in the cleaning practices at ASW2, with a failure to clear slag from the area after smithing.

Further evidence of metal-working in period B was identified during Paranavitana's excavations between the Mahapali and the Gedige in the late 1920s (1936: 3). Several fragments of crucibles with a "plumbago" (a fine powdered graphite used in foundry) coating were recovered, each measuring approximately 10cm in height, along with one complete example measuring approximately 25cm in height (*ibid.*: 08). Whether this represents on-site metal working within the Citadel, or a shift in waste disposal practices, this appears to clearly indicate a reduction in social status of the area with, once again (as seen in **5.3**), a reduction in the elite status between period F and B, again clearly indicating a massive shift in the function and role of the Citadel.

Turning back to the precious metals found within the ASW2 sequence, it is worth noting that although extremely minute quantities of gold are found naturally in Sri Lanka, these are not of sufficient concentration to allow their working (Cooray 1984: 212). As a result it is almost certain that gold (or indeed silver) would have to have been imported from the subcontinent (McDonnell et al. 2006: 85), although it would most likely have been worked locally (*ibid.*), and finds of two moulds for such metalworking at ASW2 indicate that gold was clearly worked at the site (*ibid.*). However, even though one mould was recovered from the deposits of C,D&E, both moulds were dated to around the beginning of the first millennium AD (McDonnell et al. 2006: 85) and the period C,D&E mould is likely to have been excavated from its original location by robbing activity endemic to that period.

5.5.3: *Glass artefacts (excluding beads)*

A total of 603 glass artefacts were recovered from periods B through F of the ASW2 excavations, not including glass beads which will be discussed separately due to the comparatively huge number found (Coningham 2006: 333). This represents almost all of the 637 glass artefacts (excluding beads) recovered from the ASW2 excavations (*ibid.*) and fits with the established view of glass objects becoming widespread throughout South Asia in the second half of the first millennium AD (Basa 1992: 99).

Table 5.15: Glass Artefacts recovered from ASW2

Period	Rings & bangles	Vessel fragment	Unformed glass	Other	Total (g)
B	17 (22.5)	95 (157.2)	11 (8.1)	0 (0.0)	**123 (187.8)**
C,D&E	56 (58.1)	293 (232.8)	64 (77.1)	4 (3.6)	**417 (371.6)**
F	11 (24.5)	33 (16.6)	18 (99.2)	1 (2.0)	**63 (142.3)**
Total	**84 (105.1)**	**421 (406.6)**	**93 (184.4)**	**5 (5.6)**	**603 (701.7)**

Comparing periods B and F it is interesting to see that although almost twice as many artefacts were recovered from period B, the two periods are far closer in total weight. Indeed, while the average glass artefact from period F weighed 2.26 grams, the average period B glass fragment weighed just 1.53 grams. This can also be seen in the glass artefacts recovered from periods C,D&E, where the average artefact weighed just 0.89 grams. This would appear to be indicative of the nature of the deposits themselves, with the heavily disturbed deposits of periods C,D&E resulting the greatest fragmentation of glass artefacts. The period B deposits, characterised by a series of palaeosurfaces, appear to have resulted in a similarly increased level of fragmentation – albeit from different depositional processes. Meanwhile the period F deposits, specifically the foundation and packing deposits that so characterise it, would have been formed quicker resulting in a lower level of fragmentation. As a result of this, the weight of the glass artefacts recovered could be considered more representative of the quantities of glass in circulation during each period. Examining periods F and B in this manner we would see an overall increase of approximately 25.8% between the two periods.

Table 5.16: Geographical source of ASW2 glass vessel fragments (after Coningham 2006: 333-376)

Period	Egypt	Persia	East Mediterranean	Unknown
A	0 (0.0)	0 (0.0)	0 (0.0)	4 (9.2)
B	6 (36.9)	0 (0.0)	1 (5.6)	99 (112.8)
C,D&E	18 (30.8)	2 (1.4)	0 (0.0)	340 (280.4)
F	0 (0.0)	0 (0.0)	1 (0.3)	50 (115.5)

However there is another important factor to be taken into account here, the very nature of broken glass. While it may be a prestige good when intact, when broken it becomes a hazardous waste material, something to be removed from habitation areas to prevent injury. This is arguably less so in the case of items such as unformed glass or glass ingots, but would certainly be true of shards of glass vessels. As usual little significance should be attached to the large quantity of vessel fragments recovered from C,D&E as much of this material is either disturbed or deliberate infilling of pits with waste material. Comparing period B to F is more interesting, for while period F sees just 33 vessel fragments (weighing 16.6 grams), period B produced 95 vessel shards (157.2 grams) – close to a three-fold increase in quantity, and more than a nine-fold increase by weight. This clearly demonstrates a far less rigorous clearing of hazardous materials from habitation areas. This was also seen in Ayrton's excavations of the period B 'House F', within the Citadel and forming part of his period B street, where three fragments of glass vessels (green, blue and purple) were found within rooms F7 and F9 (Ayrton 1924: 52-53).

Although glass artefacts have been found in the Citadel as early as period I (fourth to second centuries BC (Coningham & Batt 1999: 127)), glass vessels appear to be a later development and a wholly imported phenomenon (Coningham 2006: 333), with Persian, Egyptian and Eastern Mediterranean vessel fragments recovered from ASW2. As seen in Table 5.16 the majority of vessel shards were too small and fragmented to provenance. However, where such identification was possible, it is clear that glass vessels from Egypt are the most common in periods B, and C,D&E. As only one shard of a glass vessel was identifiable in period F, it is difficult to form any strong arguments about glass wares within this period.

While there are no indications of local glass vessel production, the discovery of two dark-blue glass hair curls suggest that South Asian glass-working was sufficiently advanced by the first half of the first millennium AD to produced such objects from moulds (Coningham 2006: 348). Although these artefacts were recovered from periods D and F it seems likely that they both originated from period F (*ibid.*). Both are circular moulded-glass hair curls from a Buddha figure, with circular holes in their undersides – likely for a rod or dowel attachment to the head of the figure (*ibid.*). It is possible that the figure itself was entirely made of glass, but it is equally possible that the figure would have been a composite piece. To date these artefacts are unique within Sri Lankan archaeology (*ibid.*).

Other glass artefacts worth mentioning include a glass kohl stick, likely Egyptian in origin and dating to period E, and an ear reel, from period F, in dark red glass that bears a close resemblance to an ear reel recovered from the Bhir Mound at Taxila (Marshall 1951: 690). Indeed similar ear reels have been found throughout North and South India at sites including Maheshwar, Nasik, Kaundinyapur and Ujjain – dating from Mauryan times to the end of the Satavahana period (Dikshit 1969: 15-17).

5.5.4: Glass beads

These are by far the most common glass artefacts found at ASW2, with over four thousand recovered in total. Of these, 3461 glass beads were found in periods F through A, including a horde of 2120 found within period F. The horde of 2120 beads found within period F clearly distorts the sample, however as it is neither intrusive nor *ex situ* there is no reason to in any way attach less significance to the bead count from this period. Consequently period F clearly has far and away the largest number of glass beads, with a total of 2773, in comparison ASW2 period B sees just 171 glass beads (Coningham 2006: 361).

Table 5.17: ASW2 glass bead assemblage (after Coningham 2006)

Period	Glass beads
B	171
C,D&E	511
F	2773

Elsewhere in the Citadel, Ayrton (1924: 53) recorded a green glass disc bead during his excavation of room F9 of 'House F, while at the Mahapali excavations (Paranavitana 1936), recorded a further 33 glass beads, recovered from depths ranging between 0.30 and 2.40 metres below the surface, approximately corresponding to periods B and/or D&E. Given Paranavitana's description of these deposits as "disturbed" it is impossible from depths alone to assign any structural period to these contexts (or the artefacts within), though it is likely that the disturbed deposits correspond to periods D&E. However, this again indicates just how ubiquitous glass beads appear to have been within the Citadel.

Table 5.18: Glass bead forms at ASW2 (after Coningham 2006)

Bead Form	Period A	Period B	Period C,D&E	Period F	Horde F	Total
Disc	2	20	32	22	1	77
Spherical disc	3	103	298	493	2071	2966
Tube	-	6	36	26	-	68
Hexagonal prism	-	-	-	1	-	1
Collared sphere	1	23	64	59	21	168
Sphere	-	7	21	8	-	36
Squashed collared sphere	-	-	1	8	16	25
Elliptical	-	-	15	9	-	24
Squashed sphere	-	-	1	-	-	1
Barrel	-	1	1	-	-	2
Notched prism	-	1	3	-	-	4
Rectangular spacer	-	-	1	-	2	3
Notched & collared sphere	-	1	-	3	4	8
Collared triangular barrel	-	-	-	1	-	1
Truncated bicone	-	-	1	1	-	2
Triangular spacer	-	-	-	1	-	1
Ringed sphere	-	-	2	-	-	2
Sectioned sphere	-	-	-	1	-	1
Unperforated sphere	-	2	4	1	-	7
Undiagnostic	-	7	31	19	5	62
Total	6	171	511	654	2120	3462

Period F is also the zenith of bead form variety, with 15 distinct forms of glass bead present in the archaeological record of this period. In comparison, period B sees just 9 distinct forms, none of which are unique to period B. It is clearly dangerous to attempt to attach too much significance to this drop in form variety, though there must be a temptation to interpret this as a drop in craft complexity. This can also be seen in the variety of colours in which glass beads are found. During period F fifteen different colour combinations are seen, while period B sees just eleven. Francis (2002: 136-137) describes the red spherical disc beads as the most common of all Sri Lankan glass beads, highlighting their frequency at Gedige, where they formed nearly 75% of all the glass beads recovered (Deraniyagala 1972: 137), at Tissamaharama (Weisshaar & Wijeyapala 1993: 160) and in the north of the Jaffna peninsula, where Peiris (1921: 64) recorded that *"the red discs which first led me to look for beads are exceptionally abundant"*.

The ASW2 glass bead assemblage fits within what Francis (1982) identifies as the South Indian diagnostic regional group – one of four South Asian regional diagnostic groups identified by Francis (*ibid.*). Although the four groups identified by Francis (two in North India, one in West India centred around Maharastra and one in South India centred around Arikamedu) now appear to display much more overlap than originally believed (Basa 1992), and are much less diachronically constrained than initially thought (Coningham 2006: 357). These beads also appear to have been traded over across sizeable distances, with similar beads (and indeed glass bangles) reported as far away as the site of Karang Agung in Indonesia (Manguin 2004: 288).

Despite an absence of wasters, the presence of imperforated beads, sectioned beads, glass ingots and unformed glass all argue heavily in favour of glass bead production occurring in or around the Citadel of Anuradhapura (Coningham 2006: 353) during period F, from when we see 17 examples of unformed glass, as well as one ingot of glass weighing 99.2 grams.

Such glass working would likely have been on a small scale, manufacturing glass from cullet (scraps of glass) (*ibid.*). However, the trade in unformed glass should not be underestimated. For example, an eleventh century shipwreck discovered off the coast of Turkey was found to be loaded with complete glass vessels, unformed glass and cullet, and is believed to have been en route from Syria to the Black Sea, with its cargo intended for Byzantine glass-makers (Kroger 1995: 8; Bass & van Doornick 1978: 124-131).

Such small scale production of glass beads is also supported by the findings of a technical analysis of glass roundels from Ganhdhara, which found that glass roundels apparently manufactured locally could be ascribed a Roman source (three roundels), a Near Eastern/Mediterranean source (one roundel) and a mixed source for the fifth – produced by combining glass scraps from a range of sources to produce the roundel (Wypyski 1992: 283). It should also be noted that the absence of wasters is not an argument against the production of glass beads at ASW2, such waste indicators only identify major manufacturing loci, and it is quite likely that such small scale manufacturing would be archaeologically invisible (Coningham 2006: 357). An example of such production is seen in a 19th century account of itinerant glass-workers in Madras, who would purchase raw coloured glass in assorted colours from industrial glass furnaces, and would then work this glass into bangles in domestic ovens in the city's bazaars (Buchanan 1870: III, 369-372).

5.5.5: *Worked and precious stone artefacts*

Sri Lanka has been renowned for its gemstones for over two millennia (Cooray 1984: 241), and it thus comes as little surprise to find numerous such examples within the Citadel's archaeological record. However we also see examples of gemstone artefacts from further away, in addition to a sizeable number of Indian examples, including carnelian, jasper, chalcedony, agate and amethyst beads.

Table 5.19: *Geographic source of ASW2 stone artefacts* **(after Coningham et al. 2006)**

Period	Sri Lanka	India	Egypt	Afghanistan / Baluchistan / Burma	Total
B	61 (569.1)	17 (20.6)	1 (0.8)	0 (0.0)	79 (590.5)
C,D&E	227 (4239.6)	51 (69.5)	0 (0.0)	0 (0.0)	278 (4309.1)
F	220 (2270.1)	52 (177.7)	0 (0.0)	2 (0.7)	274 (2448.5)

Such beads are found throughout the Indian Ocean region and over a wide time-span (Coningham et al. 2006: 379). Indian sites featuring such beads include Ahichchhatra, Atranjikhera and Hastinapur in the upper Gangetic plains, Ayodya in Uttar Pradesh, Garh-Kalika, Tripuri, Maheswar, Navdatoli and Nagda in central India, and Somnath, Nagara, Nagal and Dhatva in western India, as well as Taxila in Pakistan (Lahiri 1992: 274). In Southeast Asia similar beads (especially in agate and carnelian (Bellina & Glover 2004: 73)) have been recovered from the coastal sites of Ba Thê, Oc Eo (Manguin 2004: 290) and Giong Ca Vao in Vietnam (Bellina & Glover 2004: 73), Karang Agung in Indonesia (*ibid*.: 288), Noen U-Loke (Higham 2004: 61), Ban Don Ta Phet and Khao Sam Kaeo in Thailand (Bellina & Glover 2004: 73), and Gilimanuk in Bali (*ibid*.).

However, it should be noted here that, despite the established view that such beads represented trade of exotic luxury goods (Glover 1990; Glover 1996: 59; Ray 1996: 43) from the Indian subcontinent (Bellwood 1976: 276-7; Francis 1989: 23; Glover 1990; Glover 1996; Ray 1996: 43; Lamb 1965: 92-3; Wisseman-Christie 1990: 41), recent geochemical analysis of carnelian beads, archaeological debitage from production centres in Sri Lanka and India, and unworked carnelian from a Thai quarry, has now cast doubts upon this (Theunissen et al. 2000). This analysis indicated that the Thai beads and a small quantity of the Sri Lankan debitage originated from Thai quarries ((*ibid*.: 85), suggesting that Southeast Asian beads did not in fact all originate from India, but that instead a "*complex multi-source origin including some local manufacture appears likely*" (*ibid*.).

More interestingly, within a Sri Lankan context, is their interpretation of the Sri Lankan carnelian manufacturing flakes. These pieces of carnelian bead debitage originated from Deraniyagala's sondages AG, AMP and AS within the Citadel (Theunissen et al. 2000: 94), from deposits Deraniyagala ascribed to between the eighth century BC through to the second century AD. The chemical analysis of these fragments showed a clear shift in geographical origin of raw materials around the first century BC, moving from Indian carnelian to a source in or near Thailand (*ibid*.: 99). Theunissen et al. concluded that around the first century AD the bead makers of Anuradhapura began sourcing their raw material from Thailand instead of India, as well as trading the completed beads with that same region (*ibid*.: 100), casting into doubt the previous assumption that carnelian was solely imported from India.

Four other stone artefacts were recovered from the latter periods of ASW2 that were imported from beyond India, two lapis lazuli beads from period F and one Egyptian jasper bead (the only such artefact found at ASW2) from period B (Coningham et al. 2006: 377). These beads (lapis lazuli and Egyptian) clearly represent the long distance trade of luxury goods, however they are also clearly just that – a luxury, and are neither common nor widespread, unlike the trade of semi-precious stone beads and raw materials throughout the South and Southeast Asian worlds.

Table 5.20: Stone artefact forms at ASW2 (after Coningham et al. 2006)

Period	Beads	Shaped blanks & debitage	Bangles & other jewellery	Raw material	Undiagnostic
B	2 (1.7)	39 (57.7)	1 (19.5)	11 (432.1)	26 (79.5)
C,D&E	10 (5.1)	150 (493.5)	8 (8.5)	17 (3393.3)	103 (408.7)
F	32 (77.9)	177 (464.7)	3 (10.0)	7 (1720.1)	55 (175.8)

The greatest quantity of stone artefacts were recovered from periods C,D&E, with a total of 4309.1 grams of material recovered (*ibid.*). However, this is largely due to the recovery from this period of ten large fragments, weighing 3371.1 grams, of unworked greenstone (a widespread and locally available stone). Additionally the period C,D&E assemblage contained a sizeable quantity of undiagnostic fragments. In contrast period F produced both the largest quantity of beads, bangles and other such jewellery, and (by quantity) shaped blanks and debitage. Period B meanwhile produced a much smaller quantity of stone artefacts, with just 79 artefacts weighing 590.5 grams, the majority of which were either undiagnostic fragments (by weight) or shaped blanks and debitage (by quantity). Indeed just two beads were found in period B material, both of which were the imported Egyptian jasper. It is thus clear that by period B the manufacturing of beads and other stone jewellery has diminished greatly, and indeed that the number of such luxury items in circulation has also fallen greatly.

Table 5.21: ASW2 stone types (after Coningham et al. 2006)

Bead Colour	Period B	Period C,D&E	Period F	Total
Carnelian	3 (1.4)	25 (37.0)	15 (27.3)	**43 (65.7)**
Lapis lazuli	-	-	2 (0.7)	**2 (0.7)**
Greenstone	11 (450.7)	10 (3371.1)	12 (1751.8)	**33 (5573.6)**
Chert	1 (0.9)	8 (22.4)	3 (11.1)	**14 (34.4)**
Agate	-	1 (0.3)	8 (11.6)	**9 (11.9)**
Chalcedony	2 (4.6)	-	-	**2 (4.6)**
Jasper	2 (1.7)	-	-	**2 (1.7)**
Garnet	3 (2.2)	21 (14.6)	33 (22.5)	**57 (39.3)**
Amethyst	11 (13.7)	24 (28.7)	29 (138.8)	**64 (181.2)**
Amazonite	-	1 (3.5)	-	**1 (3.5)**
Clear quartz	20 (35.8)	69 (148.9)	67 (278.6)	**156 (463.3)**
Smokey quartz	4 (60.0)	29 (571.1)	26 (103.4)	**59 (734.5)**
Crystalline limestone	-	2 (1.3)	7 (10.9)	**9 (12.2)**
Coral	-	1 (61.0)	1 (30.2)	**2 (91.2)**
Quartzite	-	1 (0.6)	24 (26.9)	**25 (27.5)**
Muscovite meca	21 (18.8)	85 (44.3)	47 (34.7)	**153 (97.8)**
Biotite mica	1 (0.7)	1 (4.3)	-	**2 (5.0)**
Total	**79 (590.5)**	**278 (4309.1)**	**274 (2448.5)**	**631 (7348.1)**

It is interesting to note that the large number of pieces of debitage and shaped blanks found in conjunction with finished beads strongly suggest that their manufacturing was done on site, and that the trade of semi-precious stones was carried out in raw material, with the manufacturing process of beads, intaglios, jewellery inserts and bangles taking place at ASW2 (Coningham et al. 2006: 412). Whether the finished artefacts were for local consumption, or were then traded again, is unknown but it seems likely that the majority of such trade would have been carried out in raw-materials. A further 33 stone beads were recovered from the Mahapali excavations (Paranavitana 1936: 34-36), displaying a wide range in both bead forms and stones (predominantly clear quartz, carnelian, amethyst and chyrsoprase). However, as only their depths are recorded, little significance can be attached beyond demonstrating their ubiquity throughout the Citadel, and demonstrating that the ASW2 assemblage is representative of the Citadel as a whole.

5.5.6: *Summary*

There is a clear economic downturn between Period F and Period B, reflected in the specialised manufacturing of stone and glass beads, the production of the glass ear reels, as well as in the architectural forms discussed earlier. A similar change is also seen in the quantities of long distance trade goods within the Citadel, though these appear to peak later, during periods C,D&E. It is also interesting to note that the long distance trade appears to have been primarily focussed upon the west, with the eastern trade only really picking up around the eighth or ninth century AD. The disposal patterns of glass and metal-working residues, along with the quantities of luxury goods, also supports the earlier conclusion that the occupational nature of period B is far lower in social status and effectively sees the absence of the traditional elite.

5.6: Conclusion

This chapter presented the archaeological data relating to the final centuries of occupation within the Citadel at Anuradhapura. This has displayed a period of monumental elite occupation lasting up to the final centuries of the first millennium AD; characterised by monumental construction, regular cleaning, extensive long distance trade, craft specialisation in architecture and manufacturing, the production of glass, stone and metal jewellery and similar luxury goods, the presence of a well established elite and a subsistence package with a heavy emphasis upon marine an freshwater species. The presence of appliqué ware sherds in Periods F, C,D&E and B (albeit just a single sherd in each period) suggests the emergence of South Indian or Mahayanist influences from at least the seventh century AD.

At some point between the ninth and eleventh centuries we see a change in activity, long distance trade continues, but monumental construction and repairs are carried out using structural materials looted from earlier periods, suggesting a lack of time or labour to procure new materials. The looting pits are either left open to gradually fill or backfilled with rubbish. At this time the Citadel's fortifications are significantly improved – using much of the robbed structural materials.

There then appears to be a brief hiatus before an entirely new occupational period, one which sees ephemeral structures that have more in common with rural village architecture than the grand and monumental structures of the preceding periods. However, despite the somewhat transient nature of these structures they still show clear evidence of urban planning, following a grid-like street system. Indeed, the structures are repeatedly re-built in successive short lived structural phases, always using similar materials and following the same layout. Long distance trade items, luxury goods, and monumental construction are all either completely absent or greatly diminished in this period and the area of the Citadel occupied is reduced by around 30%. The subsistence package displays no evidence of the marine or freshwater species that previously formed such an important part. The living areas do not appear to be well cleaned and significant quantities of rubbish (broken ceramics, animal bones etc.) are found. This period appears to continue until the beginning of the thirteenth century, after which the Citadel appears to be completely abandoned. Taking into account the archaeological data presented within this chapter, the archaeological signature for the late Anuradhapura period can simply presented as shown below in table 5.22.

Having presented the archaeological data from the Citadel, and having formed an occupational sequence for its final centuries, the next chapter will now examine the final centuries of the Sacred City, the monasteries, shrines, monuments, parks and tanks surrounding the Citadel.

CHAPTER 5: THE CITADEL

Table 5.22: The Citadel's Archaeological Signature

13th	12th	11th	10th	9th	Century AD
✠	↙	←	↙	→	Population
✠	←	✠	←	→	Monumental Construction
✠	←	✠	↙	→	Traditional Elite
✠	✠	✠	←	←	New Elite
✠	✠	✠	→	→	Long Distance Trade
✠	←	←	↙	→	Craft Specialisation

KEY: ↑ High ↓ Low ↗ Rising ↘ Falling → Steady ✠ Absent

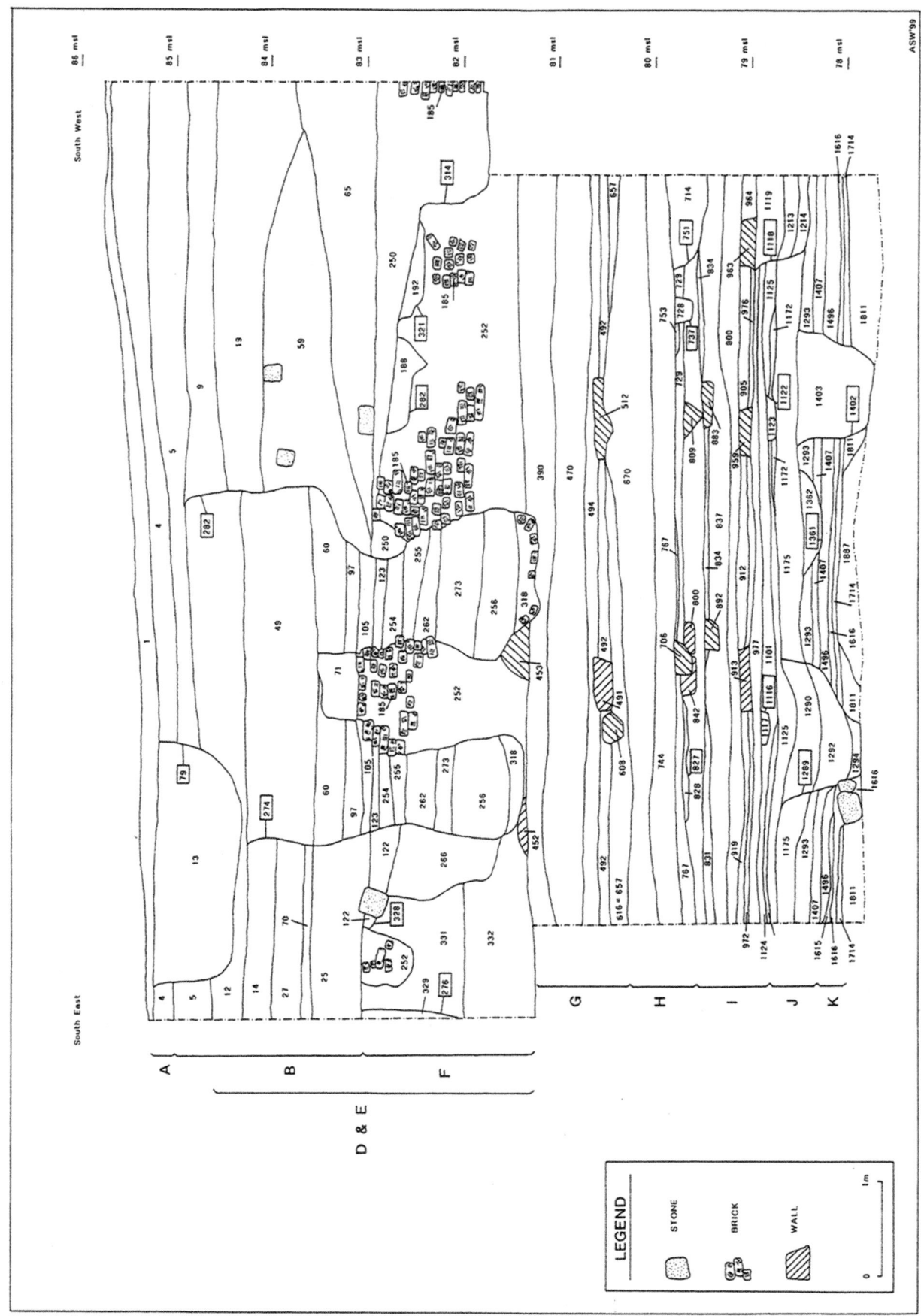

FIGURE 5.01: SOUTHERN SECTION OF ASW2 TRENCH, WITH STRATA OF STRUCTURAL PERIODS DISPLAYED ALONG THE LEFT AXIS (AFTER CONINGHAM ET AL. 1999: 87)

CHAPTER 5: THE CITADEL

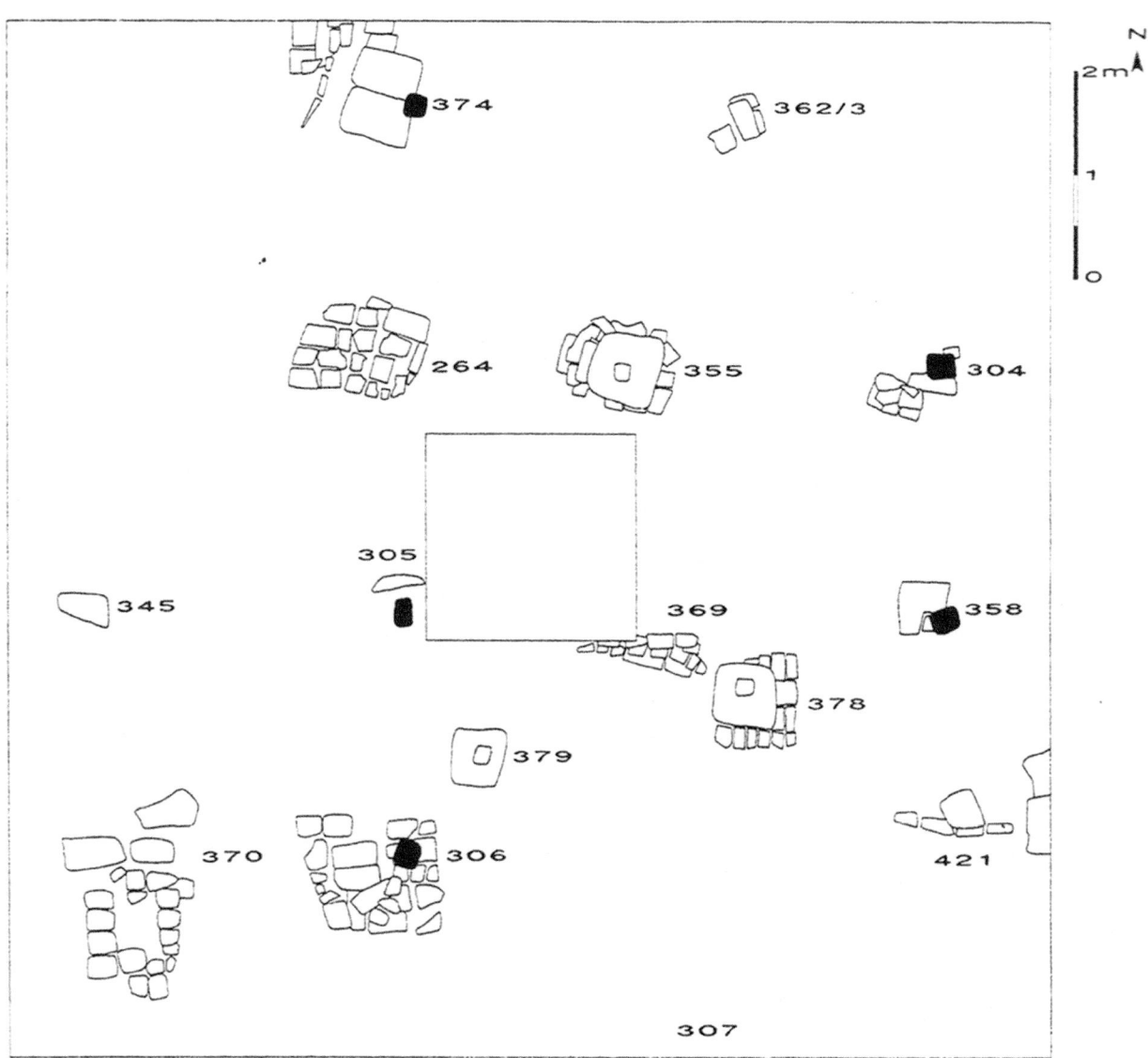

Figure 5.02: Plan of structural period F
(after Coningham 1999: 111)

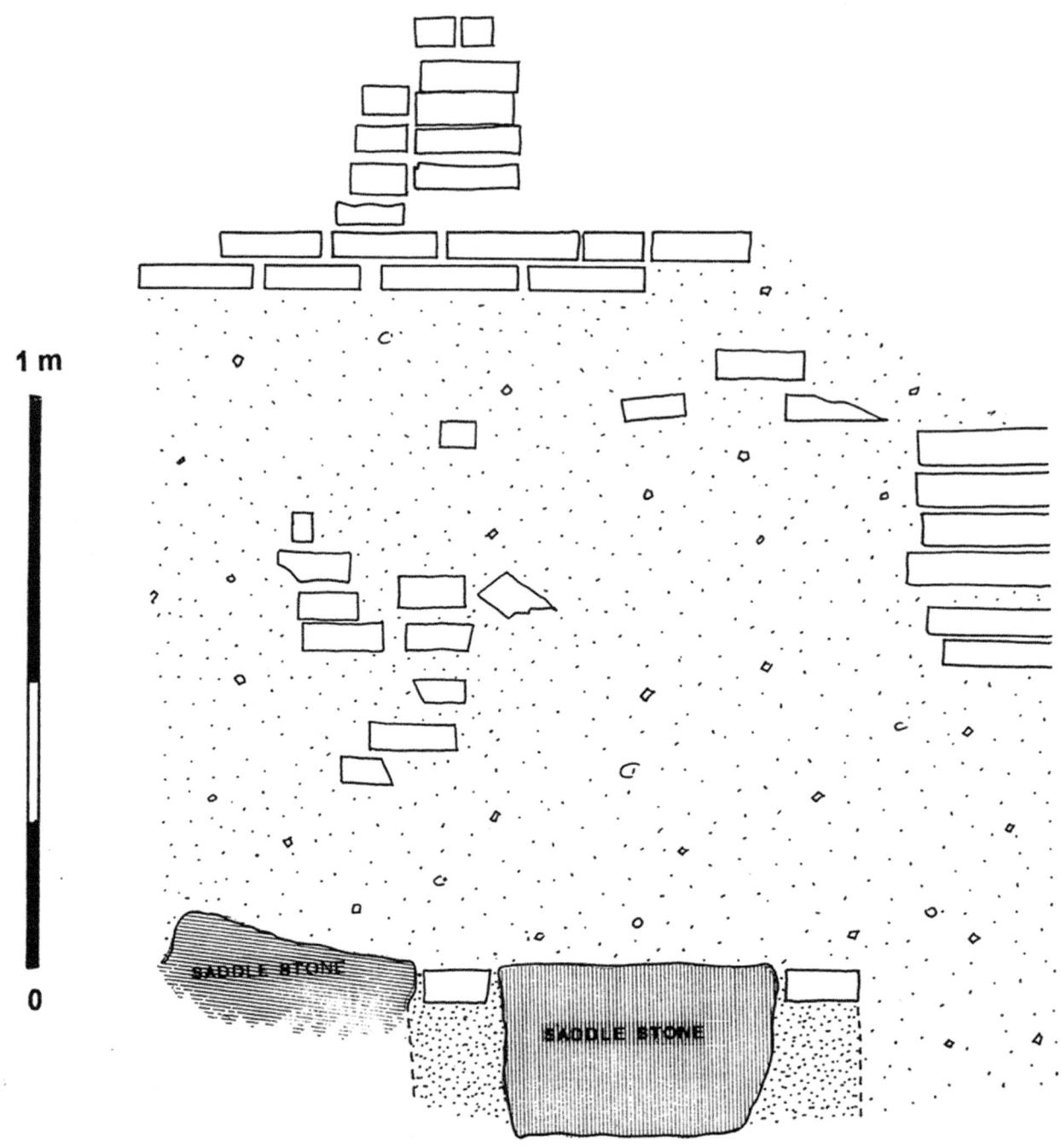

Figure 5.03: Elevation of Period F pillared hall
(AFTER CONINGHAM 1999: 113)

CHAPTER 5: THE CITADEL

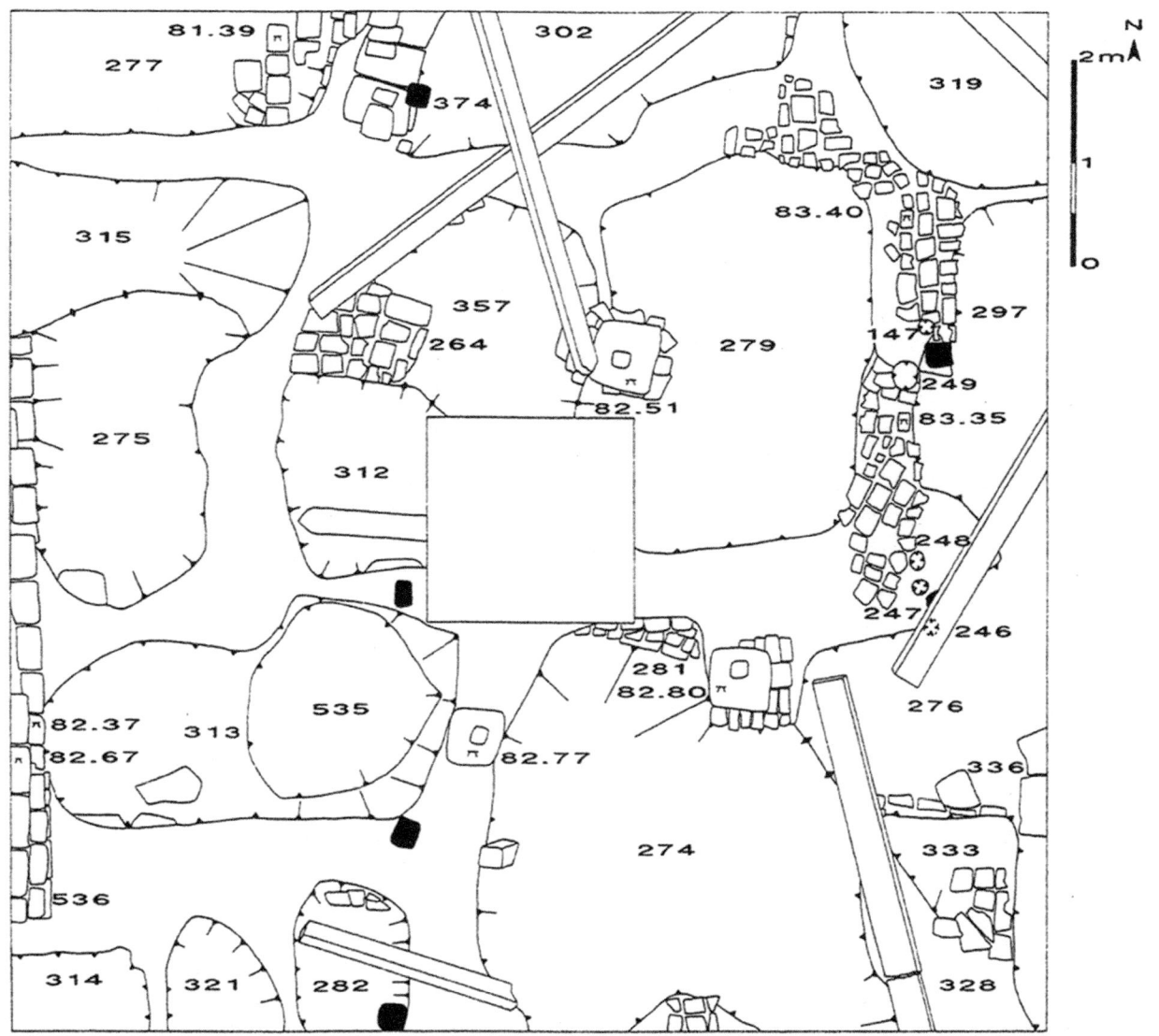

Figure 5.04: Plan of structural phase D&E of ASW2
(AFTER CONINGHAM 1999: 116)

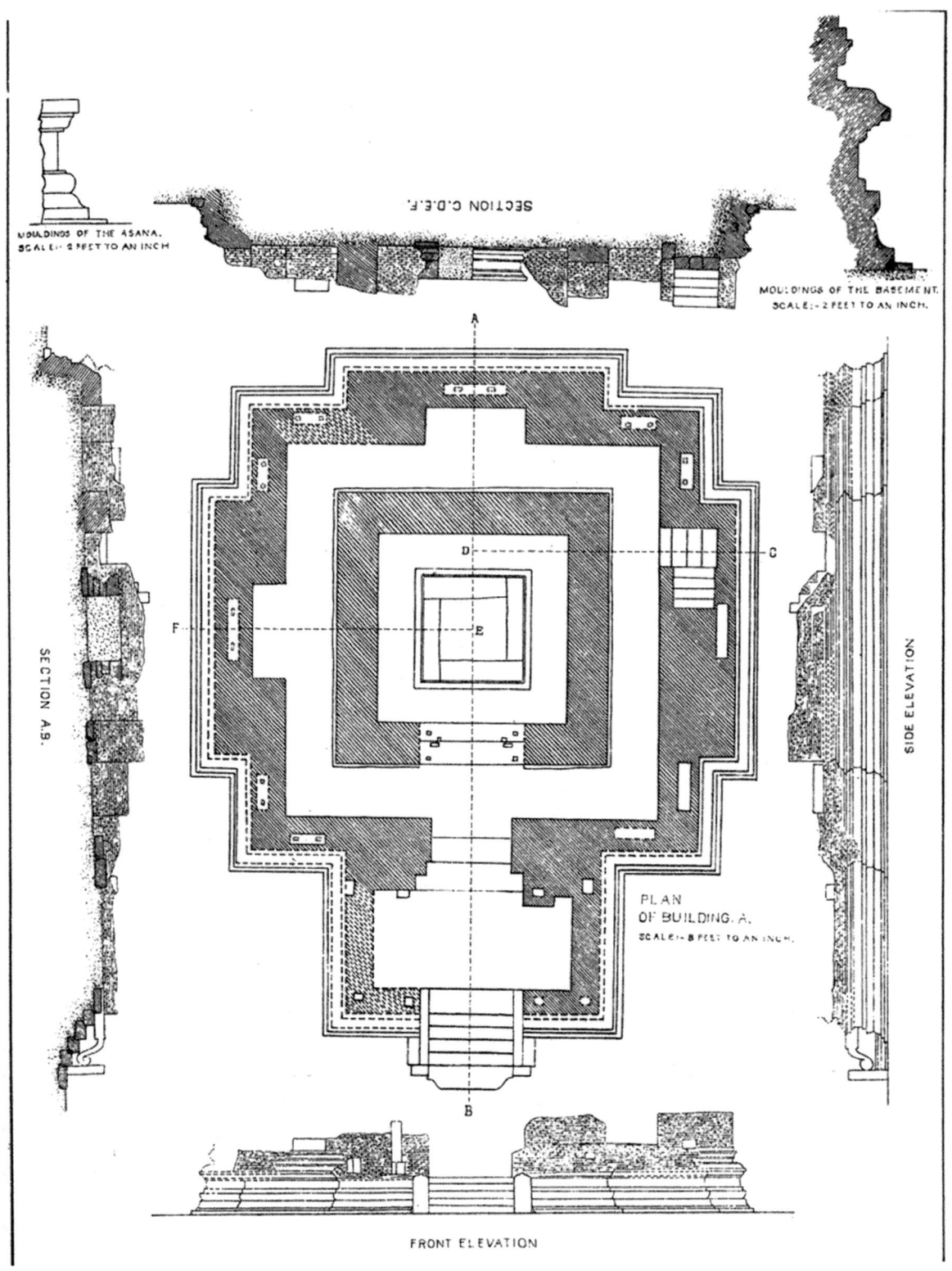

Figure 5.05: Plan of Building A
(AFTER PARANAVITANA 1936: 07)

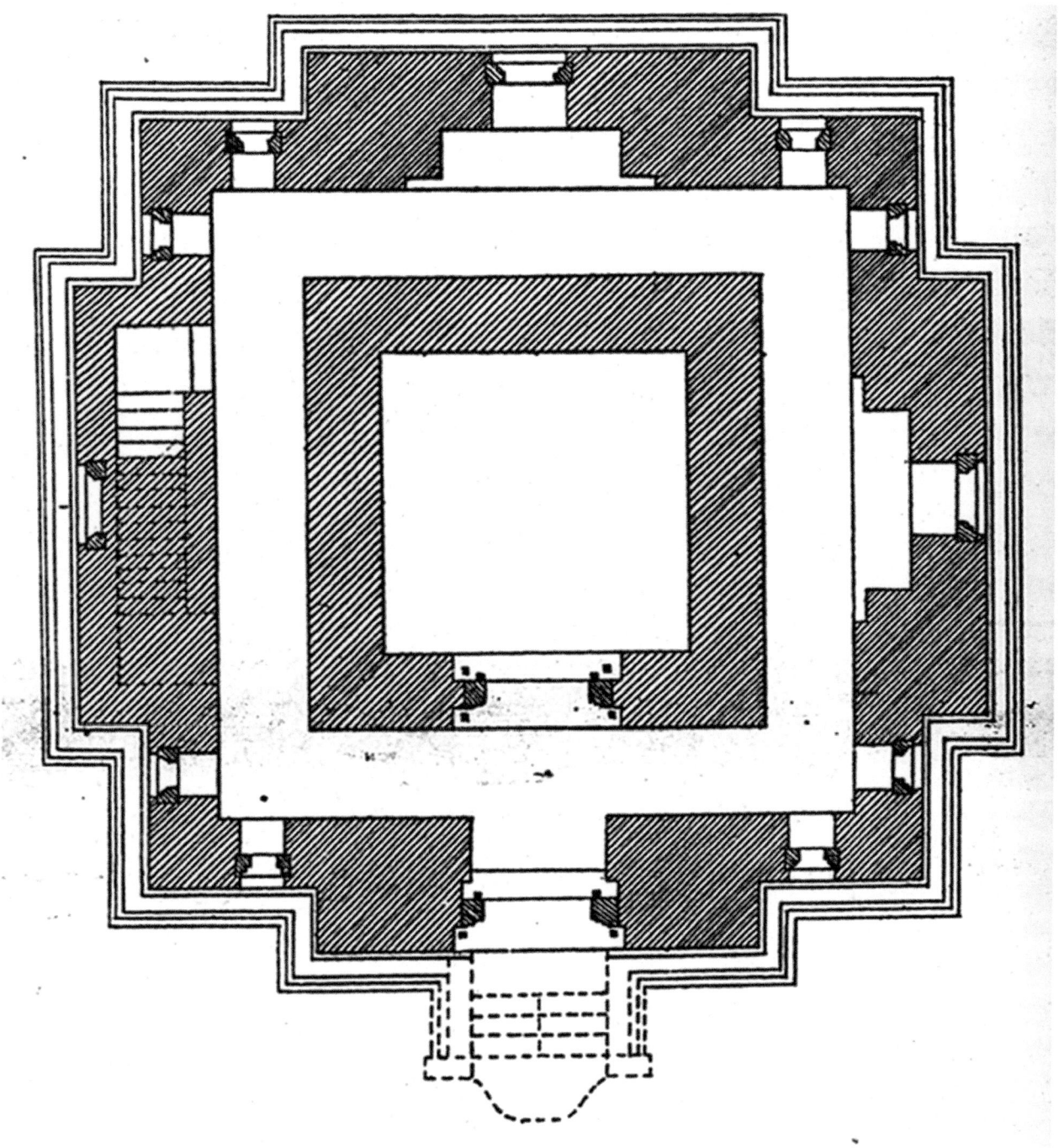

Figure 5.06: Plan of Gedige
(AFTER BANDARANAYAKE 1974: 204)

A Time of Change: The "Collapse" of Anuradhapura, Sri Lanka

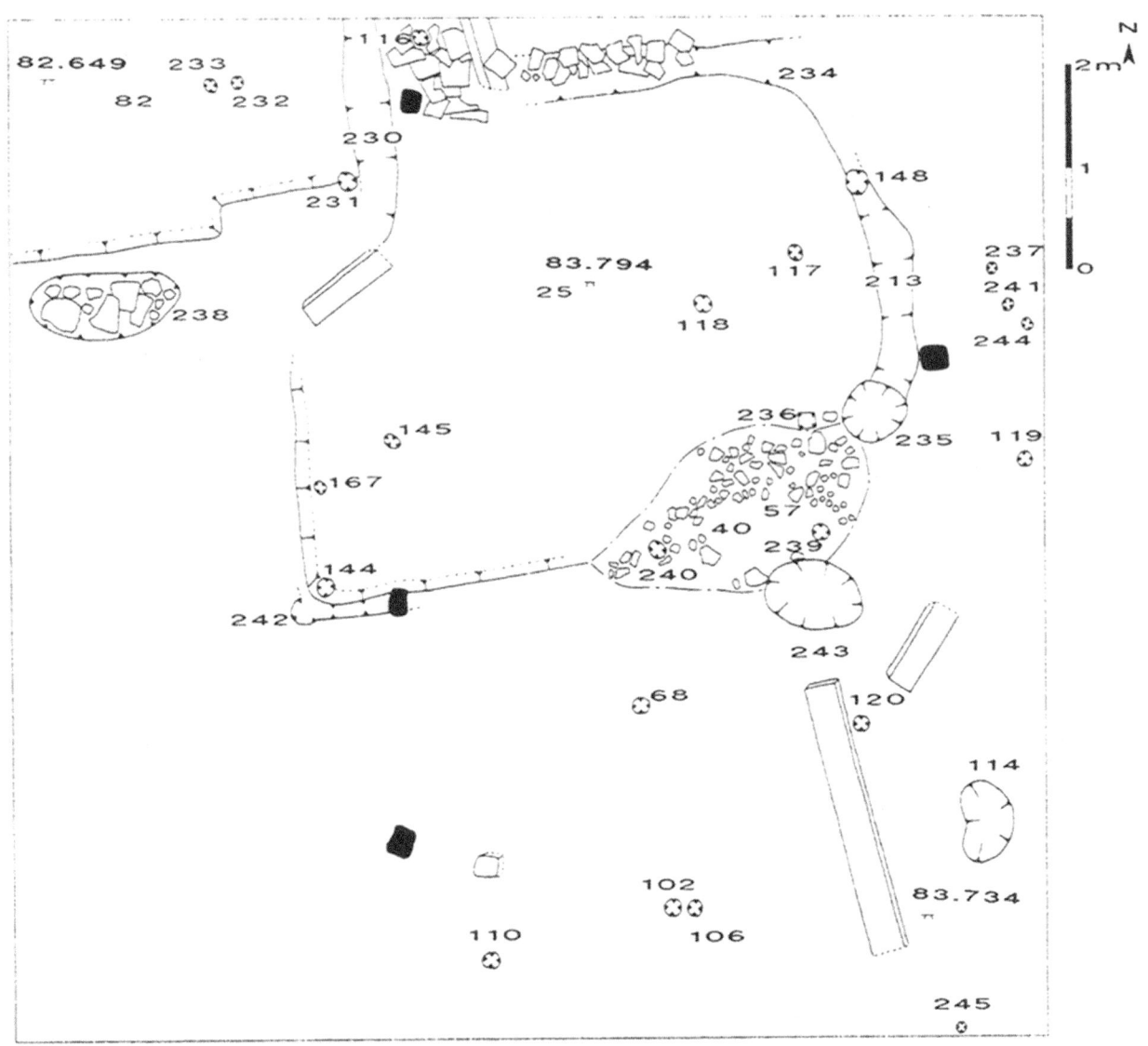

Figure 5.07: Plan of Structural Phase B1
(after Coningham et al. 1999: 119)

CHAPTER 5: THE CITADEL

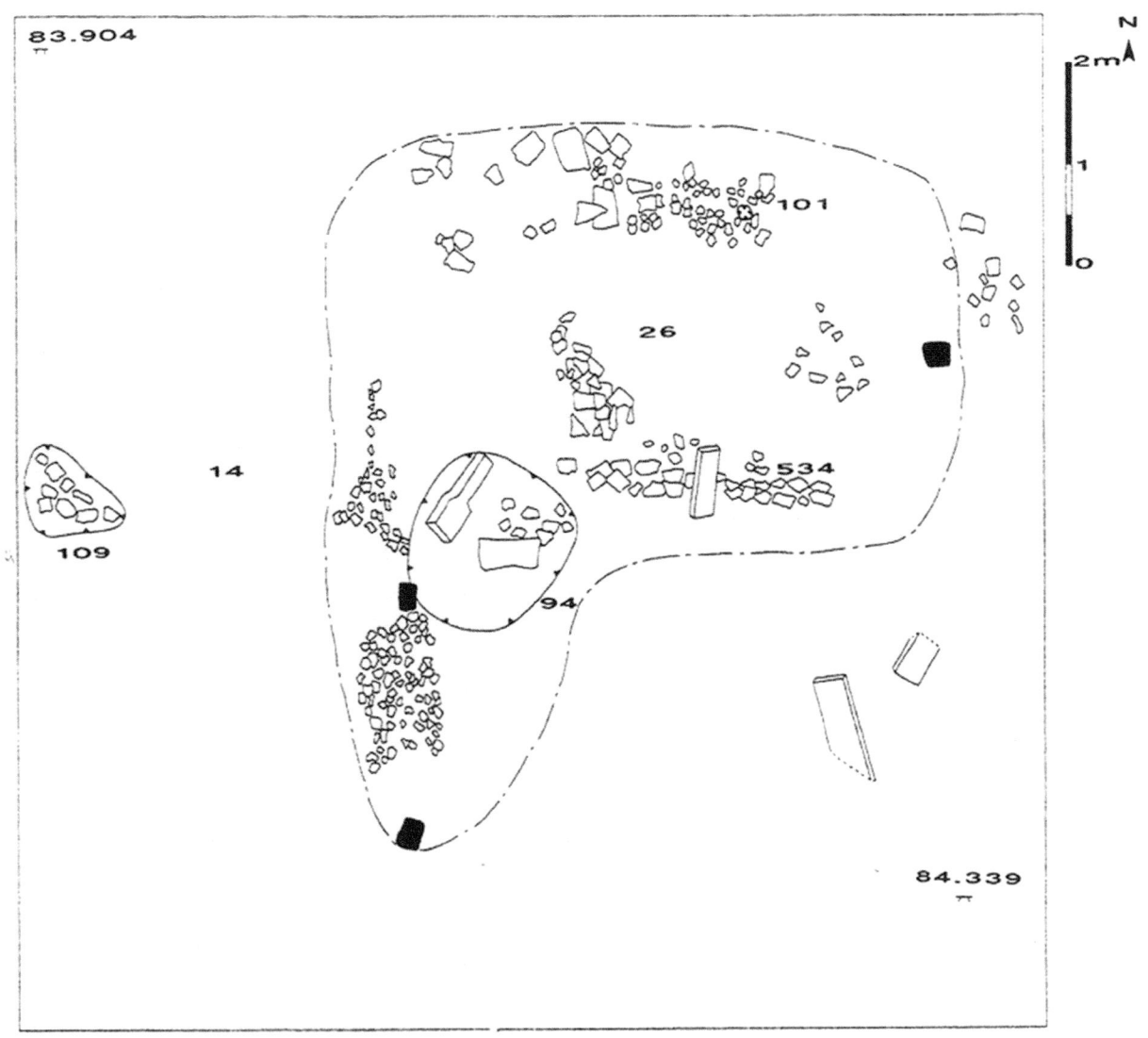

Figure 5.08: Plan of Structural Phase B3
(AFTER CONINGHAM ET AL. 1999: 120)

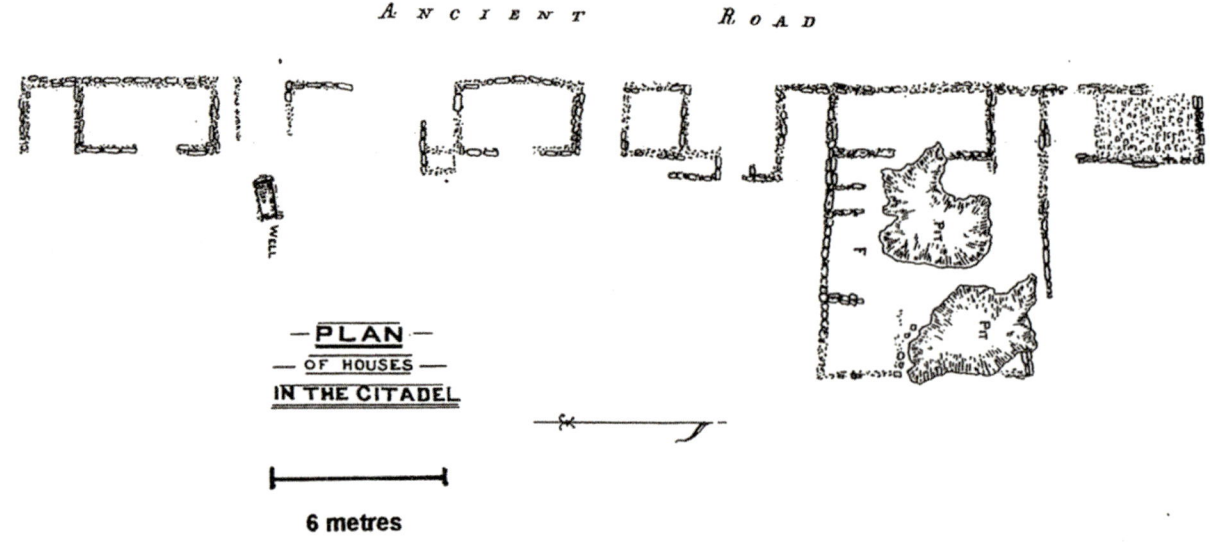

Figure 5.09: Plan of period B street
(AFTER AYRTON 1924: 51)

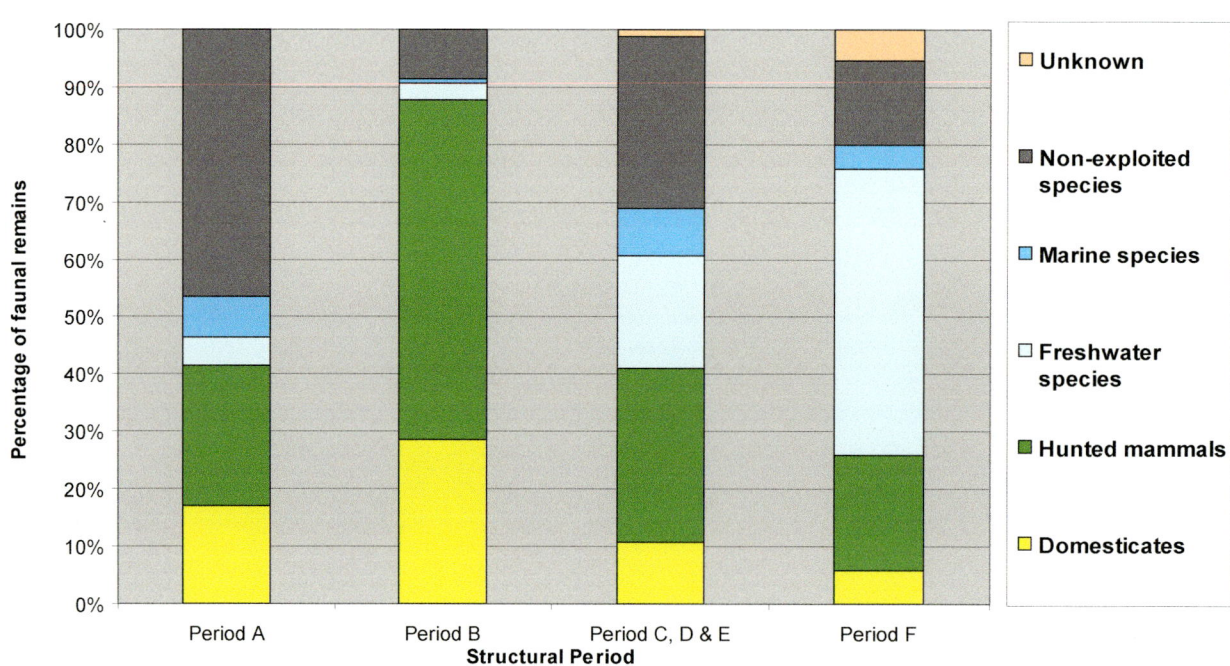

Figure 5.10: ASW2 Faunal Assemblage by Class
(AFTER YOUNG ET AL. 2006)

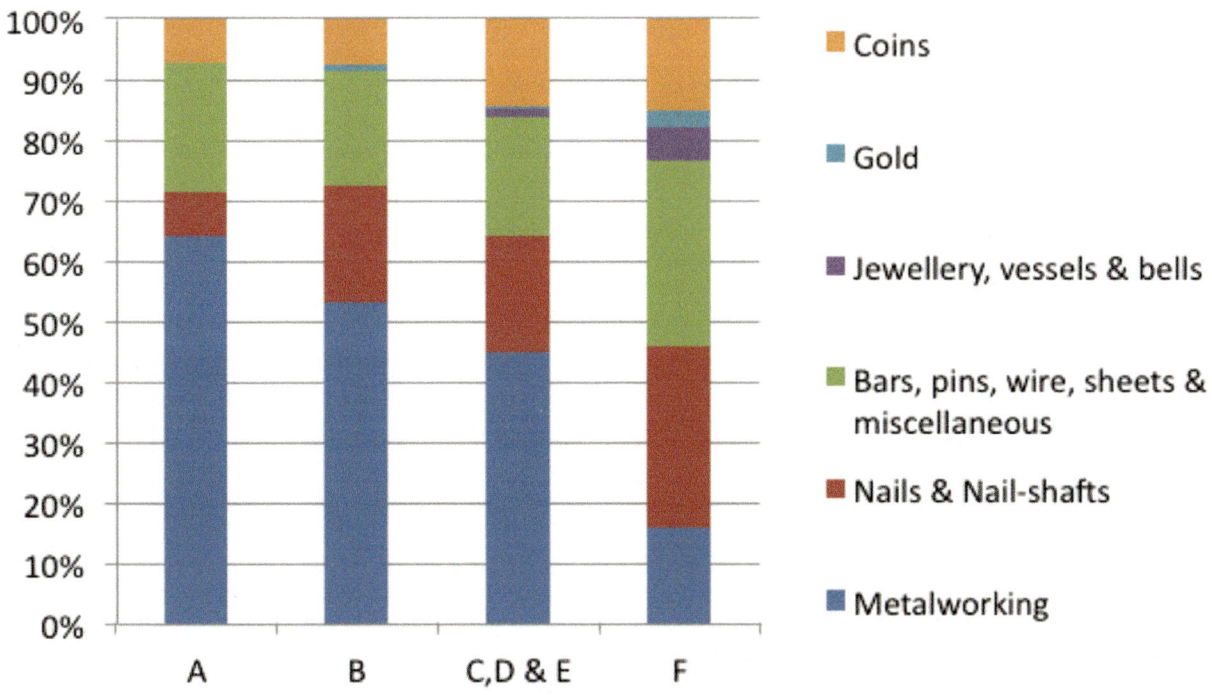

Fig. 5.11: ASW2 metal artefacts by type
(after Coningham & Harrison 2006: 27-76)

Chapter 6:
The Sacred City

"...there is no other City upon this universe that has maintained its position as a Sacred City, replete with sacred objects of diverse kind, for a period of 2,200 years, except this City"

(Harischandra 1908: preface)

6.1 Introduction

The previous chapter defined the archaeological signature of the Citadel's terminal period, Chapter Six will now present the archaeological data from the Sacred City, and establish its own archaeological signature for its terminal period. The Sacred City (Fig.6.01) has seen extensive excavation and restoration over the last 150 years, to a far greater extent than seen within the Citadel. This is due in part to the monumental nature of the Sacred City's massive stupas, and in part to the fact that these monuments were, and remain, living elements of the national religion and identity (Hettiaratchi 1990: 45-46). The drive to restore and develop the ancient stupas and shrines was far greater than for the secular palaces of the Citadel. As summarised in Chapter Two, a great deal of archaeological data has been lost from the Sacred City as a result of the extent of these early excavations and restorations. Consequently, the primary source of archaeological data for the Sacred City is the 1980s Central Cultural Fund excavations at the Jetavana and Abhayagiri viharas.

The available archaeological data from the numerous excavations and partial publications will now be collated and integrated as best as possible in an attempt to determine the archaeological characteristics of the final centuries of activity within the Sacred City following the headings laid out in the methodology (Chapter Four) as closely as possible.

6.2: Population & monumental construction

Bandaranayake described the architecture of the Sacred City as an *"...organic expression of ...the economic and technological levels reached by that society... the nature of its social organisation and expresses the forms and concepts of its cultural aspirations. It is at once the skeleton and the outer garments of the social body"* (1974: 01). However, despite the grand sentiments of Bandaranayake; *"The house that a man inhabits, the palaces and public buildings of the overlords... the temples, theatres and other cultural edifices... are all direct manifestations of the essential character of his social being"* (ibid.), archaeological studies have inherently focussed upon the monumental, the *"palaces and public buildings of the overlords"*, while paying scant attention to the *"house that a man inhabits"*, primarily due to the lower visibility of such mundane domestic structures, a result of their less prepossessing, ephemeral structural form, as well as the biodegradable materials used. Such domestic structures are typically represented by much more subtle archaeological features – typically negative features such as post- and stake-holes, drainage gullies and wall slots, as well as building platforms of packed earth and the remains of wattle and daub walling, as Oertel wrote in the report on the restoration of Anuradhapura's monuments; *"one must not expect to find any traces of ordinary domestic architecture at Anuradhapura... Commoners, however wealthy, lived in thatched bamboo huts, for strict sumptuary laws... confined the use of superior building materials, such as brick, stone or carved wood, to the king's palaces and religious edifices"* (Oertel 1903: 464).

Compare this to the stupas of Anuradhapura, and it is unsurprising that the archaeological investigations of Anuradhapura have focussed upon the monumental rather than the mundane. While this cannot be avoided within the analysis of the Sacred City, it should be borne in mind that the architecture that has been studied, mapped, recorded, discussed, examined and indeed lauded, is exclusively that of the monumental and the elite. Consequently, given the absence of domestic structures, attempts to estimate or determine population fluctuations within the Sacred City must of necessity consider several different factors. Perhaps primary amongst these considerations (and this applies to the Citadel) is actually found in the hinterland's agricultural productivity, and this will be examined in the chapter seven.

However, for at least the last two centuries the Sacred City itself has also contained a sizeable area of paddy field rice production, and it is likely that this was true of the Anuradhapura period as well. As has been established repeatedly agricultural productivity within the Dry Zone of Sri Lanka is reliant upon irrigation and water management, consequently any analysis of the Sacred City's (and indeed Citadel's) population must consider the tanks of the Sacred City. Given the monumental nature of these reservoirs they must also be considered monumental structures" and in that regard come under two headings.

Also representative of both population size and monumental construction are the residential halls of the great monasteries within the Sacred City. Writing circa 414AD, the Chinese pilgrim Faxian described Anuradhapura as home to over 10,000 monks and nuns (specifically 3000 at the Mahavihara, 5000 at the Abhayagiri vihara, and 2000 at Mihintale) (Bandaranayake 1974: 7, 92 & 288). Clearly this is several centuries prior to the Chola "sacking" of the city, though Bandaranayake estimates that by the tenth century "*it had surely doubled or trebled*" (*ibid.*). However, while we have no archaeological record of the domestic housing of the lay people within the Sacred City, we do have very detailed architectural descriptions of the residential buildings of the Sacred City (e.g. Smither 1894; Bandaranayake 1974: 247-307).

6.2.1: *The Structural Sequence of the Sacred City*

Lacking the deep stratigraphic excavations of the Citadel the architectural sequence (as we understand it) of the Sacred City owes far more to stylistic observations than stratigraphic sequence, and is effectively formed by Bandaranayake's four period sequence (1974: 19-26), presented earlier in Chapter Four (section **4.3.1**). The final period of monastic construction (Bandaranayake's Period IV and ASW2 Periods C,D&E) covers the period from around the seventh to tenth centuries AD, and is believed to be responsible for the vast majority of the extant structures across the Sacred City (Bandaranayake 1974: 25). Indeed, Bandaranayake attributes the construction of the greater part of the standing masonry in the Sacred City to the latter half of this period, specifically between the reigns of Sena I (r.833-853) and Mahinda IV (r.956-972) (ibid.). It must be stressed that the Pali chronicles were instrumental in the derivation of these dates, and must thus be viewed critically.

The Central Cultural Fund (CCF) excavations revealed an architectural sequence similar to that seen within the Citadel, although far shallower. While the ASW1 and ASW2 trenches in the Citadel reached virgin soil or bedrock at a depth of up to almost 10m (Coningham 1999: 71), excavations at Abhayagiri Vihara typically appear to have bottomed at between two and four metres (Wikramagamage 1992: 31; Bouzek et al. 1993). Unlike the ASW2 excavations, the Abhayagiri Vihara Project formed their chronology around the ceramic forms recovered (Bouzek et al. 1986). Fortunately these typological periods correspond relatively closely with the ASW2 structural periods, as shown in Fig.6.02. As the structural sequence from the Sacred City is drawn from several different excavations, each of which developed its own chronology, the ASW2 periods will be used as an umbrella periodisation. This will best allow comparative analyses with the Citadel's sequence, as well amongst the Sacred City excavations.

6.2.1.1: *Period F*

This corresponds to the Abhayagiri Vihara Project's *Strict Articulated Period* and the earliest part of the *Simplified Period*, the Jetavanaramaya Project's *Period 3* and Bandaranayake's *Phase III*. Across the Sacred City this period saw widespread new construction following the third century AD horizon of structural demolition, burning and levelling (Wikramagamage et al. 1984: 65) that the Abhayagiri Vihara Project excavators termed the Great Destruction Horizon or GDH (Wikramagamage et al. 1983: 359). This episode of widespread destruction was represented throughout the Abhayagiri excavations and was archaeologically represented by thick charcoal deposits, structural debris and episodes of levelling (*ibid.*). The majority of this construction work appears to have originated immediately preceding the beginning of Period F, around the fourth century AD (Bouzek et al. 1993: 53) though it appears to have continued throughout Period F.

In a very real sense this period is the beginning of the Sacred City as we see it today, Bandaranayake places the origins of the great institutionalised refectories within this period (1974: 307), monastic forms that reached their final phase at Anuradhapura in the tenth century AD, though they undoubtedly continued at Polonnaruva after this date (*ibid.*). The earlier timber pillared structures were re-modelled at this time, using the characteristically undressed limestone pillars of the period. This can be seen in the area immediately west of the Second Samadhi Bodhigara (AVP Site One (Wikramagamage 1984: 07)), where stone pillars were intruding into ancient surfaces were interpreted as being replacements for earlier wooden pillars (Wikramagamage et al. 1983: 345). The coin assemblage of these strata also mirrors that of ASW2 Period F, with a Lakshmi Plaque and three coins tentatively identified as Late Roman Imperial Third Brass recovered (*ibid.*). This also supports the chronological placement of this period. The replacement of the timber superstructure appears to have been part of a larger redevelopment of the structure, with the construction of a gneiss boundary wall in layer two of this site (Wikramagamage 1984: 7) occurring around the same time. Unfortunately no structural plan was determined and the function and form of this structure remain unknown.

Further early Period F construction can be seen around the edges of the monumental Elephant Pond, with AVP Sites Eight, Nine, Ten and Eleven all seeing their initial construction around the fourth century AD. The first three of these sites are all clusters of small monastic residential structures, with nine and ten representing classic forms of the *pancayatana parivena* while site eight is a small group of four *kutis* (Bouzek et al. 1993: 18). While the groups are clearly monastic in nature, Bandaranayake argues that the cells (or *kutis*) should be interpreted as residential in nature, while the central pasada (when present) would have been ritual (Bandaranayake 1974: 94). Subsequent redevelopment of all of these structures has largely obscured their original form, but the layout of the groups appears to have been consistent (Wikramagamage et al. 1984: 54, 55, 56, 57). AVP Site Eleven meanwhile is again a cluster of monastic structures, though not one in any diagnostically recognisable plan or layout. Here, once again, the initial stone and brick construction appears (from coins and ceramic wares) to date to the fourth century AD (Bouzek et al. 1993: 20) though occupation at the site undoubtedly predates this by at least a century (*ibid.*). Unfortunately none of these structures were described in any detail in the excavation reports (Wikramagame et al. 1984: 60), and very little can be said of them other than their construction date and materials.

While the majority of construction during Period F appears to have been early in nature, there appears to have been new construction occurring throughout the period. AVP Site Three, a linear series of pits across open ground south of the Abhayagiri stupa, revealed a fifth century AD stone conduit running parallel to a road of the same period (Bouzek et al. 1993: 15). Around a century later we see restoration work carried out on the Abhayagiri stupa's inner boundary walls (Salapatasala Maluva) with several new courses of bricks added (*ibid.*: 17). Later development is seen in what has been termed the Sannipatasala immediately south of the Abhayagiri stupa (AVP Site Two) (Bouzek et al. 1993: 13). This building was tentatively identified as an assembly hall where "members of the community of *bhikkus* with laymen who were concerned in the affairs of the church met" (Bandaranayake 1974: 235) and appears to have been first constructed towards the end of Period F and featured brick walls, likely timber supports for the superstructure, and a brick and timber gatehouse within the boundary wall (Bouzek et al. 1993: 13).

6.2.1.2: *Periods C,D&E*

This corresponds approximately to the latter stage of the Abhayagiri Vihara Project's *Simplified Period* and all of the *Smooth Period*, the Jetavanaramaya Project's *Period 2* and Bandaranayake's *Phase IV*. This period sees the construction or remodelling of the greater part of the extant architecture within the Sacred City (Bandaranayake 1974: 25), and can be architecturally divided into two phases; a formative one lasting until around the mid to late eighth century AD and a subsequent period of growth and consolidation lasting until the tenth century (*ibid.*).

The boundary between this structural phase and the preceding one is ephemeral, but there appears to have been continued construction within the Sacred City throughout this transitional period (dating to around the seventh century AD), with construction at AVP Sites Seven (the "monasteries" east of the Elephant Pond) and Two (the Sannipatasala). AVP Site Seven is described as a *pancayatana parivena* (like AVP Sites Nine and Ten) and lies immediately east of the monumental Elephant Pond (Bouzek et al. 1993: 19), three of which were excavated as part of the Abhayagiri Vihara Project (Wikramagamage et al. 1984: 53). Although Bandaranayake describes this characteristic monastic grouping as *"a cluster of four large, square cells or* kutis *symmetrically placed around a larger, oblong structure or* pasada" (Bandaranayake 1974: 86), in the case of site seven this central *pasada* is entirely absent (Bouzek et al. 1993: 18). Three of the *kutis* were excavated, all of which featured gneiss pillars on a low structural platform with simple gneiss curbs and appear to date to the transitional period between Periods F and C,D&E or around the seventh century AD (Bouzek et al. 1993: 19), dated by architectural style and ceramic forms (Wikramagamage et al. 1984: 53). This construction appears to have been redevelopment of earlier structures (*ibid.*), though the plan of these structures was lost when the seventh century structures were erected, likely around the same time that the Elephant Pond was expanded and completed (*ibid.*). All three are classic examples of the early part of Bandaranayake's architectural Phase IV, with simple stone elements, brick work and presumably a timber superstructure and tiled roof (*ibid.*).

At the Sannipatasala we see a new structural phase following an episode of demolition and levelling (Wikramagamage 1984: 12). This second structural phase, dating to around the seventh century AD, reused much of the earlier (Period F) structure's foundations and followed a near identical ground plan, unfortunately so little of this phase remains (due to a third and final structural phase) that little more can be said (*ibid.*: 45), beyond that the structure was primarily brick with some limestone slabs - one of which may have formed the foundations for a timber staircase (*ibid.*: 46). This second structural phase appears to have been relatively short-lived as the building was significantly rebuilt sometime around the late eighth/early ninth century AD (Wikramagamage et al. 1983: 341). This final construction phase featured classic late Anuradhapura monastic features with simple gneiss mouldings on the banisters, steps and guard-stones (Bandaranayake 1974: 313-320). This late construction was significant in its scale, as the Abhayagiri Sannipatasala is one of the largest of its kind in Sri Lanka (Wikramagame 1984: 12). Imported glazed ceramics (the precise ware is not published) found within this final structural phase appear to suggest that the building was in use until at least the tenth century AD., shortly after which it appears to be abandoned or to have collapsed (Wikramagamage et al. 1983: 342), a date that would correspond well with an early eleventh century urban abandonment.

Table 6.01: The *Bhojanasalas* of Anuradhapura (after Bandaranayake 1974: 297)

Location	Size (m)	Courtyard (m²)	Columniation	Troughs	Drains
Mahapali	39 x 37	na	na	1	yes
Mahavihara	43 x 42	565	150	1	yes
Jetavana	34 x 29	212	144	2	yes
Thuparama	26 x 25	244	na	na	yes
Mirisavati	22 x 20	84	84	1	yes
Abhayagiri	45 x 42	237	na	3	na
Mihintale	35 x 24	78	128	2	yes
Vessagiriya	18 x 16	47	56	na	yes
Veherabandigala	12 x 9	7	16	na	yes

On a smaller scale, Bandaranayake assigns the development and construction of the *bhojanasalas* (a form of refectory) and *jantagharas* (believed to be a form of bath-house), both typically elements of the large institutionalised refectories, to around the tenth century AD (Bandaranayake 1974: 307). Examples of these structures can be seen across the Sacred City, and the *bhojanasalas* of Anuradhapura are briefly tabulated in Table 6.01 to demonstrate the size and scale of these structures. While it is dangerous to attach too much significance to the late construction of these residential monastic structures, the fresh construction of refectories and bath-houses certainly suggests that the population of the Sacred City was at least maintaining at this point, if not expanding, and that the monasteries were still rich enough to construct, or influential enough to be gifted, such sizeable structures.

Unfortunately neither of these building classes has been archaeologically examined (*ibid.*: 300), but we can see archaeological evidence of late construction in the boundary walls and revetments (or *Maluvas*) of the Abhayagiri stupa (AVP Site Four) and in tenth century repairs to the "Elephant Pond" (Bouzek et al. 1993: 19). At the boundary walls not only do we see major early tenth century moulded gneiss redevelopment of the outer walls (Salapatasala Maluva) but also late tenth century moulded brick redevelopment of the inner walls (Vali Maluva) (*ibid.*: 17). Just east of the Elephant Pond we see a late redevelopment of the *pancayatana parivena* (AVP Site Seven) featuring classic late Anuradhapura period elaborate stone mouldings and pillar-capitals (*ibid.*: 19). AVP Sites Eight, Nine and Ten all show a similar sequence to that of site seven, with earlier structures being either replaced or significantly redeveloped around the ninth or tenth centuries ((Wikramagamage et al. 1984: 54,55,57; Bouzek et al. 1993: 19). In the case of one of AVP Site Eight's *kutis* this included elephant protomai and fragmentary lions (very similar to those seen at Ruanvelisaya dagoba) (Wikramagamage et al. 1984: 54), indicative of the highly sophisticated and decorative architectural form of the final centuries of Period C,D&E. Similarly late construction, though without the sophisticated ornamental decorations, was identified at the boundary walls of AVP Site Eleven where the gatehouse was tentatively dated to the ninth-tenth century AD (*ibid.*: 60).

Although the vast majority of construction work in Periods C,D&E are (as seen above) either repairs to, or redevelopments of, already existing structures there is also evidence for entirely new construction during this period. As seen at Gedige and Building A within the Citadel, this period sees the introduction of lime mortar and the brick superstructures that this technology enables. This is most visible in the massive brick structure of the gedige at Jetavanavihara, a monumental 21m square structure with a 10m square vestibule (Bandaranayake 1974: 206). Though this structure is now in extremely poor condition, it has been calculated that the standing Buddha image within would have been almost 10m tall (*ibid.*). At Abhayagiri Vihara this fresh construction can be seen at AVP Site Twelve, a monastic structure of unknown function immediately southwest of the Abhayagiri stupa (Bouzek et al. 1993: 20). These structures are described as only having existed between the ninth and tenth centuries (*ibid.*), though no reason for this interpretation is given.

Elsewhere in the Sacred City we see evidence of new construction right up to the end of this period. Nowhere is this more visible than on the periphery of the Sacred City with the construction of two new monastic forms; the *pabbata vihara* and the *padhanaghara parivena*. These were mentioned in passing in Chapter Four as diachronically significant architectural forms, and will be discussed again in **6.3**, focussing upon the political and religious significance of these late monastic forms. However, political context aside, these developments represent a significant late investment of resources in their construction. Both of these monastic forms are located on the periphery of the Sacred City and are effectively suburban in nature. The Western Monasteries (the main grouping of *padhanaghara parivenas*) lie approximately 2km west of the Abhayagiri stupa, placing them on the edge of the northwest boundary of the Sacred City, and features 13 double-platform monastic units over an area of approximately 1km^2. Meanwhile, all six Sacred City *pabbata viharas* (Vijayarama, Puliyankulama, Vessagiriya, Toluvila, Pankuliya and Pacinatissapabbata-vihara) were located around the very fringes of the Sacred City (Bandaranayake 1974: 73).

Interestingly, the Sacred City does not appear to see the endemic levels of structural looting seen within the Citadel during this period. However, there is still archaeological evidence for some structural looting during the final two centuries of the first millennium AD. This can be seen in the partial destruction of the structural platform overlying the Period F road south of the Second Samadhi Bodhigara (Abhayagiri Vihara Project Site 1) (Wikramagamage et al. 1983: 348). This platform was constructed around the eighth century AD (layer 1C – Simplified Style), but was then demolished and partially looted around one to two centuries later (layer 1B – Smooth Style) (*ibid.*). The presence of intrusive robbing pits containing chronologically ex-situ artefacts around this platform (*ibid.*) is also extremely similar to periods D&E within the Citadel. In addition to the looting of the structural platform, this period sees the final tile collapse at the structure west of the Second Samadhi Bodhigara (*ibid.*: 345) after which it appears to be completely abandoned until its 20th century excavation.

6.2.1.3: *Period B*

Effectively dating from the early eleventh century to the final abandonment of the site, this corresponds with what the Abhayagiri Vihara Project, Jetavanaramaya Project and Bandaranayake all termed the *Polonnaruva Period*. Strikingly, despite the identification of the third century AD *Great Destruction Horizon* by the Abhayagiri excavators, no such eleventh century "destruction horizon" was identified between Periods C,D&E and B. Given that the *Culavamsa* describes Anuradhapura, with implicit emphasis upon the monastic elements of the city, as being "*utterly destroyed in every way by the Chola army*" (*Cvs*.lxxiv.1), the absence of a corresponding "destruction horizon" for the Chola sacking of the city is surprising. Especially as the excavators were interpreting the archaeology through reference to the Pali chronicles, and must have been expecting to identify evidence of the eleventh century Chola sacking.

Within the Citadel Period B was characterised by successive phases of predominantly ephemeral structures that, while low in investment, still displayed clear signs of urban planning. Within the Sacred City such occupation was less clearly represented, whether due to an actual absence of such structures, or because the disturbed upper strata were paid less archaeological attention. A linear series of pits excavated south of the Abhayagiri stupa (AVP Site Three) in order to form a profile across the area, revealed late occupation amidst the debris of earlier structures in the form of "crude pottery wares" (Wikramagamage 1984: 17). Although no signs of the urban planning seen within the Citadel are found here, we do see the re-use of earlier materials in ephemeral structures built during this final structural period. At AVP Site Three stone balustrades and bricks from earlier structures were used in an ephemeral structural enclosure with what appears to be a human inhumation just outside it (*ibid.*: 18) along with "some stone cists", crude pottery that resembled Polonnaruva period wares and what appears to be an area of metalworking or a small smithy (Wikramagamage et al. 1983: 352). Several similar structures were found nearby (*ibid.*) suggesting that during Period B occupation of the Sacred City continued along with industrial activity and, somewhat surprisingly, what appears to be a small burial ground. Similar Polonnaruva style wares were also identified by the Abhayagiri Vihara Project in the vicinity of the Elephant Pond, the stupa boundary walls, and from several of the profile pits excavated to the south of the stupa (Bouzek et al. 1993: 57). Though no figures are available to compare the frequencies of the Period B Polonnaruva wares with those of the preceding periods, the Polonnaruva wares are clearly a comparative rarity with Bouzek et al. (*ibid.*) describing "*some examples*", suggesting that Period B occupation was far smaller in scale than the preceding periods. A Polonnaruva period coin was also recovered from AVP Site Seven (the *pancayatana parivena*) just east of the Elephant Pond, suggesting continued activity within the area into at least the twelfth century AD (*ibid.*: 19).

During this period there is also repair work to the Abhayagiri stupa's inner boundary walls (Salapatasala Maluva) that has been tentatively identified as twelfth century on the basis of a single coin found in associated contexts (*ibid.*: 17), this may correspond to the repairs to the Abhayagiri vihara by Parakramabahu mentioned in the *Culavamsa* (*Cvs*.lxxiv1-14; *Cvs*.lxxviii.97-107) though the dating evidence for this is far from secure and is further complicated by 19th century restorations within the area of the excavations (Wikramagamage et al. 1984: 50).

Architecturally, Bandaranayake (1974: 199) identifies what he believes to be extremely late occupation and activity in the image houses (*patimagharas*) of both Lankarama and Thuparama. The stylistic form of the so called "Trident Temple" (the Thuparama *patimaghara*) is discussed below (section **6.4.3**) as representative of South Indian influences. In brief summary, the final form of the "Trident Temple", stylistically dated to between the twelfth and thirteenth centuries AD., is described as "foreign" to Sri Lankan architecture, with its *vajra* pillar capitals (the only example of such capitals identified in Sri Lanka) and a floor-plan bearing a strong similarity to Brahmanical or South Indian Buddhist shrines (*ibid.*). Additionally there appears to be post-Polonnaruva Period (i.e. post thirteenth century AD) ritual offerings at both shrines (ibid.). Elsewhere, Bandaranayake assigns several other shrines to the Polonnaruva period, including Pilimage No.41 and 42 at Jetavanavihara (*ibid.*: 202) which are described as displaying a "mixture of Sinhalese and Chola architectural characteristics" (*ibid.*: 203) and compared to the Chola shrine of Velgamvehera near Trincomalee (*ibid.*).

6.2.2: *The Sacred City Tanks*

Anuradhapura lies within an extremely intricate and sophisticated hydraulic landscape – manifold networks of canals and tanks, bunds and sluices, all engineered to an extremely high precision and accuracy (Christie 1891). This hydraulic landscape is integral to the collection, delivery, and storage of sufficient quantities of water for the city of Anuradhapura (Citadel and Sacred City) to exist – both today and in the first millennium AD. This must be stressed, as without the wider hydraulic landscape, the monumental tanks of Anuradhapura would be rendered almost useless. Fig.6.03 shows the inter-connectivity of the Anuradhapura period hydraulic landscape, allowing for safety mechanisms to avoid or minimise the risk of disaster due to either too little, or too much, water. This wider hydraulic landscape will be examined in full in Chapter Seven, but the central Anuradhapura tanks, lying as they do within "urban" Anuradhapura, must be considered a part of the Sacred City.

Anuradhapura is served by three main tanks (Table 6.02); the major perennial Nuvaraveva (1,214ha); and the two medium-sized perennial tanks, Tissaveva (182ha) and Basavak Kulam (107ha), in addition to several smaller seasonal tanks including Bulan Kulam (Jeanes & Benthem 1994: x). Due to the importance of the irrigation system, the tanks were extensively restored and renovated by the British in the late 19th and early 20th centuries (Christie 1891; Vignarajah 1992: 03). The resources diverted into restoring the ancient tanks demonstrates just how essential they are to the maintenance of an urban population, as well as how much labour must have been required for their original construction.

Table 6.02: The Major Urban Tanks of Anuradhapura (modern state)

	Nuvaraveva	Tissaveva	Basavak Kulam
Full supply level (FSL) (m asl)**	91	92	91
Bund length (m)*	6772.7	2645.7	NA
Average bund height (m)*	10.7	6.4	NA
Area when full (ha)**	1214	182	107
Storage when full (106 m3)**	44.41	3.58	2.34
Catchment area* (km2)	83.20	5.12	9.1
Area irrigated** (ha)	980	316	149
Mean average depth** (m)	3.66	1.96	2.19
w	7.00	5.30	5.00

(FIGURES FROM THE *SRI LANKAN MINISTRY OF AGRICULTURE DAM SAFETY & WATER RESOURCES DEVELOPMENT PROJECT (HTTP://WWW.MAHAWELI.GOV.LK/OTHER PAGES/DSWRPP_WEB_NEW/) AND **JEANES & BENTHEM 1994: 10)

However, as a result of the extensive restorations the archaeological recording of the bunds, sluices and spills of these tanks has been limited and, chronologically speaking, the most that can be said of these tanks is that there is no archaeological evidence to challenge the Pali chronicles dating of their construction to the latter centuries of the first millennium BC (Brohier 1934: 14). It appears likely that that the Anuradhapura tanks did not reach peak efficiency until the construction and connection of the gigantic Kalaveva and Nachchaduwa tanks in the fifth century AD (Brohier 1934: 4, 12), and the 20th century renovation of these tanks has not notably expanded upon the Anuradhapura period infrastructure, focussing instead upon restoring the canals and tanks of the Anuradhapura period. Indeed, writing in the mid-19th century, a Colonial official described Anuradhapura as "...*so fallen, so unhealthy, so unprofitable, compared with more favoured districts that... to repair and improve these* (tanks) *must be our task*" (Liesching 1869: 193).

However, the connection of the city tanks to the huge tanks of the hinterland can be placed within Period F, and by the terminal periods of C, D & E the primary work would have been to maintain and, when needed, repair the city tanks – rather than to invest in new construction. Unfortunately, due to the absence of relevant archaeological data it is near impossible to even begin to estimate the investment expended upon this maintenance without resort to the very Pali chronicles that we are attempting to test.

There is an argument for the technological development of sluices over this period, though the argument is based upon epigraphic semantics rather than archaeological excavations (Gunawardana 1984; Seneviratna 1989). Epigraphic evidence suggests that the cistern sluice, used in Sri Lanka from around the second century AD, was replaced or complemented by a piston sluice from around the tenth century (Seneviratna 1989: 81). Gunawardana believe that this model of sluice was imported from Southern India, where the piston sluice had been in use for around two centuries prior to this exchange. An inscription from Vessagiriya (Wickremasinghe 1912: 29-38), dated to Mahinda IV (r.956-972), is argued to refer to such a piston sluice (Gunawardana 1984: 134), and this would appear to demonstrate not only that while no new tanks were being built, the tanks of Anuradhapura were being developed and maintained right up to the eleventh century AD, but also the increasing levels of interactivity with the Southern Indian kingdoms during Anuradhapura's terminal centuries, as propounded by the Imperial Model (section **4.6.3**).

It is perhaps worth noting briefly, that although there are references in the *Culavamsa* to Vijayabahu and Parakramabahu repairing tanks within Anuradhapura's hinterland (*Cvs*.lx.48-51; *Cvs*.lxxiv1-14; Cvs. lxxviii.97-107), none of the urban tanks are mentioned again. Whether this is because they were not restored due to a lack of urban population to serve, or because they were not damaged enough to warrant mention is not apparent.

The Elephant Pond: This sixth or seventh century brick and stone lined "pond" lies some 300m south-west of the Abhayagiri stupa, and was excavated as part of the Abhayagiri Vihara Project (AVP Site Six). Although not a tank in that it does not appear to have been used for irrigation, it was still part of a far larger hydraulic network to bring water from the Malvatu Oya to the Sacred City, and to both store and present it within monumental and indeed ornamental "ponds". This is seen throughout the Sacred City, most famously at the so called "Twin Ponds" or *Kuttam Pokuna* also within the Abhayagiri Vihara (Seneviratna 1994: 157). The Elephant Pond was most likely preceded by a smaller scale pond or structure, but was expanded upon around the seventh century AD, resulting in an ashlar-lined pond measuring some 153.5m x 50.0m at ground level (Wikramagamage 1992: 38). This represents the single largest such pond at Anuradhapura, or indeed Sri Lanka, and was fed by at least two stone conduits and featured both silt traps and sluices (ibid.: 40; Bouzek et al. 1993: 17), just as a tank would. Unfortunately the Abhayagiri Vihara Project excavations did not determine a date for the siltation (and thus abandonment) of the Elephant Pond, though structures surrounding the pond displayed limited evidence of continued occupation post-eleventh century AD (Period B) while the last observed repairs to the pond's brick and stone lining and steps occurred around the tenth century AD (Wikramagamage et al. 1984: 53), at which point it may have begun to silt up and fill with structural collapse from its own lining as well as nearby structures (*ibid.*).

6.3: Traditional elite

The elite of the Sacred City was clearly the *sangha*, and that power and wealth can still be seen today in the monumental monastic ruins that still dominate the archaeological city of Anuradhapura. The changing fortunes of the *sangha* can best be seen archaeologically in the monumental structures and structural sequence set out above (section **6.2**), as well as in the long distance trade of luxury goods discussed below (section **6.5**). However, such evaluations, given the low resolution of the archaeological data available, treat the *sangha* as an extremely simplistic and uniform entity. By examining the late emergence of two distinct suburban monastic forms, a slightly more nuanced understanding of the Sacred City's elite can be developed.

As described above (section **6.2**), the final centuries of the Anuradhapura period saw the emergence of two new and distinct monastic forms; the *pabbata vihara* and the *padhanaghara parivena*. Both of these monastic forms represent not only a significant investment in new construction, but also a significant cultural shift in the final centuries of the Anuradhapura period. They are even more striking in that they could be argued to represent two very different philosophies.

6.3.1: *The Padhanaghara Parivena and the rise of Asceticism*

The first, that of the *padhanaghara parivena* (or double platform) sites is typically associated with the *Pamsukulikas*, an ascetic group of monks who formed around the eighth century AD (Wijesuriya 1998: 143) as a reaction to, or rejection of, the luxurious lifestyles now enjoyed by much of the *sangha* (*ibid.*). The *Pamsukulikas*, though initially associated with the Abhayagiri vihara, soon moved to exclusive monasteries built for them away from the Sacred City, at the Western Monasteries (also referred to as the Ascetic's Grove or *Tapovana*) on the very edge of Anuradhapura (see figure 6.01) as well as more rural or remote sites such as Ritagala, Tantrimale and Veherabandigala (Gunawardana 1979: 41; Wijesuriya 1998: 145). The latter sites are discussed in Chapter Seven, but the Western Monasteries must be considered to be part, albeit suburban, of the Sacred City.

The Pamsukulikas appear to have held considerable public and Royal support, and the construction of many if not all of these sites appears to have been as donative grants from members of the royal family (Wijesuriya 1998: 145), representing a significant economic (and royal) investment in these monasteries. This investment can first (and perhaps best) be seen at the site of Ritagala, believed to have been constructed by Sena I (r. 833-853) (*ibid.*: 36) as the first and largest of the major *padhanaghara parivena* complexes, followed almost immediately by the construction of the Western Monasteries under the reign of Sena II (r. 853-887) and Kassapa IV (r. 889-914). Unfortunately while the *padhanaghara parivenas* have been dated to the final centuries of the Anuradhapura period, there is no archaeological evidence to suggest when the Western Monasteries were abandoned.

As with so much of Anuradhapura's archaeological record, the interpretation of these ruins is tied into their identification as the "Grove of the Penitents" referred to in the *Culavamsa* (*Cvs*.liii.14-19), and much of what is known, or at least written, about the Western Monasteries is drawn from the Pali chronicles, rather than from observed archaeological data (Wijesuriya 1998: 148). However, while the correlation of the Western Monasteries with the "Grove of the Penitents" attaches certain conceptions and interpretations to the sites, there are also architecturally observable traits that support the association of the *padhanaghara parivena* with the ascetic Pamsukulikas.

Bandaranayake highlights the strictly formalised asceticism of these monasteries (1974: 117), stressing the shunning of decoration, the absence of inscriptions, of common ritual elements such as the image house and of the self-imposed isolation of the central pasada (*ibid.*). This interpretation is further supported by the location of the only conspicuous decoration upon urinal stones (Wijesuriya 1998: 20). These consisted of a horizontal and vertical stone slab, both featuring lavish depictions (Fig.6.05) of domed and pillared viharas (Bandaranayake 1974: 122-123). Although there is no established explanation as to why only the urinal stones are decorated remains (Wijesuriya 1998: 21), Silva (1988: 5) suggested the placement further underlined the Pamsukulikas rejection of wealth and commitment to asceticism, writing that; *"Their edifices did not contain a single stitch of decoration, but instead showed all extravagances on ornamenting the lavatory and the toilet slabs as if it says "not that we are incapable of art or richness, but this is how we treat it""* (Silva 1988: 5).

This late monastic expansion reflects more than just an architectural shift. Previously the rural organic monasteries had traditionally been linked to the *vanavasin* (or forest monks), in contrast to the *gramavasin* (or city monks) of the Sacred City (Bandaranayake 1974: 69), and the *padhanaghara parivenas* in a sense represent the introduction of the more limnal *vanavasin* to the urban centre of Anuradhapura. Whether or not the Western Monasteries correspond directly to the *Ascetics Grove* of the *Culavamsa*, these monasteries clearly demonstrate a significant and powerful ascetic movement within the *sangha* and Sacred City during the ninth and tenth centuries AD., and as interesting as that move to asceticism, is the implied wealth and riches of the more established monasteries that the *Pamsukulikas* were rejecting.

6.3.2: *The Pabbata Vihara & the rise of Mahayanism*

The name *pabbata vihara* translates directly as "mountain monastery", but unlike the *padhanaghara parivenas* the *pabbata viharas* appear to have been rural in name only, with a great deal of similarity visible between them and the major monastic complexes of the Sacred City, far more so than with the small organic monasteries of the hinterland (see Chapter Seven) (Prematilleke & Silva 1968: 70-71). Indeed of the seven pabbata viharas identified to date within Anuradhapura and its hinterland, six lie within the suburbs of the Sacred City (shown in figure 6.01); Vijayarama, Puliyankulama, Vessagiriya, Toluvila, Pankuliya and Pacinatissapabbata-vihara (Bandaranayake 1974: 73).

The characteristic feature of these sites is a large walled or raised rectangular precinct or quadrangle, within which are found four primary shrines; a *stupa*, a *bodhigara* (or bodhi tree shrine), a *patimaghara* (or image house) and an *uposathaghara* (a large ecclesiastical hall) (Bandaranayake 1974: 73). The four entries into this central precinct are arranged cardinally and the placement of the four shrines follows certain regular patterns (*ibid.*). There were also numerous ancillary structures, and these late monastic complexes as a whole were undoubtedly monumental in their scale, and certainly represent some of the largest investments in new construction during Period C,D&E of the Sacred City. Significantly, like the *padhanaghara parivenas*, it would appear that the *pabbata viharas* were royal monasteries built and supported by the monarch of Anuradhapura (Coningham et al. 2007a: 709), and may well represent an attempt by royalty to exert greater influence over the *sangha*, this will be discussed in Chapter Eight.

However, although their construction represents an extremely significant late investment (Fig.6.06) it is not just the size of the *pabbata viharas* that is of interest here. It is widely accepted that a long-standing tension existed within the Sacred City between the dominant, orthodox, Theravadism and the heterodox Mahayanism (Thero 2007: 242), though Anuradhapura is largely considered to have been predominantly Theravada (*ibid.*: 3-4). Prematilleke and Silva (1968) have argued that the formalised and ritualised layout of the *pabbata viharas* represent a distinctly Mahayanist development, and one that demonstrates the rise in influence of both Mahayanist philosophies and of the Abhayagiri vihara in the final centuries of the Sacred City (*ibid.*: 62). Specific connections to Abhayagiri aside, strong Mahayanist influences at the six Sacred City *pabbata viharas* are clearly demonstrated by the artefactual evidence. This includes the recovery of copper plaques bearing Mahayanist mantras and double-bodied bronze images of the four principle Lokapalas from Vijayarama (Bell 1893: 4-10), bas-reliefs of either Siva or Vishnu along with either Parvati or Lakshmi, again at Vijayarama (Bell 1904b: 05), bronze statue of Indra from Puliyankulama (1914c: plate DD), and a bronze image of Sudhanakumara from Toluvila (Bell 1904e: 4). These statues and images could be argued to demonstrate a Saivite influence, but all of the personages represented also exist within Mahayanist Buddhism, and in conjunction with the associated Buddhist artefacts, especially the Mahayanist copper plaques, the Mahayanist influence appears to be irrefutable. It should also be noted that further bronze Saivite images were recovered during the CCF excavations of the 1980s (Indrapala 2005: 307), but unfortunately (if unsurprisingly) these have not been published. Whether or not we directly connect the pabbata viharas to the Abhayagiri fraternity, the consensus opinion is clearly that the *pabbata vihara* represents a Mahayanist monastic form, and one that clearly suggests a significant increase in the popularity and influence of Mahayanism during the final two to three centuries of the Anuradhapura period. It should be noted that this also underlines a key problem with the archaeological data from the Sacred City, in that it is heavily reliant upon the excavations across the Abhayagiri Vihara. While it is reasonable, and indeed unavoidable, to treat this data as representative of the Sacred City as a whole, it must be remembered that the fortunes of the three major *viharas* were not synchronised, and indeed were potentially inversely linked as different philosophies and factions gained and lost favour with both the royal family and indeed the populace of Anuradhapura.

6.4: New elite

Despite references throughout the Abhayagiri Vihara Project excavation reports to the "Chola invasion" (e.g. Wikramagamage et al. 1983: 48; Bouzek et al. 186: 255; Bouzek et al. 1993: 17) there is no direct archaeological evidence of a Chola presence within the Sacred City; no Chola coins, inscriptions, weaponry, graffiti, regalia etc., though possible explanations for this were presented in chapter five (section **5.4**).

6.4.1: Violence

Despite the absence of any Chola artefacts, there are several occasions when the excavators of the Abhayagiri Vihara invoked the Chola presence. For example, when three Buddha statues were found lying prone, with their heads apparently "removed", at AVP Site Four and this was interpreted as evidence of the Chola destruction (Wikramagamage et al. 1983: 48). Bell placed a similar interpretation upon the condition of the so called "Buddhist Railing" at Jetavana, writing that; *"The indescribable confusion in which the fragments were found heaped one upon another, and the almost entire wreck of the railing, leave little room for doubt that this unique relic of Ceylon Buddhist architecture must have perished under the ruthless destruction of those invaders from South India at whose door lies the mutilation and ruin of the best works of the sculptor's art in Anuradhapura."* (Bell 1904a: 07). While both are reasonable interpretation, it is not direct evidence of a Chola presence within the Sacred City and indeed, as with the Citadel, there is a complete absence of any indications of the inter-personal violence that might be expected as a result of a violent sacking of the city.

Surprisingly we *do* see late period human inhumations within the Sacred City, at AVP Site Three an inhumation in conjunction with several stone cists were identified within the structural layout of Period B, and interpreted as a burial ground (Wikramagamage 1984: 18). As discussed in Chapter Five, the presence of human remains within an area is considered "polluting" (*Arth.*2.xxxvi.31-33; Knusel et al. 2006: 619), making the locating of a burial ground *within* the grounds of the Abhayagiri Vihara surprising to say the least, and strongly suggestive of dramatic changes to the usage of what was previously a sacred space. Unfortunately, the analysis (see Kodagoda 1992: 160-168) of the bone assemblage was *extremely* rudimentary, and was published without any contextual information such as layer, pit, or even site. However, despite this there were no indications of pathologies caused by violence, the burials are clearly planned, and are there is thus no suggestion of deaths caused by violent conflict.

Furthermore, as mentioned above, there are no recorded finds of weaponry from this period of the Sacred City. The only artefacts that *can* be interpreted as weaponry are the large number of clay balls recovered throughout (at AVP Sites One and Three) the Abhayagiri excavations (Bouzek 1993: 91), seen in Table 6.03.

Table 6.03: Clay "bullets" from Abhayagiri Vihara Project site one (after Wikramagamage 1984: 10)

Layer	No. of Clay Balls
1A	1
1B	14
2	8
3	3
4	3
5	4

These "balls" of fired clay, typically between 1.5 and 2.5 cm in diameter, have been interpreted as sling-shot bullets (Bouzek 1993: 91), though there is no suggestion that these would have been used in inter-personal warfare, and it is far more likely that this represents early Mediaeval control of monkeys. Today Anuradhapura is home to large troops of both toque macaques (*Macaca sinica*) and grey langurs (*Semnopithecus sp.*), and the macaques in particular are well documented as serious pests to local inhabitants (Richard et al. 1989: 580, 583-584; Pirta et al. 1997: 102). Slingshots are commonly used throughout South and Southeast Asia to control monkeys (Knight 1999: 629), and the author has witnessed this very behaviour within the Sacred City of Anuradhapura, although using stones rather than fired clay balls.

Consequently, if we accept that these do not represent inter-personal weaponry, we are again left with a complete absence of evidence for violent conflict. A large number of metal artefacts were recovered from both the Abhayagiri Vihara Project (Bouzek 1993: 107) and Jetavanaramaya Project (Ratnayake 1984: 121) excavations, but all were structural (e.g. nails, sheeting, etc.), monetary (coins) or decorative (jewellery, statues, etc.) in nature, with nothing that could be interpreted as suggestive of either weaponry or armour. It is also worth noting that the large quantities of such finds (statues, jewellery etc.) argues against the extensive looting of the Sacred City described in the *Culavamsa* and thus the Invasion Model.

6.4.2: A South Indian Influence?

A key aspect of the Imperial Model, as propounded by Spencer (1983) and Indrapala (2005) is the rise in popularity and prominence of South Indian religious influences in Sri Lanka, with the weakening of the Theravada *sangha* key to the collapse and abandonment of Anuradhapura (Indrapala 2005: 251). One artefact class found within the Citadel, that might be indicative of a South Indian influence, was the appliqué wares discussed in section **5.4.2**. Examples of this late coarseware form were recovered from each of the late periods of the Citadel. However, no examples of this ware were recorded as being recovered from any of the excavations within the Sacred City.

However, there are numerous potential archaeological indicators of a South Indian influence within the Sacred City, visible in statues (Fig.6.07 and Fig.6.08), carvings, and Bell's so called "Hindu Ruins (Bell 1904c: 5) north of the Abhayagiri complex (van Schroeder 1990: 554). It should also be stressed that the rise in Mahayanism (discussed above) in the eighth-tenth centuries AD can be linked to the later appearance of Saivisim within Anuradhapura, though this will be discussed in greater detail in Chapter Eight. The so called Hindu Ruins have not been archaeologically investigated for well over a century, and Bell's ASC reports (1904c: 05; 1904d: 05) remain the only records for these ruins. Bell identified a group of 17 "temples" (12 during the 1892 season and five more the following year). The original identification of the structures as Saivite was based upon their structural plan (Bell 1904c: 05), though the recovery of several lingams in the area (Bell 1904d: 05) along with several Hindu stone sculptures, including one of Surya, supported this original interpretation (von Schroeder 1990: 616).

Unfortunately, due to the period and nature of the excavations it is difficult to securely date these (apparently) Saivite temples, and vandalism to the ruins immediately prior to Bell's excavations can only have further confused matters (Bell 1904c: 5). Although there were suggestions that they could be eleventh century in date, and thus date to the period of Chola rule (Bandaranayake 1974: 199), they have now been dated to the late ninth or tenth century through analysis of the two Tamil inscriptions found within the ruins (Indrapala 1971b), which date respectively to the reign of an unspecified Sena, believed to be Sena II (Patmanatan 2002b: 695), and a ruler referred to as Samghabodhi, believed to be Mahinda IV (Veluppillai 2002: 691).

However, the translation and analysis of these Tamil inscriptions (Indrapala 1971b; Patmanatan 2002a; Patmanatan 2002b; Veluppillai 2002) has also challenged the analysis of these ruins as being Saivite or Hindu, and strongly suggest instead that at least some of the ruins were in fact Buddhist in nature, and were founded by a group of South Indian Tamil merchants (*ibid.*: 694). This will be further discussed in Chapter Eight, in conjunction with contemporary religious power-shifts in Southern India. A further Tamil slab inscription was identified within the Abhayagiri stupa platform, and appears to record an eighth century AD act of merit (the construction of a platform for a nearby shrine and a gift of money) (Patmanatan 2002a: 683). Although it does not record whether the individuals concerned were Tamil, the very existence of the inscription in Tamil strongly suggests that there were Tamils within the Sacred City during Period C,D&E.

In addition to the so called "Hindu Ruins" north of Abhayagiri, the Thuparama patimaghara (the so called "Trident Temple") displays Brahmanical influences in its floor-plan, and has far more in common with Saivite shrines from Polonnaruva and South India than the other *patimagharas* of Anuradhapura (Bandaranayake 1974: 199). Interestingly, though no appliqué wares have been recovered from the Sacred City, the *vajra* symbol that is so common upon those wares (discussed in Chapter Five) is prominent upon the pillar capitals of the Thuparama *patimaghara* (*ibid.*). There is also evidence of Saivite appropriation of Buddhist shrines at Building 21 of Pankuliya (Bell 1904d) where Saivite stucco-heads (Fig.6.09) were recovered by the ASC, similar to those recovered from Building 11 of the "Hindu Ruins" (Fig.6.0) (*ibid.*). While von Schroeder assigns these to the twelfth or thirteenth centuries AD (1990: 606), Bandaranayake suggests a slightly earlier date (1974: 345). Elsewhere the increased influence of Saivism is seen in other sculptures, including at least two Durga statues (one pictured above), unfortunately both of these statues are *ex situ*, one at the Anuradhapura Museum and one at the Colombo Museum. It is interesting to note that while Renfrew's characterisation of the aftermath of collapse featured the emergence of a "New Elite", this emergence of "Saivism" (or indeed South Indian influenced Buddhism) in Anuradhapura appears to originate *prior* to Anuradhapura's collapse. Indeed a recent paper by Ratnayake (2010) ascribes an ex-situ discovery of Saivite bronzes at Jetavanramaya to around the tenth century AD – although such a date, derived at from stylistic observations, is tentative at best.

Interestingly, the disappearance of the bull from moonstones (von Schroeder 1990: 431; Siriweera 2004: 289), seen at Polonnaruva, is not seen within the Sacred City. The classic moonstone of the Anuradhapura period featured several decorated bands, the penultimate of which characteristically featured lions, horses, bulls and elephants (Wikramagamage 1998: 18). However, in the moonstones of Polonnaruva the bull is absent, and is instead typically found upon the accompanying balustrades on either side of the entranceway (von Schroeder 1990: 431). The bull being a sacred animal within Hinduism, it is suggested that the increased popularity of Saivism in Sri Lanka (and Polonnaruva in particular) that it was considered offensive to walk upon such images (*ibid.*). While the significance, and indeed validity, of this "disappearance" has been challenged by some scholars who have argued that the motifs, symbols, and animals featured upon Anuradhapura period moonstones were never so stylistically uniform in the first place (Wikramagamage 1998: 21), there is an undoubted movement of the bull post-tenth century. However, there is no such development visible within the moonstones of Anuradhapura's Sacred City, despite the other indications (listed above) of a Saivite presence within the area.

6.5: Long distance trade, craft specialisation & manufacturing

Unlike the ASW2 assemblage, which was comprehensive in its publishing, the Abhayagiri Vihara Project and Jetavanaramaya Project artefactual assemblages are hugely incomplete in their publishing and frequently inconsistent in the detail and formatting of what has been published. Thus within the single report from the Jetavanaramaya Project we see some artefacts described by depth below surface, some by archaeological level, and some with no contextual data at all (Ratnayake 1984). However, despite this it is possible to make some observations of regarding long distance trade, craft specialisation and manufacturing within the Sacred City.

6.5.1: Imported Artefacts

6.5.1.1: *Glazed Ceramics*

Like the excavations within the Citadel, excavations at Abhayagiri produced a quantity of glazed ceramics from both the Near East and East Asia. Unfortunately all that has been published, from the Abhayagiri excavations, is a breakdown of the imported glazed wares found across the first three seasons of excavation (1982-1984) (shown below in Table 6.04). Unfortunately this assemblage is effectively completely ex-situ, as no contexts are published and it should also be stressed that the identifications of the above glazed wares are preliminary, and cannot be regarded as certain. However, it is clear that, as was the case in the Citadel, the long distance trade of glazed ceramics to China and the Near East was in existence for at least four centuries before ceasing after the tenth century. This will be discussed further in Chapter Eight.

Table 6.04: Abhayagiri Vihara Project glazed ceramics (after Bouzek et al. 1993: 87)

Type:	Date*:	Quantity	Glazed ware assemblage
Near Eastern	-	*60*	*50.0%*
Parthian	3rd C. BC – 3rd C. AD	6	5.0%
Sassanian-Islamic	3rd C. AD – 9th C. AD	41	34.2%
Samarran	7th C. AD – 9th C. AD	13	10.8%
East Asian	-	*51*	*42.5%*
Tang	7th C. AD – 10th C. AD	15	12.5%
Xing	9th C. AD – 10th C. AD	24	20.0%
Yue green ware	9th C. AD – 10th C. AD	8	6.7%
Changsha Painted stone ware	9th C. AD – 10th C. AD	4	3.3%
Unidentified	-	*9*	*7.5%*
Total		120	100%

N.B.*Date ranges given for the Near Eastern wares taken from the Abhayagiri excavation reports due to the grouping of different wares, thus dates given here differ from those of the ASW2 assemblage which are more precise as regards both ware and date.

A single sherd of "blue glazed" pottery was also recovered from the Jetavana excavations (Ratnayake 1984: 109), and a single mention made elsewhere within the single excavation report of a sherd "from Parthia" (*ibid.*: 59). The two are presumably one and the same, but due to the exceedingly poor publishing of the Jetavanaramaya Project no import can be attached to this single sherd. This is demonstrated clearly by a reference in the same report to the recovery of "two fragments of Sassanian Islamic" from pit $S_5W_8E_4$ (Ratynayake 1984: 31). Indeed, a single visit to the Jetavana museum makes it clear that a far larger quantity of imported glazed wares have been recovered from the Jetavana Vihara excavations; unfortunately none of this has been published.

6.5.1.2: Glass artefacts (excluding beads)

As seen in the ASW2 assemblage, the Abhayagiri Vihara Project and Jetavanaramaya Project excavations recovered a quantity of fragments of glass artefacts, including vessels, reliquaries, ornaments, bangles, and beads. The latter will be discussed below (along with the stone beads), due in part to the local nature of bead production as well as the number of bead-caches recovered (see Ratnayake 1984: 36-44). As with many other classes of artefacts, the Jetavana Museum strongly demonstrates that a far greater quantity of glass artefacts was recovered, but have not been published.

The Jetavana excavations recovered a total of 20 vessel fragments from three vessels, all of which were a pale translucent green (Ratnayake 1984: 119). While the limited publishing of the Jetavana excavations hinders any attempts at dating these artefacts, their location in layers I (14 sherds, two vessels) and II (six sherds, one vessel) of pit $S_5W_8E_4$ (*ibid.*) suggest that these belong to the later group of imported wares identified at ASW2, dating to the ninth and tenth centuries AD (Coningham 2006: 334). Unfortunately, layer I of the Jetavanaramaya Project excavations is effectively the topsoil (forming the top 20-25cm of the excavations), and cannot be considered stratigraphically secure, despite the corroborating find of two fragments of Sassanian glazed wares from the same layer of the same pit (Ratnayake 1984: 31). As discussed in Chapter Five (section **5.5.3**), glass vessels in early Mediaeval Sri Lanka were an entirely imported phenomenon (Coningham 2006: 333), and are thus indicative of long distance trade to the west. Unfortunately the vessel fragments from the Sacred City have not been geographically provenanced, though they likely originate from Mesopotamia, the Eastern Mediterranean or Egypt, as these three regions produced all the glassware identified within the ASW2 assemblage (*ibid.*). Twenty further glass fragments were recovered from the Abhayagiri excavations (Bouzek et al. 1993: 97-98), of which eight fragments were identified as Late Roman, dating to Period F or between the fourth and fifth centuries AD (*ibid.*). None of the twelve further glass vessel fragments were provenanced, though they are all almost certainly post-Roman (*ibid.*: 98). As was the case with the Jetavana vessel fragments, the Abhayagiri fragments were confined to the upper strata, with only two of the twenty fragments originating from Layer 2 (the other eighteen were all recovered from Layer 1) (*ibid.*).

Unlike the glass vessels, the provenance of Anuradhapura period glass bangles, while relatively common in both the Citadel and Sacred City, is unclear. However, while it is possible that they were manufactured locally, it appears more likely that this category of artefact originates from the subcontinent, with comparable glass bangles having been identified at Taxila (Marshall 1951 cited in Coningham 2006: 349) and Nevasa (Dikshit 1969: 34). Some nineteen fragments of glass bangles were recovered from the Abhayagiri excavations (Bouzek et al. 1993: 98-100) with a further two fragments published by the Jetavanaramaya Project (Ratnayake 1984: 119). Unfortunately, this category of artefacts have not been well studied, and not only is their provenance uncertain, but their diachronic window is broad, stretching from as early as 500BC (Bouzek et al. 1993: 100) to Period B of both ASW2 and Abhayagiri. In addition to glass vessels and bangles, several miscellaneous glass artefacts were recovered from the Jetavana excavations, including a fragment of a "reliquary" and three "ornaments" (Ratnayake 1984: 119). Unfortunately the publishing of these artefacts is such that any further analysis is impossible.

While the dates and provenancing of the Sacred City glass vessels are clearly lacking, they further demonstrate both that Anuradhapura was within an extensive long distance trade network, but also that the Sacred City attracted a significant quantity of such luxury goods (whether through purchasing, votive offerings or tax), and did so for several hundred years, from before Period F through to at least Periods C,D&E. Unfortunately it is impossible to either confirm the presence of absence of artefacts such as imported glass vessels in the post-tenth century Period B, as the residuality of such artefacts, the disturbed nature of the upper strata, and the piecemeal publishing of the CCF excavations have compromised this dataset.

6.5.2: Manufacturing

Due to limited recording and publishing from the Sacred City excavations very little can be said diachronically about manufacturing within the Sacred City due to the quality of the publishing of these excavations. Thus, while we can highlight the discovery of fragments of crucible and iron slag near the Period B structures at AVP Site Four (Wikramagamage et al. 1983: 352) as indicative of twelfth to thirteenth century metalworking within the Sacred City, due to the publishing only of what the excavators deemed noteworthy we cannot say with any certainty whether this represents a change in the zoning or levels of craft specialisation and manufacturing. Manufacturing does appear to have occurred within the Sacred City in the preceding structural periods, with a workshop manufacturing glazed tiles identified in the Period F strata in the vicinity of the second Samadhi Bodhigara (Bouzek et al. 1993: 13), while a small mould for manufacturing a seated Buddha image discovered within the fill of the Elephant Pond (Wikramagamage 1992: 45) suggestive of specialist metal-working occurring locally. This mould was tentatively dated to the early part of Periods C,D&E, around the seventh to eighth centuries AD (Bouzek et al. 1993: 19), though this dating is derived entirely from stylistic observations. Further evidence of such manufacturing, and the growing trade to the east, is seen in the discovery of a bronze Buddha figure in Thailand (Fig.6.10), believed to have originated from Anuradhapura and dated to the 10th century (von Schroeder 1990: 206).

Another problem presented by the Sacred City is that the vast majority of the statues (bronze or stone) and carved panels were removed to museums during the initial phases of archaeological research at the city, removing all contextual evidence from these artefacts. Meanwhile, the more recent recovery of further bronze figures from Anuradhapura during the CCF excavations in the 1980s (Indrapala 2005: 307) have not been published. Consequently studies of, for example, Anuradhapura period sculptures have tended to be heavily reliant upon the Pali chronicles and form (e.g. Wikramagamage 1990) but very weak on technical aspects and periodisation. Recent scientific studies, for example Thantilage's (2010) study on the manufacturing and origins of two collections of Anuradhapura period bronzes, have begun to move beyond this, but even here they are hindered by the ex-situ nature of such collections. Ratnayake, building upon recent research such as Thantilage's, argues strongly for the existence of an Anuradhapura school of bronze figural casting in the tenth century AD (Ratnayake 2010: 279), but once again is restricted by the ex-situ nature of such materials.

6.5.2.1: Stone and glass beads

The ASW2 bead assemblage demonstrated that beads (both glass and stone) were manufactured locally (Coningham 2006: 353). However, while Bouzek et al. (1993: 103) also assert that stone beads were sourced and manufactured locally, very little archaeological evidence of this manufacturing was identified during the CCF excavations at either Abhayagiri or Jetavana. The only evidence published is two glass artefacts described as "bead making material" in the single Jetavana preliminary report, one of which came from the disturbed topsoil "Layer 1" (Ratnayake 1984: 119). This may indicate that although such manufacture occurred locally, it did not occur within the Sacred City. However, it is also quite possible that this is simply a reflection of the publishing quality for the CCF excavations.

Diachronically, Bouzek et al. (1993: 103) attribute the majority of precious- and semi-precious stone beads to Period F and earlier, prior to being largely replaced by glass beads at the beginning of Periods C,D&E (around the fifth or sixth century AD) (ibid.). Although glass beads appear to increase in frequency from this point (the fifth/sixth century AD on), they are found in Abhayagiri contexts prior to the Great Destruction Horizon of the third century AD, albeit in far smaller quantities (*ibid.*). Unfortunately no actual quantities of Abhayagiri glass or stone beads have been published, and so we are with only generalised statements. Conversely, the Jetavana bead assemblage (Ratnayake 1984: 115-116) *does* contain quantities (Table 6.06 above), but lacks any stratigraphic information (such as layer or even depth below surface), rendering them virtually meaningless beyond the simple presence of such artefacts.

Table.6.05: *Jetavanaramaya Project Bead Assemblage* **(after Ratnayake 1984: 115-116)**

Material	Quantity
Stone	161
Glass	355
Clay	1217
Bone	12
Total	1745

The published Jetavanaramaya Project bead assemblage shown in Table 6.05 (Ratnayake 1984: 115-116) is clearly incomplete, as not only does the Jetavana Museum display many more beads, but within the same report quantities of beads founds cached in ceramic vessels (*ibid.*: 36-44) are recorded, none of which appear to be included in the assemblages published. These caches, seventeen in total, all appear to have been recovered from an extremely localised area in the upper terrace of the Jetavana stupa (*ibid.*), with sixteen of the seventeen caches recovered from a confined stratum of 0.70-1.01m below the surface at the foot of the Northern Ayaka (*ibid.*). However, no further description of these excavations is given (such as description of layers, strata, structural elements etc.), and given the extensive restoration of the Northern Ayaka by Bell in the late nineteenth century (*ibid.*: 18) it is dangerous to attach significance to these caches as they now exist solely *ex-situ*.

6.5.2.2: Architectural masonry

Another aspect of localised craft specialisation is the stone masonry used within the Sacred City, which displays clear evidence of highly skilled craft specialists. This is especially true in the final phase of moulded gneiss, around the ninth and tenth centuries AD (Bouzek et al. 1993: 120). The dressing of stone at this point becomes "perfect" (*ibid.*) and previously utilitarian and functional stone elements become increasingly sophisticated in their decoration (*ibid.*).

This can be seen in the development of moonstones, with the plain, austere, moonstones of late-Period F early Period C,D&E (fifth-seventh centuries AD) replaced by highly ornate moonstones from the ninth century onwards, such as that seen at the tenth century AD Pankuliya image-house, or at the entrance to the "Trident Temple" at Thuparama (Bandaranayake 1974: 328). A similar evolution of ornamental complexity can be seen in the pillar capitals (Fig.6.11), guardstones, and balustrades across Anuradhapura (*ibid.*: 329) (Fig.6.12). The guardstones that served as a terminal slab to the sloping balustrades on either side of entrance-ways can be seen to develop from (conjectured) painted wooden planks, through plain stone slabs, followed by slabs decorated with a *purnaghata* (initially incised, subsequently carved in relief), then figural representations (typically of Sankha and Padma) and finally *nagaraja* (*ibid.*). While this sequence is not strictly consecutive, it is believed to be representative of the stylistic and technical development of the guardstones. While the shift from wood to stone appears to date to Period F, or around the fifth or sixth century AD, and the fully developed *nagarajas* are attributed to the ninth century AD onwards (*ibid.*), there are unfortunately no dates available for the intermediary stages (*ibid.*: 330). Similarly the balustrades or railings of the entranceways see a similar developmental sequence (albeit one incorporating moulded brickwork as well as worked stone), culminating in the "fully articulated *makara* wingstones of the" ninth century onwards (*ibid.*).

However, while this "perfection" of stone working within the Sacred City is the culmination of centuries of development, the subsequent Period B (eleventh and twelfth century) structures at Abhayagiri showed none of these characteristics and were almost entirely reliant upon reclaimed and recycled material from earlier structures (Wikramagamage et al. 1983: 352; Wikramagamage 1984: 17-18). Elsewhere the tentatively dated twelfth century repairs of the Abhayagiri stupa's inner boundary walls (Salapatasala Maluva) (Bouzek et al. 1993: 17) displays new moulded brickwork, but none of the sophisticated ornamental stone working of the ninth and tenth centuries (Wikramagamage et al. 1984: 50). While the sophisticated and highly decorative ninth and tenth century stonework of the Sacred City clearly represents the existence of highly skilled craft specialists, it also demonstrates a significant expenditure of resources in the scale and scope of the ornamental carvings and decorations throughout the Sacred City.

6.6: Conclusion

The archaeological analysis of the centuries preceding, during and immediately following the Sacred City's "sacking" is massively hindered by the publishing quality of the CCF excavations at the Jetavana, and to a lesser degree Abhayagiri, Viharas in the 1980s. As a result of the piecemeal publication of these excavations it is difficult to draw firm conclusions from the available data, as there can be no certainty (or indeed anything approaching certainty) that the published data is fully representative.

With the above caveat in place, the Sacred City can be viewed overall as displaying several centuries of steady growth, peaking around the 9th century AD, before a dramatic abandonment around the eleventh century AD. Structurally we can see continuous construction and redevelopment across the area of the Abhayagiri Vihara (the only area with reasonable quality archaeological data), in addition to late construction in the suburbs of the Sacred City with the development of the *padhanaghara parivenas* and *pabbata viharas* in the final centuries of the first millennium AD. Specialist craftwork, manufacturing and trade all appear to flourish until the eleventh century AD, though the actual levels are unquantifiable due to the publishing of the Sacred City's excavations. Religiously, we appear to see a rise during Periods C,D&E in the prominence of asceticism, heterodox Mahayanism and Saivism. The latter two in particular could be argued to represent an increase in the South Indian influence within the Sacred City as posited by the Imperial Model.

Post tenth century we appear to see a massive reduction in the population and maintenance of the Sacred City. Structurally we see ephemeral and transient occupation (AVP Site Three) attributed to the eleventh century and twelfth centuries, reusing structural elements of earlier, more elaborate, structures combined with organic materials (Wikramagamage 1984: 18), and while there are sporadic indications of new construction (AVP Site Three (Bouzek et al. 1993: 15)) and renovations (AVP Site Four (*ibid.*: 17)) there is a notable dearth of Polonnaruva period artefacts, with just three Polonnaruva period coins (the latest being a single thirteenth century Parakramabahu II coin) (Bouzek 1993: 109), and only a few crude examples of Polonnaruva pottery (Bouzek et al. 1993: 57).

However, it must be highlighted that almost all of the dating within the Sacred City is built around stylistic assessments of architecture or sculpture (e.g. Bandaranayake 1974 and much of both the Abhayagiri Vihara Project and Jetavanaramaya Project excavations), and that these assessments are heavily reliant upon the Pali chronicles. There is an almost complete absence of scientific dates, and very few (the glazed wares are the exception that proves the rule) of the late period artefactual dates (i.e. ceramic typologies) incorporate comparatives from outside Sri Lanka. Consequently, it should not be surprising to see that the Sacred City's sequence appears to display wide-scale abandonment in the eleventh century, as the formation of the archaeological chronology has been *a priori* bookended by the Pali chronicles' eleventh century Chola sacking of the city. Despite this, there remains a complete absence of any direct evidence to place the Cholas within the Sacred City.

Taking into account the archaeological data presented within this chapter, the archaeological signature for the late Anuradhapura period can simply presented as shown below (table 6.06).

This chapter has presented the archaeological data for the centuries leading up to, during, and immediately preceding the apparent eleventh century abandonment of the Sacred City. As a result of the quality and scope of the available published data, this is far less comprehensive than the preceding chapter for the Citadel. The next chapter will present the archaeological data for the same period within the hinterland of Anuradhapura, something essential to any understanding of the events and processes occurring in the Citadel and Sacred City of Anuradhapura during their apparent "collapse".

Table 6.06: The Sacred City's Archaeological Signature

Century AD	9th	10th	11th	12th	13th
Population	→	→	←	↘	✠
Monumental Construction	→	→	✠	←	✠
Traditional Elite	→	→	✠	←	✠
New Elite	←	←	←	✠	✠
Long Distance Trade	→	→	✠	✠	✠
Craft Specialisation	→	→	←	←	✠

KEY: ↑ High ↓ Low ↗ Rising ↘ Falling → Steady ✠ Absent

A Time of Change: The "Collapse" of Anuradhapura, Sri Lanka

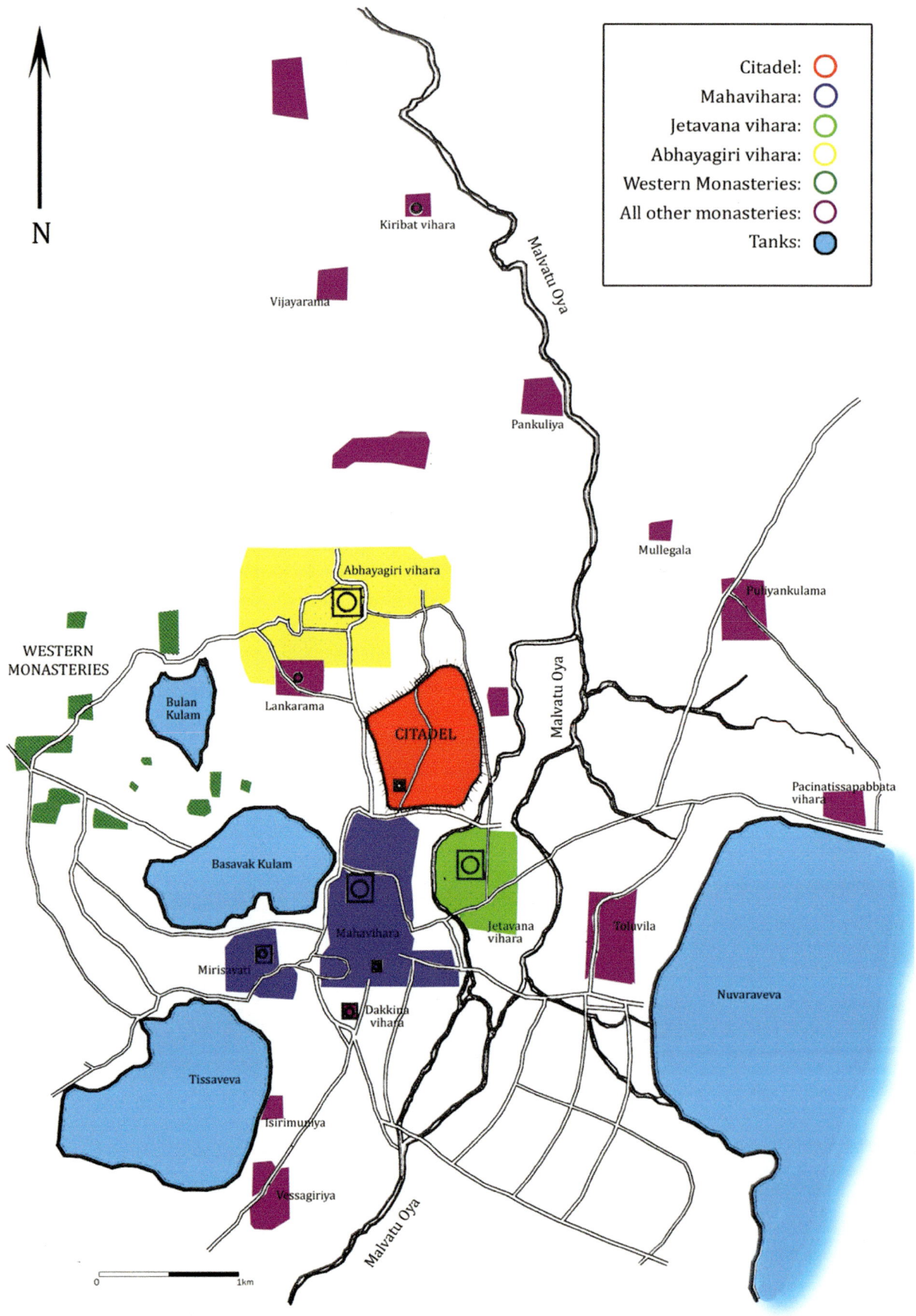

Figure 6.01: The Sacred City, Anuradhapura
(AFTER WIJESURIYA 1998: 172 & BANDARANAYAKE 1974: 34)

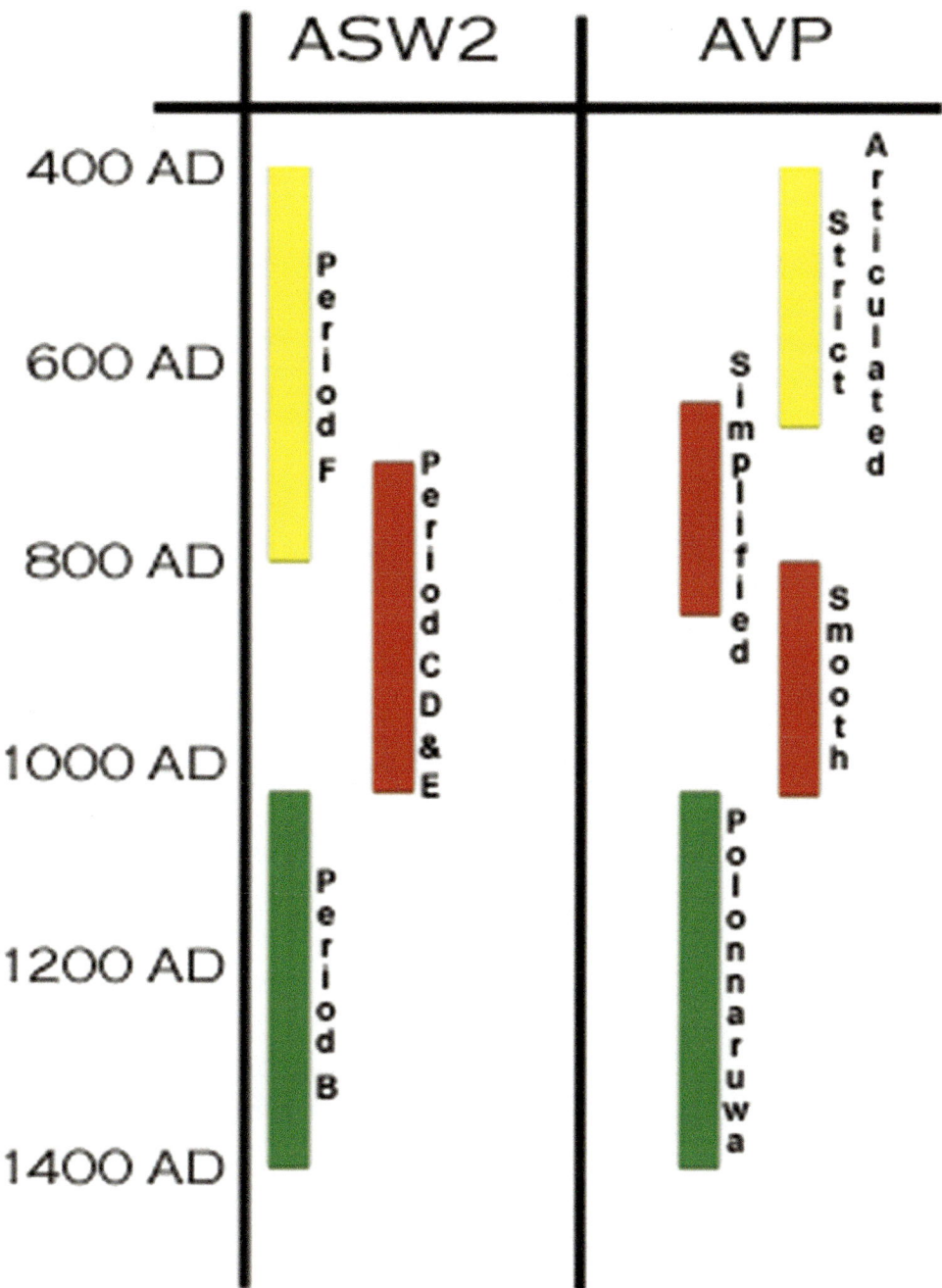

Figure 6.02: ASW2 structural periods and Abhayagiri Vihara Project typological periods

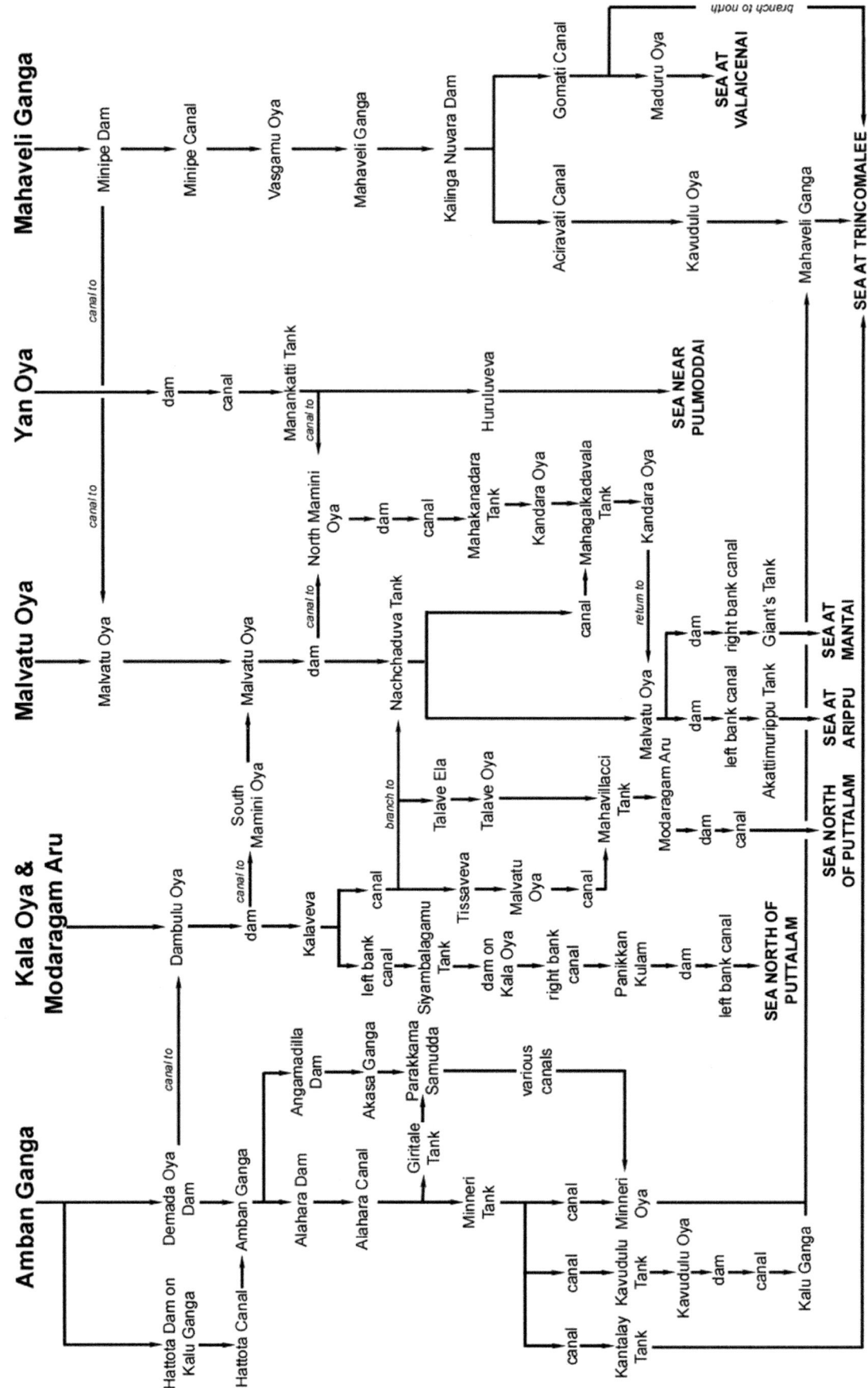

Figure 6.03: Anuradhapura's Hydraulic Network
(AFTER NICHOLAS 1960; SENEVIRATNA 1989: 94)

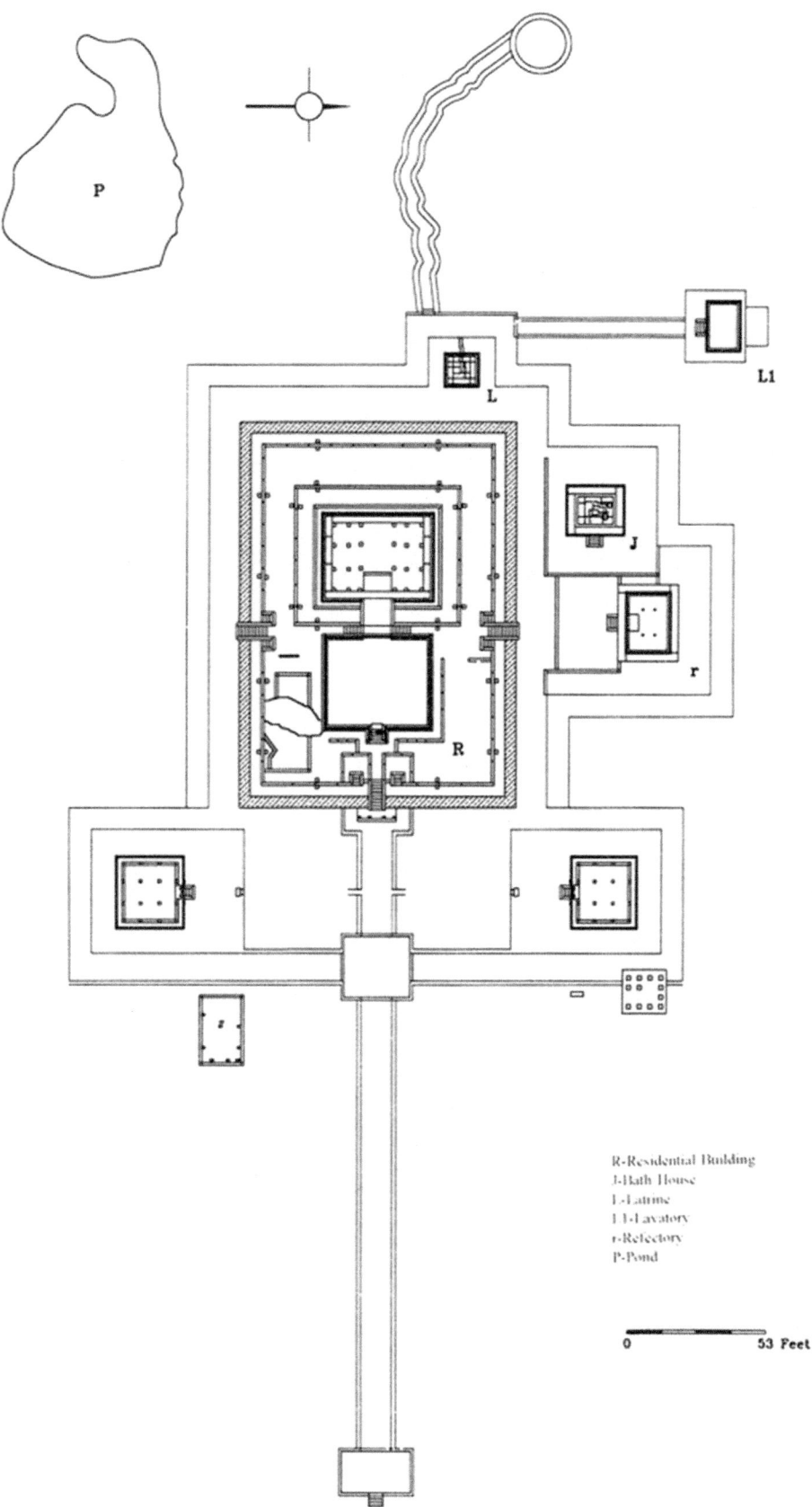

Figure 6.04: Example of double-platform monastery from the Western Monasteries
(AFTER WIJESURIYA 1998: 56)

A Time of Change: The "Collapse" of Anuradhapura, Sri Lanka

Figure 6.05: Example of a decorated urinal stone from the Western Monasteries
(after Bell 1914d: Plates IV & V)

CHAPTER 6: THE SACRED CITY

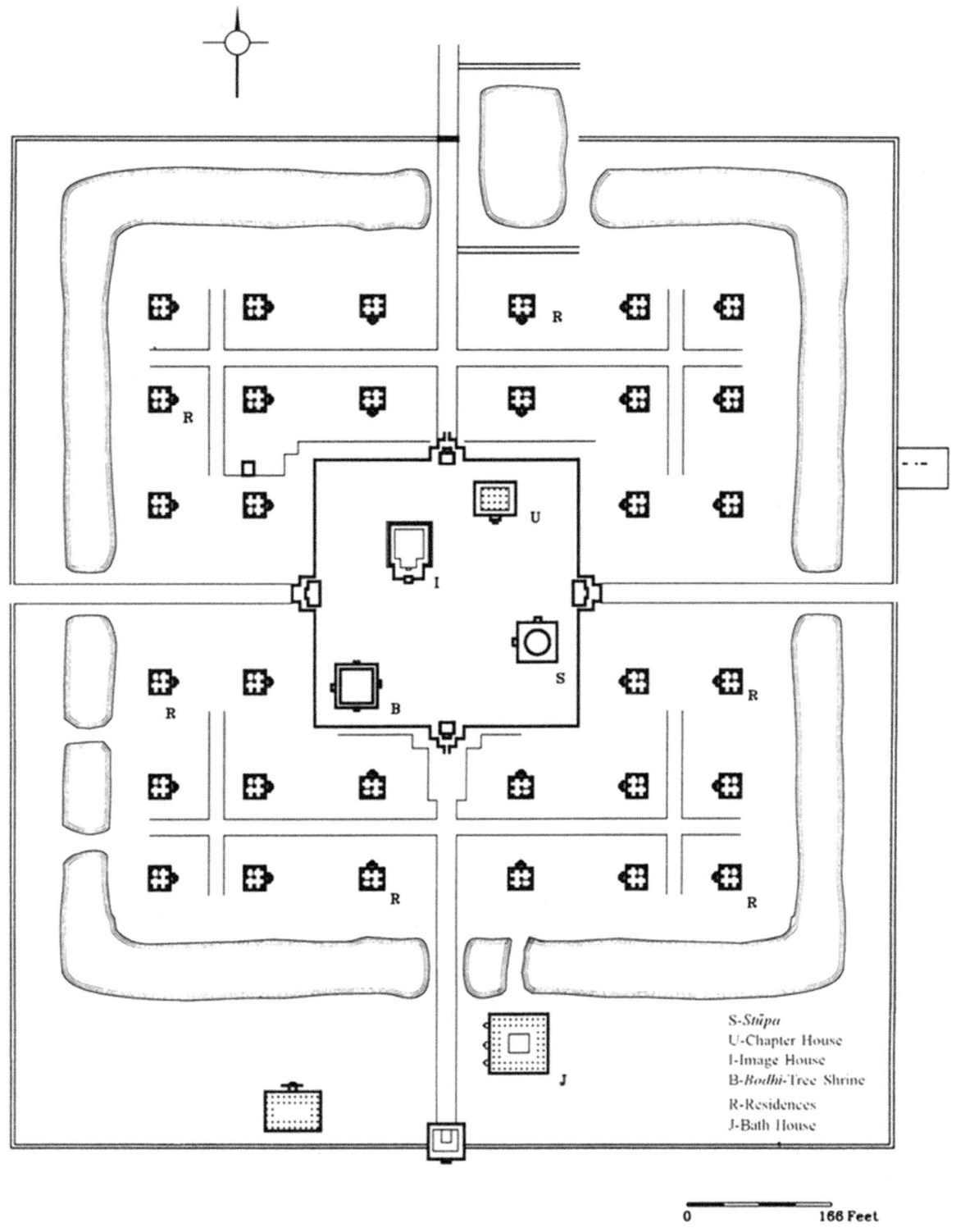

Figure 6.06: Site plan of Puliyankulama
(AFTER WIJESURIYA 1998: 54)

Figure 6.07: Bronze figure of Indra recovered from Puliyankulama
(AFTER BELL 1914C: PLATE DD)

CHAPTER 6: THE SACRED CITY

Figure 6.08: 10th century Durga statue from Anuradhapura (ex situ)
(HTTP://LANKAPURA.COM/2009/11/ANCIENT-HINDU-GODDESS-DURGA-AT-ANURADHAPURA)

Building 21, Pankuliya   Building 11, "Hindu Ruins"

Figure 6.09: Stucco heads from Building 21, Pankuliya & Building 11 of the "Hindu Ruins"
(AFTER BELL 1914A: PLATES XXIX, XXX; BELL 1914B: PLATE XXXV)

Figure 6.10: 10th century Sri Lankan bronze seated Buddha, found in Thailand
(IMAGE REF. VON SCHROEDER 1990: 206)

CHAPTER 6: THE SACRED CITY

Figure 6.11: 9th and 10th century Sacred City ornamental pillar capitals
(AFTER BANDARANAYAKE 1974: 349)

Figure 6.12: Evolution of balustrades and guardstones
(AFTER BANDARANAYAKE 1974: 335)

Chapter 7:
The Hinterland

7.1 Introduction

Chapters Five and Six presented the archaeological signature for the terminal periods of the Citadel and Sacred City. However, no such city could develop, let alone thrive, without a hinterland operating as an economic catchment for the city, providing the resources of food, raw materials and labour that the city needed to trade, build and feed its inhabitants. Furthermore, as established in Chapter Four, the city of Anuradhapura was not a city in the Classical Western model of a city and can instead be described as "low density urbanisation" (Fletcher 2009: 05), with primarily the elite "living" within the "urban core", while the general populace lived in a highly populated hinterland.

However, due in part to the ephemeral nature of lay residential architecture during the Anuradhapura period, the archaeological focus has tended to fall upon the monumental city – ignoring the rural populace. The ASC surveys of the late nineteenth and early twentieth century ventured outside of the city, but focussed upon monastic structures, the only structures within the hinterland built in stone, brick and tile. Consequently, much of the organisation and form of rural settlements in Early Mediaeval Sri Lanka remains a mystery (Leach 1961:17), and *"we have no knowledge of the form or function of its surrounding villages and secondary sites"* (Coningham 1994b: 65).

There have been a number of attempts by scholars to examine the nature of Early Mediaeval Sri Lankan and South Indian rural settlements, typically focussing upon issues of land ownership and revenues, agricultural technologies, or of caste and feudalism (e.g. Gunawardana 1971; Subbarayalu 1973: 89-95; Gunawardana 1979; Stein 1980; Lemercinier 1981; Balambal 1998; Karashima & Subbarayalu 2007; Chakravarti 2008 or Karashima 2008). However, these works are historical in their approach, drawing from epigraphic and textual sources, and the rural and urban hinterlands of Early Mediaeval South Asia have been largely ignored archaeologically. As established in Chapter's Two and Three, this leaves us entirely reliant upon a single data source, the recent British-Sri Lankan *Anuradhapura Hinterland* survey (Coningham & Gunawardhana 2013).

This chapter will now present the archaeological data relevant to the terminal period of Anuradhapura, in an attempt to test the three collapse models as set out in Chapter Four, and to create an archaeological signature for the collapse of Anuradhapura within the hinterland. While the structure of this chapter will mirror that of the preceding chapters where possible, some differences are unavoidable due to the very different nature of the hinterland in terms of both form and data.

7.2 Population

To determine changes in population levels within the hinterland it is necessary to first identify rural settlements and then to constrain their occupation diachronically. This poses two problems; firstly, there is the dating of such settlements. The chronologically significant exotic glazed wares of the Citadel and Sacred City are not generally found in secular rural settlements, nor are there typically inscriptions, coins, or indeed even long stratigraphic sequences. Secondly, as has been stressed before, the residential architecture of all bar the elite was largely organic in nature (Godakumbura 1963; Bandaranayake 1980). Consequently, it survives poorly within the archaeological record and making the identification of such settlements within the archaeological record difficult, especially during transect survey when only visibly extant surface remains are identifiable.

Due to the ephemeral nature of rural architecture there are two approaches to settlement identification. The first while simplistic, is ethnographically supported, and focuses upon the ancient tanks (whether abandoned or still in use) of the hinterland, specifically the "village tanks", and the model of *"one tank – one village"* (Gunawardana 1971: 3), frequently described as the structure of rural society in Sri Lanka, from the Early Historic period through to the early twentieth century (Gunawardana 1971: 3; Seneviratna 1989: 33). This system of rain-fed tanks functioned, and in many areas still functions, in relative isolation from each other; trapping and storing rain-water for use by the villagers around it. Setting aside the arguments surrounding hydraulic societies (the agency behind the construction of tanks, the function of the tanks and the nature of the administration of this hydraulic system (e.g. Wittfogel 1957; Leach 1959; Panabokke 1992: 02; Disanayaka 2000: 85; Gunnell et al. 2007: 210)) and focussing upon the *"one village – one tank"* concept, we might theoretically identify the existence of an ancient village by the presence of an ancient tank, indeed Brohier argues the two are in fact synonymous (1934: 02).

However, there are several factors that argue against such an approach, laid out succinctly by Wikkramatileke (1957: 364):

> *"(2) All the ancient "tanks" may not have been in operation at the same time... (3) Lake areas of old "tanks" are silted up and areas below most "bunds" so overgrown that it is difficult to estimate the area which might at sometime have been irrigated. (4) The large number of "tanks" may be indicative of population movements rather than actual numbers... (5) Some of the smaller "tanks" may have been designed primarily for domestic water supplies. Less paddy would have been grown and more importance attached perhaps to the "dry" crop millet as a staple, this were so it is likely that there would have been fewer people. The average yield of millet is seldom more than one-fourth that of paddy."*

As can be seen the number of assumptions that must be made to accommodate the simple equation of "tanks = villages" render it unviable. Issue four of Wikkramatileke's points, that of population and settlement movements, corresponds to recent data from the Anuradhapura hinterland survey (Coningham et al. 2007a) that posited a rural landscape in which settlements were short lived and moved frequently, while it is the monastic sites that are long lived and, in a sense, provide the stability and permanence within the urban hinterland. Furthermore, such a methodology provides no further information; no indication as to the period or longevity of the settlement, no indication of settlement size, no information regarding the nature of the settlement – for example whether or not metalworking or ceramic production was present, or whether long distance trade items were present.

Table 7.01: Anuradhapura Hinterland Survey Ceramic Scatters

Ceramic Scatters	493
Transect Survey	385
just ceramics	287
with brick	27
with tile	8
with brick & tile	12
with slag	49
with brick, tile & slag	2
Canal Survey	45
just ceramics	29
with brick	1
with slag	15
with brick and slag	1
River Survey	62
just ceramics	43
with brick	14
with brick & tile	2
with slag	2
with brick and slag	1

Having discarded such an approach we turn to ceramic scatters, presented in Table 7.01 above. Such sites indicate human activity during the Anuradhapura period, and are arguably of greater interest in moving beyond simply identifying the number and distribution of settlements, as Skibo (1999: 102) wrote; *"pottery like any piece of material culture, is woven into the complex tapestry of people's lives"*. Coarseware ceramics in particular, through their ubiquitousness, could thus be argued to be most representative of this interaction between people and material culture, and of the rural populace of the Anuradhapura hinterland. Through analysis of these ceramics, along with the association of any other artefacts we can not only infer more about the nature of the rural settlements of the hinterland, but also *attempt* to locate these settlements within a diachronic framework. As can be seen above (Table 7.01) the great majority of settlements across the hinterland contained no elite structural materials (brick and tile), and no signs of metalworking. These are the sites that can best be said to represent the most basic rural settlements – settlements not directly associated with monastic or Royal activities, nor with metalworking.

Looking at the size of these settlement sites we see that they were primarily small, typically less than 10m2 in area as shown in Table 7.02 below. Furthermore, the majority (64%) of the ceramic scatters were the absolute minimum sherd density to be identified as archaeological sites (five sherds per square meter). Thus from the survey alone we see a picture of small settlements with a relatively low level of activity, and Coningham et al. (2007a: 707) interpreted these smaller order scatters as representative of peripatetic villages engaged in *chenna* (slash and burn) agriculture. Such agriculture is still common in the hinterland of modern Anuradhapura, especially in areas where rice cultivation is impractical (*ibid.*).

Table 7.02: Size and sherd density of Transect Survey Ceramic Scatter sites

	Sherd Density (sherds per m2)				
		5	6-10	11-15	15>	Total
Site Size	<5 m2	86	21	3	5	115
	5-9 m2	36	18	1	0	55
	10-14 m2	27	16	3	3	49
	15> m2	34	15	9	10	68
	Total	183	70	16	18	287

This picture of small, transitory, settlements was reinforced by excavations carried out (Coningham *et al.* 2013) at three of the larger ceramic scatter sites (B009, F102 and B062, shown in Fig.7.01). The site of Siyabalagasveva (B009) appears to represent just such a small order, transient, rural settlement and an exploratory 4m^2 trench excavated at the core of the ceramic scatter (measuring 225m^2) exposed a single structural phase consisting of four shallow postholes cut into an earth platform (Fig.7.02). This small structure, (2.4m in diameter) was part of the only structural phase at the site and only coarseware ceramics were recovered during excavation (and surface collection), with no finewares, metal artefacts, brick, stone, tile or worked bone etc.

Similar results were produced from the excavation and auger core survey of site F102 (Coningham *et al.* 2013), the largest (approximately 60,000m^2) and densest ceramic scatter found within the hinterland (see Fig.7.01). This revealed a relatively shallow spread of cultural material (Fig.7.03) and despite the geophysical identification of several rectilinear features interpreted as either kilns or burnt floors (Schmidt 2005: 20), excavation failed to identify either, or indeed any further structural features. Despite the absence of structural features, the excavations did yield small quantities of slag, glass sherds, bone, a glass bead, burnished ceramics, decorated ceramics, a roof tile fragment, a roof finial fragment and the base of an oil lamp within the disturbed plough soils, and below the plough soil an *in situ* silt deposit yielded similarly impressive finds including a large quantity of slag, one bone fragment, one ore fragment and two sherds of fine ware. These artefacts clearly indicate a higher social status to the simple ceramic scatter of B009 and structurally we can infer the potential presence of a tiled roof on site from the fragments of roof tile and terracotta roof finial, suggesting the presence of an elite, either royalty or *sangha* (Bandaranayake 1974: 16).

However, despite this we again see a short term occupation, with shallow cultural deposits recovered during both excavation and auger coring (Coningham et al. 2007a: 707). Thus we are presented with a picture of rural settlements that, while predominantly small in area, range in size up to 60km². However, occupation at all such settlements, large and small, is short lived and relatively temporary in nature. As a result of the short occupational sequences at ceramic scatter sites, it is very difficult to develop a structural sequence demonstrating their structural and architectural development over time. Two OSL samples were taken from F102, targeted at dating the *terminus post quem* of site abandonment, and the *terminus ante quem* of ceramic accumulation at the site respectively (Simpson et al. 2008a: 16). Unfortunately, one was never measured, while the second appears to represent residual sediment age, yielding a date of 5600±400 BC (*ibid.*: 33).

This problem with dating was seen across the hinterland, with very few diachronically diagnostic artefacts found across the hinterland survey. No imported glazed wares were found by the *Anuradhapura Hinterland* survey, either on the probabilistic transect surveys, the non-probabilistic river and canal surveys, or during excavations. One "late" diagnostic ceramic sherd found within the hinterland was a single sherd (SF1647) of Polonnaruva style appliqué ware (Fig.7.04) found on non-probabilistic river survey at site F524, an undiagnostic pillared site. Elsewhere, just five of the 891 archaeological sites identified on transect survey featured any of the six post period C,D&E coarsewares identified earlier (section **4.3.2**), as shown below in Table 7.03. All five of these sites were ceramic scatters, with no indications of elite social status (either artefactual or architectural) present at any of the five. Of course, due to the longevity of so many of the ASW2 coarseware forms this is not an indication of a complete abandonment, as 196 of the ASW2 coarseware forms are found across periods B through F and beyond, with a further 17 forms that cover periods B through C,D&E. However, this dramatic paucity of late ceramic forms is certainly suggestive of very low levels of occupation during and after Period B.

Table 7.03: Late chronologically significant ASW2 coarseware forms

Site	Coarseware form	Site Type	Quantity	Weight
C161	28/C/A/1	Ceramic Scatter	1	43.2g
D176	8/H/A/1	Ceramic Scatter	1	89.2g
D180	2/D/C/1, 28/C/A/1	Ceramic Scatter	2	74.6g
D183	28/C/A/1	Ceramic Scatter	1	180g
D190	8/H/A/1	Ceramic Scatter	1	24.4g

As a result of the lack of secure dating for these rural settlements, and as a result of the transitory nature of the sites, it is very difficult to draw up a clear picture of the hinterland's rural population at any one moment in time. With settlements apparently occupied for relatively short periods there is clearly a great deal of movement within the hinterland, and the theoretical 31,639 ceramic scatters earlier posited as existing across the full 7857km² hinterland would represent an accumulation of archaeological sites over more than a millennium, only a fraction of which would ever have been occupied simultaneously. While it is impossible to identify the number of settlements occupied in the centuries immediately preceding and following the Chola sacking of Anuradhapura in 1017 AD, it is possible to posit that occupation and activity within the hinterland was minimal after the tenth century given the almost universal absence of late ceramic forms, or indeed other late artefacts, within the hinterland.

The other key indicator of human activity and presence within the hinterland, as mentioned earlier, is the hydraulic landscape – the tanks, canals and channels that enabled intensive agriculture. As has been established, a simple counting of tanks is not a viable method of inferring numbers of settlements. However, the maintenance of the hydraulic landscape is key to the maintenance of both the urban and rural population, and this will be examined shortly (section **7.5**).

7.3: Traditional Elite

As established in Chapters Three and Four, the traditional elite of Anuradhapura is represented by the *sangha* and royalty. However, while the Sacred City may represent the monumental core of the Buddhist fraternity in Anuradhapura, the elite of the hinterland appears to have been primarily formed by the Buddhist monasteries (Coningham et al. 2007), forming a Buddhist temporality surrounding and linking (both symbolically and economically) the rural communities to the city of Anuradhapura – in effect a "sacred hinterland" (*ibid.*). Within the hinterland monastic sites range from small single structure archaeological sites identified by the Anuradhapura Hinterland survey, to extensive monastic complexes such as those at Dambulla (just over 60km south-southeast of the Citadel), Ritagala (approximately 38km southeast) or at Hathttikuchchi (approximately 37km south-southwest). The latter will be examined shortly, but first the monastic sites from the Anuradhapura Hinterland survey will be presented.

Table 7.04: *Monastic Sites identified on transect survey*

Monastic Sites	97
On Outcrop	**64**
lena, stupa & stone pillars	5
lena & stupa	4
stupa & stone pillars	9
lena & stone pillars	7
stone pillars & other Buddhist features	14
lena	12
stupa	7
other monastic features	6
On plain / hill	**33**
lena, stupa & stone pillars	0
lena & stupa	0
stupa & stone pillars	4
lena & stone pillars	2
stone pillars & other Buddhist features	7
lena	18
stupa	1
other monastic features	1
Inscription	**1**
Undiagnostic site with pillars	**48**

The Anuradhapura Hinterland transect survey (Manuel et al. 2013) identified 98 monastic sites, in addition to a further 48 undiagnostic pillared sites, predominantly likely to be monastic in nature. Overall the form and size of these monastic sites varied greatly, including one monumental *pabbata vihara* (site Z00 as shown in Fig.7.01), several *Padhanaghara Parivena* or double platforms, to single *lena* (caves or rock shelters with associated drip ledges and/or inscriptions). It is impossible to perform a detailed analysis of the majority of the monastic sites identified during the transect survey within the Anuradhapura Hinterland as the majority were recorded as monastic after the identification of a "monastic feature", thus while there is a record of whether or not a lena was present, or a stupa is present, there is not enough recorded data to judge what period that monastery belongs to, although it is possible to attribute the majority to Bandaranayake's "organic monastery" classification (seen above in Table 7.04). As discussed in Chapter Four, sites defined solely by the presence of *lena* pre-date the period of interest here. However, the presence of *lena* in conjunction with other monastic features, especially late developments such as stone pillars (Bandaranayake 1974: 25), demonstrates continuity of occupation at these monastic sites – something further supported by Anuradhapura Hinterland excavations (Coningham *et al.* 2013) at the site of Veheragala (A155). This site is characteristic of the "organic monasteries" identified on transect survey, located on and around a large granite outcrop and featuring a *lena*, several *in situ* stone pillars, rock-cut steps, ponds, figural limestone sculpture, *yantrigala*, *Sri pada*, brick foundations and a large stupa. The presence of the *lena* indicates early monastic occupation (c.300 BC – 100 AD), a supposition supported by geoarchaeological investigation of the nearby bund and tank site (E400), where an OSL sample from a section through the bund yielded an OSL dates of 400 BC ±100. This suggests that construction of this tank was part of the first wave of hydraulic construction in the hinterland and was very likely associated with the presence of the Buddhist monastery at Veheragala, demonstrating the strong link between the *sangha* and the hydraulic landscape – an issue that will be returned to later in this chapter.

While the tank and *lena* provide evidence of early occupation, the stone pillars were clearly a later development, likely dating to no earlier than the seventh century AD (Bandaranayake 1974: 25). A 4m² trench, situated over an in-situ pillar, (Fig.7.05) identified two Anuradhapura period structural phases (in addition to a twentieth century structure that burned down in 1989). The earliest structural period consisted of a large brick retaining wall, built directly onto the granite outcrop, and appears to represent the creation of a level platform or terrace. As this structural phase is then sealed by an old land surface, containing fragments of Black and Red Ware, it appears apparent that this initial phase dates to the first millennium BC – likely around the same time as the tank construction and urbanisation of Anuradhapura.

The second structural phase is of more interest here, featuring stone pillars, stone paving, a brick wall and a tiled superstructure, and dating to Bandaranayake's Architectural Phase IV (seventh to eleventh centuries AD). The end of this second phase of occupation at the site is archaeologically represented by the collapse of the tiled roof onto the adjacent land surface and brick paving. Although the upper level of this tile collapse was disturbed by bioturbation, charcoal fragments throughout the tile collapse suggest that the collapse occurred after the timber roof structure was burnt. There then appears to have been no activity at the site until the construction of a new monastic building in the twentieth century, ending several centuries of abandonment at Veheragala.

The range of artefacts and structures at the site, in combination with the sheer depth of deposits, indicate that the site was very long lived with a possible origin in the Early Historic period (c. 250 BC) and was occupied until the burning of the pillared hall and the collapse of its roof. Unfortunately, while charcoal samples were taken from the roof collapse, no radiocarbon dates are available at this time, making the dating of the site's collapse and abandonment difficult. Unfortunately, there is no way to date the collapse and abandonment of the monastery, however once again we see no indications of occupation post-tenth century – there are no Polonnaruva period artefacts, no Kandyan period structural or artistic phase, and it appears likely that the site was abandoned between the eighth and eleventh centuries AD, and with the charcoal within the tile collapse it appears to have occurred rapidly and due to fire.

Thus we can see a stark contrast between the continuous and long lived occupation at Veheragala, and almost certainly other organic monastic outcrop sites, and the ephemeral short lived rural settlement sites represented by the ceramic scatter sites. While the secular rural settlements shifted and moved around the hinterland the monasteries on their granite outcrops remained fixed points in an otherwise fluid landscape.

7.3.1: *Late monastic construction*

While the majority of the hinterland's archaeological monastic sites were apparently long lived and occupied throughout the Anuradhapura period, there is a clearly visible late wave of monastic construction within the hinterland. This can most clearly be seen in the *padhanaghara parivenas*, or "double-platforms" (Bandaranayake 1974: 102), and *pabbata viharas* (Bandaranayake 1974: 58), though the hinterland excavations (Coningham *et al.* 2013) have shown monastic construction occurring during the final centuries of the first millennium AD on a far smaller and simple scale.

This can be seen at site F517 (see Fig.7.01), initially identified as an 'undiagnostic pillared site', where excavation revealed a rectilinear single room structure (orientated E-W) with a moonstone. The building had no internal divisions, and was structured around 20 granite gneiss pillars arranged in four columns of five pillars. Of these pillars the two outside columns, and the first and last row (effectively those pillars on the edge of the plan) were thicker and larger, and it seems likely that they bore the greater part of the superstructural load. Around these 20 pillars ran a carefully constructed brick wall of which seven full courses and three foundation courses were still extant. Despite the presence of a moonstone and the discovery of several terracotta oil-lamps within the structure, no further Buddhist features were identified, though it is quite possible that any such artefacts were removed during the heavy looting of the site in the late twentieth century.

As a result of this it is difficult to assign the structure precisely to any known class of monastic buildings, but it appears that it was either a small *pasada* (Bandaranayake

1974: 251), or, more likely, a large *kuti* (*ibid.*: 278). Both of these were residential structures, but the *kuti* is both more typical of the late Anuradhapura period, and typically around the same size as F517. The architectural plan of the structure typologically dates the structure to post seventh century AD (Bandaranayake 1974: 327), but this typological date was brought forward by an OSL sample taken from the siltation of a palaeochannel beneath the foundations of the building. This returned a date to 970 AD ($\pm$ 60), indicating that the construction likely occurred after the tenth century AD, thus placing construction around the period of Anuradhapura's collapse and challenging all three collapse models.

However, there is no evidence to suggest that the site was occupied for long. A clear tile collapse lying upon the external land surface, including several roofing nails and the upper element of a stone pillar was identified, and while no dating evidence, either scientific or typological, is available to date the collapse, there is a complete absence of any Chola or Polonnaruva period ceramics, coins etc., let alone artefacts from later periods (Kandyan etc.). Coupled with the absence of any structural repairs, the absence of a deep stratigraphic sequence and absence of multiple structural phases, this suggests that the site was likely abandoned by the end of the eleventh century AD if not earlier, less than a century after the site's construction.

7.3.1.1: *Padhanaghara Parivenas*

While site F517 represents late Anuradhapura period monastic construction on a small scale, and very much in keeping with what had come before, the emergence of the *pabbata vihara* and *padhanaghara parivena* (discussed in Chapter Six, section **6.3**) is very different. The *padhanaghara parivena* has been identified at several rural sites (Fig.7.06). Unfortunately, while sites such as Tantrimale, Ritagala (Fig.7.09) and Tapovana have been well mapped, all were cleared and exposed by the ASC at the turn of the century, and consequently very little archaeological data is available for the sites (Bandaranayake 1974: 118).

However, the transect survey (Manuel *et al.* 2013) identified and excavated a previously unrecorded *padhanaghara parivena*, site C112, south of Nachchaduwa (see Fig.7.01). This monastic complex appears to be a solitary unit and conforms to Wijesuriya's Single Residential Unit Monastic Plan (1998: 57). As is typical with such sites, the monastery is located on rocky terrain within a forest, with the double-platform itself lying directly on-top of a rock outcrop (Wijesuriya 1998: 15), though less typically (*ibid.*: 74) there is no evidence of a boundary wall. The two platforms were located on an east-west axis, with the "front" platform facing west. This is somewhat unusual as it is typical for such sites to face east (Bandaranayake 1974: 119).

A stone bridge over the central moat connects the two platforms and appears to be only the element of the site that is in any way decorated or adorned – something common to the ascetic *Pamsukulikas* and *padhanaghara parivenas*. The double-platform itself appears to be fairly central within the monastic complex. To the south lay the remains (pillars and pillar bases) of at least four further small structures, one of which appears to have been a small *jantaghara* or hot-water bath. Around 25m south of the *jantaghara* a further two tentative double platforms were identified upon the western edge of the low outcrop, along with at least one further cluster of residential structures. Around 10m to the east of the primary double-platform lay the structural remains of what was tentatively identified as a refectory (based upon the structures size and position in the monastery (Wijesuriya 1998: 56)), as well as a plain urinal stone.

Unfortunately the double-platform had been looted, with a large robber-pit dug into the moat between the platforms, just below the bridge, as well as a smaller robber-pit at the base of the pillar on the southwest corner of the rear platform. An exploratory trench across the moat and western face of the rear-platform revealed a clear construction and abandonment sequence. Construction appears to have occurred in a single phase with no remodelling or repairs identified. On top of the packing deposits low brick walls and brick paving were identified, and would have formed the front-left corner of the residential structure upon the rear platform. The stonework of the two platforms display a combination of two architectural styles, with the front platform featuring rubble construction, while the rear platform displayed cleanly dressed ashlar blocks. This combination places the double-platform within Bandaranayake's transitional Phase II of the stylistic development of *padhanaghara parivenas* (Wijeysuriya 1998: 88), the same as much of Ritagala's double-platforms (*ibid.*), and tentatively places construction at C112 to the second half of the ninth century AD (*ibid.*: 36), though it could be as much as a century earlier (*ibid.*: 27).

However, of more interest here than the site's construction is its abandonment. The section through the moat fill revealed a thick tile collapse deposit (Fig.7.07) lying almost *directly* on top of the bed rock, with only an extremely shallow (approximately 2-3cm thick) siltation deposit beneath it. This strongly suggests that the moat was being cleaned on a regular basis during the occupation of the site, and that the structural collapse occurred while the site was still occupied. This is based upon field observations of the speed at which the moat silted up during excavation, with 0.10m of silt deposited in just two days. An OSL sample taken from this ephemeral siltation deposit beneath the tile collapse produced a date of 1090 AD $\pm$ 50 (Simpson et al. 2008a: 27), placing the collapse and subsequent abandonment of the monastery to the period of Anuradhapura's apparent abandonment and the brief Chola rule of Sri Lanka. It is striking to observe that the structural collapse must have occurred while the site was still occupied, as any period of abandonment would have resulted in a far greater siltation deposit below the tile-collapse. While it would be a stretch indeed to interpret this as violence or an "invasion" it would support an interpretation of either the deliberate destruction of the tiled superstructure, or a structural collapse during habitation of the site, directly leading to the site's complete abandonment. The latter was inferred from the complete absence of any repairs, squatter occupation, secondary structural phases, or Polonnaruva period artefacts. The tile collapse, at its deepest approximately 0.40m thick, was sealed by an initial brick collapse and subsequently by a thick deposit that appears to have been predominantly surface material swept into the moat by wind and rain, mixed with some material from the packing of the rear platform. This deposit was capped by a silt deposit containing large sections of ashlar masonry, representative of a slow gradual silting of the channel during which a major structural collapse occurred.

Although there are no dates available for the abandonment of Ritagala, the thick tile spreads of Ritagala's final phase suggest that abandonment of this site was also sudden, and in the absence of any identified Polonnaruva Period artefacts, likely no later than the eleventh century AD.

7.3.1.2: Pabbata Viharas

The generic lay-out (see section **4.3.1.3**) and religious significance (see section **6.3.2**) of these monasteries has already been examined. However, although the *pabbata viharas* were primarily suburban, with no examples of such sites found any real distance from Anuradhapura, the hinterland survey identified an extensive *pabbata vihara* on the southern edge of Nachchaduwa. Parthigala (or site Z00) covers some 480m east to west and 440m north to south, and features a central group of monuments including pillared halls, stupa and image houses within a sacred precinct. In this case with the stupa located to the north-east of the central cluster of buildings (Bandaranayake 1974: 68) and, as such, its date may be attributed to between the mid-eighth and twelfth centuries AD (*ibid.*: 81). Within the associated structures was a large pond featuring lime-mortared brick construction and, as with the monastic form, this dates the site to between the eighth and eleventh centuries AD (*ibid.*: 25). Unfortunately, excavations at Parthigala revealed very little, and did not provide any artefacts or evidence relating to the site's abandonment. However, geoarchaeological investigations at a tank and bund (Z021 and Z021a) associated with Parthigala provided an OSL sample from the tank fill (dating the beginning of siltation, the abandonment of the tank) produced a date of 1100AD±70 (Simpson et al. 2008a: 27). This at least suggests that this *pabbata vihara* was abandoned around the end of the eleventh century AD. Interestingly, although the *pabbata vihara* at Parthigala is clearly a very late development, recent thermoluminescence (TL) dating of the stupa's bricks provided a date of 471AD±110, suggesting that the *pabbata vihara* was built around or over an existing monastic site, and once again demonstrating the long lived nature of rural monastic sites. This imposition of a *pabbata vihara* upon an extant monastic site may indicate a late Anuradhapura period royal attempt to either consolidate or secure influence within the hinterland (Coningham et al. 2007a: 717), this will be examined in Chapter Eight.

Finally, it must be stressed that despite the abandonment of monastic sites such as C112, A155, F517 or Z00, the sacred hinterland does not completely vanish between the eleventh century and the arrival of the British. The presence of two Kandyan period *tampita viharas* (one at modern day Habarana, just over 50km southwest of Anuradhapura, and site D361, a previously unrecorded site located approximately 34km southwest of the Citadel) within the hinterland clearly indicates at least some Buddhist monastic activity post-abandonment.

7.4: New Elite

Not only does Renfrew characterise the aftermath of collapse as featuring the emergence of a new elite, but the Imperial Model posits an increase in South Indian influences in the centuries leading up to Anuradhapura's collapse. Additionally, all three collapse models invoke a Chola invasion as one of the prime movers in the collapse, but, despite the recent exhaustive hinterland survey (1339 sites and 1229 special finds) and over a century of archaeological research there is no direct archaeological evidence for a Chola presence within the hinterland, brief or otherwise.

7.4.1: South Indian Influence

Turning to the Imperial Model's late South Indian influence upon monastic sites, we might highlight the Mahayanist influences present in the development of the *pabbata vihara* as a monastic form (Prematilleke & Silva 1968: 62) as already discussed (**6.3.2**). The site of Parthigala did not contain any of the South Indian architectural forms, sculptures, or carvings seen at sites like Puliyankulama (Bell 1914b: DD; von Schroeder 1990: 605), Toluvila (Bell 104e: 4) or Vijayarama (Bell 1893: 4-10) in the Sacred City, though it must be highlighted that only a 4m² trench was excavated at the site, and also that the site has been extensively looted. Consequently Parthigala appears more representative of royalty attempting to establish greater control upon the hinterland (Coningham et al. 2007a: 717) than of an increase in South Indian influence upon the monastic sites of the hinterland.

7.4.2: After Collapse

Renfrew (1984: 369) describes the emergence of a new elite as being characteristic of the aftermath of collapse, although no such emergence was seen in either the Citadel (see section **5.4**) or Sacred City (see section **6.4**). However, within the hinterland we appear to see the emergence of cultic behaviour some time after the eleventh century. Anurdhapura Hinterland site D339 (shown in Fig.7.01) was initially identified as an undiagnostic pillared site, and thus likely monastic in nature. An interpretation supported by the subsequent discovery of a stupa and pillared hall approximately 150m to the south.

However, an explorative $4m^2$ trench, opened around an extant ashlar pillar, revealed something quite different. The pillars appear not to have been structural, and appear instead to have been re-used (likely from the nearby monastic site) for the erection of a small shrine centred upon a terracotta statue of an unidentified female figure. Surrounding the extant pillar was a shallow tile collapse deposit sealing thick votive deposits of small terracotta figurines that have been linked to agricultural fertility associated with paddy fields and water (Coningham *et al.* 2012). An OSL sample from the earliest terracotta deposit produced a date of 1060AD±80 (Simpson et al. 2008a: 27), suggesting that the emergence of this cultic behaviour post-dates the abandonment of Anuradhapura, and the abandonment of the hinterland's monastic sites.

7.5: Monumental Construction

The construction and maintenance of monumental public works requires a high level of organisation, necessitating significant economic investment in the form of both materials and labour, and requiring a high level of craft expertise. Within the hinterland this falls into two very distinct groups; monastic and hydraulic. The former has already been examined (section **7.3**) and will only be recapped briefly, with the emphasis upon the monumental, while the latter can be seen in the bunds, canals, and annicuts of the hinterland, and will be examined in greater detail.

7.5.1: Monumental monastic architecture within the hinterland

Clearly, not all monastic structures within the hinterland are monumental, and the majority of the 97 monastic and 48 undiagnostic pillared sites recorded on transect survey by the Anuradhapura Hinterland project are unremarkable in size and scale. However, the large monastic complexes seen at Ritagala, Mihintale, Dambulla, Parthigala (Z00), and Hathttikuchchi (all previously mentioned), as well as Aukana (c.45km south-southwest of the Citadel) and Tantrimale (c.28km northwest of the Citadel) all contain monumental elements; from the stupas at Mihintale and Parthigala to the monumental rock-cut standing Buddha statues at Aukana and Sasseruva.

However, the majority of these sites saw their monumental construction occurring significantly before the period of interest here, and only Ritagala, Parthigala and Hathttikuchchi represent late Anuradhapura period monumental construction. Tantrimale contains a ninth century *padhanaghara parivena*, but this is an isolated element and merely demonstrates the long-lived nature of monastic sites. Ritagala, Hathttikuchchi and Parthigala were discussed earlier, and little more can be added other than to emphasise that they represent significant investments of resources during the eighth to ninth centuries, though none display any indications of construction or repairs post tenth century AD.

7.5.2: The Hydraulic Landscape

The hydraulic infrastructure of the hinterland represents a colossal and sustained investment, one that was vital to the enablement and preservation of the city, economy and population of Anuradhapura. Although the hydraulic landscape was effectively already in place long before the final centuries of the Anuradhapura period, the ownership, administration and maintenance of this landscape is still of critical importance to understanding Anuradhapura's collapse.

As established in Chapter Two (section **2.2.3**) a combination of high run-off, high evapotranspiration and limited "wet" seasons create an environment in which the effective planned management of water is vital for the maintenance of any sedentary communities in the northern Dry Zone (Farmer 1954: 23; Jayatilaka et al. 2001: v). The hydraulic landscape of northern Sri Lanka (and indeed south-eastern India) was thus a response to the high level of monsoon variability at low frequencies, and is effectively a method of; "*correcting the spatio-temporal heterogeneity and low predictability of rainfall by harnessing rainwater through a dense... and widely distributed net of interconnected reservoirs*" (Gunnell et al. 2007: 210). This system depended upon a mixture of both the numerous small runoff tanks within the valleys of the undulating landscape (Farmer 1954: 23-25; Jayatilaka et al. 2001: 3) and canals with a bund on the lower side only, thus trapping rainfall run-off from the higher ground and diverting it into tanks (Karunananda 2006: 264), as well as a number of larger tanks that function as "*drought hazard mitigation structures*" and "*flash flood moderators*". These are fed by diverting the streams and rivers that carry this rainfall from the hill-country to the south of the North Central Province to the sea in the north-west, through the construction of weirs, or *anicuts*, to divert the water into major systems of canals that then feed water into major tank cascade systems (Farmer 1954: 23). Effectively the larger tanks are built and calibrated to accommodate large storm floods. Indeed the system depends upon extreme rainfall events (rather than a steady median) to perform successfully and efficiently in the longer term

(Gunnell et al. 2007: 210). Thus, the hydraulic landscape was designed to provide both a minimum level of agricultural sustainability during drier years (with the small tanks providing sufficient water for a single crop), and a capacity for the generation of huge surplus during the wetter years through the collection and storage of rainfall surplus in the large tanks.

This system of small scale tanks will be examined first, although not as large as the monumental royal tanks, they still represent public works that required cooperation and organisation on a significant scale to build and maintain.

7.5.2.1: *Small Tanks*

The "one village – one tank" (Leach 1959: 08) system of small, rainfall or cascade fed, tanks which can be seen today across the North Central Province, and is indeed concentrated around Anuradhapura and its hinterland (Seneviratna 1989: 73) was also identified by the British administration of the province in the nineteenth century. The diary of an unnamed government agent in 1874 records that within the Anuradhapura district there existed a total of 1086 operational tanks associated with inhabited villages, in addition to a further 1427 abandoned tanks in uninhabited areas (Karunananda 2006: 246). Even today there remains an estimated 1170 abandoned small (less than 80ha) tanks within the Anuradhapura District, in addition to 1870 functional small tanks (Panabokke 1999). Archaeologically, the Hinterland survey identified 255 tanks on transects which, as mentioned earlier, covered approximately 2.44% of the survey universe (the semi-circular 3928.5 km2). Working on a purely mathematical basis, this would produce a figure of 20,902 within the 50km radius survey universe. Clearly this is an extremely inflated figure as tanks are undoubtedly the largest and most visible of all site types, and the real figure almost certainly lies far closer to the 2513 tanks identified by the British administration in 1874, but the transect survey results do suggest at least that the true number of Anuradhapura period small tanks may have been significantly underestimated.

These small tanks are typically constructed by building an earthwork (the bund) transversely across the line of a natural stream and damming up the seasonal water flow from rainfall and run-off behind this bund. Due to the relatively flat nature of the landscape these bunds are typically built long rather than high, and create a large but shallow tank behind them (Leach 1959: 8). Typically several small tanks would be built within the same drainage area/watershed, within a three to four mile radius from one another, all fed by the same drainage system forming a cascade system that sees the tank situated at the top of the drainage system filled first during the rainy season, the water would then flow through the spill to the next tank, filling each subsequent tank in turn (Jayatilaka et al. 2001: 3). For example the Thirapane tank cascade system (Fig.7.08), displaying a cascade system of six tanks within the larger Nachchaduwa watershed (*ibid.*).

In addition to cascade systems there also exists simple, solitary, rain-fed tanks that do not form part of a cascade and are not linked into a larger hydraulic network, these are effectively the crudest forms of water management and storage within the North Central Province and are not indicative of large scale cooperation or administration in the way that the construction and maintenance of cascade systems are.

Although when the British arrived in the North Central Province the overwhelming majority of small tanks were owned by their respective villages (Karunananda 2006: 246), it seems clear from epigraphic and proto-historical records that during the Anuradhapura period these small irrigation works were owned either by private individuals or by the *sangha* (Paranavitana 1958: 01; Seneviratna 1989: 33), with the majority of village tanks constructed, maintained and owned by individuals who were designated as *Vavihamika* (or Lord of the Lake), and belonged to the noble class called *Parumakas* (*ibid.*).

However, from as early as the first and second centuries BC there are epigraphic records of tanks and channels that, while owned privately by the *Parumakas*, the income from which was donated to the *sangha* (*ibid.*: 32). This involvement in irrigation management and ownership by the *sangha* appears to have started gradually but accelerated rapidly, including the direct donation of tanks or canals to monasteries (*ibid.*: 105 & 108). This appears to have been a somewhat contentious issue, with Paranavitana writing that; "*The acceptance of such gifts of lands by a bhikkus... was not strictly in keeping with the spirit of the Buddhist religion, and various devices were adopted to reconcile this enjoyment of a share of the produce of land with the Vinaya rules expressly prohibiting the practice...*" (Paranavitana 1958: 02).

This practice of making donative grants to monasteries appears to have continued throughout the Anuradhapura period and, judging by epigraphic records (Dias 1990: 151) had increased dramatically during the final two-three centuries of the millennium so that by the end of the tenth century AD the *sangha* appear to be hugely influential in the ownership, administration and management of the tank system (Gunawardana 1979: 58).

Small tank administration: The administration of any irrigated landscape requires its society to perform several tasks peculiar to irrigation. Most obviously it must be constructed and maintained (Hunt & Hunt 1976: 390). Although Leach argued that the construction and maintenance of small tanks was carried out by the villagers, and no large scale administrative action was necessary for the system to function (Leach 1959: 8). Ethnographic observations during the recent Anuradhaura

Hinterland project have shown that villagers work together to de-silt the village tank, and to clear vegetation, repair, and strengthen the bund. However, these were purely field observations, and there was no assessment of the quality or efficaciousness of these repairs. Early British observations also showed that villagers would either make basic repairs to their own tanks, or hire in tank menders ("*Kulankattis*") from Jaffna (Karunananda 2006: 246). However, these repairs appear to have been of poor quality and unmethodical; "*the bunds were not properly sloped, the earth was not rammed and the sluices were repaired by unskilled masons. The inevitable result was that at the occurrence of the first heavy rains, these bunds were subjected to destruction*" (*ibid.*). Thus not only were the most important rains of the year, i.e. the heaviest, lost, but the tank was severely damaged at a great cost. For example the Rampathawila tank, repaired at a cost of £400 in 1870, was destroyed by the first floods (*ibid.*). Furthermore, when the British arrived in the North Central Province there was not a single functioning sluiced tank (*ibid.*: 287), with villagers simply breaching the bund to allow water flow. This clearly indicates that without a reasonable level of skilled labour and/or supervision even the maintenance of small scale tanks is difficult, resulting in the ineffective collection and storage of water, and thus resulting in a greatly limited agricultural productivity and increased risk of malarial vectors. Indeed Brodie, the first British government agent to tour Anuradhapura district, identified the neglect of irrigation works as the main hindrance to the development of agriculture in the area, describing the repairs and maintenance carried out by villages as; "*...a crude patching up of the tanks to serve their bare needs*" (*ibid.*: 248).

The necessity for centralised administration of even small scale irrigation works is further supported by the comprehensive legislatures implemented both by the British in the nineteenth century, and during the Anuradhapura period. The *Samantapasadika*, a collection of Pali commentaries on the Vinayas dated to the fifth century AD, details at length the manners in which an individual could be classed as "stealing" water from the irrigation system, and the penalties for each specific crime; from deliberately diverting water, to allowing cattle to weaken the bund through trampling and resulting in seepage or a breach (cited in Seneviratna 1989: 121). The passage below, cited by Paranavitana (1958: 03), demonstrates the exhaustive nature of these regulations:

"*With regard to the matter of breaching the dams (of reservoirs), he who has breached a dam with trees growing thereon has committed a* dukkata *offence, as it is a stratagem for theft, and the offence is committed at each blow. One who breaches the dam by taking his stand inside the reservoir and working outwards, completes his offence when the outer extremity is reached. When cutting inwards from outside, the act is completed when the inner extremity is reached. When breaching from inside as well as outside, leaving the middle, the act has been committed when the middle is reached. If any person, after having weakened the dam (of a reservoir) drives cattle over it, or causes village boys to drive cattle over it, and the cattle thus driven come and cause the dam to be breached with their hoofs, it has to be held that the breach of the dam had been caused by that person himself. If any person, after having weakened the dam (of a reservoir) drives cattle into the reservoir, or causes village children to drive cattle (into it), and the dam gets breached by the waves raised by such cattle, or (if a person) asks the village boys to sport in the water, or frightens boys who are sporting in the water, and the dam gets breached by the waves raised by them; or fells or cause someone else to fell down a tree growing in the water inside the reservoir, and the waves raised thereby breach the dam, the dam has been breached by that person himself.*"

These regulations were mirrored by the nineteenth century publications of the Ceylon Department of Irrigation (1892 & 1894), laying out duties of anyone in charge of irrigation works. There were literally hundreds of matters that needed careful attention and regulation, from the clearing of sluices to the prevention of cattle wandering onto the bund, how to proceed in the event of both floods and droughts, where bathing and fishing are allowed and prohibited, guidance on construction of, and repairs and damages to the irrigation system. Again this clearly indicates how important the irrigation system was, and how tightly it was controlled, with every single offence change and alteration to the system carefully monitored and controlled at a centralised level.

Small tank abandonment: While there are epigraphic records and mentions in the Pali chronicles of major tank construction or repair, small tanks rarely got such attention, and (unsurprisingly) the abandonment of tanks was never recorded. However, recent Anuradhapura Hinterland geoarchaeological investigations (Gilliland et al. 2013) have identified twelfth and thirteenth century abandonment of hydraulic sites within Anuradhapura's hinterland, suggesting that the abandonment of the rural landscape occurred within a century of the central collapse.

All three sites, two small tanks and a channel, were located around Nachchaduwa, and were initially identified during the transect survey. Site C009, a small abandoned bund and tank (shown in Fig.7.01), was not associated with any other site, suggesting that the tank was originally associated with a small settlement. Here OSL samples from the lower bund and lower tank fill yielded dates of 340AD+60 and 1200AD+60 respectively. Simpson et al. (2008a: 31) interpret these dates as indicative of bund construction in the fourth century, consistent with the Pali chronicles dating of the initiation of the major Nachchaduwa bund by Mahasena (r. 277-304 AD), and abandonment around the end of the twelfth century. Prior to 1200AD+60 the tank appears to have been regularly de-silted, and the siltation of the tank from this point clearly represents the abandonment of the tank and any associated settlement. This twelfth century abandonment date is supported by OSL dates from site C018, a buried channel associated with a metalworking site (Fig.7.01). A sample taken from a layer at the base of the channel produced an OSL date of 1120AD+40, interpreted as representing the beginning of a steady siltation without cleaning (either manual or scouring through use) from the first half of the twelfth century AD onwards (*ibid.*).

While C009 and C018 were interpreted as being associated with secular sites, site Z021 is a larger tank and bund system associated with the *pabbata vihara* Parthigala (Z00), as shown in Fig.7.01. Here, although the date of the original tank construction is unknown, OSL samples suggest the tank was developed (with a secondary bund) around 590AD±60, shortly after the massive fourth century construction of Nachchaduwa and around the same period as the initial monastic construction at Parthigala (the stupa dated to 471AD±110), though several centuries before the *pabbata vihara's* construction (Simpson et al. 2008a: 31). Of greater significance is the date of tank siltation, taken from an OSL sample from the lowest level of tank fill, dating the beginning of siltation (and thus abandonment) to 1100 AD ±70. This date is around a century earlier than those of C009 or C018, which may relate to the connection with a monastic site rather than a secular site, this will be discussed in Chapter Eight.

7.5.2.2: Large tanks

The urban tanks of Nuvaraveva, Tissaveva and Basavakkulam were examined in Chapter Six (section **6.2.3**), consequently it is the hinterland's major tanks that are examined here, though they directly impact upon urban Anuradhapura. Although the small village tanks were capable of supporting a rural population, they were heavily dependent upon local rainfall which, as established earlier, was unreliable and often insufficient (Karunananda 2006: 264). To support a larger population, and provide economic and agricultural stability, larger tanks and canals were needed to store and distribute water across a large area of the hinterland. By the middle of the twentieth century, of the 850,000 acres under rice cultivation across Sri Lanka, 530,000 were dependent upon irrigation (Mills 1943: 173), 160,000 acres of which were dependent upon the restoration of major irrigation works, and 370,000 were dependent upon small scale village tanks (*ibid.*).

This reliance would have been far greater within the northern Dry Zone, where not only were the small scale tanks vital in of themselves, but they were in turn reliant upon the major irrigation works that provided security and support to the smaller tanks. The first major restoration project in the Anuradhapura district was the Kalaveva tank project, completed in 1887 (Karunananda 2006: 280), and a government report upon at the time stated that; "*the repair of Kalaveva with its Yoda-ela of 53 miles was of paramount importance as a feeder to village and other large tanks in and about Anuradhapura*" (cited in Karunananda 2006: 281). Not only did the Yoda-ela (ancient canal) carry water from the Kalaveva to Anuradhapura, but it also collected the drainage between Elagamuwa and the Malvatu Oya along its course, which otherwise was lost (*ibid.: 263*), and allowed a considerable area between Anuradhapura and the Kalaveva tank to utilise this water for irrigation (*ibid.*). This is supported by papers laid before the Legislative Council of Ceylon in 1891, which stated that: "*Before restoration of Kalaveva and its canal the taxation lists show that few, if any, of the villages obtained a yala harvest... I find that for the yala harvests alone they have reaped crops amounting to a total of 98,000 bushels of paddy since the restoration of the tank*" (Christie 1891: 38).

However, the importance of the Kalaveva and Yoda-ela was not restricted to the rural areas it supplied directly or passed through. At the time of its restoration, the work's main objective was to provide a sufficient water supply to two of Anuradhapura's primary tanks, Basavakkulam and Tissaveva, after both had been found incapable of supplying even the minimum required for Anuradhapura (Karunananda 2006: 263). Writing in 1891 Christie echoed this, stating; "*...the very existence of the town and settlement of Anuradhapura depends on Kalaveva. Unless the town tanks were filled from it, the lands now cleared and cultivated would relapse back into jungle, and the population would probably fall to what it was in 1871 (=702 persons), the cultivation under the town tanks being 12 acres!*" (*ibid.*).

Administration of Large Tanks: The construction and maintenance of such monumental tanks and canals clearly required greater administration. While it is arguable that small tanks were built and maintained at a local level (Leach 1959: 8), there can be no doubt that the larger tanks required a centralised authority to organise their planning, construction and maintenance. This is seen in the royal construction of all of the monumental tanks (Brohier 1934; Seneviratna 1989), clearly significant command of power and resources was needed to construct such monumental feats of engineering. Indeed, even with the resources available to the British governance of Sri Lanka in the nineteenth century the first attempt to repair the Nachchaduwa tank, in 1891 had to be abandoned (Karunananda 2006: 263), and was not successfully completed until fifteen years later in 1906 (Samad & Vermillion 1999: 28). Similarly, although the critical restoration of Kalaveva and its Yoda-ela was first initiated in 1876, the restoration was not completed until 1887 (Karunananda 2006: 280).

Another indication of the high level of expertise involved in the construction of the major Anuradhapura period irrigation works comes, again, from the nineteenth century British restoration. During the restoration of the larger irrigation works they frequently found that the ancient canals, sluices and bunds were placed perfectly and simply needed repair. Unlike the unreliable small rainfed tanks, the Kalaveva was guaranteed a reliable supply of water due its watershed of the Mirisgoni Oya and Dambulla Oya flowing down from the Matale Hills (Karunananda 2006: 265). Indeed, the only thing needed to render Kalaveva practically inexhaustible was "*a perennial river be linked... This link is found in an ancient connection with the Amban-ganga*" (Christie 1891: 39). This report of the ancient canal, whose levels were judged to be perfect, is representative in general of the British repairs to the ancient irrigation system and it is clear that it was often more expensive for the British to repair an ancient channel than build a new one. However, the ancient system was constructed and located ideally for the landscape, climate and agricultural system, resulting in channels, tanks and canals being surveyed, and then restored rather than constructing new irrigation works (Ceylon 1892: 27-110). Indeed, Farmer remarked in 1954 that "*It is incredible how often when one clears the jungle and tries to make a channel, or to prepare a bund, one finds one there already*" (Farmer et al. 1954: 32). In addition to the accuracy and precision of the hydraulic framework, there is also the question of the scale and scope of the system. By the tenth century AD there was a total of 506 miles of artificial canals diverting water from the principal rivers of the North Central Province as follows:

Table.7.05: Yoda-elas of the North Central Province (after Seneviratna 1989: 92)

River	Length of Canals
Mahaveli Ganga	132 Miles
Amban Ganga	197 Miles
Kala Oya, Modaragam Aru & other rivers	177 Miles
Total	506 Miles

The complexity and scale of this system (Fig.6.02) to it being listed by the International Council of Monuments and Sites (ICOMOS) as worthy of consideration for World Heritage status (Hughes 1996). This is intriguing as the ICOMOS list was; "*mainly concerned with waterways whose primary aim was navigation*" (*ibid.*: 01), something the panel deemed highly probable within the Sri Lankan system, albeit as a secondary function

(*ibid.*: 73). This is in addition to the sheer size of the largest tanks of the period; the bund at Kalaveva is nearly 25m at its highest point, over 60m in width at its base, and almost 5km in length (Brohier 1934: 06). Indeed, when the British restored the Yoda-ela between Kalaveva and Anuradhapura they encountered severe labour problems, and were forced to resort to hiring labourers from Jaffna to complete the work (Karunananda 2006: 278). The importance of labour during the Anuradhapura period can be seen in the *Mahavamsa*'s declaration that; "*the warrior, Labhiyavasabha, achieved a great reputation by his ability to move more earth when tank-building than, it is said, ten or twelve men*" (*Mvs*.xxiii.90-95).

State level control of hydraulic maintenance can also be seen in the *sannas* granted to the *sangha*. Many of these donative grants exempted villagers living within gifted lands from *vari* or forced labour (Dias 1990: 154-55), in one example this been translated as; "*labourers shall not be impressed for river-work*" (Wickremasinghe 1928: 8) which suggests the state could forcibly demand labour from the general populace to maintain the tanks and canals of the hydraulic landscape. Indeed, after the nineteenth century restoration of the Yoda-ela there were protests from villages charged with maintaining the canal (repairing minor breaches to the bund, keeping the channel clear and removing vegetation) who felt that "*Rajakariya*" (feudal service to a lord or king) was being extracted from them and that they were thus being oppressed (*ibid.*: 279).

Large tank abandonment: The majority of the major tanks were constructed centuries before the period being examined here, and by the seventh century AD the hydraulic landscape was, to all intents and purposes, complete (Seneviratna 1989: 46). Unfortunately, however, no archaeological dates are available for the failure of the major tanks; for the siltation of canals, the breaching of bunds and the siltation of the tanks themselves. All that is available are references in the Pali chronicles to repairs to the system during the reigns of Mahinda II (r. 777-797 AD) and Sena II (r. 853-887 AD), and, during the reign of Kassapa V (r. 914-923 AD) and Mahinda IV (r. 956-972 AD), references to famine and crop failures that Seneviratna attributes to a "*major breakdown of the irrigation system*" (1989: 55). However, these chronicle descriptions are of course the *very* sources that we are attempting to test here, and while they will be discussed in Chapter Eight, such an inference cannot be considered here as archaeological evidence.

Finally, there are anecdotal references to four large breaches identified in the ancient bund of Nachchaduwa during its 1906 reconstruction, leading to suggestions that this damage might be a result of either catastrophic flooding, or of deliberate damage due to invasion and occupation (Brohier 1965; Shaw & Sutcliffe 2003). Unfortunately, no further details of these breaches is recorded anywhere, making any analysis impossible.

7.6: Trade and Manufacturing

Artefactual analysis of trade and manufacturing within the hinterland is extremely difficult, due to the reliance upon survey data and the lack of well published excavations – both of which make diachronic constraining very difficult. However, even with these disclaimers the lack of luxury goods and items of long distance trade is striking.

7.6.1: Long Distance Trade

Not a single sherd of imported glazed wares were recovered during five seasons of transect survey and excavation in the recent Anuradhapura Hinterland survey. While such trade would be expected to centre upon the urban core of Anuradhapura, the complete absence in the hinterland is still surprising – especially given the large number of monastic sites, and the presence of large monastic complexes such as Parthigala, within the hinterland. Furthermore, this absence is despite non-probabilistic survey along potential trade-routes to the city; the Malvatu-Oya, ancient canals, and excavation at a major riverside ceramic scatter (B062), in an attempt to identify trade routes and break of bulk points. However, the absence of imported glazed wares (diachronically a late development) is not an indication that the hinterland did not receive luxury goods, and a small number of fineware sherds *were* recovered during transect survey and excavation. These finewares are all early in date, and of no relevance to the examination of the hinterland's terminal period beyond indicating that luxury goods were found within the hinterland.

One late traded item, a carnelian barrel bead, was recovered from monastic site F517 (discussed in section **7.3.2**), dating from around the tenth century AD. Carnelian is not found in Sri Lanka and would almost certainly have been imported from either India (Coningham et al. 2006: 379) or Thailand (Theunissen et al. 2000: 94). However, while the raw material was imported, it is also likely that the bead shaping occurred locally (Coningham et al. 2006: 380), though there with no debitage found at F517 there is no suggestion that the site was associated with bead production. One garnet bead was also identified, from a surface collection at site D613 (an undiagnostic pillared site), but while garnet was imported from India it was also sourced locally within Sri Lanka, and there are no dates associated with the bead or site D613.

7.6.2: Craft Specialisation

As with trade artefacts, an absence of dates and published excavations make the analysis of craft specialisation and production in the hinterland extremely difficult. Thus, while it is clear from the Anuradhdapura Hinterland survey results that metalworking occurred at sites throughout the hinterland, and from ethnographic observations that brick manufacturing would likely have been extremely local to construction occurring, there is neither quantitative data for such production, nor any way to diachronically constrain such data. It is possible to highlight the difference in construction quality between late Anuradhapura period sites, such as Parthigala or F517, and the cultic shrine D339 which appears to have relied upon reused granite pillars from a nearby monastic site. Similarly, the failure to maintain the hydraulic landscape post-eleventh century might indicate the loss of the necessary skills and expertise, though it might just as well be a direct result of the abandonment of the hinterland.

7.7: Conclusion

Chapter Seven has described the form of Anuradhapura's hinterland, and summarised the archaeological data relating to the centuries leading up to, and immediately succeeding, the eleventh century collapse of urban Anuradhapura. Clearly a number of problems were encountered when it came to diachronically constraining sites and artefacts, especially in regards to the rural secular population, trade and manufacturing. However, from the data available it is possible to identify what appears to be a relatively clear point of abandonment of the hinterland, starting with monastic sites around the eleventh century AD and ending with the siltation of the hydraulic landscape around a century later. This is visible in the tile collapses indicating sudden abandonment at monastic sites such as C112 and Ritagala, the siltation and abandonment of the hydraulic landscape, and the near complete absence of Polonnaruva period artefacts or architectural forms. Despite this sudden abandonment, which superficially at least fits with the established Chola invasion model, there remains no direct archaeological evidence for a Chola presence within the hinterland. This can be summarised as show in table 7.06 below.

The archaeological data at the core of this volume has now been presented, along with the archaeological signatures for the terminal periods of the Citadel (Chapter Five), Sacred City (Chapter Six) and hinterland (Chapter Seven). The next chapter will now establish whether Anuradhapura's terminal period represents a true "collapse", and will discuss the archaeological agreement of each of the three collapse models.

Table 7.06: The Hinterland's Archaeological Signature

Century AD	9th	10th	11th	12th	13th
Population	↓	↓	↙	←	←
Monumental Construction	→	→	✠	✠	✠
Traditional Elite	→	→	✠	✠	✠
New Elite	✠	✠	←	✠	✠
Long Distance Trade	✠	✠	✠	✠	✠
Craft Specialisation	↓	↓	←	←	✠

KEY: ↑ High ↓ Low ↗ Rising ↘ Falling → Steady ✠ Absent

CHAPTER 7: THE HINTERLAND

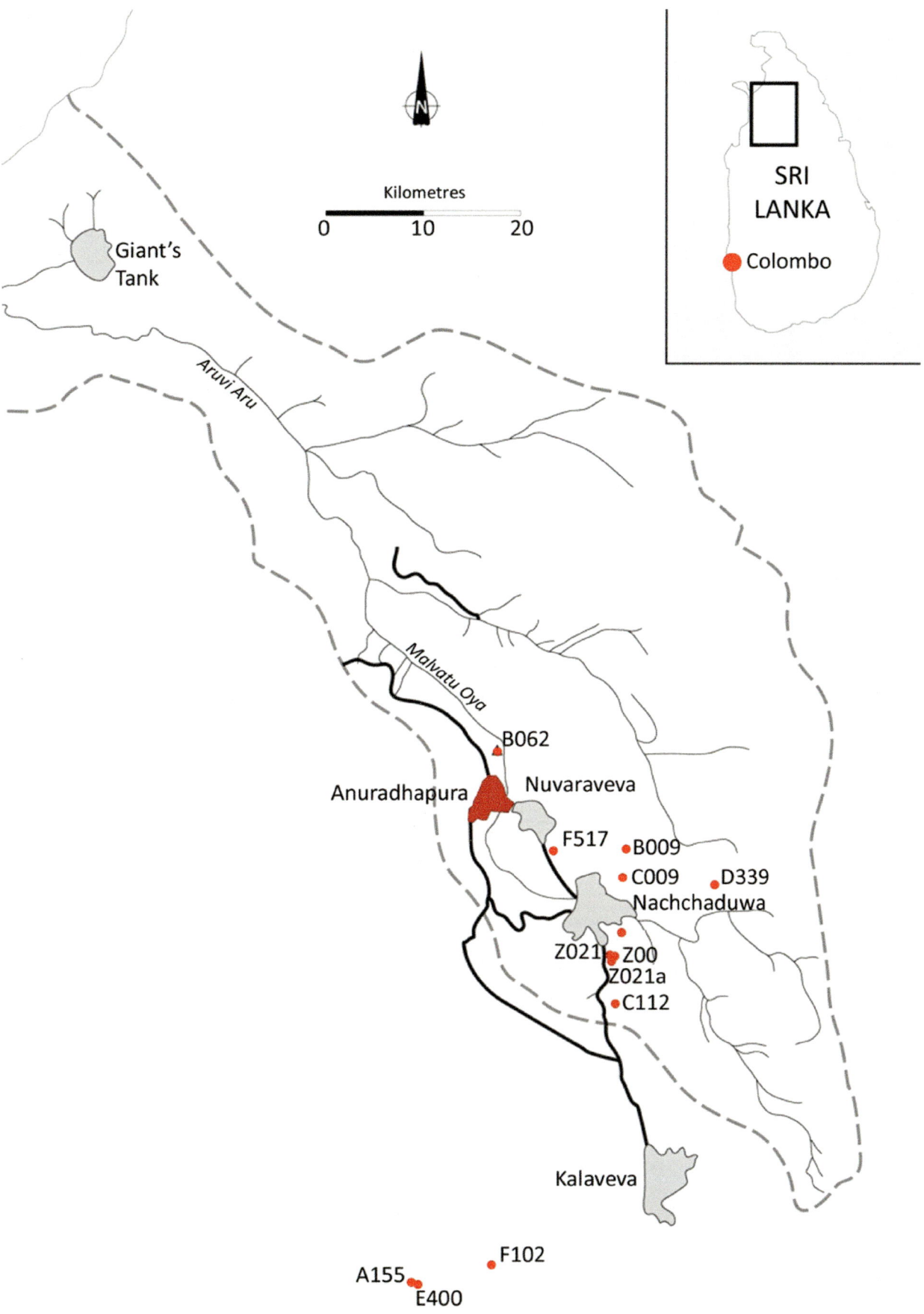

FIGURE 7.01: MAP OF HINTERLAND SITES DISCUSSED IN CHAPTER 7
(IMAGE BY AUTHOR)

Figure 7.02: Site B009 showing postholes of single structural phase (image by Anuradhapura Hinterland project)

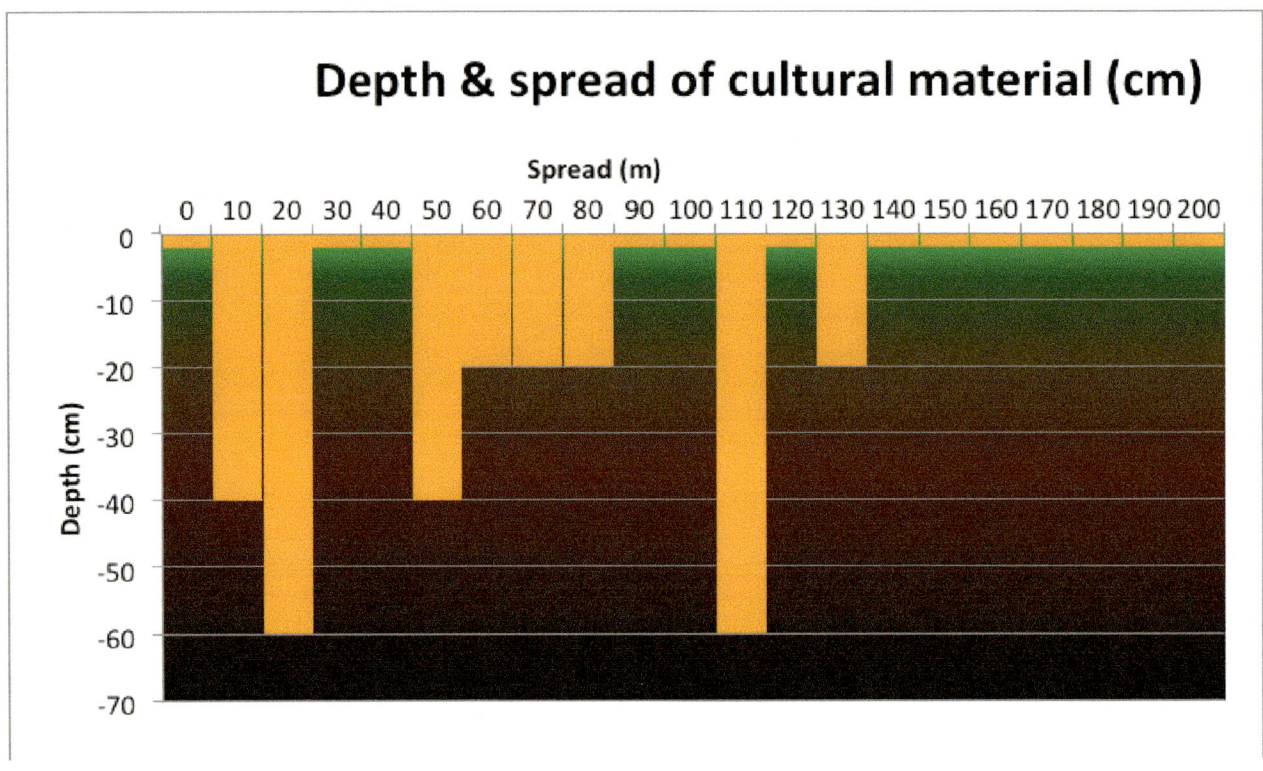

Figure 7.03: Depth of cultural material at F102

CHAPTER 7: THE HINTERLAND

Figure 7.04: SF1647 Polonnaruva style appliqué ware
(image from Anuradhapura Hinterland project)

FIGURE 7.05: TRENCH AT A155 (VEHERAGALA) SHOWING STRUCTURAL SEQUENCE
(IMAGE FROM ANURADHAPURA HINTERLAND PROJECT)

CHAPTER 7: THE HINTERLAND

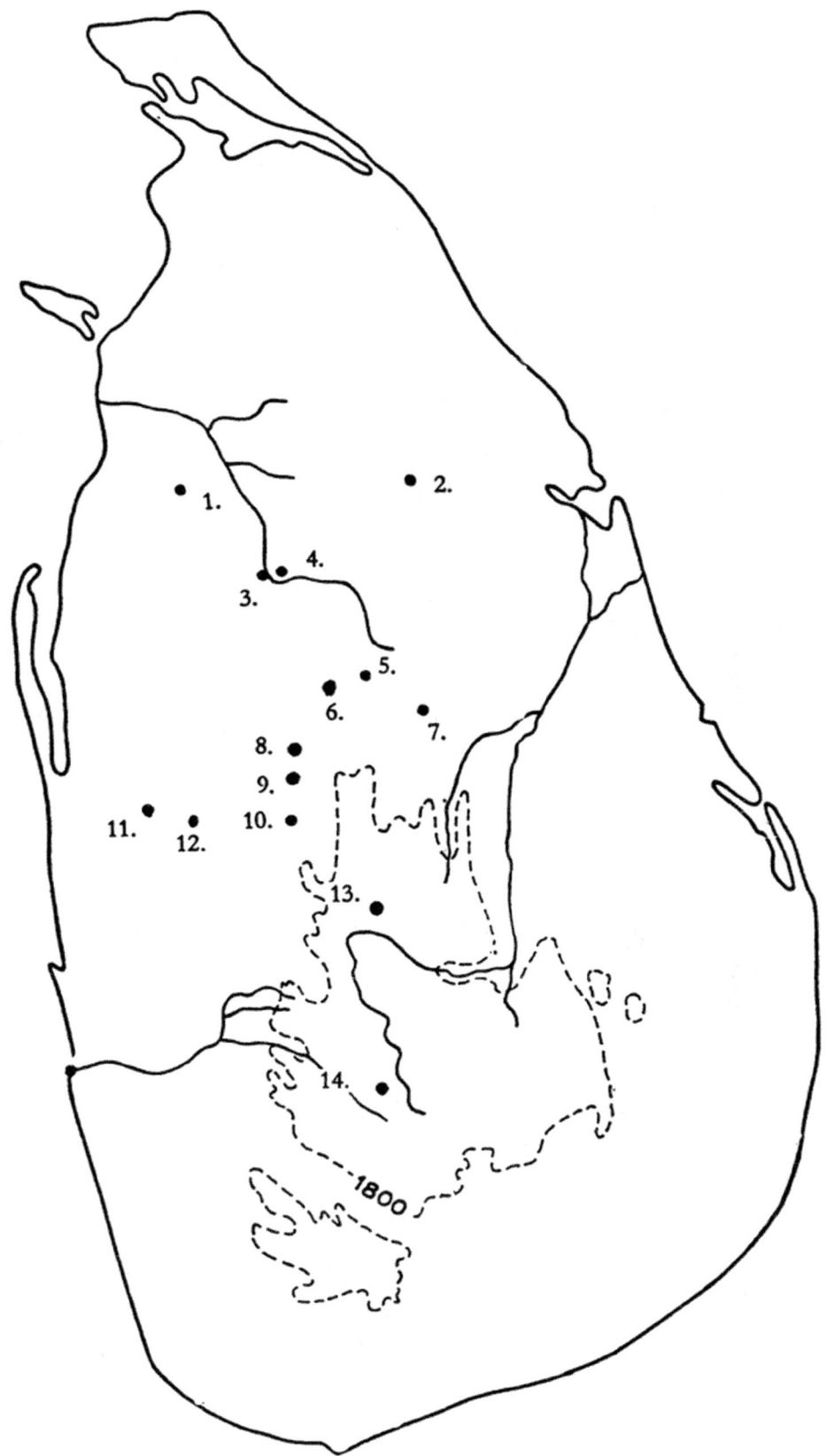

FIGURE 7.06: MAP OF PADHANAGHARA PARIVEṆA SITES
(AFTER WIJESURIYA 1998: 171)

A Time of Change: The "Collapse" of Anuradhapura, Sri Lanka

Figure 7.07: Section showing tile collapse in moat of C112
(image from Anuradhapura Hinterland project)

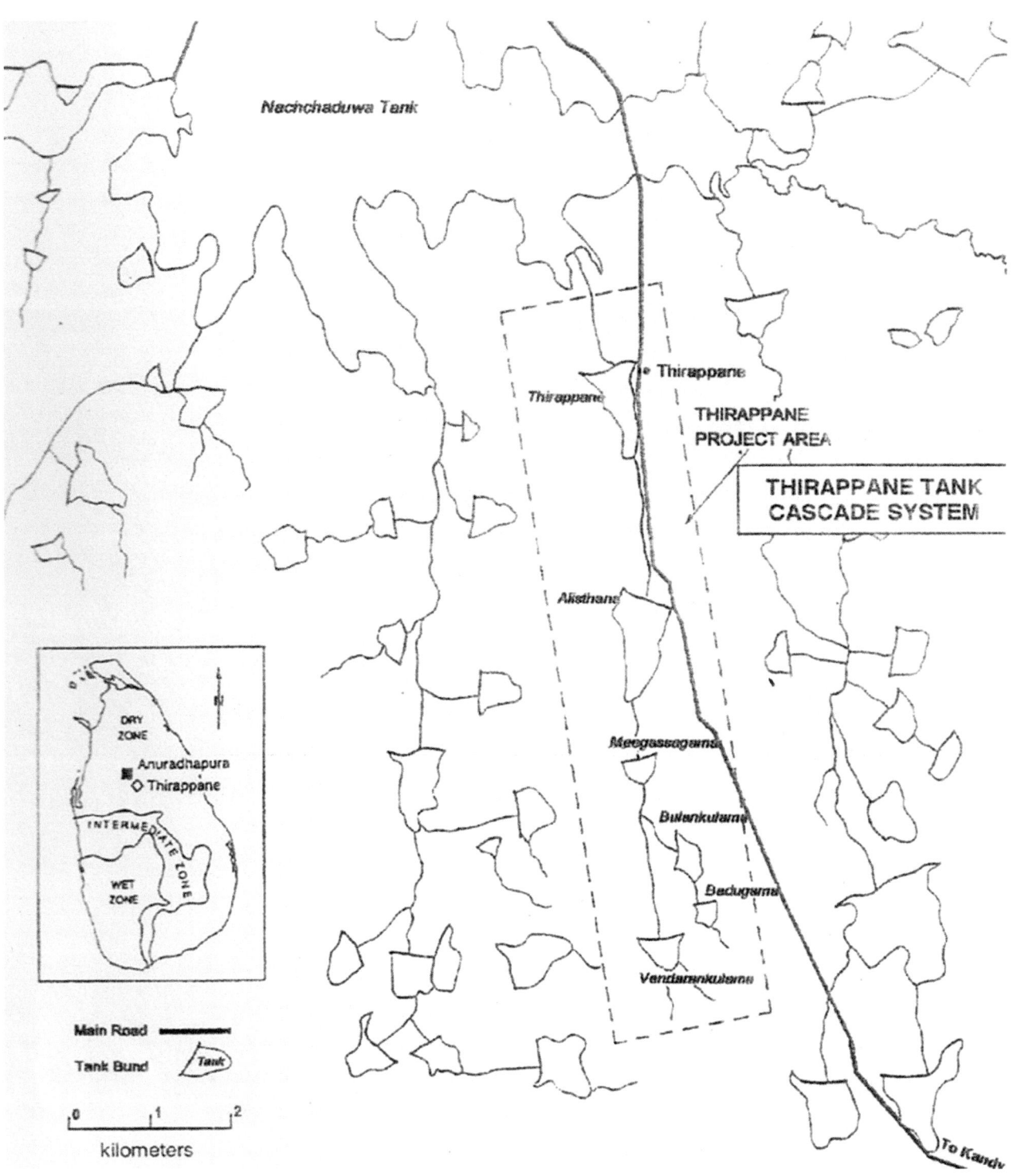

FIGURE 7.08: THIRAPPANE CASCADE SYSTEM
(AFTER JAYATILAKA ET AL. 2001: 02)

A Time of Change: The "Collapse" of Anuradhapura, Sri Lanka

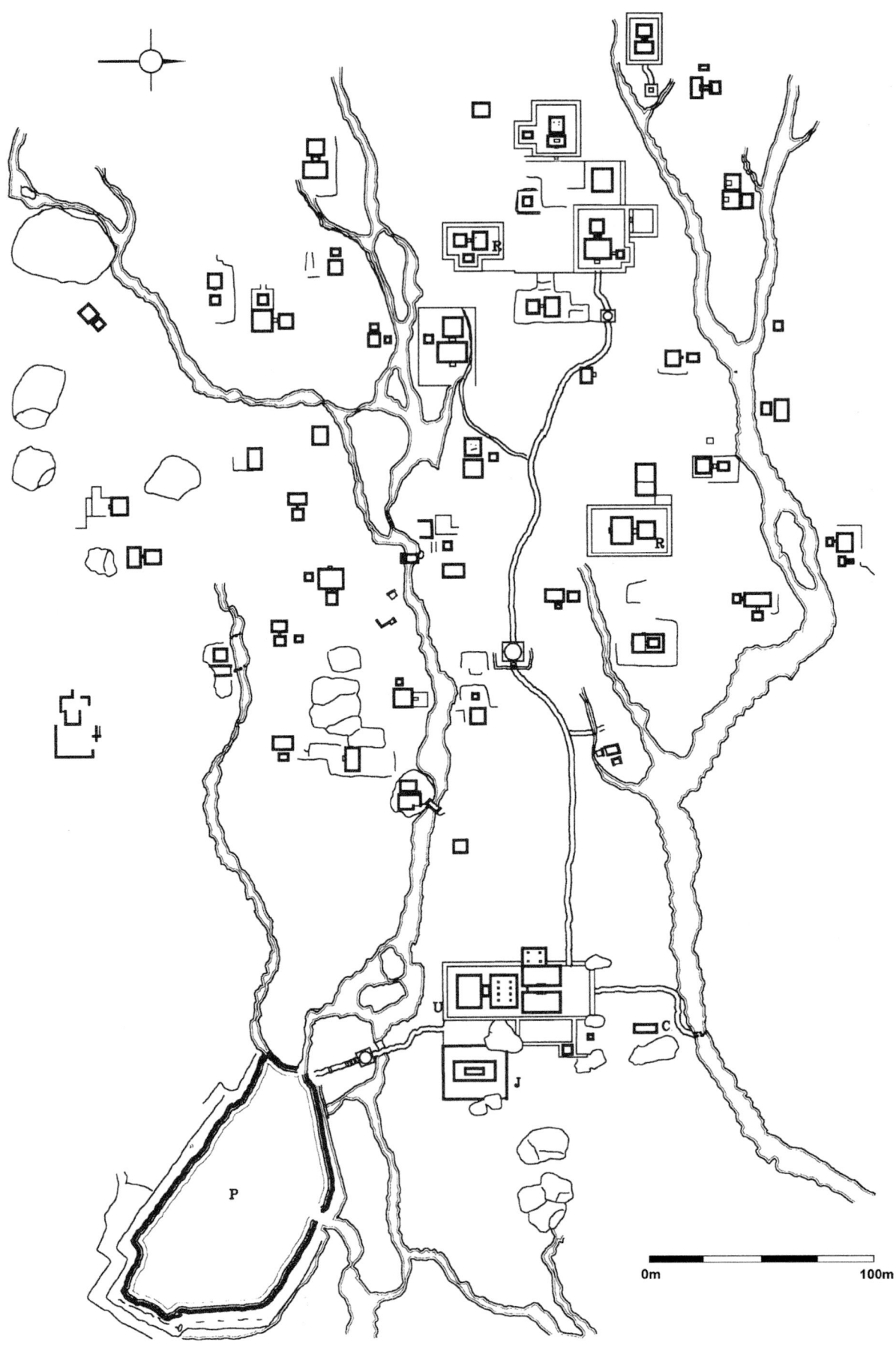

FIGURE 7.09: SITE PLAN OF RITAGALA
(AFTER WIJESURIYA 1998: 192)

Chapter 8: The Discussion

8.1: Introduction

This chapter will now assess how the archaeological data from each of Anuradhapura's zones fits with the predicted archaeological signatures developed in Chapter Four (section **4.6**). After comparing the predicted archaeological signatures for the three existing models with the actual archaeological signatures of the three Anuradhapura zones the archaeological data will be placed into a national context, integrating the archaeological data from Anuradhapura with archaeological data from sites such as Mantai, Polonnaruva, and Tissamaharama, as well as epigraphic evidence. The focus will then shift to the wider Indian Ocean milieu, considering contemporaneous developments within the Indian subcontinent and in Southeast Asian polities, in an attempt to better understand the eleventh century developments at Anuradhapura.

However, before moving on to examining the individual models the first question is whether or not we actually see Anuradhapura "collapse"? Or do we in fact see a decline, or even a transition?

8.2 Does Anuradhapura Collapse?

Revisiting Renfrew's characterisation of Systems Collapse (discussed in section **3.2.1**), we can compare his generic predictions (Renfrew 1984: 367-370) with the archaeological data. Characteristics that were never true of Anuradhapura (for example "2.a: cessation of rich traditional burials") have been omitted.

During Collapse

1) *Collapse of central administrative organisation of the early state* (Renfrew 1984: 367-368):

   a. *Disappearance or reduction in number of levels of central place hierarchy.*
   b. *Complete fragmentation or disappearance of military organisation into small, independent units.*
   c. *Abandonment of palaces and central storage facilities*
   d. *Eclipse of temples as major religious centres (often with their survival, modified, as local shrines).*
   e. *Effective loss of literacy for secular and religious purposes*
   f. *Abandonment of public building works.*

The central administrative organisation of Anuradhapura has been archaeologically shown to break down around the tenth or eleventh century AD; the palaces and monasteries of the Citadel and Sacred City have been predominantly shown to have been abandoned around the eleventh century AD (points 1.C and 1.D), with the monastic sites of the hinterland show contemporary abandonment (point 1.D). The disappearance of the central place hierarchy is more complex issue because, as demonstrated by Coningham et al. (2007a) there is no archaeological evidence for a true central place hierarchy within the Anuradhapura hinterland. However, what hierarchy was archaeologically visible is clearly lost - the hinterland monastic sites that appear to be abandoned around the eleventh century AD (e.g. Anuradhapura Hinterland project sites C112, F517, A155 and even the *pabbata vihara* of Z00) have been argued to represent the second order sites within the hinterland, (Coningham et al. 2007a: 717). These sites represented the administrative infrastructure of the Anuradhapura Kingdom, forming a *"network of long-lived centres of literacy, administration, education, production and the accumulation of economic surplus"* (*ibid.*), and with their abandonment we effectively see the archaeological disappearance of a centralised administration (point 1.A).

2) *Disappearance of the traditional elite class* (Renfrew 1984: 368):

   b. *Abandonment of rich residences, or their re-use in impoverished style by "squatters".*
   c. *Cessation in the use of costly assemblages of luxury goods, although individual items may survive.*

Across the board, in the Citadel, Sacred City and across the hinterland, we see the abandonment of "rich" residences, the structures that utilised the restricted building materials (Bandaranayake 1974: 16), predominantly monastic in nature but also including the palaces of the Citadel (point 2.B). Additionally, while Anuradhapura does not appear to have ever been characterised by hordes of precious metals or other luxury goods, we see a cessation in the importation of luxury items, a reduction in precious metals, jewellery and other prestige goods (point 2.C).

3) *Collapse of centralised economy*
   (Renfrew 1984: 368):

a. *Cessation of large-scale redistribution or market exchange.*

b. *Coinage (where applicable) no longer issued or exchanged commercially, although individual pieces survive as valuables.*

c. *External trade very markedly reduced, and traditional trade routes disappear.*

d. *Volume of internal exchange markedly reduced.*

e. *Cessation of specialised or organised agricultural production. With agriculture instead based upon on a local 'homestead' basis with diversified crop spectrum and mixed farming.*

f. *Cessation of craft-specialist manufacture.*

The archaeological data from all three zones of Anuradhapura has demonstrated that, around the eleventh century AD, the levels of both craft specialist manufacturing and specialised agricultural productivity fall dramatically. The latter is clearly visible in the failure to maintain the sophisticated hydraulic landscape (as seen in Chapter Seven), while the former is visible in the massive loss of architectural sophistication post- tenth century in both the Citadel and Sacred City, along with the absence of late glass working, long distance trade, working of precious metals and sculpture.

4) *Settlement shift and population decline*
   (Renfrew 1984: 368):

a. *Abandonment of many settlements.*

d. *Marked reduction in population density.*

As shown in Chapters Five and Six, the Citadel and Sacred City both see large scale abandonment around the beginning of the eleventh century, with occupation after this point confined to smaller areas of both zones. Outside of the "urban" core we see a clear abandonment of monastic sites around the eleventh century AD, and while it has been difficult to securely date the abandonment of rural settlements, the apparent eleventh century abandonment of the hydraulic landscape, coupled with the absence of post tenth century artefacts strongly suggests that the majority of these settlements were also abandoned around the eleventh century AD.

After Collapse

6) *Development of romantic Dark Age myth*
   (Renfrew 1984: 369):

b. *Tendency among early chroniclers to personalise historical explanations, so that change is assigned to individual deeds, battles, and invasions, and often to attribute the decline to hostile powers outside the state.*

d. *Paucity of archaeological evidence after collapse compared with that for preceding period (arising from loss of literacy and abandonment or diminution of urban areas).*

e. *Tendency among historians to accept as evidence traditional narratives first set down in writing some centuries after the collapse.*

f. *Slow development of Dark Age archaeology, hampered both by the preceding item and by focus on the larger and more obvious central place sites of the vanished state.*

Renfrew's characterisation of a mythologised "Dark Age", one that carries over from the narratives of the period to the modern historical and archaeological study of the period is clearly seen in the collapse, and that is the correct term, of Anuradhapura. The dominance of the *vamsas* in the study and discussion of Sri Lankan history and archaeology has already been discussed at length, as has the failure of Sri Lankan archaeology to critically question the *vamsas*.

It therefore seems reasonable, given the above points, to state that, around the eleventh century, Anuradhapura does indeed collapse. Not only are all of the relative characteristics (Renfrew 1984: 367-370) of the collapse and its aftermath present, but the speed at which it occurs is clearly "rapid", occurring in less than century. Although there is a longer, more drawn out, post-collapse aftermath – characterised by the so called "squatter" occupation within both the Citadel and Sacred City, this not only fails to ever restore the individual zones to their former complexity, but also critically fails to ever unite or even link the separate zones. In and of itself this confirmation of Anuradhapura's collapse should perhaps not be surprising; it has after all been widely accepted for centuries as this is what the *Culavamsa* describes. Despite this though, the fact that the archaeological record, with minimal reference to the proto-historical sources that have been such a crutch (simultaneously supporting while hindering further development) to Sri Lankan archaeology, explicitly supports the existence of Anuradhapura's collapse is still noteworthy, given the failure of archaeologists to tackle this question before now.

However, just because Anuradhapura can be archaeologically seen to collapse, does not inherently support or validate the *Culavamsa's* explanation for the causes of that collapse, and it is to the causes and models that our attention must now turn. As discussed in Chapters Three and Four, the models are all developed from the same foundations (the *vamsas*), and all agree that the primary cause of the initial abandonment of Anuradhapura is the Chola invasion around 1017 AD. Consequently, they are also near identical in their portrayal of the period immediately preceding the collapse. Thus, before considering each of the three models in relation to the archaeological record of Anuradhapura's three zones, we shall examine whether the archaeological record supports the *Culavamsa's* narrative of the centuries preceding the eleventh century Chola invasion, and the invasion itself.

The *Culavamsa* repeatedly describes how complete the Chola sacking of the city was; Anuradhapura is "*violently destroyed*" (*Cvs.*lv.21), the city "*had been utterly destroyed in every way by the Chola army*" (*Cvs.* lxxiv.1), yet despite this there was a marked absence of archaeological evidence for violent conflict within either the Citadel or the Sacred City. There is no "great destruction horizon", as the Abhayagiri Vihara Project identified in the third century deposits of the Sacred City (Wikramagamage et al. 1983: 359), in the late deposits of either the Citadel or the Sacred City - no thick deposits of charcoal suggestive of widespread burning, no weaponry, and no skeletal remains suggestive of violent deaths. There were skeletal remains recovered from both the Citadel (Knusel et al. 2006) and the Sacred City (Wikramagamage 1984: 18), but no evidence in either case to suggest violence or conflict, and in the case of the Citadel there were also human remains from Period F (albeit in smaller quantity (Knusel et al. 2006: 219)), from an apparently stable and prosperous period. Furthermore the human remains recovered from the Sacred City appear to post-date the collapse, while the majority of the ASW2 remains were fragmented, disarticulated and recovered from the fills of the robber pits of periods D&E (*ibid.*).

The same is true of the hinterland sites, where although we see evidence of eleventh century abandonment of monastic sites such as C112, Parthigala, F517, Ritagala, A155 etc., there is again no direct archaeological evidence of conflict, violence or forced evacuation. Indeed there is no direct archaeological evidence of a Chola presence within the Citadel, Sacred City or hinterland at any point. As established in Chapter Six (sections **6.3.2** and **6.4.2**), we do see a late rise in Mahayanism, and possibly Saivism, at Sacred City sites such as Puliyankulama, Toluvila, Vijayarama and the so called "Hindu Ruins" and "Trident Temple", but nothing comparable is seen in either the Citadel or the hinterland, and there is no significant Saivite presence seen post-collapse anywhere in Anuradhapura. Finally there is the damage to the "Buddhist Railing" at the Jetavana vihara, interpreted by Bell (Bell 1904a: 07) as deliberate vandalism caused during the Chola sacking of the city. This is certainly possible, the railing was badly fragmented. However, without any way to diachronically connect the damage to the Buddhist railing to the eleventh century, let alone any evidence to connect it with the Cholas this appears once more to be an example of archaeologists looking for events described within the *vamsas*.

However, despite the absence of direct evidence of the "sacking" of the Citadel, Chapter Five did demonstrate a significant investment into the reinforcing and expanding of the Citadel's fortifications late within the Anuradhapura sequence – tentatively dated to around the tenth or eleventh century AD (Coningham 1999: 54). This work appeared to have either been carried out in a hurry, or at a time of vastly reduced resources, as structures within the Citadel appear to have been structurally robbed to provide building materials for this reinforcing and expanding of the ramparts. While there are many symbolic reasons for the construction of ramparts around a settlement (see Uziel 2010 for full discussion), the hurried expansion of the existing Citadel's ramparts (already well over 4m in height), at the cost of the very structures the ramparts are protecting, appears likely to be a direct response to a perceived threat. Unfortunately there is no way to date this late expansion of the ramparts precisely enough to tie this construction to any eleventh century Chola invasion, and if we are to interpret this rampart expansion through reference to the *vamsas* we might equally attribute the work to the ninth century Pandyan invasion(*Cvs.*l.12-36), or the civil unrest caused by the 95,000 Tamil mercenaries brought over by Senapti Sena in the during the reign of Sena V (*Cvs.*liv.64), or indeed the besieging of the Royal Palace by the same Tamil mercenaries a generation later after Mahinda V was unable to pay them (*Cvs.*lv.4-6) – the very events that the *Culavamsa* attributes with sparking the Chola subsequent Chola invasion. Consequently it is impossible to positively archaeologically identify the supposed Chola sacking of Anuradhapura. Indeed it is entirely possible, given the archaeological data available, that the Citadel at least was already at least partially abandoned before the Chola invasion of Sri Lanka. The description provided by the *Culavamsa* of the ninth and tenth centuries is one of instability, conflict and misrule (as was discussed in Chapter Three), and despite Codrington's dismissal of this period as causing "*no very great damage*" (Codrington 1960: 94), the available dates for the structural robbing, extension of the ramparts and the subsequent period of abandonment (seen in the slow siltation of the robber-pits (Coningham 1999: 80)) allow these archaeological events to be associated with either (or indeed both) the eleventh century Chola invasion or the century of conflict that preceded it.

The Sacred City does not show the same endemic levels of structural looting that so disturbed the later deposits within the Citadel, and there is no archaeological evidence to suggest that either the Sacred City or hinterland were in any kind of turmoil or decline prior to the eleventh century AD. Indeed in both areas the converse appears to be true, with significant monastic construction in the suburbs of the Sacred City and further afield in the hinterland. The construction of the ascetic *padhanaghara pariveṇa* monasteries at both the Western Monasteries, and further afield at Ritagala and Anuradhapura Hinterland project site C112, is matched by the massive investment of resources into the construction of the monumental *pabbata viharas* around the fringes of the Sacred City, as well as within the hinterland on the shores of Nachchaduwa (Anuradhapura Hinterland project site Z00). Although the monastic site of F517 is far smaller and less grandiose in nature, the late construction of this site also points to new monastic construction, perhaps even expansion, within the Anuradhapura hinterland towards the right at the end of the tenth century AD (OSL date 970 AD ($\pm$ 60)). So while the Citadel appears to go through a significant period of instability during which time endemic structural looting occurs, in conjunction with the hasty expansion of the Citadel's ramparts. Further afield though, in the Sacred City and hinterland, we see significant monastic construction and expansion right up to the point of collapse. Interestingly, this is as described earlier (in section **4.4.1**), with the secular rulers of Anuradhapura encountering severe financial difficulties in the second half of the tenth century, while the monasteries appear to continue to flourish right up to their abandonment. Thus while we can archaeologically identify a distinct collapse within the Citadel we can neither archaeologically confirm nor refute the *Culavamsa*'s account of the centuries preceding that collapse. This is in many ways unsurprising, given the Tolstoy-esque focus upon the actions of individuals – events and actions that will always be extremely difficult to identify archaeologically. Furthermore, although there is no direct evidence of the Chola sacking of Anuradhapura, neither does the archaeological data necessarily challenge this potential event. Additionally the *Culavamsa*'s description of economic problems for the secular rulers can perhaps be seen in the disturbed deposits of Periods D&E within the Citadel.

The next question then is one of the collapse itself, and the subsequent period of occupation prior to the complete abandonment of Anuradhapura. Does the archaeological data support one of the three models propounded? Or do we need to turn elsewhere to explain the archaeological signature of Anuradhapura's collapse.

8.3 Testing the Invasion Model

Let us start with the oldest, and the most widely accepted, of the three models. The simple Invasion Model, in which the destruction inflicted upon Anuradhapura by the Cholas directly results in its collapse and abandonment. As discussed above, there is a lack of direct archaeological evidence for the Chola sacking of either the Citadel or the Sacred City. This is of course a key event in all three models, but this is *especially* true of the Invasion Model, where the Chola sacking of the Citadel and Sacred City is seen as being so complete that Anuradhapura is of necessity abandoned as an urban centre, and then deliberately abandoned as capital when Vijayabahu claimed rule of Sri Lanka in 1072AD.

As it has not been possible to identify the actual Chola sacking of the city, our attention must now turn to other key characteristics of this collapse model, in order to determine whether or not it can be supported by the archaeological evidence. As set out in Chapters Three and Four, the Invasion model describes an initial complete abandonment of the city after "*all the monasteries*" of Anuradhapura are "*violently destroyed*" by the invading Cholas (*Cvs*.lv.21). Anuradhapura is then abandoned for just over 50 years before Vijayabahu's consecration there in 1073 AD (Codrington 1960: 95; *Cvs*.lix.8). Around this time repairs are carried out to the Bodhi Tree shrine and "the *vihara*" are repaired (*Cvs*. lx.62-63). After this Anuradhapura appears to be largely abandoned, and is only mentioned in conjunction with two further episodes of repairs and restorations, firstly in the latter half of the twelfth century AD (*Cvs*.lxxiv1-14; Cvs.lxxviii.97-107) and then again almost a century later (*Cvs*. lxxxviii.80-85). In Chapter Four the archaeological signature of the Invasion model was summarised in table form (table 4.06), while Chapters Five, Six, and Seven have produced similar representations of the archaeological sequence for each of Anuradhapura's zones (tables 5.22, 6.06 and 7.06). Each of these will now be compared and discussed, starting with the Citadel. Once more, it is important to note that this is not a quantitative summary of the Citadel's archaeological sequence, simply an aid in graphically summarising a large amount of archaeological data.

8.3.1: *The Invasion Model – The Citadel*

The walled Citadel was, spatially at least, the core of Anuradhapura as an urban centre, though perhaps not as a polity, as well as effectively providing the core of the archaeological data for this volume through the monumental archaeological sequence that the ASW2 project produced, and of course the comprehensive publishing of that data (Coningham 1999; Coningham 2006). The archaeological data (table 8.01) clearly demonstrates a significant shift in the occupation within the Citadel around the beginning of the eleventh century

AD, moving from monumental structures of stone and brick to more ephemeral, rural style, structures of wattle and daub (Ayrton 1924: 51; Coningham 1999: 81-82). The area occupied also shrinks by around 30% (from approximately 100ha to 70ha) and stylistically resembles a rural Mediaeval Sinhalese village more than it does the monumental urban Citadel of the preceding centuries (Godakumbura 1963: 02). Long distance trade appears to cease at this point, with no imported artefacts (whether glazed wares, glass vessels, coins or similar) that can be securely attributed to post eleventh century dates, and the frequencies of precious metals and similar luxury goods decrease. This then is the actual "collapse".

Comparing the anticipated signature of the Citadel (table 8.02) with the archaeological signature of the Citadel (see table 8.01), we see a relatively close correlation with just two notable differences. The first is the absence within the archaeological record of the twelfth and thirteenth century "restorations" described by the *Culavamsa*, with their accompanying spikes in population, construction and presence of elite, while the second is the continued presence of long distance trade items in the period after the collapse. The latter can be relatively easily explained through the residuality of ceramics, certainly there were no trade artefacts that can be conclusively dated to post eleventh century AD, and so the existence of imported glazed wares within Period B deposits is far more likely to represent the sherds from preceding periods than from freshly imported vessels. This is reinforced by the existence of east Asian glazed wares dating from the eleventh – thirteenth centuries AD at Polonnaruva, Jaffna, Yapahuwa, Sigiriya, and other sites outside of the Anuradhapura region (Mikami 1992: 152), clearly demonstrating that long distance trade to continued during this period, albeit not within the Citadel. Moving on to the issue of restorations, again this is perhaps unsurprising, as although the *Culavamsa*, and thus Invasion Model, describes repeated attempts to restore Anuradhapura, these attempts appear to have focussed upon the Sacred City, and were apparently motivated by religious considerations; Anuradhapura being *"specially deserving of honour, since its soil was hallowed while he lived by the feet of the Master, distinguished by the wheel with its thousand spikes and its rim, and because it was the place where the southern branch of the Sacred Bodhi tree (was planted) and where a dona of relics was preserved"* (Cvs.lxxiv.2-4). At this point It should of course be remembered that the *Culavamsa* was compiled by Buddhist monks, and thus that it is far from impartial when it comes to areas such as this.

There is of course, as discussed in Chapter Five (section **5.2.1.3**), one probable example of post-collapse monumental construction within the Citadel, in the form of the so called Vijayabahu's Palace. This structure, interpreted as an eleventh century construction, was unfortunately excavated and restored between 1949 and 1950 with no excavation report ever published (Coningham 1999: 21). As a result, it is difficult to tie into the structural sequence of the Citadel with any certainty, though architecturally it does indeed appear to date to the eleventh or even twelfth century AD and does appear to represent an example of post-collapse monumental construction. However, the extensive use of timber pillars in this structure, and the conspicuous lack of worked stone or other decorative features (Seneviratna 1994: 138) almost suggests a certain token symbolism in its construction. Thus, while it partially substantiates the *Culavamsa*'s account, it appears to be an exception rather than representative of post-collapse occupation within the Citadel (best represented by the ephemeral "squatter" occupation identified by Coningham (1999: 81-82) and Ayrton (1924: 51)), suggesting that the Polonnaruva period restorations described in the *Culavamsa* (Cvs. lx.62-63; Cvs.lxxiv1-14; Cvs.lxxviii.97-107; Cvs. lxxxviii.80-85) were symbolic rather than genuine efforts to restore the former capital. This is further supported by the apparently punctuated nature of this occupation, with several distinct episodes (structural periods B1-5) of occupation identified, suggesting that the occupation of the Citadel was at best fluid, and possibly even related directly to the symbolic episodes of restoration.

8.3.2: *The Invasion Model – The Sacred City*

As already discussed, there is a lack of clear archaeological evidence for the Chola sacking of the Sacred City, and while this in no way proves the contrary, this has to be considered surprising. The Invasion Model is built upon the theory that the damage inflicted by the invading Chola army was so great that Anuradhapura was still being repaired nearly 300 years later, and was never again fit to serve as capital. This damage, at least from the *Culavamsa*'s perspective, appears to have focussed upon the temples of the Anuradhapura – quite literally the Sacred City. Spencer cites the relevant passage while discussing the Chola invasion;

"In the three fraternities and in all Lanka [breaking open] the relic chambers, [they carried away] many costly images of gold, etc., and while they violently destroyed here and there all the monasteries, like bloodsucking yakkhas they took all the treasures of Lanka for themselves" (Cvs.lv.16-22 cited in Spencer 1976: 412).

The three fraternities are of course the Mahavihara, Abhayagiri vihara and Jetavana vihara, and yet archaeologically we cannot identify this violent destruction of the monasteries, beyond the possible deliberate smashing of the Buddhist railing at Jetavana (Bell 1904a: 07). We do archaeologically see the apparent abandonment of the Sacred City around the eleventh century AD, but there is simply no identifiable evidence for the wilful destruction of shrines, stupas, statues or similar.

Turning from the supposed sacking of the Sacred City, we see Period B occupation similar in nature to that seen within the Citadel and characterised by the use of ephemeral structures utilising robbed and organic structural materials (Wikramagamage 1984: 18). As was the case within the Citadel, this post-collapse structural period displays evidence of continued planning in the layout of structures, suggesting that this period of occupation, although vastly reduced in scale, grandeur and density, was still relatively well established. This is further borne out by the identification of a metalworking site (Wikramagamage et al. 1983: 352) and what appears to be a burial ground in conjunction with the structures in the Abhayagiri area (Wikramagamage 1984: 18). As seen in the Citadel, the presence of human remains within a settlement is surprising (*Arth*.2.36.31-33; Knusel et al. 2006: 619), even more so given the essentially holy nature of the Sacred City.

Clearly then the Sacred City does see continued occupation post-collapse, and, unlike the Citadel (with the possible exception of 'Vijayabahu's Palace') there is archaeological evidence of scattered repairs and restorations to monastic structures within the Sacred City. These repairs include the apparent twelfth century repairs to the Abhayagiri stupa's inner boundary walls (Bouzek et al. 1993: 17), though there remains doubt about this identification due to the 19th century restorations to the stupa (Wikramagamage et al. 1984: 50), as well as Polonnaruva period repairs to Mirisavati (Bandaranayake 1974: 198).

Elsewhere there also appears to be new construction with Bandaranayake Period B dates (between the twelfth and thirteenth centuries AD) to the final forms of the so called 'Trident Temple' (Bandaranayake 1974: 199), as well as Pilimage No.41 and No.42 at Jetavanavihara (*ibid*.: 202). It should be noted here that the dating of all three of these structures is based upon their architectural form, and they are thus not securely tied into the archaeological sequence of the Sacred City. Although this construction work appears relatively small in scale, it must be remembered that a great deal of the Sacred City was renovated and restored by organisations such as the Atamasthana Committee as well as the ASC during the early part of the 20th century, severely complicating and obfuscating the archaeological record of these structures (Hettiariatchi 1990: 45).

Structurally then, at least, we appear to see a clear and significant reduction in the presence of an (indeed any) elite within the Sacred City. This is also borne out artefactually (as presented in Chapter Six), with what appears to be a significant post-eleventh century reduction in the quantities of all forms of luxury goods (at least all forms that might be archaeologically visible), including long distance trade goods, precious metals, glass artefacts, precious stones and jewellery. However, due to the exceedingly limited nature of that publishing (see discussion in Chapters Four and Six), it is important that any such observation is heavily qualified as, unlike the Citadel data from the ASW2 sequence, such an observation is based upon the absence of reference to such artefacts within the Period B deposits of the Abhayagiri and Jetavana excavations. As has been established in Chapters Three and Four, the Invasion Model sees a massive depopulation of the Sacred City, specifically of the elite, the *sangha*. Indeed this depopulation is so severe that upon his ascension to the throne, Vijayabahu was forced to send for Buddhist monks from Myanmar, such was the shortage (*Cvs*.lx.4-6). However, where the Invasion Model suggests we should see a return of the elite, during the repeated restorations of the Sacred City, we do not archaeologically see returns of luxury goods within the Period B sequence. There are no twelfth or thirteenth century imported glazed wares, indeed no post tenth century long distance trade goods were recovered from the Sacred City, and once again we find that the archaeological record does not support suggestions of significant restorations or repopulations of the Sacred City.

8.3.3: The Invasion Model – The hinterland

Unfortunately, the Invasion Model makes virtually no reference to the hinterland of Anuradhapura. This is perhaps due in part to the culture-historical period in which the model was archaeologically codified, and likely also to the very nature of the *vamsas* that formed this model, proto-historical chronicles that focussed so heavily upon the actions of the elite. As a result any hypothetical archaeological modelling of the hinterland as seen by the Invasion Model is at best tenuous and vague. Taken from the general description of the utter devastation caused by the invading Cholas, the "blood-sucking yakkhas" (*Cvs*.lv.16-22), the suggestion is that this devastation would not have spared the land around Anuradhapura. Obviously, such an interpretation is clearly extremely open to challenge.

However, taken as a simplistic reading, the expectation is that the hinterland would have been abandoned at the same time as the Citadel and Sacred City, and without references to either full repopulations of Anuradhapura as an urban centre or to restoring or repopulating the hinterland, we can only assume the region that once acted as an urban hinterland to Sri Lanka's capital saw a significant reduction in population density, productivity, investment, trade and elite. This is shown in the graphical summary of the hinterland as seen by the Invasion Model (Fig.8.03) while the actual archaeological signature of the hinterland is shown in Fig.8.12. Once again, it is important to note that the latter is not a quantitative summary of the archaeological sequence, simply an aid in graphically summarising a large amount of archaeological data.

The Invasion Model would appear to suggest a sudden and largely permanent rural abandonment of the hinterland, and this is seen in the abandonment of monastic sites around the beginning of the eleventh century AD, as identified by OSL date at C112 and the complete absence of Polonnaruva period ceramics, coins or similar artefacts. Although the hinterland never saw a significant quantity of luxury goods or long distance trade artefacts there is a complete absence of such artefacts post eleventh century (the Carnelian barrel bead from F517, dated to around the tenth century AD, represents the last such artefact). The elite then do appear to vanish from the hinterland at the same time as the Citadel and Sacred City are initially abandoned.

However, the siltation and abandonment of the hydraulic landscape (such as Z021, C018 or C009) appears to date to well over a century later, certainly later than would be expected in the Invasion Model. Unfortunately, although settlement distribution patterns were archaeologically discernable, it proved near impossible to diachronically constrain or sequence these rural settlements. Consequently changes to population density and distribution resulting from the collapse of the Citadel and Sacred City can only be inferred from the archaeological record. The later siltation of the tanks and channels suggests that the abandonment of the hinterland by the general populace may have post-dated the abandonment of the monastic sites, however this abandonment appears just as final. Perhaps significantly, albeit unsurprisingly, there is once again a complete absence of direct archaeological evidence for the presence of an invading Chola army within the hinterland of Anuradhapura, this absence will be tackled after considering the Malarial and Imperial models.

8.3.4: *The Invasion Model – Summary*

Unsurprisingly, the Invasion Model is not *directly* challenged by the archaeological record of the Citadel, Sacred City or hinterland of Anuradhapura. However, neither can it be said to receive strong support. The complete absence of evidence for the violent sacking of the Sacred City, or even any evidence of a Chola presence, is deeply troubling. Indeed, the only archaeological evidence for major unrest around the tenth or eleventh century is seen in the endemic structural looting of the Citadel and the corresponding expansion of the Citadel's ramparts. However, these cannot be dated securely to the eleventh century, and could potentially pre-date the Chola invasion of 1017AD.

The lack of a direct archaeological challenge to the Invasion Model is unsurprising. This model is after all *the* established model and as such has broadly incorporated the available archaeological data. However, in the absence of of archaeological evidence for the dreadful destruction described within the *vamsas,* the Invasion Model cannot be said to satisfactorily explain either the initial abandonment or the subsequent failure of later monarchs to restore Anuradhapura. The absence of archaeological support for the Chola invasion allows the real possibility that an alternative model could better explain the archaeological record for the collapse of Anuradhapura. Certainly the reliance upon the external *deus ex-machina* of the Chola invasion to explain the collapse of a City and indeed Kingdom that had survived for over a millennium must be considered as unsatisfactorily simplistic and crude, and Tainter would dismiss such an explanation for collapse as *"unsatisfactory in that a recurrent process – collapse – is explained by a random variable, by historical accident"* (Tainter 1990: 64).

8.4 Testing the Malarial Model

Chronologically, the second explanation to be put forward for Anuradhapura's collapse (Nicholls 1921; Still 1930: 90-91; Brohier 1941: xvii), the Malarial Model might be considered something of a fringe theory. However, it is undoubtedly true that malaria was a major obstacle to the Colonial re-settlement of the North-Central Province (Knighton 1854: 140), and it is an explanation for Anuradhapura's collapse that has never been satisfactorily challenged.

It is in the period following the collapse that the three models differ significantly, in the scale, nature, and rate of the abandonment, and it is in the latter that the Malarial Model differs significantly (see table 8.03) from the other two explanations for Anuradhapura's collapse. However, it is also here that the Malarial model differs from the archaeological record (table 8.01).

8.4.1: *The Malarial Model – The Citadel*

Within the Citadel, the Malarial Model still relies upon the Chola invasion as the primary trigger of collapse, as this has been discussed at length above little more can be added here, other than to reiterate the lack of archaeological evidence for such an event. More problematic is that the Malarial Model describes a rapid decline and subsequent *total abandonment* of the Citadel, yet this cannot be seen in the archaeological record. Instead, while the initial abandonment appears rapid, there is then a prolonged period of occupation lasting likely around two to three centuries. Period B is clearly distinct from the preceding period, reflecting the collapse that has occurred, and is greatly reduced in scale with its absence of long distance trade, greatly reduced manufacturing, reduction in quantity of luxury goods, crude and ephemeral structures, reduction in area space, and lack of repairs to the monumental buildings. But the sheer length of this period argues clashes with the slower decline of the Malarial model; Nicholls' "decay" that *"slowly* insinuated itself through the cities"

(Nicholls 1921: 2 (emphasis added)), or Stills' epidemic that "*eventually*" resulted in the complete abandonment of Anuradhapura to the jungle tide (Still 1930: 91). It can be argued that Nicholls and Still were referring more to rural Anuradhapura than the walled Citadel at the Kingdom's heart, but if malarial was as endemic as they suggest, even the attenuated occupation of Period B would appear surprisingly high, especially if we accept the 'Vijayabahu Palace' as a Period B construction.

Moving from the general features of collapse and their rates, it should also be noted that the ASW2 faunal assemblage demonstrated a significant reduction in the number of freshwater species exploited between Period F and Period B. Still (1930: 90) argued that the damage to the tanks of Anuradhapura would result in a depopulation of the fish that inhabit them, but the ASW2 assemblage displayed a reduction in all exploited freshwater species, falling from 50% of the faunal assemblage for Period F to just 2.7% of the Period B assemblage. This included the freshwater snails (*Pila* and *Thiara*) and freshwater clam (*Parreysia corrugate*) which vanish completely in the post-collapse Period B, freshwater turtles (*Lissemys*) and terrapins (*Melanochelys*) which fall from 366g in Period F to just 39g in period B, and various freshwater fish species which fall by over 75% between F and B (Young et al. 2006).

This strongly suggests that these species are either unavailable for exploitation in Period B, or that a decision is made not to exploit them. Given that all of the above species are exploited today (Young et al. 2006), the latter would appear unlikely, lending weight to the possibility that during Period B the paddy fields and tanks of Anuradhapura were no longer viable habitats for these species. This in no way confirms a hypothesis of deliberate sabotage of the tank system during conflict, but does strongly suggest that the habitats of these species had been lost, though whether this was due to the sabotage of the hydraulic landscape, climate-change, or even a shift in subsistence package is unknown. It might be possible that a severe storm could result in a catastrophic breaching of one the major tanks, resulting in a similar breakdown of the hydraulic landscape. This would be especially true of Kalaveva, which played such a key role in reinforcing the irrigation system (see section **7.5.2.2**). Unfortunately, due to the restoration of these tanks, it is extremely difficult to identify such breaches, let alone date them.

8.4.2: *The Malarial Model – The Sacred City*

The problems with the Malarial Model here are the same as those encountered in the Citadel's archaeological sequence. Again, the lack of archaeological evidence for the Chola sacking has already been covered, though this is again a problem for the Malarial Model, built as it is around the premise of a Chola invasion that not only destroyed the Citadel and Sacred City, but also severely damaged the hydraulic landscape – including the three major Anuradhapura tanks. Archaeologically, this was unfortunately impossible to either corroborate or challenge due to the extensive restorations of those tanks by the British, but the lack of corroborating archaeological indicators of a Chola presence, or even violent sacking, must cast doubt upon such events having occurred.

Also challenging the Malarial Model is the speed of the initial abandonment, and the subsequent length of Period B occupation within the Sacred City, with architectural and numismatic evidence suggesting a low level of occupation until around the twelfth to thirteenth century AD. Combined with new construction and repairs (discussed above in **8.2.1**), we simply do not appear to see the irrevocable decline into endemic epidemic malaria that this model suggests.

However, despite these two significant challenges to the Malarial Model, the suggestion that malaria played a part in Anuradhapura's abandonment should not be rejected completely. While no archaeological data is available for the major urban tanks of Anuradhapura, the excavations within the Elephant Pond demonstrated a gradual siltation dating from around the eleventh century. Recent scientific studies (Amerasinghe et al. 1997, 2001; Klinkenberg 2001; Kilinkenberg et al. 2004) in Sri Lanka have demonstrated that tanks or channels that are allowed to become silted and overgrown serve as excellent vectors for the *Anopheles sp.*. This will now be discussed in greater detail in relation to the hydraulic landscape of the hinterland.

8.4.3: *The Malarial Model – The hinterland*

It is within the hinterland that the Malarial Model can best be applied, as here we can move beyond considering the rates of abandonment (observed and conjectural), to examining the actual hydraulic landscape of early Mediaeval Anuradhapura in a manner rendered impossible in the Sacred City by nineteenth and twentieth century restorations.

It is within the hinterland that the Chola destruction to the monumental irrigation system would have occurred, here that the "*...clean running water ...would dry rapidly under the tropical sun into a string of pools; millions of small fish would be left to perish of drought and millions more would be captured by birds where they still fought for life in water all too shallow for them; and mosquitoes would multiply at an appalling rate*" (Still 1930: 90), and thus here that the Malaria epidemic would have begun. The geoarchaeological investigations of the Anuradhapura Project demonstrated at several sites that the tanks and channels of the hinterland were well maintained (including of necessity regular de-silting) up to around the twelfth century AD., though these were seemingly abandoned at different times over that period with tank Z021 abandoned c.1100 AD ±70, channel C018 abandoned c. 1120 AD ±40 and tank C009 abandoned c.1200 AD ±60. Left unmaintained these small tanks and channels would have begun to silt up, and become clogged with vegetation, creating shallow pools with vegetative cover, perfect habitats for *Anopheles* sp. Mosquitoes and thus an ideal malarial vector (Amerasinghe et al. 1997; Amerasinghe et al. 2001; Klinkenberg et al. 2004). In the case of all three of these smaller scale tanks or channels there is no archaeological evidence of deliberate damage being inflicted to the bunds or similar. However, there is anecdotal evidence (referred to in Chapter Seven) of four large breaches in the gigantic Nachchaduwa bund, identified during the 1906 restoration of that tank (Brohier 1965; Shaw & Sutcliffe 2003). This may have been deliberately inflicted, but unfortunately no detailed records of these breaches exists and it is just as possible that they were the result of severe flooding and the absence of regular repairs to the bund.

It appears likely then, given the geoarchaeological evidence from the Anuradhapura Hinterland project, that malaria would have become an increasingly serious problem for the inhabitants of the rural hinterland surrounding Anuradhapura. However, the dates for the beginning of siltation, and thus presumably the cessation of maintenance, would suggest that the formation of malarial vectors would not have occurred until at least the latter half of the twelfth century AD, well over a century after the Cholas are supposed to have sacked Anuradhapura, and around a century after the Citadel and Sacred City appear to see their initial period of abandonment.

Coupled with the absence of archaeological evidence for a Chola presence within the hinterland, and the lack of clear archaeological evidence for the deliberate sabotaging of the hydraulic landscape, it is difficult to support Still's argument that the invading Chola army targeted the rural hinterland as a means to bringing about the collapse of the urban centre; "*tanks and channels suffered terrible damage in the war. Their bunds must have been cut as an ordinary tactic, or as reprisal... with disastrous results*" (Still 1930: 89).

8.4.4: The Malarial Model – Summary

The invocation of malaria as a causal *factor* in the abandonment of the hinterland of Anuradhapura appears to be both archaeologically and scientifically supported. The geoarchaeological investigation of tanks and channels within Anuradhapura's hinterland has shown a steady siltation that is likely to have lead to the formation of malarial vector habitats for the *Anopheles sp.*, and the faunal assemblage of ASW2 (Young et al. 2006) shows a significant reduction in the exploitation of freshwater species post-collapse, suggesting the loss of habitats that the hydraulic landscape provided. However, the Malarial Model, as propounded by Nicholls (1921) and Still (1930) cannot be archaeologically validated, with no evidence of the long slow decline that they described. Furthermore, despite recent attempts (see for example Sallares & Gomzi (2000) or Soren (2003)), it is extremely difficult to identify malaria skeletally (Chilvers 2004; Roberts 2005), even if such assemblages existed for any of Anuradhapura's zones, which of course they don't.

Malaria should still be considered to be a factor in the final abandonment of the urban hinterland, and therefore the city (both Sacred and Citadel), but it is clearly a contributory factor rather than a prime mover. It should also be noted that the formation of malarial vectors through the breakdown of the hydraulic landscape appears to be a *consequence* of the initial abandonment, rather than a causal factor in it, and as such malaria should be considered a factor in the failure of later generations to resurrect Anuradhapura, rather than as a reason for the initial collapse.

8.5 Testing the Imperial Model

Having found both the Invasion and Malarial models to be unsatisfactory in explaining the archaeological record of Anuradhapura, and thus unsatisfactory in explaining Anuradhapura's collapse, we now turn to the most recent model for Anuradhapura's collapse; the Imperial Model. More complex than the Invasion or Malarial models, the Imperial model differs significantly in its portrayal of a far more turbulent tenth century leading up to the final Chola sacking of the city, including the abandonment of Anuradhapura by King Udaya III. The description of the actual Chola sacking of 1017AD broadly mirrors the Invasion model's description of catastrophic damage inflicted upon the Citadel and Sacred City as the invading Cholas removed the traditional elite. However, the Imperial model then differs significantly in its description of the hinterland during the Chola invasion and subsequent rule, as well as its consideration of the monastic sites of the hinterland, both in the centuries leading up to the Anuradhapura's collapse and the period immediately after.

8.5.1: The Imperial Model – The Citadel

The archaeological signature of the Citadel (see table 8.01) appears to closely mirror the anticipated signature of the Imperial Model (table 8.04), with an identifiable period of unrest (the structural looting of periods D&E) that some have identified with the tenth century unrest; Paranataka's invasion, royal abandonment of Anuradhapura, economic unrest, and the rebellion of the Tamil mercenaries (Indrapala 2005: 231). This is followed, as described by the Imperial Model, by a complete collapse of Anuradhapura in the eleventh century, following the Cholas decapitation and replacement of the kingdom's administrative structure.

The Imperial model's depiction of the Citadel post-collapse is similar to that presented by the Invasion Model, though the reasons given for the damage inflicted by the invading Chola army are different. While the *vamsas* portray the destruction as mindless vandalism, the Imperial model suggests that the removal of the traditional elite was key to the Chola conquest in order to not only redirect the collection of surplus, but also to shift long-distance trade routes away from Mantai and Anuradhapura (and thus the Citadel) and instead to the northeast (Spencer 1983: 60). Post-collapse, and despite the different motives, we would expect to see roughly the same archaeological characteristics as seen in the Invasion Model's portrayal of the Citadel's collapse. Consequently, the same archaeological agreements, absences and challenges that were identified above for the 1017AD sacking model in the Citadel can be seen for the Imperial model.

In terms of post-collapse occupation, the Imperial model clearly dismisses any possibility of Chola rule from, or even occupation of, Anuradhapura (Indrapala 2005: 231). Consequently, we should expect a period of abandonment lasting until Vijayabhau's coronation in Anuradhapura (c.1073AD). After this, while the Invasion model portrays the attempts to restore Anuradhapura as meaningful, if scattered, the Imperial model places far less emphasis upon these attempts, instead portraying them as largely symbolic. Again, the apparently punctuated Period B structural sequence could be tentatively linked with episodes of restoration or repairs, whether in the Sacred City or Citadel, as Polonnaruva rulers put resources and labour into restoring elements of Anuradhapura.

Overall the archaeological agreement is largely good, both in the century leading up to the collapse, the speed and scale of that collapse, and in the subsequent absence of long distance trade goods, and indeed other luxury goods. However, as with the Invasion model, the absence of archaeological indicators of a Chola presence at any point remains surprising.

8.5.2: The Imperial Model – The Sacred City

The hypothetical archaeological characteristics of the Imperial model's Sacred City are broadly similar to those of the Invasion model, more so than in the case of the Citadel as the Imperial model does not see describe same level of turmoil in the tenth century Sacred City as it does within the Citadel. While the Imperial Model describes the abandonment of Anuradhapura by the monarchy c.950 AD, and the subsequent economic problems that the ruler of Anuradhapura encountered (Indrapala 2005: 231), no such mention is made of the either the *sangha* in general or in terms of the three great fraternities, and there is no reason to assume they were either economically or physically threatened until the early eleventh century sacking. As with the Invasion model, the invading Cholas are presented as causing devastating damage to the Sacred City, resulting in its complete abandonment. Again, as with the Citadel, the Imperial model sees this destruction as being a deliberate removal of the established traditional elite, allowing the conquering Cholas to redirect the flow of economic surplus to their own agents, whether by completely replacing the administrative structure or by adding a Chola superstructure to it, all while ruling from a place more favourable to them (Indrapala 2005: 232).

However, again as was the case in the Citadel and with the Invasion Model, there is a lack of archaeological evidence for the violent Chola sacking of the Sacred City. Consequently, while the abandonment of the Sacred City can be archaeologically identified, there is neither archaeological evidence placing the Cholas in the Sacred City nor evidence of a violent sacking of the monasteries of the Sacred City. Although there is no archaeological evidence for the presence of the invading Cholas, we do see archaeological evidence for a rise in South Indian, or Tamil influences within the Sacred City in the centuries leading up to its collapse. This is interesting as the Imperial Model sees the power struggle between South Indian Saivism or Mahayanist Buddhism and the orthodox Theravada Buddhism of Anuradhapura as key to the collapse of Anuradhapura (Indrapala 2005: 236-8).

Although the weakening of the Theravada Buddhist *Sangha* is often seen as a consequence of the Chola invasion (Seneviratna 1998: 44), the Imperial Model suggests that this weakening of the Orthodox Theravada *sangha* had started around two centuries earlier as the rulers of Anuradhapura became increasingly embroiled, both politically and economically, with the Tamil kingdoms of South India (Indrapala 2005: 230). This resulted in an increasingly significant South Indian Tamil presence within Sri Lanka, specifically in the north and north-east of the island, but also within Anuradhapura itself, where recent epigraphic studies have identified the so called "*Hindu ruins*" of Bell (1904c: 05) as being, at least in part, Mahayanist Buddhist structures, constructed by Tamil merchants who had fled religious conflicts in South India (Veluppillai 2002: 693). Epigraphic studies (Indrapala 1971b; Patmanatan 2002; Veluppillai 2002) have suggested that these structures, the so called "*Hindu ruins*", indicate the existence in the ninth and tenth centuries AD, of a Tamil community living within the northern fringe of the Sacred City.

However, *if* we accept such an interpretation, then we are faced with a visible emergence of Saivism within the Sacred City alongside a dramatic and highly visible increase in the apparent power and wealth of the Mahayanist *sangha* within the Sacred City, visible in the late development of the monumental *pabbata viharas* and the ascetic *padhanaghara parivena*. This again supports the Imperial Model, which sees the rise of Mahayanism and Saivism tied to an inverse decrease in the power of the orthodox Theravadist *sangha*, a religious sea-change that is completed by the choice of Polonnaruva as capital, where Saivisim and Mahayanist Buddhism continue to exist relatively peacefully alongside Theravadist Buddhism. However, despite the broad agreement seen above, it still remains archaeologically impossible to identify the catastrophic sacking of the Sacred City described by all collapse models.

8.5.3: *The Imperial Model – The hinterland*

As established, the Citadel and Sacred City both broadly archaeologically support the Imperial Model, if not completely, then at least more so than the archaeological record can be said to support the Invasion or Malarial models. However, as established in Chapters Three and Four, the hinterland is key to the Imperial Model, as in contrast to the other models, the Imperial Model does *not* invoke wide-scale destruction. Instead, the Imperial Model predicts the focussed removal of the rural Buddhist infrastructure, leaving the wider population unharmed and able to continue its production of economic surplus, primarily though intensive irrigated agriculture.

Examining the first element, the monastic collapse, we saw clear archaeological evidence in Chapter Seven of the sudden abandonment of Buddhist monastic sites around the eleventh century AD, best seen in the sudden abandonment of the *padhanaghara parivena* site C112, which was abandoned around 1090 AD ± 50. Although this was the only monastic site with a precise scientific date for its abandonment, there were no archaeological indicators present at any of the monastic sites (such as the organic monastery A155, the *Pabbata Vihara* Z00, or the small and simple pasada at F517) to suggest occupation beyond the eleventh century AD. Geoarchaeological investigations at the tank (Anuradhapura Project sites Z021 and Z021) associated with the *Pabbata Vihara* Z00, showed signs of siltation from 1100 AD ±70, suggesting abandonment around the same time as C112. The siltation of the tank strongly suggests that the *Pabbata Vihara* was either abandoned already, or abandoned at this time. Although with the Imperial Model we would expect to see monastic sites abandoned, or even destroyed, around that date of 1017 AD, the OSL age determinations above are unfortunately not precise enough to confirm or reject such a date. If we take the earlier of the date for Z021 and C112 we see abandonment occurring at 1030 and 1040 AD, shortly after the Rajendra I's conquest of Anuradhapura. Equally however, both sites could have been occupied until as late as 1170 and 1140 AD respectively, long after Vijayabahu's coronation had taken place in Anuradhapura. Although the dates of that rural monastic abandonment are indeterminate, the *nature* of that abandonment is clearly sudden and rapid, seen in the thick tile collapses of monastic sites such as Ritagala, Anuradhapura Hinterland project site A155, and most strikingly Anuradhapura Hinterland project site C112. Although no direct indications of violence were identified, the speed at which sites like C112 were abandoned is striking and suggestive of a hurried or even forced abandonment, rather than a slow withdrawal or fall into disuse.

The Imperial Model postulates a rural collapse that is confined to the administrative elite, and thus implicitly the monastic sites that appear to have formed the administrative infrastructure of rural Anuradhapura (Coningham et al. 2007a). However, while we would thus expect monastic sites to be abandoned around the beginning of the eleventh century, we would conversely expect to see secular settlements left undamaged as it was in the interest of the invading Cholas to preserve the agricultural productivity of the region. This was an invasion both imperial and mercantile in form and nature, not a punitive smash-and-grab, and gaining access to the agricultural productivity of the intensively farmed and irrigated North Central plains was key to this aim. Archaeologically this was difficult to identify due to the ephemeral nature of secular rural architecture, the seemingly transitory nature of rural villages (Coningham et al. 2007a) and the difficulty in securely and precisely dating sites consisting of little more than negative features and coarseware ceramic forms that are extremely long lived.

Fortunately, it was possible to determine the dates of abandonment for several hydraulic sites within the hinterland, hydraulic features that were (and indeed remain) vital to the agricultural productivity and even viability within Anuradhapura's hinterland. The Anuradhapura Hinterland project geoarchaeological investigations demonstrated at these sites that the hydraulic infrastructure of the hinterland appears to have been maintained until around the twelfth century AD., with channel C018 abandoned c. 1120 AD ±40 and tank C009 abandoned c.1200 AD ±60. Interestingly the tank associated with the Pabbata Vihara Z00, Z021, appears to have been abandoned earlier, around 1100 AD ±70, which would fit with the Imperial Model's targeted removal of monastic sites by the Cholas.

As with the Sacred City and Citadel, the one stumbling block for this model is the complete absence of archaeological indicators of a Chola presence within the Anuradhapura hinterland. However, unlike the Citadel and Sacred City, although there is no direct suggestion that the Cholas ever maintained a significant presence or interest in Anuradhapura (Indrapala 2005: 232), this appears to be a matter of urban disinterest and it is generally considered that the area of the modern day North Central Province was under direct Chola rule for the duration of Chola rule (*ibid.*: 237), and there is no suggestion as to why they would be disinterested in a previously economically productive region.

8.5.4: *The Imperial Model – Summary*

The Imperial model is well supported archaeologically across the three zones of Anuradhapura, with the greatest single challenge emerging from the continued absence of direct archaeological indicators for a Chola presence within the Citadel, Sacred City or hinterland of Anuradhapura, both in the centuries leading up to and following its collapse. However, the disturbed late deposits of the Citadel, the pre-collapse emergence of a significant South Indian presence within the Sacred City, the associated rise in Mahayanism, and rapid monastic abandonment of the hinterland coupled with a later agricultural abandonment, all fit well with the sequence of events described by the Imperial Model.

However, for the Imperial Model to be truly archaeologically supported it is necessary to expand our focus, considering archaeological sites across the north of Sri Lanka. It is widely accepted that the Cholas ruled Sri Lanka from Polonnaruva for over half a century, but the Imperial Model highlights the mercantile drive behind the eleventh century Chola invasion of Sri Lanka, and stresses the importance of the ports in the North-East of Sri Lanka – specifically within the region of Trincomalee (Gunasingam 1999; Spencer 1983: 61). Furthermore the return of Sinhalese rule with Vijayabahu failed to alter either the location of the island's capital, or the increased popularity and prominence of both Mahayanism and Saivism (Indrapala 2005: 236). Consequently it is to these areas, and to the question of *why* Vijayabahu rules from Polonnaruva, that we must now turn.

8.6: The Wider Early Mediaeval Milieu

As laid out above (section **8.5**) the archaeological record of Anuradhapura broadly supports the Imperial Model – that is to say, *of the explanations propounded* for Anuradhapura's collapse the Imperial Model is the best supported. However, the Imperial Model is a synthetic model developed from the works of multiple scholars explicitly studying either the Cholas (Spencer 1976; Spencer 1983) or Tamils (Indrapala 2005) in Sri Lanka, and consequently the overall narrative described by this model primarily takes place outside of Anuradhapura (which the Cholas apparently had little interest in), in the areas that the Cholas did show an interest in. The archaeological record of these areas demonstrates that, as described by the Imperial model, while the Cholas appear to have shown no interest in Anuradhapura, they were extremely active in the north and east of the island, as well as at Polonnaruva.

8.6.1: *Mantai*

One of the difficulties encountered in examining Anuradhapura's collapse was in distinguishing cause from effect, and this was particularly true of the cessation of long distance trade in Period B. It was possible to state that long distance trade to both the west and east appeared to cease *around* the point of collapse, but not to identify whether this was a consequence of the collapse, a *cause* of the collapse, or an indication of the Cholas taking control of, and moving, these long distance trade routes – as described within the Imperial Model (Spencer 1983: 56-60). Excavations at the site of Mantai, next to the modern town of Manaar on the north-western tip of Sri Lanka, strongly suggest the latter.

The site of Mantai, excavated in the 1980s (Carswell & Prickett 1984), has unfortunately never produced a final excavation report. However, the preliminary reports clearly demonstrate that the site was a major early Mediaeval hub for trade between China and the Near East (*ibid.*: 10). Indeed, the quantities of imported glazed wares at Mantai were so great that a preliminary field visit in 1974 recorded abundant glazed Islamic and Chinese wares on the surface (*ibid.*: 15). The presence of Adam's Bridge, an underwater chain of rock formations between Sri Lanka and the southern tip of India, is thought to have made Mantai a natural break-of-bulk point for trade between the Near East and Far East (*ibid.*). Goods would be ferried either overland, or by smaller vessels, around Adams Bridge and to new ships that could continue the long distance journey. Crucially for Anuradhapura though, is the internal link between Mantai and Anuradhapura by the Malvatu Oya, along which it has been speculated trade goods were carried to the Island's capital, and to its rulers and monasteries. Indeed, the party of Robert Knox followed the Malvatu Oya through the Anuradhapura region (during his escape from the Kandyan Kingdom) in the 17th century, leading his party past Anuradhapura and eventually to Manaar (Knox 1681: 255-272). The suggestion of a direct link between Mantai and Anuradhapura is further supported by epigraphic evidence placing Anuradhapura at the cross-roads of the major north-south and east-west internal trade routes and Mantai at the northern end of those same routes (Dias 2008: 81; Vidanpatirana 2008: 222). This connection is further supported by the presence of a pillar inscription granting immunities to three villages a few km north of Mantai in the name of the Mahavihara, Anuradhapura (Wickremasinghe 1933: 105), such immunities will be discussed shortly.

Consequently, with a direct link between Mantai and Anuradhapura established, the close resemblance between the glazed ceramics assemblage from the ASW2 excavations and those of the Mantai excavations is unsurprising, with the vast majority of wares present at one site also found at the other (Seely et al. 2006: 117). In turn, the assemblages of Mantai and Anuradhapura closely mirror the imported ceramics assemblages of Indian Ocean and Persian Gulf trade centres such as Siraf, Basra, Sohar, Banbhore, Manda and Kilwa (Carswell & Prickett 1984: 61), reinforcing both Mantai's and Anuradhapura's important position within the Indian Ocean trade network.

However, just as the ceramic assemblage of Mantai so closely mirrors that of Anuradhapura, so too does the date of its abandonment. The site's final phase (in over a millennium of occupation), the phase to which the vast majority of the imported wares belong to, ends in the eleventh century AD (Carswell & Prickett 1984: 59). Just like the ASW2 assemblage, and just like the Sacred City at Anuradhapura, there are no examples of the typical twelfth thirteenth and fourteenth century trade wares (*ibid.*). The precise reason for Mantai's abandonment is unclear, and once again there is an element of obfuscated cause and effect. However, the eleventh century abandonment fits well with the Imperial Model's description of Chola merchants taking control of, and redirecting, long distance trade routes (Spencer 1983: 58), as well as reinforcing the suggestion that Mantai and Anuradhapura shared a significant connection (Carswell & Prickett 1984: 21) and that without the market and/or protection provided by the elite of Anuradhapura, Mantai's position was untenable in the face of aggressive, and often violent (Hall 1977: 215), South Indian merchant groups. Additionally. there is a strong suggestion that the Cholas were more interested in trade with, and expansion into, the east than the west (Schalk 2002: 674). Mantai's position on the northwest coast was perfect for Indian Ocean trade coming from the Near East, controlling as it did a direct route from the Arabian Sea in the west to the Bay of Bengal in east, and this can be seen in the glazed ceramic corpus of ASW2, with 308 of the 329 glazed ceramics sherds originating from the west (Seely et al. 2006: 91. However, without the patronage of Anuradhapura, and with a new focus upon the east, Mantai failed.

8.6.2: *North and East of Sri Lanka*

The archaeology of the north and east reinforce the Imperial Model's depiction of the Cholas taking control of the long distance Indian Ocean trade. Unlike Mantai, the artefactual assemblages for the majority of these sites suggest they were occupied continuously from shortly after the beginning of the first millennium AD until around the thirteenth century AD (Ragupathy 1987: 11). This analysis is crude in that it is based upon surface collections in the absence of any published excavations. However, it strongly suggests that, unlike Mantai, the northeast of Sri Lanka remained heavily involved in long distance Indian Ocean trade throughout the period of Chola rule, and for approximately two centuries after the collapse of Anuradhapura and Mantai. The scale of such trade can clearly be seen across the northeast of Sri Lanka, but is perhaps most strikingly visible in the quantities and distribution of imported glazed ceramics found by Ragupathy's archaeological survey of Jaffna (1987). At Anuradhapura (the capital of the island and a significant trade centre in its own right) these highly prestigious wares were tightly restricted to the urban centre (the Citadel and Sacred City), with not a single sherd of an imported glazed ware found (either on transect survey or during excavation) by the recent Anuradhapura Hinterland project survey of the hinterland. However, during the survey of archaeological settlements in Jaffna, glazed wares (Chinese or Islamic) dating from between the ninth and thirteenth centuries AD (Ragupathy 1987: 11) were recovered from more than half (16 of 26) of the sites surveyed (*ibid.*: 14). It is also worth noting Bell's description (1911a: 26) of a surface collection of artefacts carried out in dunes near Mantai, where he collected; "*...copious debris ...washed up to the surface by the monsoons of centuries. This contains coins of various Pandiyan and Choliyan types - and a few Sinhalese massas. The commonest coin is of the "bull and fishes" type. There are also found innumerable fragments of glass bangles and of other objects of glass, many pieces of glazed pottery, and carved chank shell bangles*" (Still 1911: 26).

This artefactual evidence further supports the Imperial Model and suggests that long distance trade in the northeast of Sri Lanka was primarily controlled by Tamil mercantile groups (collectively referred to as the Ainnurruvar (Schalk 2002: 675), and that this trade flourished during the eleventh and twelfth centuries AD (Schalk 2002: 675). Trincomalee in particular appears to have been a major focus for Chola and Tamil activity (Schalk 2002: 503). This can be seen architecturally in the construction of temples such as those at Velgamvehera in the Trincomalee district (approximately 15km northwest of modern Trincomalee town). Here we see the Rajarajapperumpalli at Periyakulam, a large brick image house, excavated by the ASC in 1929 and then again in 1953 (Paranavitana 1953: 9-12), that appears to have been dramatically redeveloped in the eleventh century AD, producing a Buddhist shrine of characteristic South Indian style (Bandaranayake 1974: 203). Inscriptions at the site indicate that there had been a Buddhist temple on the site since at least the second century AD. (*ibid.*), but that in the eleventh century, during the Chola hegemony over the region, it was radically reconstructed (Patmanatan 2002c: 769) fusing Sinhalese and Chola, and indeed Buddhist and Saivite, architectural styles in a manner unique within Sri Lanka (Bandaranayake 1974: 203; Patmanatan 2002c: 776). It is similar in certain aspects to both the so called Trident Temple at Anuradhapura (Bandaranayake 1974: 203) and the Chola temples of Polonnaruva (Paranavitana 1953: 12) (discussed shortly), combining Dravidian style mouldings with moonstones and balustrades that appear to be directly influenced by local Buddhist architectures, and it has been suggested that it is effectively an adaptation of the standard Saivite shrine form for the requirements of Buddhist ritual (Patmanatan 2002c: 776). The 16 Tamil inscriptions found at the shrine all date to the period of Chola imperial rule, and record various endowments given to the temple by local employees of the Chola administration (*ibid.*). Although there are also records of several Saivite temples within the Trincomalee region, it is striking that we see such clear archaeological evidence of the Cholas constructing a large and lavish Buddhist temple, clearly within the north and east of Sri Lanka Buddhist and Saivite practices appear to have coexisted during the period of Chola rule.

This is further suggested in the 1909 annual report of the ASC, when, during an archaeological survey of the Northern Province (then the Vanni) of the island, Still records the ruins of a "buried town" that contain "*a thorough mixture of Buddhist and Hindu ruins*" (Still 1909: 34). This "buried town", named as Kuruntan-Ur, had previously been identified and described by Lewis (1895) in his *Manual of the Vanni*. Still, contesting Lewis' interpretation, wrote that; "*I cannot help thinking that the kovils in the town were built by some later Sinhalese King, who while upholding the ancient religion, like Solomon, tolerated the introduction of the new.*" (Still 1909: 34). Unfortunately, this site has not been further investigated in the subsequent century.

It should be noted that although, just as seen archaeologically in Anuradhapura's Sacred City (as discussed above in **8.5.2**), there was a significant Tamil presence in the north and east of Sri Lanka centuries before the period of Chola rule, there is little doubt that the eleventh and twelfth centuries represent a peak in Tamil activity across Sri Lanka, and the northeast of Sri Lanka is widely accepted to have remained predominantly Tamil long after the Cholas as an imperial force had been defeated by Vijayabahu I (de Silva 1977: 44-47).

8.6.3: *Polonnaruva*

This religious duality seen in the now strongly Tamil north and east is even more striking at Polonnaruva, where we see eleventh century construction and veneration of both Saivite and Buddhist temples and shrines (Seneviratna 1998: 35). Polonnaruva had existed as a sizeable settlement for centuries before its eleventh century selection as capital by the Cholas (Seneviratna 1998: 13), and indeed was, for a period, believed to have been Sri Lanka's capital from the eighth or ninth centuries onwards (e.g. Enriquez 1884: 68; Hocart 1926: 01). However, this was based heavily upon the earlier translations of the *Mahavamsa*, and it is now widely accepted that it was the Cholas who first made Polonnaruva the capital of Sri Lanka (e.g. de Silva 1981: 565-70; Coningham 1999: 155-58). Whether Polonnaruva was used as a royal capital prior to the Cholas eleventh century rule or not, it appears likely that Polonnaruva was already an important site by the eighth century (Bandaranayake 1974: 159). Unfortunately in the absence of any deep sequence excavations (such as ASW2 at Anuradhapura) our understanding of the structural sequence of Polonnaruva is limited (Bandaranayake 1974: 8) and restricted to a combination of stylistic observations, epigraphic records and the *vamsas*. As with Anuradhapura's Sacred City, the only archaeological excavations carried out since the early 20th century work of the ASC were carried out in the 1980s by the CCF (Premetilleke 1982a, 1982b, 1982c, 1985, 1987 and 1989) and have never produced a final publication.

Interestingly, while the glazed ceramics assemblages of the Citadel, Sacred City and Mantai are virtually identical (Mikami 1992: 152) none of these wares (dating to the second half of the first millennium AD) have been found at Polonnaruva. However, East Asian glazed wares dating from the eleventh to thirteenth centuries AD have been found at Polonnaruva, Jaffna, Yapahuwa, Sigiriya, and other sites outside of the Anuradhapura region (*ibid.*). This clearly demonstrates the shift in long distance trade routes from Anuradhapura to Polonnaruva, and from sites like Mantai on the west coast to the northeast of Sri Lanka. This shift in elite and economic focus, from Anuradhapura to Polonnaruva, is clearly demonstrated in the distribution of inscriptions before and after Anuradhapura's collapse (shown in Figs.8.01 and 8.02). In the five centuries leading to the eleventh century AD the vast majority (57%) of inscriptions recorded in the volumes of the Epigraphia Zeylanica were located within the Anuradhapura District (modern boundaries), with just 8% located in the nearby Polonnaruva District. However, between the eleventh and fourteenth centuries this shifts dramatically, with 53% of all inscriptions found in the Polonnaruva District, and just 5% in the Anuradhapura District – clearly suggesting a massive abandonment of not only the city of Anuradhapura, but also of the hinterland surrounding it.

However, it is also clear is that Polonnaruva displays both clear architectural and artistic continuity with Anuradhapura, as well as clear and strong South Indian influences across the city (Bandaranayake 1974; Seneviratna 1998: 13). Thus we see large *Pabbata Vihara* complexes such as the Alahana Parivena and Daladamaluva (Bandaranayake 1974: 85), just as we saw in the Sacred City, alongside Saivite and Vaishnavite shrines and temples (Bell 1911a: 43; Paranavitana 1953: 9; Bandaranayake 1974: 208). These Hindu temples, described by Bell as being; "*laid out with the customary precision and conformity to broad universal Southern Indian canons*" (Bell 1911a: 19) are architecturally similar to the eleventh and twelfth century Saivite and Vaishnavite temples seen in southern India. They were named by the ASC excavators as simply as "Siva Devale" 1-7 and "Visnu Devale" 1-5 (von Schroeder 1990: 635), and contained a number of sophisticated Saivite and Vaishnavite bronze images (see Arunachalam 2004), along with inscriptions in Tamil, stone *yoni* and *linga* (Bell 1911a: 22; von Schroeder 1990: 661). There can be no doubt that these Hindu shrines date to the period of Chola rule, though the vast majority of the extant structural remains at Polonnaruva are thought to post-date the period of Chola occupation, typically being attributed to either Vijayabahu I (r.1070-1110 AD), Parakramabahu I (r.1153-1186 AD) or Nissankamalla (r.1187-1196 AD) (von Schroeder 1990: 636-677; Seneviratna 1998).

However, the predominantly twelfth and thirteenth century Buddhist shrines share a great deal of stylistic features with the eleventh century Saivite and Vaishnavite temples (von Schroeder 1990: 637), and there is no suggestion that there was any significant conflict between Buddhism and Hinduism within the city. Furthermore the Hindu temples and shrines within Polonnaruva appear to have flourished after the departure of the Cholas, with the eleventh and twelfth centuries often portrayed as a period of religious harmony (e.g. Still 1909: 34; Seneviratna 1998: 40, 125; Indrapala 2005: 251). Consequently it would certainly appear that, even after the period of Chola rule had well and truly ended, Vijayabahu and his successors not only chose to rule from Polonnaruva, building Buddhist shrines, Buddhist monasteries and royal palaces throughout the city, but also that throughout the Polonnaruva period Saivism was not only tolerated but even royally patronised.

8.6.4: *Indian Ocean Region*

It is perhaps self-evident, but the most significant event in the Indian Ocean area during the period of Anuradhapura's collapse is the sudden expansion of the imperial Cholas. Not only do they subdue the greater part of South India, conquer Sri Lanka and the Maldives, but they claim to have sent armed expeditions as far north and east as the Ganges Valley and even Srivijaya (now Java) (Subbarayalu 1973: 12; Spencer 1983: 1; Thirunavukkarasu 1985: 3-6). Furthermore, there are historical records of Chola merchants sending a delegation to China in 1077 AD (Thapar 2002: xv), and of a Cambodian trade delegation to the Chola court in the early part of the eleventh century (*ibid.*: 382). However, looking beyond the tenth and eleventh century imperial expansionism of the Cholas, there is a wider spread of Indian influence across the region. This was visible archaeologically from around the eighth century onwards in the Sacred City (sections **6.3.3** and **6.4.3**) of Anuradhapura, but is equally visible as far away as central Thailand where the Buddhist Dvaravati kingdom adopts a number of Indian cultural elements (including religious beliefs, languages, coinage, and artistic and architectural styles) between the seventh and tenth centuries AD (Indrawooth 2004: 142). This appears to reflect increased mobility and interaction between the kingdoms of South and Southeast Asia during this period, with a marked increase in not only long distance trade at this time (Manguin 2004: 305), but also in inter-polity conflict (Southworth 2004: 228-229; Miksic 2004: 247). These events do not in of themselves directly impact upon the eleventh century collapse of Anuradhapura, but they do reflect the growing interconnectivity of the polities and trade centres of the early Mediaeval Indian Ocean world, and the growing regional economy that develops at this time, an economy which could be argued to be at the heart of Anuradhapura's collapse.

8.7 Anuradhapura's Collapse

The "Imperial" Model could just as well be termed the "Economic" Model, effectively arguing that the critical damage inflicted by the invading imperial and mercantile Cholas was not the violent and catastrophic sacking of Anuradhapura's palaces, monasteries or tanks, but was the restructuring of the economic administration within Early Mediaeval Sri Lanka around a new focal point - Polonnaruva.

The *Culavamsa*, and consequently the Invasion Model, has always portrayed the eleventh century Chola conquest of Sri Lanka as an act of extreme violence, one that resulted in the demolition of the island's capital, in the decimation of the *sangha*, and in the plundering of the islands treasures (*Cvs*.lv; Codrington 1960; Seneviratna 1994: 73-74). However, the motivation for this conquest is absent from this long established narrative, and this would appear to be key to any understanding of why Anuradhapura collapsed. Implicitly, and sometimes explicitly, the collapse of Anuradhapura is portrayed as being a direct result of a clash between the invading Tamils and the defending Sinhalese, or the invading Saivites and the defending Buddhists (Schalk 2002: 674). These Indian, Saivite, Tamil invaders are portrayed as ending over a millennium of Buddhist rule at Anuradhapura, and thus ending its "golden age" of Buddhist "history" in Sri Lanka (Coningham & Lewer 2000).

Nevertheless, contrary to the claims of the *Culavamsa*, there is very little archaeological evidence for the destructive sacking or devastation of Anuradhapura's Citadel or Sacred City. What we do see archaeological evidence for, is the disappearance of a centralised economy centred upon Anuradhapura's monasteries and palaces. We see the reorganisation of trade routes away from Anuradhapura, the disappearance from Anuradhapura of craft specialists, of manufacturing, of the elite, of monumental construction, effectively the loss of all the characteristics of an urbanised complex society, all the characteristics of a centralised economy.

Yet, if the Cholas did not devastate the city, why then did Vijayabahu not fully restore Anuradhapura? Why did he and subsequent monarchs not rule from the ancient capital of Sri Lanka? Furthermore, why did the great Buddhist fraternities not return to the Sacred City of Anuradhapura, a site; *"specially deserving of honour, since its soil was hallowed while he lived by the feet of the Master, distinguished by the wheel with its thousand spikes and its rim, and because it was the place where the southern branch of the Sacred Bodhi tree (was planted) and where a dona of relics was preserved*" (*Cvs.*lxxiv.2-4)? The answer to these questions appears to lie in the role that the *sangha* played in the economic administration of Sri Lanka, and the role of kingship within Early Mediaeval Sri Lanka.

The Imperial Model argues that the Cholas, requiring control of the means of production and of long distance trade, removed an economic administrative structure that had developed, crystallised, over more than a thousand years. There is no doubt that Chola merchants were ruthless, and more than willing to use violence or the threat of violence to ensure trade (Hall 1977: 215), and there can be little doubt that the Cholas primary interest in imperial expansion, and thus in their invasion of Sri Lanka, was economic, as Schalk wrote in 2002;

"*The rational reason for conducting the wars was for territory. It was not for the preservation of ethnicity, for Tamilness or for Caivam, but for resources. The Cholas objectified the island as a source of income to maintain institutions in Tamilakam and as a springboard for further military and economic expansions to the East.*" (Schalk 2002: 674).

This is also seen in the claimed Chola invasion of the Gangetic Valley in the tenth century AD (Spencer 1983: 44). The Ganges formed the; "*artery of east-west trade in north India*" (Ray 1989: 440), and there is a strong argument that Chola mercantile groups (such as the Ainnurruvar, Manigramam and Anjuvannam) were at the forefront of the Chola growth both politically and imperially (Indrapala 2005: 240). It is also worth noting that, from the beginning of the eleventh century AD, epigraphic studies within the Chola heartland have highlighted a significant rise in the centralised control of taxes and economic administration as smaller "feudal" areas succumbed to the royal dominance (Heitzman 1987: 54).

Consequently, although the Cholas were not motivated by religion, to take control of the economy of Sri Lanka it was necessary to remove the Buddhist *sangha* from its position at the heart of that economic administration. Recent archaeological research within the Anuradhapura hinterland by Coningham et al. has produced a working hypothesis that sees the Buddhist monasteries of the hinterland performing the; "*...administrative, economic and political functions usually associated with towns*", acting as; "*...a network of long-lived centres of literacy, administration, education, production and the accumulation of economic surplus*" (Coningham et al. 2007a: 717). This administrative structure had developed over more than a millennium and, as discussed in Chapter Seven, many of the monastic sites within the Anuradhapura hinterland were occupied throughout the Anuradhapura period (*ibid.*: 709-10), not to mention the three major fraternities of the Sacred City.

8.7.1: *The Economic Power of the Sangha*

Individual members of the *sangha* were prohibited by their faith from accepting, owning, or even using money (Olivelle 1974: 61), and though the storing of goods was considered a practical necessity, they were also forbidden from engaging in trade (*ibid.*). However, from the beginning of Indian Ocean trade in the Early Historic period we see a synergy between Buddhist monasteries and trade centres (Ray 1989: 437 & 456), with monasteries initially clustering along trade routes (Ray 1989: 455) before becoming directly involved in the trade, and through that involvement accumulating significant wealth (Kosambi 1955: 60-61). At Anuradhapura it is worth noting Faxian's fifth century description of foreign (including Chinese) merchants living within the city in "*very grand dwellings*" (Hulagalle 2000: 15; Dias 2008: 82), again demonstrating that Anuradhapura was a major centre within the long distance trade network of the Indian Ocean.

Over the subsequent centuries, as the Buddhist fraternities became increasingly involved in land ownership and management, revenue collection and day-to-day economic administration, a "*...type of legal fiction pretended that nothing substantial had changed. All changes were treated as exceptions or at the most as allowances granted by the Buddha himself*" (Olivelle 1974: 61). Furthermore, the *sangha* was formally recognised as an incorporate body, and while individual members were not permitted to own property, the *sangha* as a body could (Liyanarachchi 2009: 105). However, even this rule appears to have been bent or broken, with a number of *sannas* (or grants) appearing to be gifted to individual *bhikkus* (Seneviratna 1989: 108).

There can be little doubt that, world renunciants or not, by the tenth century the *sangha* were becoming increasingly wealthy and increasingly powerful (Dias 2001; Liyanarachchi 2009: 102), due in no small part to the donative tradition of *sannas* granting lands, immunities and other resources, such as water rights, to monasteries (Gunawardana 1979: 58; Dias 1990: 151; Liyanarachchi 2009: 106-108). This practice started around the second century BC (Seneviratna 1989: 32) and had not only continued throughout the following centuries, but judging by epigraphic records had increased dramatically during the final two centuries of the millennium (Dias 1990: 151). These grants, frequently recorded through inscription on a rock or pillar, granted a range of facilities to the monasteries and *bhikkus*, and were gifted by kings, officials and private individuals (Liyanarachchi 2009: 106). It is likely that a significant number of land grants went unrecorded, or at least unrecorded on stone, as no inscriptions exist detailing solely a grant of land (Perera 2003: 96). Instead all such epigraphic records detail gifts of land (or water rights) *and* the immunities conveyed upon it (*ibid.*), and it is the immunities that are of particular interest here. They typically granted exemption from taxes, barred royal officials from entering the specified area (for *any* reason), and/or exempted villagers living within gifted lands from *vari* or forced labour, including working on the hydraulic landscape (Dias 1990: 154-55). Indeed, from epigraphic evidence and from clarifications of *vinaya* (or conduct) within the Samantapasadika (e.g. Kopp 1977 vol.3: 121-124, 345-346, 679), it would appear that the influence and control that the *sangha* wielded over the hydraulic system of Anuradhapura had grown steadily throughout the first millennium AD, resulting in the creation of ever increasing quantities of legislature to control access to and management of that system (Paranavitana 1958: 3; Seneviratna 1979: 125).

It is also striking that monasteries were frequently granted immunities for lands a significant distance away. For example, the three villages near Mantai granted immunities in the name of the Mahavihara, Anuradhapura (Wickremasinghe 1933: 105). Because these immunities were granted in perpetuity to institutions that had, by the tenth century, often existed for as long as a thousand years, each of these donative grants effectively permanently reduced the area and resources that the King or Queen of Anuradhapura ruled over. Conversely, as the estate of the monarch was steadily weakened and eroded by the immunitive grants, the monasteries became ever more powerful and wealthy as the land and resources they commanded grew steadily larger (Liyanarachchi 2009: 108). This led to the *sangha* wielding increasing influence upon the general populace, both spiritually and economically, forcing the monarchy to woo the *sangha* to ensure a good relationship and to maintain peaceful and successful governance (Rahula 1993: 70).

Indeed the *sangha* had become so wealthy, and weakened royal power to such a degree, that by the ninth century epigraphic records suggest there were significant problems, including the misappropriation of wealth in the monasteries, as well as conflict between royal officials and monasteries over the arrest of criminals taking refuge within these havens from royal rule (Liyanarachchi 2009: 108). Significantly it appears that the monasteries, and thus the *sangha*, were either unwilling or unable to address these issues and throughout the ninth and tenth centuries we increasingly see epigraphic records of (the more powerful) monarchs attempting to introduce checks and balances to address an increasingly corrupt or inefficient *sangha* (Perera 2005: 274; Liyanarachchi 2009: 108).

8.7.2: *Royal power and legitimation*

The relationship between the king and the *sangha* was always a complex one, with the king regarded as both the secular head and defender of the *Sasana* (Rahula 1993: 66), a role that variously saw different monarchs command, serve, and come into conflict with the *sangha*. The latter appears to have been a reasonably common occurrence, and from time to time the monarch would "purify" the *Sasana*, "*...whenever they found it to be disorganised or corrupt*" (Rahula 1993: 67).

However, such a balance was undoubtedly extremely difficult, and would only have been possible for the more powerful monarchs (Liyanarachchi 2009: 111). Indeed the position of king in Early Historic and Early Mediaeval Sri Lanka appears to have described the title rather than the succession (Coningham 1993a: 296 & 312). Usurping was common, and appears to have been readily accepted within the Pali chronicles and epigraphic records, meaning that the power and security of a king appears to have been only as great as that which they could command (*ibid.*). The support of the *sangha* was thus vital in legitimising royal rule, while at the same time representing a significant economic and political rival, this relationship is depicted in figures 8.03 and 8.04.

This complex and dynamic relationship between the monarchs of Anuradhapura and the *sangha* can be seen in the descriptions of various kings in the Pali chronicles. We know the Pali chronicles were compiled by *bhikkus*, and as such are open to bias in *how* events and individuals are portrayed, as well as *which* events are described. This issue has been long recognised, with de Zoysa accusing the annalists of the *Mahavamsa* and *Culavamsa* of omitting "*some unpleasant episodes*" as early as 1873 (de Zoysa 1873: 76), while Burrows, writing in 1887, argued that the *Mahavamsa* had ignored the works of Nissanka Malla (r.1187-1196) because; "*it does not appear that he did much for, or interested himself much in, the priesthood. His tastes seem to have lain rather in the direction of foreign conquest... than of the endowment of viharas*" (Burrows 1887: 54-55). Furthermore, Burrows highlights inscriptions from the Mahavihara of Anuradhapura recording Nissanka Malla tackling corruption within the *sangha* and making donations to a Saivite temple (*ibid.*). Burrows ends by stating that "*If we had before us a fair secular and political history as well, it is more than probably that we should form a very different estimate of the various kings whose reigns are detailed in it.*" (*ibid.*). Clearly then, the relationship between the *sangha* and royalty was not always harmonious, yet despite this it is also clear that the *sangha* was vital not only in legitimising royal rule (Houtart 1977: 208), but also in providing the connection between the rural production of surplus, and the centralised collection and storage of that surplus (Houtart 1977: 209; Coningham et al. 2007a: 717).

However, by the ninth century AD the economic and political structure of Sri Lanka had crystallised over move than a millennium, the great fraternities of Anuradhapura had become immensely economically powerful institutions and in so doing were alienating resources and authority from the royal rulers of Anuradhapura. The *sangha* was able to withhold villagers from labour upon the hydraulic landscape (Seneviratna 1979: 125), to deny royal officials entry to their holdings, all while collecting ever greater amounts of revenue which, even as it made the monasteries richer, simultaneously diminished the revenues that the king received, and further, diminished the power that the king could wield. This system was so established around the *sangha* that by the tenth century AD we see extensive inscriptions publicly detailing the accounting and auditing requirements of the monasteries, such as those seen at Mihintale (Perera 2005: 275; Liyanarachchi 2009: 112).

8.7.3: *Theoretical Perspectives*

Phillips (1979: 138) has suggested that, "*the problem is not that states collapse... but rather that some states last so long*". Philips argued that it takes time for a state to utilise its resources efficiently (*ibid*.: 140), however, efficiency results in a lack of flexibility in resource allocation (*ibid*.). Although Phillips was explicitly writing about the Mayan collapse, such theoretical models may aid in the examination of the mechanisms and causal factors behind Anuradhapura's collapse.

Effectively, Phillips argued that during its early phase a state controls a large and often expandable resource base, but has not yet developed the complex institutions that will efficiently derive a significant return from this resource base. At this time a large proportion of these resources will always be utilised in non-critical ways (for example monumental construction). This can be seen in the case of Anuradhapura in the construction of both the monumental stupas and monumental tanks, all of which were constructed between the third century BC and the fifth century AD. This results in the creation of a hidden resource reserve, as such non-essential activities can be suspended at times of crisis (*ibid.*).

However, Phillips argues that, over time, social and political institutions then emerge that are able to efficiently exploit these resource bases, and in turn use greater resources themselves (*ibid*.: 141). Within the case of Anuradhapura's collapse we might highlight the monastic institutions here, over time taking greater and greater control of the economic management of the state, as seen in the growing number of *sannas* (Dias 2001; Liyanarachchi 2009: 102). Eventually the state reaches a point where the majority of resources are allocated to supporting these institutions, leaving no reserves and thus no flexibility in resource allocation, leaving the centre susceptible to disruptions (Phillips 1979: 142).

Here it is possibly helpful to integrate Tainter's (1988) *Marginal Productivity of Increasing Complexity* model with Phillips' (1979) *Insufficient Response to Circumstances* model. At its most basic, Tainter's model argues that more complex societies are more costly to maintain, and as societal complexity increases so too does the cost (Tainter 1988: 93). At a certain point of this socio-political evolution, that cost reaches a point of diminishing marginal returns, at which time increased investment fails to yield proportionately increased returns (shown in figure 8.05).

The marginal costs continue to increase, but the marginal returns decline and the very complexity that so defines that society becomes increasingly costly, less productive and thus less beneficial to the members of that society (*ibid*.: 121). At this point the state is now vulnerable to what Phillips terms "historical accidents"; crises that an emerging state would manage comfortably, but that a society experiencing declining marginal returns, a society already operating at peak efficiency, simply cannot respond to. This theoretical model can be seen in flowchart form in figure 8.06.

This could easily be applied to, for example, the agricultural productivity of Anuradhapura. The hydraulic landscape appears to have been effectively complete from around the seventh century AD (Seneviratna 1989: 46), after this point the cost of increasing agricultural productivity would have risen exponentially, and the marginal returns would have declined sharply. Indeed the law of diminishing marginal returns has been particularly successfully applied to agriculture (Clark & Haswell 1966: 83-84; Boserup 1981: 45; Tainter 1988: 94-99).

8.7.4: *Choosing to Collapse*

Consequently, both archaeologically and theoretically, the Anuradhapura of the ninth and tenth centuries could be described as being in decline, despite the accepted view that this represent's Anuradhapura's golden age. Of course, as was established in Chapter Three (**3.2.2**), Anuradhapura's collapse is urban, not societal, as the Polonnaruva period is quite clearly a cultural and societal continuation. Therefore, did the collapse of Anuradhapura, and the shift of political, religious and economic power to Polonnaruva, represent a coping mechanism to manage the crisis posed by South Indian mercantile and imperial aggression, and the Monastic marginalisation of royal power? As discussed above (**8.7.2**) Anuradhapura had reached a level of socio-political complexity and economic efficiency that greatly hindered any attempts to counter this threat, but by moving the capital, moving the "city" to Polonnaruva the state could grow and develop for several more centuries. Recent research in the hinterland has demonstrated that rural settlements in the Anuradhapura hinterland were transitory (Coningham et al. 2007a), and there is the Indian example of Fatehpur Sikri, the site of an (unsuccessful) imposed sixteenth century urban development and shift of capital (Brand et al. 1985). Furthermore, after the collapse of Polonnaruva we see the capital in Sri Lanka shifting several times (Fig.8.07), with Dambadenyia, Yapahuwa, Kurunagala, Gampola and Senkadagala (modern Kandy) all serving as capital after the abandonment of Polonnaruva in the thirteenth century (De Silva 1981: 82) – clearly the nature of the capital had transformed from the geographically grounded sacred land of Anuradhapura, to a mobile symbolism represented by the Tooth Relic and the monarchy, and moving capital was now an established and accepted response to adverse circumstances.

This transition of power from Anuradhapura to Polonnaruva appears to have been facilitated by the period of Chola rule, it was they who first ruled from Polonnaruva, and they who appear to have re-routed trade, stripped the *sangha* of its holdings built up by over a millennium of donative grants. But, given the nature of the relationship between the king and *sangha* by the eleventh century AD, Vijayabahu's decision to rule from Polonnaruva and to maintain the administrative structure of the Cholas could be argued to be a deliberate decision to keep the recently decimated *sangha* in a comparatively weakened state, and by doing so secure his own power base both economically and politically. This would seem even more important given the description in the *Culavamsa* (*Cvs*.lix) of rivals raising civil unrest in the south of Sri Lanka immediately after Vijayabahu's coronation. Clearly in the aftermath of the victory over the Cholas, some effort is made to restore both the *sangha* and Anuradhapura, Vijayabahu is after all, as king of Sri Lanka, the defender of the Buddhist faith (Houtart 1977: 214). He is described as importing Buddhist monks from Southeast Asia (*Cvs*.lx.4-6; Indrapala 2005: 239), so decimated was the *sangha* after the period of Chola rule, and he and several of his successors are described as carrying out repairs to Anuradhapura (*Cvs*.lxxiv.8-14). Coronations and similar ceremonies are frequently held at Anuradhapura (e.g. *Cvs*.lix.8), but it appears clear that by the twelfth century AD, Anuradhapura had been transformed from the economic, administrative, royal and spiritual capital of Sri Lanka to a symbolic ceremonial site. The distribution of inscriptions (Fig.8.01 and Fig.8.02) demonstrates the change of focus, with the only post-tenth century inscriptions at Anuradhapura recording repairs carried out by Polonnaruva period rulers – a seemingly symbolic gesture.

Finally, it is interesting to note that there have been suggestions that the thirteenth century failure of the Chola imperial state was caused by precisely the same alienation of wealth and resources by religious institutions in South India. Heitzman suggests that;

"*...the donation of lands to temples, and the verification in inscriptions of the particular rights enjoyed by all participating parties, were thus the signs of an increasing flight from royal control and the creation of tax shelters in religious institutions... as the central state fell apart, temple endowments expanded until the temples themselves became the greatest institutions in South India, major landlords and political forces themselves*" (Heitzman 1987: 58).

It could thus be argued, that Anuradhapura did not in fact collapse, but was deliberately abandoned as the only available response to similar circumstances to those that contributed to the Chola collapse two centuries later. As discussed earlier the South Asian city was understood to be at the centre of the world – not simply in a geographical, political or economic sense, but as the centre of the cosmos and of order (Eck 1987: 04). Consequently, when the "city" was moved to Polonnaruva, Anuradhapura lost not only its economic and political importance, but also lost its place within the Early Mediaeval Sri Lankan world-view. It is also interesting to note the shift in ritual focus post-Anuradhapura. During the Anuradhapura period the emphasis was upon static fixed objects that made Anuradhapura sacred; the Bodhi tree, Mihintale, the gigantic stupas with their reliquaries (Seneviratna 1994). However, after this the focus moves to mobile forms of religious veneration. The focus is not upon Polonnaruva as a sacred centre, it is upon the Temple of the Tooth, and this (as is subsequently seen) is a mobile object. Even now Anuradhapura remains a centre of pilgrimage, a sacred *place* – Polonnaruva today is purely an archaeological reserve. Almost as if there was a recognition that mobility was a necessary response mechanism, and that anchoring the state to one site, as Anuradhapura did for over a millennium, was a mistake. Thus, just as rural settlements moved in search of new resources within the Anuradhapura hinterland (Coningham et al. 2007a), perhaps too the capital, the "city" of Sri Lanka (as arguably Anuradhapura, and subsequently Polonnaruva, were the only true cities in Sri Lanka during their respective periods as capital) required mobility to adapt to changing economic and political climates.

8.7: Conclusion

This chapter started by identifying Renfrew's characteristics of systems collapse (Renfrew 1984: 367-370) within the archaeological record of Anuradhapura's three zones, confirming that Anuradhapura can indeed be said to collapse around the beginning of the eleventh century AD. It then went on to fulfil the second aim of the book, testing the established explanation for Anuradhapura's collapse through explicit reference to the archaeological record. By comparing the archaeological signatures of collapse for each of the three models (Invasion, Malarial and Imperial) with the actual archaeological signatures developed in Chapters Five, Six and Seven, it was possible to identify the Imperial Model as the most analogous to the observed archaeological record. Moreover, the Imperial Model demonstrates synergy with recent archaeological research (Coningham et al. 2007a) into the administrative system of rural Anuradhapura, and can not only explain the initial abandonment of Anuradhapura, but also makes a compelling argument for the deliberate decision by later Polonnaruva rulers to marginalise Anuradhapura. Chapter Nine will now conclude this volume by relating Anuradhapura's collapse to collapse theory, in addition to considering the significance and difficulties encountered within this work, and future directions of study on Sri Lanka's low-density urban states.

Table 8.01: *Anuradhapura's Archaeological Signature*

13th	12th	11th	10th	9th	Century AD	
✠	↘	←	↘	→	Citadel	Population
✠	↘	←	→	→	Sacred City	
←	←	↘	↓	↓	Hinterland	
✠	←	✠	←	→	Citadel	Monumental Construction
✠	←	✠	→	→	Sacred City	
✠	✠	✠	→	→	Hinterland	
✠	←	✠	↘	→	Citadel	Traditional Elite
✠	←	✠	→	→	Sacred City	
✠	✠	✠	→	→	Hinterland	
✠	✠	✠	←	←	Citadel	New Elite
✠	✠	←	←	←	Sacred City	
✠	✠	←	✠	✠	Hinterland	
✠	✠	✠	→	→	Citadel	Long Distance Trade
✠	✠	✠	→	→	Sacred City	
✠	✠	✠	✠	✠	Hinterland	
✠	←	←	↘	→	Citadel	Craft Specialisation
✠	←	←	→	→	Sacred City	
✠	←	←	↓	↓	Hinterland	

KEY: ↑ High ↓ Low ↗ Rising ↘ Falling → Steady ✠ Absent

Table 8.02: *The Invasion Model's Archaeological Signature*

13th	12th	11th	10th	9th	Century AD	
✠	←	✠	→	→	Citadel	Population
✠	←	✠	→	→	Sacred City	
✠	←	←	→	→	Hinterland	
✠	←	✠	→	→	Citadel	Monumental Construction
✠	←	✠	→	→	Sacred City	
✠	←	✠	→	→	Hinterland	
✠	←	✠	→	→	Citadel	Traditional Elite
✠	←	✠	→	→	Sacred City	
✠	✠	✠	→	→	Hinterland	
✠	✠	→	✠	✠	Citadel	New Elite
✠	✠	→	✠	✠	Sacred City	
✠	✠	✠	✠	✠	Hinterland	
✠	✠	✠	→	→	Citadel	Long Distance Trade
✠	✠	✠	→	→	Sacred City	
✠	✠	✠	↓	↓	Hinterland	
✠	←	✠	→	→	Citadel	Craft Specialisation
✠	←	✠	→	→	Sacred City	
✠	✠	✠	→	→	Hinterland	

KEY: ↑ High ↓ Low ↗ Rising ↘ Falling → Steady ✠ Absent

Table 8.03: *The Malarial Model's Archaeological Signature*

13th	12th	11th	10th	9th	Century AD	
✣	↘	←	→	→	Citadel	Population
✣	↘	←	→	→	Sacred City	
✣	↘	←	→	→	Hinterland	
✣	↘	←	→	→	Citadel	Monumental Construction
✣	↘	←	→	→	Sacred City	
✣	↘	←	→	→	Hinterland	
✣	↘	↘	→	→	Citadel	Traditional Elite
✣	↘	↘	→	→	Sacred City	
✣	↘	↘	→	→	Hinterland	
✣	✣	→	✣	✣	Citadel	New Elite
✣	✣	→	✣	✣	Sacred City	
✣	✣	→	✣	✣	Hinterland	
✣	↘	↘	→	→	Citadel	Long Distance Trade
✣	↘	↘	→	→	Sacred City	
✣	↘	↘	↓	↓	Hinterland	
✣	↘	↘	→	→	Citadel	Craft Specialisation
✣	↘	↘	→	→	Sacred City	
✣	↘	↘	→	→	Hinterland	
KEY: ↑ High ↓ Low ↗ Rising ↘ Falling → Steady ✣ Absent						

Table 8.04: *The Imperial Model's Archaeological Signature*

13th	12th	11th	10th	9th	Century AD	
✠	↙	←	↙	→	Citadel	Population
✠	↙	←	→	→	Sacred City	
✠	↙	↙	→	→	Hinterland	
✠	←	✠	↙	→	Citadel	Monumental Construction
✠	←	✠	→	→	Sacred City	
✠	↙	↙	→	→	Hinterland	
✠	←	✠	↙	→	Citadel	Traditional Elite
✠	←	✠	↘	→	Sacred City	
✠	✠	✠	↘	→	Hinterland	
✠	✠	✠	↘	←	Citadel	New Elite
✠	✠	✠	↘	←	Sacred City	
✠	✠	↘	↘	✠	Hinterland	
✠	✠	✠	→	→	Citadel	Long Distance Trade
✠	✠	✠	→	→	Sacred City	
✠	✠	✠	↓	↓	Hinterland	
✠	↙	↙	↙	→	Citadel	Craft Specialisation
✠	↙	↙	→	→	Sacred City	
✠	↙	↙	→	→	Hinterland	

KEY: ↑ High ↓ Low ↗ Rising ↘ Falling → Steady ✠ Absent

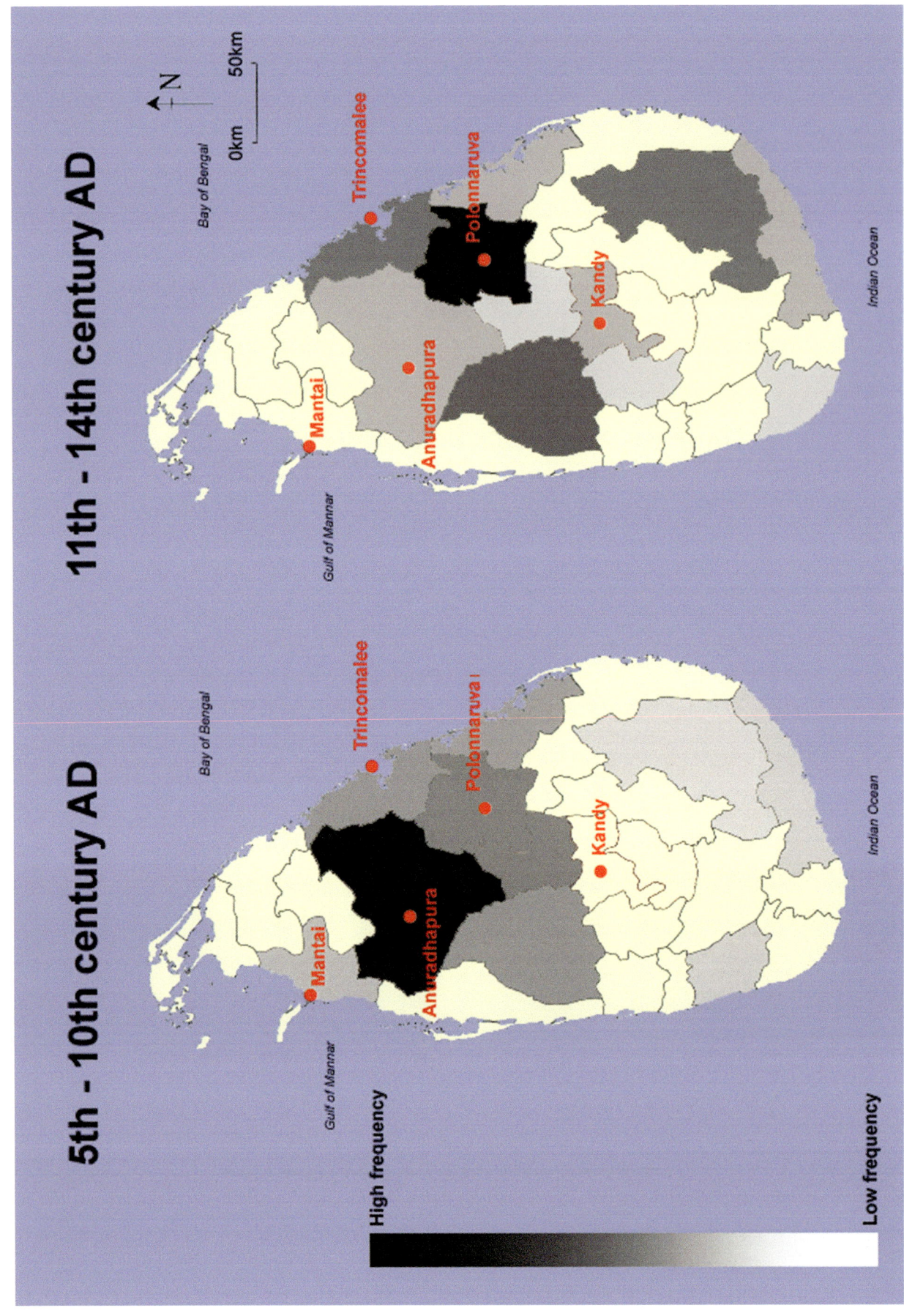

FIGURE 8.01: DISTRIBUTION OF EPIGRAPHIA ZEYLANICA INSCRIPTIONS (IMAGE REF: AUTHOR)

CHAPTER 8: THE DISCUSSION

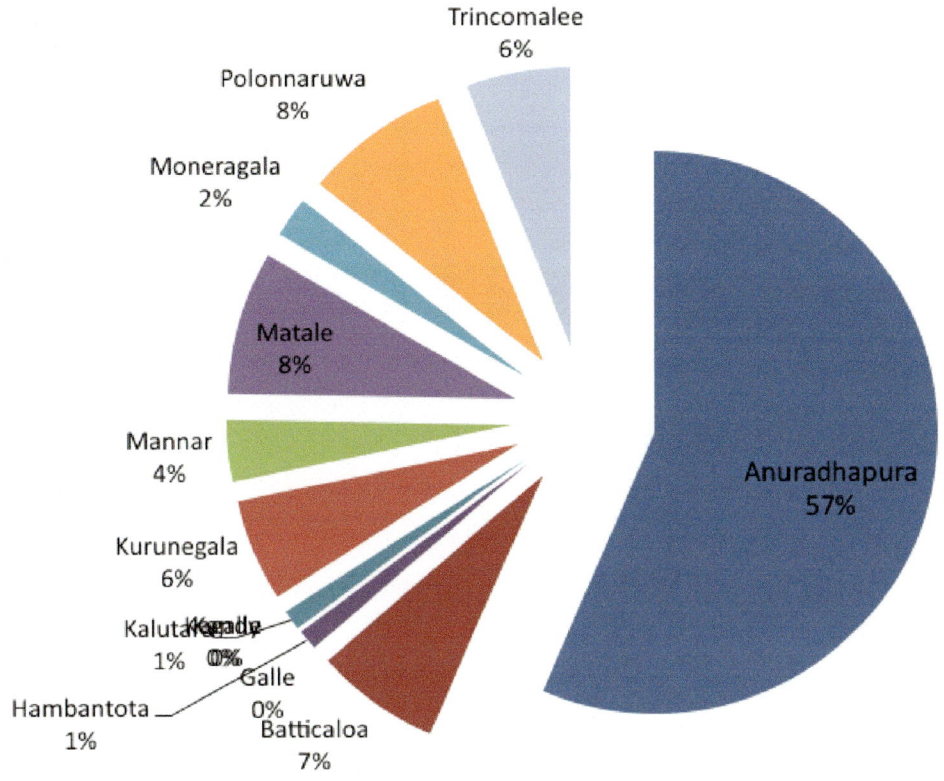

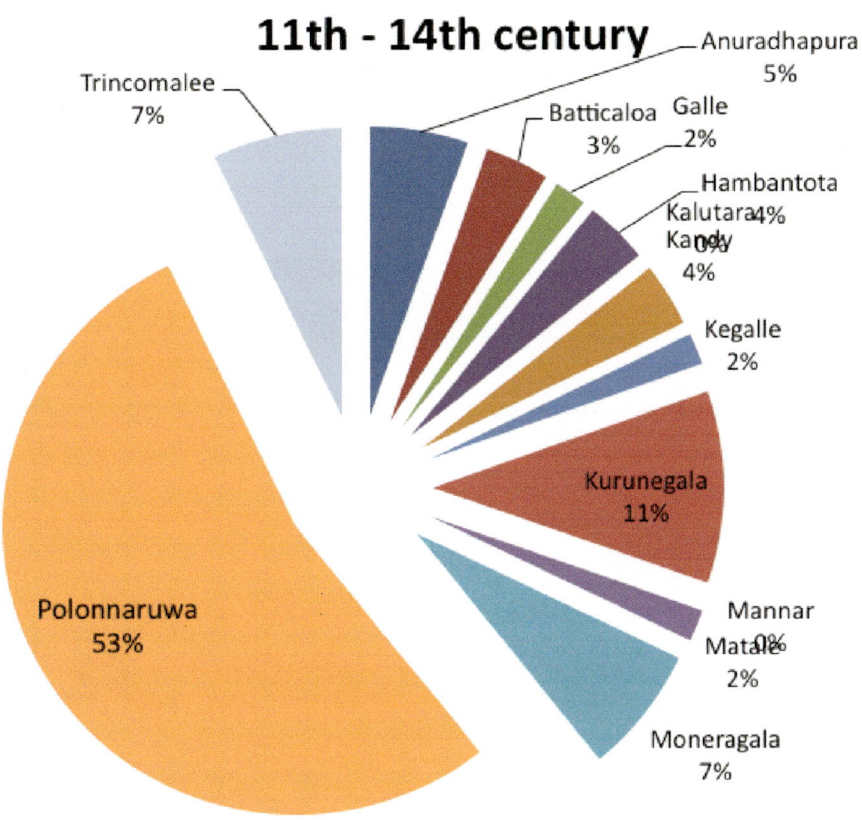

FIGURE 8.02: DISTRIBUTION OF EPIGRAPHIA ZEYLANICA INSCRIPTIONS (IMAGE REF: AUTHOR)

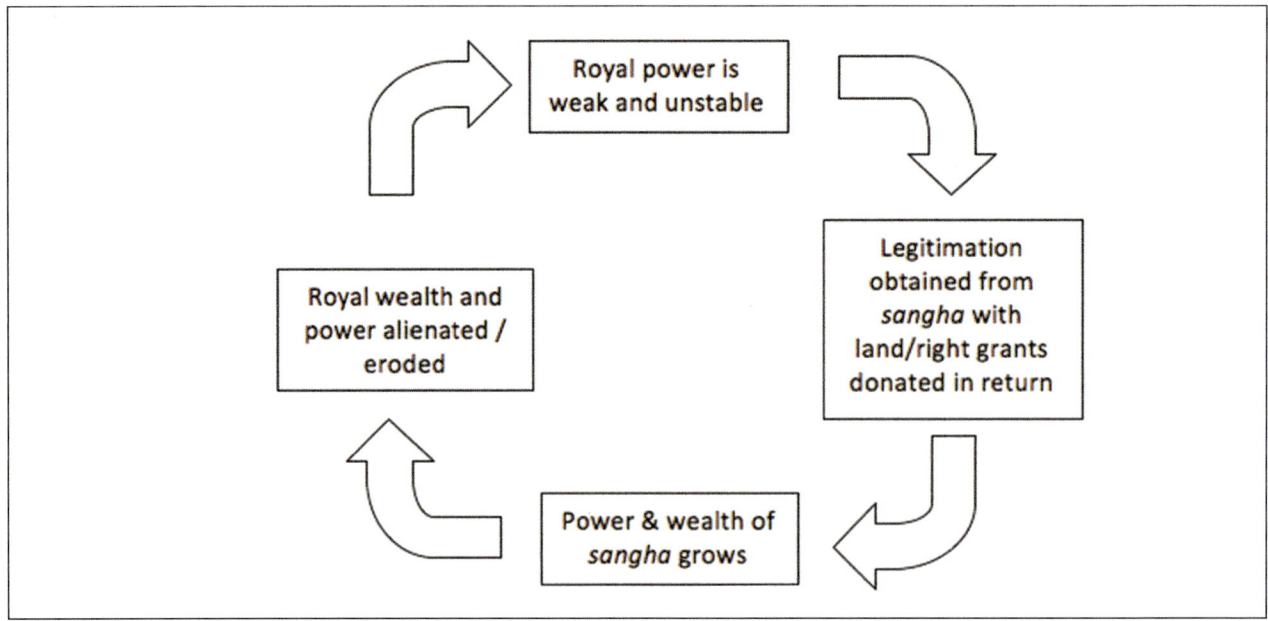

Figure 8.03: Positive feedback loop of alienation of Royal power

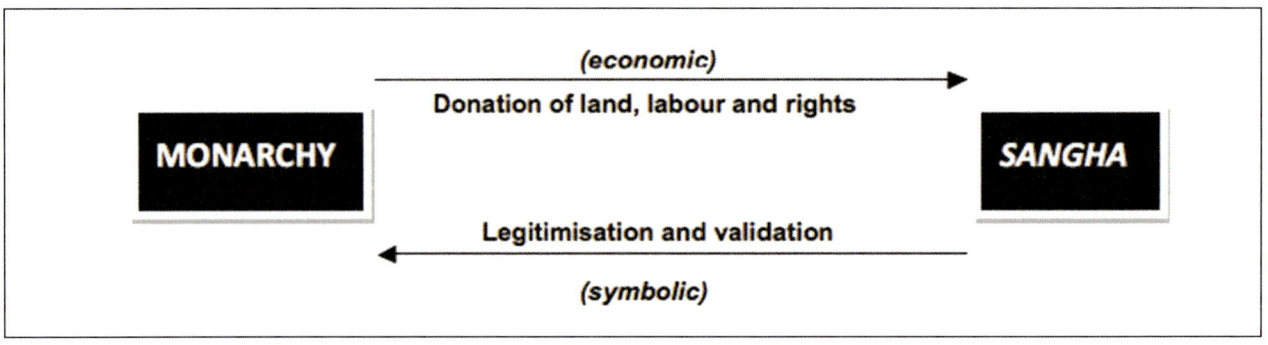

Figure 8.04: Graphic visualisation of exchange between monarchy and sangha

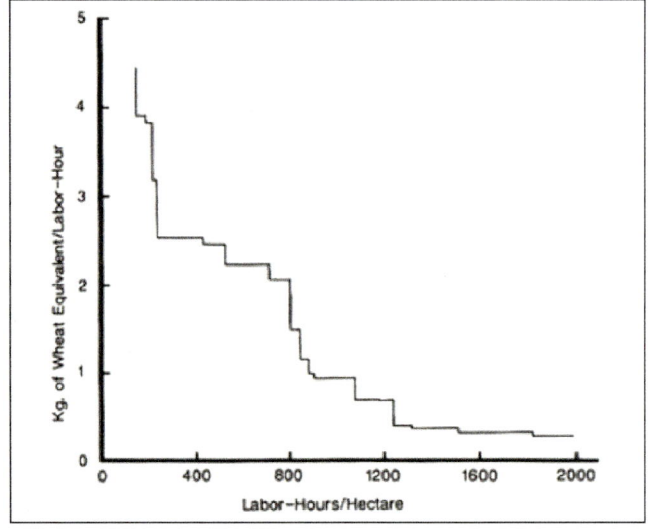

Figure 8.05: The marginal product of increasing complexity in Greek agriculture
(image ref. Tainter 1988: 97)

CHAPTER 8: THE DISCUSSION

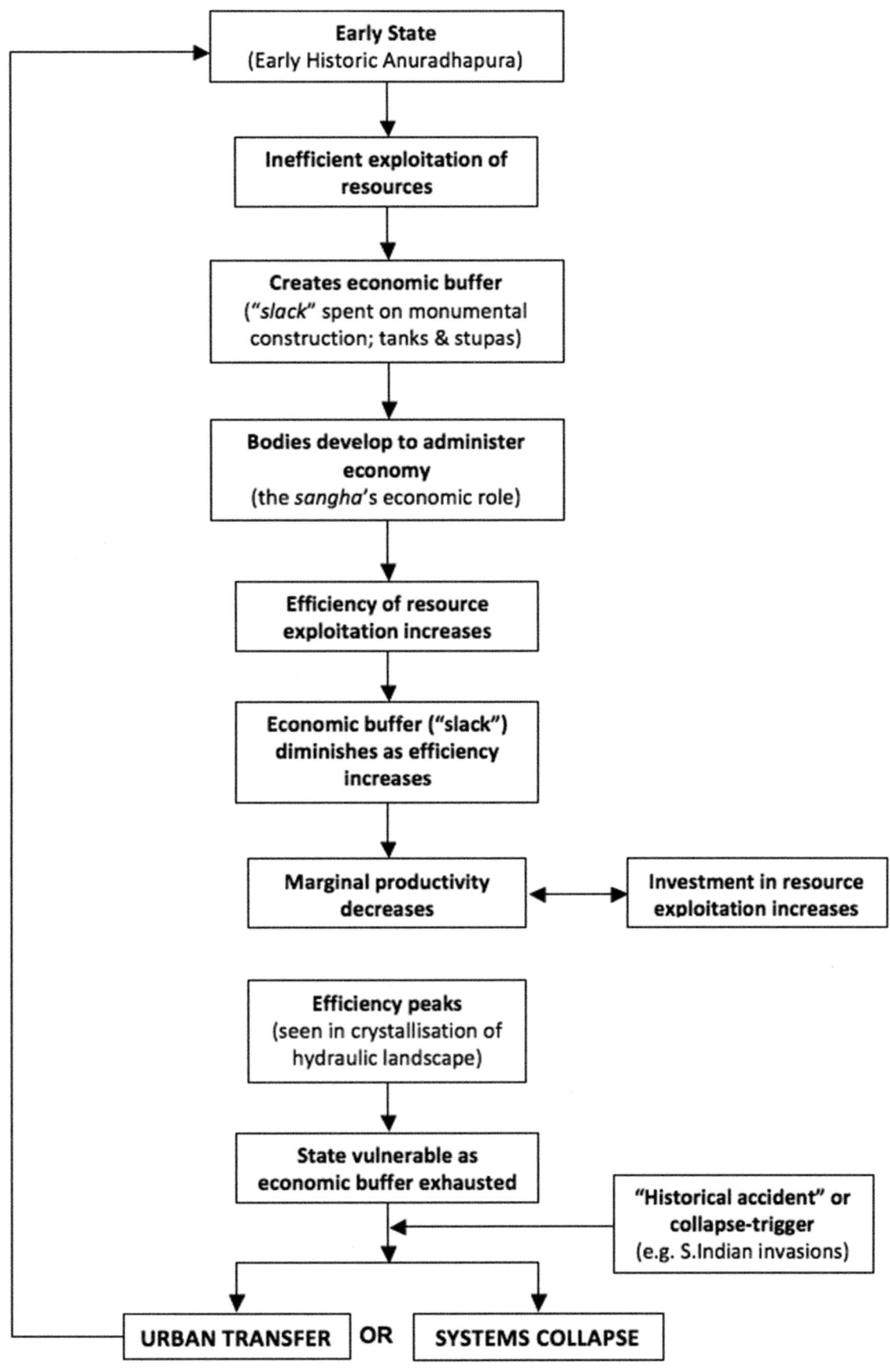

FIGURE 8.06: PARENTHETICAL FLOW CHART OF ANURADHAPURA'S COLLAPSE
(AFTER PHILLIPS 1979; RENFREW 1987; TAINTER 1988; MORTAZAVI 2004)

A Time of Change: The "Collapse" of Anuradhapura, Sri Lanka

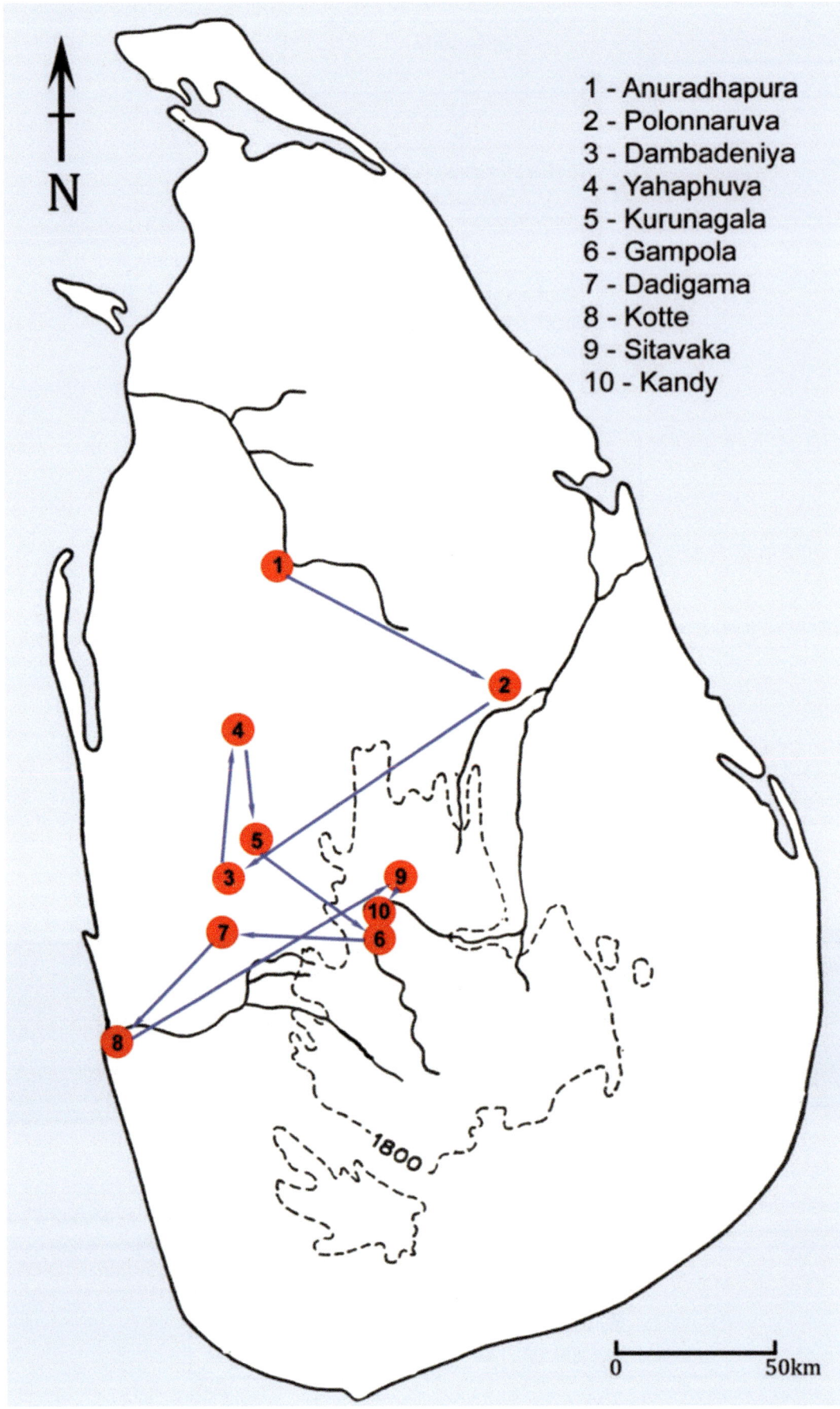

Figure 8.07: Mobility of Sri Lanka's Capitals (Image by author)

Chapter 9: Conclusion

9.1 Introduction

This book set out (section **1.4**) to establish whether or not Anuradhapura "collapsed", and to reassess the established explanation for Anuradhapura's eleventh century "collapse", through explicit reference to the archaeological record of Anuradhapura. In the case of the former, the answer is relatively simple and affirmative; Anuradhapura appears, archaeologically at least, to collapse during the eleventh century AD. Accepting the characteristics of collapse as laid out by Renfrew (1984), the terminal period of Anuradhapura matches all applicable characteristics (**8.2**), as well as fitting Tainter's more generic definition of a; "*rapid, substantial decline in an established level of complexity*" (Tainter 1988: 38) or Diamond's slightly more specific definition of; "*a drastic decrease in human population size and/or political/economic/social complexity, over a considerable area, for an extended time*" (Diamond 2005: 03).

The conclusion to the second aim is somewhat more cautious. Clearly the collapse of Anuradhapura cannot be attributed to malaria, though it may have been a factor in discouraging re-settlement after the collapse. However, the Chola invasion, while almost impossible to archaeologically identify, cannot be dismissed, and the difficulties in identifying warfare in South Asian archaeology have been discussed. Despite this, the established narrative of the Pali chronicles, that attributed the Anuradhapura's collapse completely and solely to the Chola sacking of the city, must be considered an insufficient explanation of a number of complex processes occurring during the final centuries of the first millennium.

The Imperial Model is clearly the best supported of the three collapse models, and found broad archaeological agreement across all three zones of Anuradhapura, as well as across Sri Lanka (**8.6**). However, as already stressed, the Imperial Model is a synthetic model the source texts of which never explicitly attempt to explain Anuradhapura's collapse, and consequently it was both necessary and rewarding to unpack the Imperial Model in chapter 8 (**8.7**), in effect creating an "Expanded Imperial Model" that successfully combined and related the archaeological signatures of Anuradhapura's terminal period across its three key zones, concurrent archaeologically observable developments across Sri Lanka and the Indian Ocean region, historical records, extant regional scholarship (i.e. Spencer 1983; Indrapala 2005), in addition to and both universal (Tainter 1988) and comparative (Phillips 1979) theoretical collapse models.

Chapter nine will now concisely present the *Expanded Imperial Model*, effectively the final product of this volume and certainly an entirely new understanding of Anuradhapura's collapse, before going on to examine the successes and failures of this volume, along with the significance of this study and future avenues of research that might be pursued.

9.2: The Expanded Imperial Model

The growth and development of Anuradhapura into a major economic and cultural Indian Ocean centre has been comprehensively mapped, most significantly and recently by the ASW2 excavations (Coningham 1999 & 2006) and Anuradhaura Hinterland project (Coningham & Gunawardhana 2013). However, its terminal period has been both intellectually neglected and extremely poorly understood until now.

Anuradhapura at the start of Period F, around the 3rd or 4th century AD, was a thriving, and growing, city – and within this context the concept of the city may be extended to its fullest extent, one in which the immediate hinterland effectively forms the outer zone of that low-density urban form (Fletcher 2011). Right around this time we see huge investment goes into developing not only the Citadel and Sacred City's monumental viharas, stupas and palaces, but also into the final wave of construction of gigantic tanks and canals – in effect the finishing touches to an extraordinarily vast and complex hydraulic landscape. This was seen within the recent Anuradhapura Hinterland survey in the dating of sites such as the stupa at Parthigala (site Z00) to the 5th century AD and its associated bund and tank system (site Z021) to the 6th century AD. This development can be seen as the fine-tuning, or maximising, of economic productivity within that hinterland, and it would appear clear that not only were monastic sites closely linked to the construction of this hydraulic landscape, but also that these monastic sites acted as managers, administrators, and often owners, of these hydraulic sites. As predicted by Phillips (1979: 141) the *sangha*, a "social and political institution", appears to have acted as a facilitator for improving the efficiency and scale of this resource exploitation, as well as being heavily involved in resource consumption and redistribution (*ibid*.).

Anuradhapura appears to have then continued to flourish during the first half (c.6th to 8th centuries AD) of the subsequent structural macro-period (Period C,D&E), with clear evidence of fresh construction across the Citadel, Sacred City, and Hinterland. This is perhaps most visible in the massive brick gediges of the Citadel, the Pabbata Viharas and Padhanaghara Parivenas of the Sacred City and hinterland, the flourishing westwards trade with the Middle East, and the scale and sophistication of the stonework of so much of the extant architecture across the Citadel and Sacred City.

However, while the hinterland and Sacred City can be archaeologically seen to flourish right up to the end of Period C,D&E (around the beginning of the 11th century) with only low levels of robbing of structural materials identified within the Sacred City, the Citadel sees clear evidence of an extremely turbulent period. The endemic structural robbing and re-use of material identified within the ASW2 sequence (Coningham 1999) is striking and, combined with the late remodelling of the ramparts (Coningham & Cheetham 1999: 54), indicates at least the *threat* of violence, in addition to either a significant lack of resources or time. Given that within the hinterland we see fresh monastic construction as late as 970 AD ($\pm$60) at site F517, and the apparent continued success of the Sacred City's viharas, it is reasonable to link these apparently disparate fortunes to the centuries of donative *sannas* leaching land, resources, and power away from the monarchy, leaving the monarchy attenuated. It is also extremely likely that, by this point, Anuradhapura had reached something approaching peak efficiency in its economic productivity, reaching a stage of declining marginal returns (Tainter 1988: 93), and unable sufficiently respond to the apparent Chola invasion of Sri Lanka.

Of course, the legendary Chola sacking of Anuradhapura remains troubling, in the complete absence of any direct archaeological evidence of either a Chola presence or violence or warfare in any of Anuradhapura's zones. However, in a sense the question of the Chola sacking is secondary, as the critical damage done to Anuradhapura lies in the altering of the economic administrative network; the neglecting of the hydraulic landscape, the rerouting of the system of economic surplus gathering and redistribution, the redirecting of trade routes to Polonnaruva and the east, the religious sea-change of Polonnaruva period Sri Lanka.

However, this period of Chola imperial rule lasts less than a century, and archaeologically it is clear that Anuradhapura (in any of its zones) has not been utterly laid waste to. Consequently, it is not unreasonable to suppose that Anuradhapura, at this point, might have been restored, repaired and returned to its place as Sri Lanka's capital and pre-eminent city. This appears to have occurred in the past, certainly the chronicles describe several earlier incursions by South Indian armies (for example see *Cvs*.l.12-36 or Codrington 1960), even going as far as suggesting that for brief periods several monarchs attempted to shift the capital away from Anuradhapura (e.g. *Cvs*.ixxxx; *Cvs*.l). However, this time a clear and irreversible decision is made by Vijayabahu I (and his successors) to abandon well over a millennium of rule, of tradition, and to invest resources into further sustaining, and further developing, Polonnaruva ahead of Anuradhapura.

The displacement of the *sangha* by the Cholas was arguably an economically motivated move, allowing the Cholas access to, and control of, the economic administration of Sri Lanka. However, it also effectively reset the clock on centuries of accumulation of power by the major monastic fraternities of Anuradhapura and re-empowered the monarchy, and this must surely be considered as a prime mover behind Vijayabahu's decision not to restore Anuradhapura as capital, of Sri Lanka. Furthermore, by relocating Sri Lanka's capital the Cholas and Vijayabahu effectively relocated the city's hinterland – thus enabling new growth, and combating the declining marginal returns and peaked efficiency that would have posed continuing problems at Anuradhapura.

Back at Anuradhapura, now deposed as capital, as Sri Lanka's "city", we can archaeologically see that around the early part of the 11th century AD, the Citadel and Sacred City are largely abandoned, as the economic and political focus shifts to Polonnaruva, as illustrated in figures 8.13 and 8.14. Following this abandonment, occupation continues in both the Citadel and Sacred City, albeit on a far smaller scale, and largely in a cruder form. Despite the dramatic shift in structural form, with a predominance of organic and re-used structural materials (Coningham 1999; Coningham & Batt 1999: 129), there is still clear evidence of the existence of a street-plan (Ayrton 1924: 51; Coningham 199: 20), and even fresh construction of "monumental" buildings as seen in the so-called "Vijayabahu's palace" (albeit fresh monumental construction of a smaller, far simpler and less lavish form than those that preceded) (Coningham 1999: 21). Occupation also continues for a few more centuries in the Hinterland, although monastic sites appear to be abandoned relatively early, with sites such as C112 and Z00 being abandoned late in the 11th century AD (1090AD$\pm$50 and 1100AD$\pm$70), and the hydraulic sites such as C018 and C009 that were so vital to the functioning of the hinterland abandoned to siltation around the 12th century AD (1120AD$\pm$40, 1200AD$\pm$60). By around the beginning of the 13th century Anuradhapura appears to be largely abandoned across all its zones, and although there is continued ephemeral settlement activity within the hinterland in areas such as the Citadel and Sacred City there is almost no further occupation until the colonial period.

9.3 Future Directions

As with all archaeological research, this current volume, and all of its conclusions, hypotheses and arguments, is a product of the archaeological dataset *currently* available. Long term, this dataset will (hopefully) continue to expand, be refined and analysed using new techniques, and consequently this very subject, the collapse of Anuradhapura, will doubtless be revisited at a future date. However, in the short term, there are several avenues that could greatly benefit our understanding of Anuradhapura's collapse; perhaps most importantly palaeoenvironmental research, greater focus upon the archaeology of the "Tamil" north and east of Sri Lanka, and further archaeological research into both the emergent and terminal periods of Polonnaruva.

The first, a focus upon archaeological research in the north and east of Sri Lanka, has realistically been impossible for several decades due to the conflict in these areas. However, with a lasting end to this conflict, it may now be possible to once again carry out such archaeological research in an area that is vital to any understanding of the early Mediaeval period of Sri Lanka, and especially to our understanding of the 11th century period of Chola imperial rule in Sri Lanka. As touched upon in section **8.6.2**, the ASC identified a significant number of Chola inscriptions and Saivite shrines in this region, but the majority of excavations and surveys in these areas were carried out *by* the ASC, over a century ago. Since then the region has, rather sadly become the subject of something of an academic divide with scholars of Tamil (e.g. Indrapala 1971b; 2005; Schalk & Veluppillai 2002) or South Indian (e.g. Spencer 1976 & 1983; Spencer & Hall 1974) history studying region, while Sinhalese archaeologists have tended to focus upon the former strongholds of the Sinhalese rulers (i.e. Anuradhapura, Polonnaruva, Tissamaharama, Dambulla, Sigiriya etc.). In particular, an archaeological survey of the Trincomalee region would be of huge interest to any analysis of Chola rule and their involvement in long distance Indian Ocean trade. It is further hoped that future archaeological research within this field will be more collaborative and more polyvocal. It is a great shame that there appears to exist an academic divide within Sri Lanka, with only "Tamil" academics and institutions studying the Tamils in ancient Sri Lanka (e.g. Schalk & Veluppillai 2002; Indrapala 2005), and only Indian historians studying the Cholas in ancient Sri Lanka (e.g. Spender 1976 and 1983). This same research problem might also be addressed by the conducting of new excavations at the so called "Hindu Ruins" of Anuradhapura, in order to better understand the complex interactions and relationships of ethnicity and religion during Anuradhapura's apparent fluorescence.

A further avenue of research that could provide fascinating new perspectives upon the terminal period of Anuradhapura, and more specifically Polonnaruva, is that of palaeoenvironmental research. It seems in recent years that environmental causes for collapse have gained a new popularity (see Haug et al. 2003; Diamond 2005), and indeed when discussing Anuradhapura's terminal period with Dr. Roland Fletcher (Fletcher *pers. comm.* 2007) he suggested the key role climate change or environmental degradation could have played, citing his research into Angkor's early Mediaeval collapse as an analogous example (Fletcher et al. 2008). Unfortunately this was not an avenue that could be pursued at this time due to a lack of palaeoenvironmental data. Sri Lanka has; *"no tradition of studying Late Quaternary vegetation and climate history"* (Premathilake & Risberg 2003: 1525), and its distinct weather patterns rendering palaeoenvironmental data from South Asia (e.g. Yadava et al. 2004; Yadava & Ramesh 2005; Caner et al. 2006; Gunnell et al. 2007), the Middle East (e.g. Fleitmann et al. 2003), East Asia (e.g. Gasse et al. 1991; Liu et al. 2004; Maher & Hu 2006) and North Africa (e.g. deMenocal et al. 2000) too remote to analyse Sri Lankan climate change during the early Mediaeval period. However, the current research being carried out by Dr. Kathleen Johnson, has the potential to produce an extremely fine resolution mapping of rainfall fluctuations over the past 2000 years (Johnson 2008 *pers. comm.*). Such higher precision palaeoclimatic data could examine the hypothetical dramatic increase in rainfall between the "Mediaeval Warm Period" and "Little Ice Age" suggested by Premathilake and Risberg (2003: 1538) (discussed in **2.2.4**), though this is more likely to have been a factor greater in the subsequent collapse of Polonnaruva (some three centuries after Anuradhapura).

Such research brings us neatly to another avenue for future archaeological research in Anuradhapura. The site of Polonnaruva has been widely excavated and restored during the work of the ASC in the first half of the 20th century (Karunaratne 1990). However, it has not been the subject of a multidisciplinary research project with a clear research question such as those that have focussed upon Anuradhapura in the past two decades (Coningham 1999 & 2006; Coningham et al. 2005, 2006a, 2006b, 2007a & 2007b). The collapse of Polonnaruva in the fourteenth century ripe for an archaeological examination, much as was the case with Anuradhapura the accepted narrative is one that has been formed almost solely through reference to the Pali chronicles. More significantly within the current context though, is the formative stages of Polonnaruva. What little is known of the city's developmental sequence is primarily sourced from epigraphic records and the Pali chronicles. For some time it was believed that Polonnaruva first became capital of Sri Lanka during the eighth century (e.g. Enriquez 1884: 68; Hocart 1926: 01), and though this has now been largely rejected, this would pose fascinating questions about the shift of power from Anuradhapura to Polonnaruva. It was posited above that Anuradhapura was abandoned as means of overcoming a crystallised socio-economic structure and diminishing marginal returns. However, it must currently be assumed that this transfer of power was only enabled by the Chola invasion. However, if Polonnaruva was intentionally developed as capital from the eighth century it would suggest a far more deliberate urban transfer as a mechanism to cope with economic stress. Of course until such archaeological investigations are carried out this remains entirely hypothetical. Finally, more detailed archaeological investigation of "Vijayabahu's Palace" within Anuradhapura's Citadel might also greatly assist our understanding of the urban transition from Anuradhapura to Polonnaruva.

9.4 Problems encountered

Undoubtedly the most significant problem encountered during this volume was the number of archaeological excavations that have not been published. It cannot be stressed enough just how damaging to Sri Lankan archaeology the continued failure to publish final reports from major excavations is. Normally under the heading of "future directions" (**9.3** above) one might suggest archaeological investigation of areas of Anuradhapura that are perhaps poorly understood at this moment in time, but these excavations by and large already been carried out, but they have *not* been published. During the 1980s excavations were carried out at Mantai (Carswell & Prickett 1984), at Anuradhapura's Jetavana (Ratnayake 1984) and Abhayagiri (Wikramagamage 1984 & 1992) monasteries, within Anuradhapura's Citadel (Deraniyagala 1986), and at Polonnaruva's Alahana Parivena (Prematilleke 1982a, 1982b, 1982c, 1985, 1987 & 1989). Additionally the first major settlement survey was carried out in the Sigiriya-Dambulla region (Bandaranayake et al. 1990).

Not one of these projects has produced a final report, and in the majority of cases just a *single* preliminary report is the only published data produced by multiple field seasons of excavation at some of Sri Lanka's most important archaeological sites. Such a state of affairs is lamentable, and can only hinder the development of Sri Lankan archaeological research. Certainly within this volume alone, the consideration of the Sacred City was hugely hindered by the sporadic publication of the CCF excavations.

A secondary problem encountered was one of chronological resolution. It is always difficult to refine the chronological dating of archaeological episodes as precisely as might be liked. However, within the secular hinterland, away from deep sequences, imported ceramics, epigraphic records and other such diachronically diagnostic artefacts this proved impossible. The one local coarseware that was identified as chronologically diagnostic of late occupation, the appliqué wares, was found at just a single site and from surface collection – limiting the significance that could be attached to it.

9.5 Significance of research

Perhaps, most obviously, this volume has established the eleventh century collapse of Anuradhapura (Chapter Eight), in addition to establishing that to developing an archaeological signature for that collapse across the three zones of Anuradhapura (Chapter Five, Six and Seven). Confirmation of Anuradhapura's collapse might seem relatively unimportant – it has, after all, been accepted for over a century. However, previously understanding of this collapse was built upon relatively superficial textual readings and utilised archaeology only to support claims made within the Pali chronicles – rather than truly analysing the archaeological data within a clear methodological and theoretical framework. This volume has succeeded in identifying the characteristics of collapse (as defined by Renfrew 1984) within the archaeological record of Anuradhapura, clearly identifying the collapse of the city around the eleventh century AD.

However, and of far greater significance, the eleventh century Chola invasion, long blamed for that collapse, has been found to be a wholly inadequate explanation for that collapse. Its reliance upon individuals and a *dues ex machina* to explain the failure of a previously highly successful social and economic urban form were rejected, and the far more sophisticated synthetic polycausal Imperial Model has been identified as broadly supported through explicit reference to the archaeological record, presenting for the first time an archaeologically supported explanation for Anuradhapura's eleventh century collapse.

On a wider scale, it is hoped that this volume has succeeded in contributing to the linking of theoretical collapse literature (e.g. Renfrew 1984, Tainter 1988) with an explicitly archaeological approach to testing and modelling collapse. It is approaches such as this that will enable the formation of *archaeological* collapse theory, rather than historical, economical or environmental theories that are then applied to archaeological data.

Finally, it is hoped that this volume will in some small way assist in removing the collapse of Anuradhapura from the nationalist political debate, which has for far too long framed this event in confrontational ethnic and religious language (see Coningham & Lewer 1999 and 2000). Such abuse of archaeology is sadly more relevant than ever in Sri Lanka, with recent accusations that archaeologists are working alongside the Sri Lankan armed forces in the north and east of the island to identify Buddhist sites within the former "Tamil strongholds" (Page 2010). Coningham stated recently that; *"that debate will never be answered archaeologically"* (*ibid.*). While this may be true, it is incumbent on archaeologists working in Sri Lanka that the abuse of archaeology for political aims is minimised, and this is only possible through poly-vocal collaborative archaeological projects, and the full and complete publishing of all data (*ibid.*).

Certainly, the collapse of Anuradhapura was not the result of Saivite, Indian or Tamil aggression, instead it would appear to have been the victim of its own economic success, as Phillips wrote; *"the problem is... that some states last so long"* (1979: 138).

References

Abu-Lughod, J., 1969. 'Varieties of Urban Experience: Contrast, Coexistence, and Coalescence in Cairo'. In I.M.Lapidus (ed.) *Middle Eastern Cities: A Symposium on Ancient, Islamic and Contemporary Middle Eastern Urbanism*: 159-187. Berkeley; University of California Press.

Agnihotri, R., Dutta, K., Buhshan, R. &Somayajulu, B.L.K., 2002. 'Evidence for solar forcing on the Indian monsoon during the last millennium'. *Earth and Planetary Science Letters* **198**: 521-527.

Allchin, F.R. (ed.), 1995.*The Archaeology of Early Historic South Asia: The Rise of Cities and States*. Cambridge; Cambridge University Press.

Amerasinghe, F.P., Konradsen, F., Fonseka, K.T. & Amerasinghe, P.H., 1997. *Anopheles (DipteraL Culcidae) breeding in a traditional tank-based village ecosystem in north central Sri Lanka.* Journal of Medical Entomology **34**: 290-297.

Amerasinghe, F.P., Konradsen, F., van der Hoek, W., Amerasinghe, P.H., Gunawardena, J.P.W., Fonseka, K.T. & Jayasinghe, G., 2001. *Small irrigation tanks as a source of malaria mosquito vectors: A study in north-central Sri Lanka.* Research Report 57.Colombo; International Water Management Institute.

Aristotle. 1984. *The Politics* (translated by C.Lord). Chicago; University of Chicago Press.

Arthur, P. & Patterson, H., 1994. 'Ceramics and Early Medieval central and Southern Italy: A "Potted History"'. In R.Francovich & G.Noyé (eds.) *La Storia dell'alto Mediovo Italiano (VI-X Secolo) alla Luce dell Archeologia*:409-441. Firenze; Instituto della Mediovo Italiano.

Arthur, J.W., 2006. *Living with Pottery: Ethnoarchaeology among the Gamo of Southwest Ethiopia.*Salt lake City; University of Utah Press.

Arunachalam, P., 2004. *Polonnaruva bronzes and Siva worship and Symbolism*. New Delhi; Asian Educational Services.

Ayrton, E.R., 1924. *Memoirs of the Archaeological Survey of Ceylon Vol.1*. Colombo; Archaeological Survey Department.

Bailey, S.D., 1952. *Ceylon*. London; Hutchinson's University Library.

Bairoch, P., 1988. *Cities and Economic Development: From the Dawn of History to the Present*. Chicago; University of Chicago Press.

Balambal, V., 1998. *Studies in Chola History.*Delhi; Kalinga.

Bandaranayake, S.D., 1974. *Sinhalese Monastic Architecture: The Viharas of Anuradhapura*. Leiden; E.J.Brill.

Bandaranayake, S.D., 1980. 'Hypotheses on the Unity and Differentiation of Cultures: Patterns of Architectural Development in Monsoon Asia'.*Diogenes* **25**: 65-82.

Bandaranayake, S.D., 1984. *Sigiriya Project: First Excavation and Research Report*. Colombo; Ministry of Cultural Affairs.

Bandaranayake, S.D., Mogren, M. & Epitawatte, S. (eds.) 1990. *The Settlement Archaeology of the Sigiriya-Dambulla Region*. Colombo; University of Kelaniya.

Barrow, G.,1857. *Ceylon: Past & Present*. London; John Murray.

Basa, K.K., 1992.'Early glass beads in India'.*South Asian Studies* **8**: 91-104.

Basham, A.L., 1973. 'The Background to the rise of Parakkamabahu I'. In S.D.Saparamadu (ed.) *The Polonnaruva Period (3rd ed.)*: 11-24. Dehiwala; Tisara Prakasakayo.

Bass, G.F. & van Doornick, F.H., 1978.'An eleventh century shipwreck at Serce Liman, Turkey'. *International Journal of Nautical Archaeology* **7**: 119-132.

Begley, V., 1981. 'Excavations of Iron Age burials at Pomparippu, 1970'. *Ancient Ceylon* **4**: 49-96.

Bell, H.C.P., 1891. 'Numismatics: a find of Roman coins in Ceylon'. *Ceylon Literary Register* **6**(17): 133-135.

Bell, H.C.P. (ed.), 1892. *Archaeological Survey of Ceylon, Annual Report 1892*. Colombo; Ceylon Government Press.

Bell, H.C.P., 1893. *Archaeological Survey of Ceylon. Anuradhapura. Fifth Progress Report, April to June, 1891*.Colombo; Ceylon Government Press.

Bell, H.C.P. (ed.), 1904a. *Archaeological Survey of Ceylon, Annual Report 1890*. Colombo; Ceylon Government Press.

Bell, H.C.P. (ed.), 1904b. *Archaeological Survey of Ceylon, Annual Report 1891*. Colombo; Ceylon Government Press.

Bell, H.C.P. (ed.), 1904c. *Archaeological Survey of Ceylon, Annual Report 1892*. Colombo; Ceylon Government Press.

Bell, H.C.P. (ed.), 1904d. *Archaeological Survey of Ceylon, Annual Report 1893*. Colombo; Ceylon Government Press.

Bell, H.C.P. (ed.), 1904e. *Archaeological Survey of Ceylon, Annual Report 1894*. Colombo; Ceylon Government Press.

Bell, H.C.P. (ed.), 1911a. *Archaeological Survey of Ceylon, Annual Report 1907*. Colombo; Ceylon Government Press.

Bell, H.C.P. (ed.), 1911b. *Archaeological Survey of Ceylon, Annual Report 1910-1911*. Colombo; eylon Government Press.

Bell, H.C.P., 1914a.*Archaeological Survey of Ceylon, Plans and Plates for Annual Report 1892 (Tenth Report)*.Colombo; Ceylon Government Press.

Bell, H.C.P., 1914b.*Archaeological Survey of Ceylon, Plans and Plates for Annual Report 1893 (Eleventh Report)*.Colombo; Ceylon Government Press.

Bell, H.C.P., 1914c.*Archaeological Survey of Ceylon, Plans and Plates for Annual Report 1896 (Fifteenth Report)*.Colombo; Ceylon Government Press.

Bell, H.C.P., 1914d.*Archaeological Survey of Ceylon, Plans and Plates for Annual Report 1901 (Twentieth Report)*.Colombo; Ceylon Government Press.

Bellina, B. & Glover, I., 2004. 'The Archaeology of early contact with India and the Mediterranean world, from the 4th century BC to the 4th century AD.'In I.Glover & P.Bellwood (eds.) *Southeast Asia: From Prehistory to History*: 68-88.London; Routledge.

Bellwood, P., 1976.'Archaeological research in Minhasa and the Talaud Islands, Northeastern Indonesia'. *Asian Perspectives* **29**(2):240-288.

Birley, M.H., 1991. 'Guidelines for Forecasting the Vector-Borne Disease Implications of Water Resources Development'. PEEM Guidelines Series no. 2.Geneva; World Health Organization.

Bopearachchi, O., 1998. 'Archaeological Evidence on Changing Patterns of International Trade Relations of Ancient Sri Lanka'.In O.Bopearachchi & D.P.M.Weerakkody (eds.) *Origin, Evolution and Circulation of Foreign Coins in the Indian Ocean*: 133-178. New Delhi; Manohar.

Bopearachchi, O., 2006. 'Coins'.In R.A.E.Coningham (ed.) *Anuradhapura: The British-Sri Lankan Excavations at Anuradhapura Salgaha Watta 2, Vol. 2: The Artefacts*: 7-26. Oxford; Archaeopress.

Bopearachchi, O. & Weerakkody, D.P.M. (eds.), 1998.*Origin, Evolution and Circulation of Foreign Coins in the Indian Ocean*. New Delhi; Manohar.

Boserup, E., 1981. *Population and Technological Change*. Chicago; University of Chicago Press.

Bouzek, J. (ed.), 1993. *Ceylon, Between East and West: Anuradhapura Abhayagiri Vihara 1981-1984*. Prague; Charles University.

Bouzek, J., 1993. 'Other Clay Objects'.In J.Bouzek (ed.) *Ceylon, Between East and West: Anuradhapura Abhayagiri Vihara 1981-1984*: 91-96. Prague; Charles University.

Bouzek, J., Břeň,J., & Charvát, P., 1986. 'The chronology of the local pottery and other finds and features uncovered in the SW sector of the Abhayagiri Vihara (Anuradhapura, Sri Lanka)'. *Archeogické rozhledy* **38**: 241-262.

Bradley, R.S. & Jones, P.D., 1993. '"The Little Ice Age" Summer temperature variations: their nature and relevance to recent global warming trends.' *The Holocene* **8**: 477-483.

REFERENCES

Brand, M., Lowry, G.D., Desai, Z-D.A. & Petruccioli, A., 1985. *Fatephur-Sikri: A Sourcebook*. Cambridge, Mass.; MIT Press.

Brodie, A.O., 1853. 'Rock Inscription at Gurogoda Vihare in the Magul-Ko'rale, Seven Korales'. *Journal of the Royal Asiatic Society of Ceylon* **2**(6): 59-64.

Brohier, R. L., 1934.*Ancient Irrigation Works of Ceylon.Part II, Northern and North-Western Sections of the Island.*Colombo; The Ministry of Mahaweli Development.

Brohier, R.L., 1941. *The History of Irrigation and Agricultural Colonization in Sri Lanka: The Tamankaduwa District and the Elahera-Minneriya Canal*. Colombo; Ceylon Government.

Buchanan, F., 1870.*A Journey through the Countries of Mysore, Canares and Malabar.*Madras; Government Press.

Burrows, S.M., 1886. *Report on Archaeological Work in Anuradhapura and Polonnaruva, Sessional Paper X*. Colombo; Government of Ceylon.

Burrows, S.M., 1887a. 'Jottings from a Jungle Diary'. *Journal of the Royal Asiatic Society of Ceylon* **10**(34): 01-13.

Burrows, S.M., 1887b. 'A Year's Work At Polonnaruwa'. *Journal of the Royal Asiatic Society of Ceylon* **10**(34): 46-82.

Caner, L., Lo Seen, D., Gunnell, Y., Ramesh, B.R. & Bourgeon, G., 2006. 'Spatial heterogeneity of land cover response to climatic change in the Nilgiri highlands (Southern India) since the last glacial maximum.' *The Holocene* **17**(2): 195-205.

Carswell, J., & Prickett, M., 1984. 'Mantai 1980: A Preliminary Investigation. *Ancient Ceylon* **5**: 03-80.

Cartman, J., 1957. *Hinduism in Ceylon*. Colombo; M.D.Gunasena.

Casal, J.M., 1949.*Fouilles de Virampatnam-Arikamedu.*Paris; Publications de la Commission des Fouilles archéologiques.

Ceylon. 1892. Reports of the Central and Provincial Irrigation Boards for 1890. In *Papers Laid Before the Legislative Council of Ceylon During the Session of 1891 (vol.1)*: 27-110. Colombo; Ceylon Government Press.

Ceylon Department of Irrigation., 1892. *Memorandum for the Information and Guidance of Provincial Boards*. Colombo; Ceylon Government Press.

Ceylon Department of Irrigation., 1894. *Memorandum on the Duties of Guardians and others in charge of Irrigation Works*. Colombo; Ceylon Government Press.

Chakravarti, R., 2008.'Agricultural Technology in Early Medieval India (c. A.D. 500 1300).*The Medieval History Journal* **11**(2): 229-258.

Chanda, R., 1926. 'The Indus Valley in the Vedic Period'. *Memoir of the Archaeological Survey of India* **31**: 2-5. Calcutta; Government of India Central Publications Branch.

Chandra, R.G., 1996. *Indian Symbolism: Symbols as Sources of Our Customs and Beliefs.*New Delhi; Munshiram Manoharlal.

Chattopadhaya, B., 1977. *Coins and Currency Systems in South India c. AD 225-1300.*New Delhi; Munshiram Manoharlal.

Chetty, S.C., 1848. 'A Royal Grant, Engraved on a Copper Plate'.*Journal of the Royal Asiatic Society of Ceylon* **1**(3): 109-110.

Childe, V.G., 1950. 'The Urban Revolution'. *Town Planning Review* **21**: 3-17.

Childe, V.G., 1951. *Social Evolution*. London; Watts & Co.

Chilvers, E.R., 2004. *Ancient DNA and Palaeopathology: Malaria in Ancient Greece*. University of Manchester' unpublished PhD thesis.

Chittick, N., 1974.*Kilwa: An Islamic Trading City on the East African Coast.*Nairobi; British Institute in Eastern Africa.

Chhabra, B.C., Sircar, D.C. & Desai, Z.A., 1953. 'Epigraphical research'. *Ancient India* **9**: 207-232.

Christie, T..N., 1891. 'Kalawewa Water Supply: Return to an Order of the Legislative Council of Ceylon dated November 5, for – A Return showing the Periods from March 1, 1888, to September 30, 1890, during which the Water in Kalawewa has been above Spill-level'. In *Papers Laid Before the Legislative Council of Ceylon During the Session of 1890*: 37-40. Colombo; Ceylon Government Press.

Clark, C. & Haswell, M., 1966. *The Economics of Subsistence Agriculture*. London; Macmillan.

Codrington, H.W., 1924. *Ceylon Coins & Currency*. Colombo; Colombo Museum.

Codrington, H.W., 1960. 'The Decline of the Medieval Sinhalese Kingdom'. *Journal of the Ceylon Branch of the Royal Asiatic Society* n.s.**7**(1): 93-103.

Codrington, H.W. & Paranavitana, S., 1934. *Epigraphia Zeylanica Vol.IV*. Oxford; Oxford University Press.

Codrington, K. de B., 1969. 'Excavations at the Gedige site'. *Ceylon Today* **18**(9): 32-34.

Coningham, R.A.E., 1991. 'Anuradhapura Citadel Archaeological Project: Preliminary Report of the Second Season of Sri Lankan British Excavations at Salgaha Watta, June-August 1990'. *South Asian Studies* **7**: 167-175.

Coningham, R.A.E., 1992. 'Anuradhapura Citadel Archaeological Project: Preliminary Report of a Geophysical Survey at the Citadel, 1991'. *South Asian Studies* **8**: 179-188.

Coningham, R.A.E., 1993a. *Urban Texts: An Interpretation of the Architectural, Textual, and Artefactual Records of a Sri Lankan Early Historic City*.Cambridge University; Unpublished PhD thesis.

Coningham, R.A.E., 1993b. 'Anuradhapura Citadel Archaeological Project: Preliminary Results of the Excavation of the Southern Rampart, 1992'. *South Asian Studies* **9**: 111-122.

Coningham, R.A.E., 1994a. 'Anuradhapura Citadel Archaeological Project: Preliminary Results of a Season of Geophysical Survey, 1993'. *South Asian Studies* **10**: 179-188.

Coningham, R.A.E., 1994b.'Notes on the construction and destruction of ancient Sri Lankan buildings'. In B.Allchin (ed.) *Living Traditions: Studies in the Ethnoarchaeology of South Asia*: 69-82.New Delhi; Oxford & IBH.

Coningham, R.A.E. (ed.), 1999. *Anuradhapura: The British-Sri Lankan Excavations at Anuradhapura Salgaha Watta 2.Vol. 1: The Site*. BAR International Series 824. Oxford; Archaeopress.

Coningham, R.A.E. (ed.), 2006. *Anuradhapura: The British-Sri Lankan Excavations at Anuradhapura Salgaha Watta 2. Vol. 2: The Artefacts*. BAR International Series 1508. Oxford; Archaeopress.

Coningham, R.A.E. & Allchin, F.R., 1992. 'Anuradhapura Citadel Archaeological Project: Preliminary Report of the Third Season of Sri Lankan British Excavations at Salgaha Watta, June-September 1991'. *South Asian Studies* **8**: 155-167.

Coningham, R.A.E. & Allchin, F.R., 1995. 'The rise of cities in Sri Lanka' In Allchin, F.R. (ed.) *The archaeology of early historic South Asia*. Cambridge; Cambridge University Press. 152-183.

Coningham, R.A.E. & Batt, C.M., 1999. 'Dating the Sequence'.In R.A.E. Coningham (ed.) *Anuradhapura: The British-Sri Lankan Excavations at Anuradhapura Salgaha Watta 2.Vol. 1: The Site*: 125-133. BAR International Series 824. Oxford; Archaeopress.

Coningham, R.A.E. & Cheetham, P., 1999. 'The Fortifications'.In R.A.E. Coningham (ed.) *Anuradhapura: The British-Sri Lankan Excavations at Anuradhapura Salgaha Watta 2.Vol. 1: The Site*: 47-69. BAR International Series 824. Oxford; Archaeopress.

Coningham, R.A.E. & Harrison, P., 2006. 'Metal Objects'. In R.A.E.Coningham (ed.), *Anuradhapura: The British-Sri Lankan Excavations at Anuradhapura Salgaha Watta 2. Vol. 2: The Artefacts*: 27-76.BAR International Series 1508. Oxford; Archaeopress.

Coningham, R.A.E. & Lewer, N., 1999. 'Paradise Lost: The Bombing of the Temple of the Tooth – A UNESCO World Heritage Site in South Asia'. *Antiquity* **73**: 857-866.

Coningham, R.A.E. & Lewer, N., 2000. 'The Vijayan colonisation and the archaeology of identity in Sri Lanka'. *Antiquity* **74**: 707-712.

REFERENCES

Coningham, R.A.E. & Strickland, K.M., 2007. 'South Asia - Sri Lanka'. In D.M.Pearsall (ed.) *Encyclopaedia of Archaeology*. Miamisburg, Ohio; Elsevier.

Coningham, R.A.E. & Gunawardhana, P. (eds.) 2013. *Anuradhapura Volume 3: The Hinterland*. BAR International Series 2568. Oxford; Archaeopress.

Coningham, R.A.E., Gunawardana, P., Adikari, G., Schmidt, A., Simpson, I., Young, R. & Adderley, P., 2005. *Upper Malvatu Oya Exploration Project Seasons I & II (2005)*. Report for the Director General of Archaeology, Sri Lanka.

Coningham, R.A.E., Gunawardana, P., Adikari, G., Katugampola, M., Simpson, I., & Young, R.L., 2006a. 'The Anuradhapura (Sri Lanka) Project: the hinterland (phase II), preliminary report of the first season 2005. *South Asian Studies* **22**: 53-64.

Coningham, R.A.E., Gunawardana, P., Adikari, G., Schmidt, A., Simpson, I., Stern, B., Young, R., Adderley, P. & Strickland. K., 2006b. *Upper Malvatu Oya Exploration Project Season III (2006)*. Report for the Director General of Archaeology, Sri Lanka.

Coningham, R.A.E., Gunawardana, P., Manuel, M.J, Adikari, G., Katugampola, M., Young, R.L., Schmidt, A., Krishnan, K., Simpson, I., McDonnell, G., & Batt, C.M., 2007a. 'The State of theocracy: defining an Early Medieval hinterland in Sri Lanka'. *Antiquity* **81**: 699-719.

Coningham, R.A.E., Gunawardana, P., Adikari, G., Schmidt, A., Simpson, I., Young, R., Adderley, P., Strickland. K. & Manuel, M.J., 2007b. *Upper Malvatu Oya Exploration Project Season IV (2007)*. Report for the Director General of Archaeology, Sri Lanka.

Coningham, R.A.E., Gunawardana, P., Davis, C.E., Adikari, G., Simpson, I.A., Strickland, K.M., Gilliland, K. & Manuel, M.J. 2012. 'Contextualising the Tabbova-Maradanmaduva 'Culture': Excavations at Nikawewa, Tirappane Division, Anuradhapura District'. *South Asian Studies* **28**(1): 01-14.

Coningham, R.A.E., Gunawardhana, P., Adikari, G., Strickland, K.M., Manuel, M.J., Senanayake, J., Namalgamuwa, H. & Rammungoda, U.R., 2013. 'Chapter 7: Excavation'. Pp. 135-190 in R.A.E. Coningham & P. Gunawardhana (eds.) *Anuradhapura Volume III: The Hinterland* 2568. BAR International Series. Oxford; Archaeopress.

Gilliland, K., Simpson, I.A., Adderley, W.P., Burbidge, C.I., Cresswell, A.J., Sanderson, D.C.W., Coningham, R.A.E., Gunawardhana, P., Adikari, G., Manuel, M.J., Strickland, K.M., Young, R.L., Namalgamuwa, H., Rammungoda, U.R. & Senanayake, J., 2013. 'Chapter 8: Environment and Water Management'. Pp. 191-228 in R.A.E. Coningham & P. Gunawardhana (eds.) *Anuradhapura Volume III: The Hinterland*. BAR International Series 2568. Oxford; Archaeopress.

Coomaraswamy, A.K., 1906. 'Sinhalese earthenware'. *Spolia Zeylanica* **4**(13): 1-18; (14 & 15): 135-141.

Cooray, P.O., 1984. *An Introduction to the Geology of Sri Lanka (2nd ed.)* Colombo; National Museum of Sri Lanka.

Costa, P.M. & Wilkinson, T.J., 1987. 'The Hinterland of Sohar: Archaeological Surveys and Excavations within the Region of an Omani Seafaring City'. *Journal of Oman Studies* **9**: 01-238.

Cousins, L.S., 1996. 'The Dating of the Historical Buddha: A Review Article'. *Journal of the Royal Asiatic Society (3rd Series)* **6**(1): 57-63.

Crowley, T.J. & Lowery, T.S., 2000. 'How warm was the Medieval warm period?' *Ambio* **29**:51-54.

Culbert, T.P., 1973. *The Classic Maya Collapse*. Albuquerque; University of New Mexico Press.

Cunliffe, B. (ed.), 1984. *Danebury: an Iron Age Hillfort in Hampshire, Vol. 1, the Excavations, 1969-1978: The Site*. London; Council for British Archaeology.

Dales, G.F. 1964 (Reprinted 1979). The Mythical Massacre at Mohenjo-daro. In G.L.Possehl (ed.), 1979, *Ancient Cities of the Indus*: 293-296. New Delhi; Vikas.

Dales, G.F., 1966 (Reprinted 1979). 'The Decline of the Harappans'. In G.L.Possehl (ed.), 1979, *Ancient Cities of the Indus:* 307-312. New Delhi; Vikas.

Dales, G.F., 1987. 'The Phenomenon of the Indus Civilisation'. In M.Jansen, M.Mulloy & G.Urban (eds.) *Forgotten Cities on the Indus:* 129-144. Mainz; Verlag Philipp von Zabern.

Davis, C., 2008. *The Antiquity of Caste: a British colonial construct?* MA Durham University, Department of Archaeology; Unpublished MA thesis.

Deraniyagala, P.E.P., 1933. 'Cured Marine Products of Ceylon'. *Ceylon Journal of Science* **5**: 49-77.

Deraniyagala, P.E.P., 1957. *Administrative Report for the Acting Archaeological Commissioner for 1957.* Colombo; Government of Ceylon.

Deraniyagala, P.E.P., 1960. *Administrative Report for the Acting Archaeological Commissioner for 1958.* Colombo; Government of Ceylon.

Deraniyagala, S.U., 1972. 'The Citadel of Anuradhapura: excavations in the Gedige area.' *Ancient Ceylon* **2**: 48-169.

Deraniyagala, S.U., 1984. 'A Classification System for Ceramics in Sri Lanka'. *Ancient Ceylon* **5**: 109-114.

Deraniyagala, S.U., 1986. 'Excavations in the Citadel of Anuradhapura: Gedige 1984 a preliminary report.' *Ancient Ceylon* **6**: 39-48.

Deraniyagala, S.U., 1990. 'The proto and early Historic radiocarbon chronology of Sri Lanka'. *Ancient Ceylon* **12**: 251-292.

Deraniyagala, S.U., 1992. *The Prehistory of Sri Lanka (2 vols.).* Colombo; Archaeological Survey Department.

Dewaraja, L.J. 1988. *The Kandyan Kingdom of Sri Lanka (1707-1782).* Colombo; Lake House Investments.

Diamond, J., 2005. *Collapse: How Societies Choose to Fail or Survive.* London; Allen Lane.

Dias, M., 1990. 'Inscriptions – 800 -1200 A.D.'. In N.Wijesekera (ed.) *Archaeological Department Centenary Commemorative Series Volume Two: Inscriptions*: 151 – 212. Colombo; Department of Archaeology.

Dias, M., 2001. *The Growth of Buddhist Monasteric Institutions in Sri Lanka from Brahmi Inscriptions.* Colombo; Department of Archaeology.

Dias, M., 2008. 'Trade in Ancient Sri Lanka: Epigraphical Evidence (3rd BC – 7th AD)'. In N.Chutiwongs & N.de Silva (eds.) *Roland Silva: Felicitation Volume*: 78-83. Colombo; Postgraduate Institute of Archaeology.

Dikshit, M.G., 1969. *History of Indian Glass.* Mumbai; University of Bombay.

Disanayaka, J.B., 2000. *Water Heritage of Sri Lanka (2nd ed.).* Colombo; University of Colombo.

Eck, D.L., 1987. 'The City as a Sacred Center'. In B.L.Smith & H.B.Reynolds (eds.) *The City as a Sacred Center: Essays on Six Asian Contexts*: 01-11. Leiden; E.J.Brill

Erdosy, G., 1995. 'City States of North India and Pakistan at the time of the Buddha', in F.R.Allchin (ed.) *The Archaeology of Early Historic South Asia: The Emergence of Cities and States*: 99-122. Cambridge; Cambridge University Press.

Fagan, B.M., 2007. *People of the Earth: An introduction to world prehistory.* 12th ed. New York; Longman.

Farmer, B.H., 1954. 'Problems of Land Use in the Dry Zone of Ceylon'. *The Geographical Journal* **120**(1): 21-31.

Ferguson, D., 1905. 'Roman coins found in Ceylon'. *Journal of the Royal Asiatic Society for 1905*

Flannery, K.V., 1972. 'The Cultural Evolution of Civilisations'. *Annual Review of Ecology and Systematics* **3**: 399-426.

Flannery, K.V., 1994. 'Childe the evolutionist: A perspective from Nuclear America'. In D.R.Harris (ed.) *The Archaeology of V. Gordon Childe: Contemporary Perspectives*: 101-119. London' UCL Press.

Fleitmann, D., Burns, S.J., Mudelsee, M., Neff, U., Kramers, J., Mangini, A. & Matter, A., 2003. 'Holocene forcing of the Indian monsoon recorded in a stalagmite from Southern Oman.' *Science* **300**: 1737-1739.

Fletcher, R., 2009. 'Low-Density, Agrarian-Based Urbanism: A Comparative View'. *Institute for Advanced Studies: Insights* **2**(4): 01-19.

REFERENCES

Fletcher, R., 2011. 'Low Density, Agrarian Based Urbanism'. Pp. 285-320 in M.Smith (ed.) *Comparative Archaeology and Complex Societies*. Cambridge; Cambridge University Press.

Fletcher, R., Penny, D., Evans, D., Pottier, C., Barbetti, M., Kummu, M. & Lustig, T., 2008. 'The water management network of Angkor, Cambodia.' *Antiquity* **82**: 658-670.

Forbes, J., 1841. *Eleven Years In Ceylon: Comprising sketches of the field sports and natural history of that colony and an accountof its history and antiquities*. London; Richard Bentley.

Foss, C., 1979. *Ephesus after Antiquity: A Late Antique, Byzantine and Turkish City*. Cambridge; Cambridge University Press.

Francis, P., 1982.*The Glass Beads of India.*New York; Lapis Route Books.

Francis, P., 1989.'Beads and Bead Trade in Southeast Asia'. *Contributions of the Centre for Bead Research* **4** (Lake Placid, New York).Centre for Bead Research.

Francis, P., 2002. *Asia's Maritime Bead Trade: 300 B.C. to the Present*. Honolulu, HI; University of Hawaii Press.

Geiger, W., (ed.), 1929.*Culavamsa (2 vols.)*. London; Pali Text Society.

Geiger, W., (ed.), 1934.*The Mahavamsa*. London; Pali Text Society.

Geiger, W., (ed.) 1960.*Culture of Ceylon in Medieval Times*. Wiesbaden; Otto Harrassowitz.

Geiger, W., (ed.), 2003. *The Mahavamsa: The Great Chronicle of Ceylon*. Dehiwela; Buddhist Cultural Centre.

Gill, R., 2000. *The Great Maya Droughts*. Albuquerque; University of New Mexico Press.

Glover, I. C., 1990. 'Early Trade between India and Southeast Asia: A Link in the Development of a World Trading System'. *Occasional Papers* 16. Hull; The University of Hull, Centre for Southeast Asian Studies.

Glover, I. C., 1996.'The southern Silk Road: archaeological evidence for early trade between India and Southeast Asia'. In A.Srisuchat (ed.) *Ancient Trades and Cultural Contacts in Southeast Asia*: 57-94. Bangkok; The Office of the National Culture Commission.

Godakumbura, C.E., 1961. *Administrative Report for the Archaeological Commissioner for 1961*. Colombo; Government of Ceylon.

Godukumbura, C.E., 1963.*Sinhalese Architecture.*Colombo; Government of Ceylon.

Goonetileke, H.A.I., 1963. 'A Bibliography of Ceylon Coins and Currency: Ancient, Mediaeval and Modern'. *The Ceylon Journal of Historical and Social Sciences* **6**(2): 187-242.

Grove, J.M., 1988. *The Little Ice Age*. London; Routledge.

Gunasekera, B., 1882. 'Two Sinhalese Inscriptions'. *Journal of the Royal Asiatic Society of Ceylon* **7**(25): 181-207.

Gunasekera, U.A.Prematilleke, P.L. & Silva, R., 1971. 'A corpus of pottery forms found in Ceylon'.*Ancient Ceylon* **1**: 166-192.

Gunasingam, M., 1999. *Sri Lankan Tamil nationalism: a study of its origins*. Sydney; MV.

Gunawardana, R.A.L.H., 1971. 'Irrigation and hydraulic society in early medieval Ceylon.' *Past and Present* **53**: 3-27.

Gunawardana, R.A.L.H., 1979.*Robe & Plough*. University of Arizona Press.

Gunawardana, R.A.L.H., 1984. 'Inter-Social Transfer of Hydraulic Technology in Pre-Colonial South Asia: Some Reflections Based on a Preliminary Investigation'. *Southeast Asian Studies* **22**(2):115-142.

Gunnarsson, B.E. & Linderholm, H.W., 2002. 'Low frequency summer temperature variation in central Sweden since the tenth century inferred from tree rings.' *The Holocene* **12**(6): 667-671.

Gunnell, Y., Krishnamurthy, A. & Sultan, B., 2007. 'Response of the South Indian runoff-harvesting civilization to northeast monsoon rainfall variability during the last 2000 years: instrumental records and indirect evidence.' .' *The Holocene* **17**: 207-215.

Hall, K.R., 1977. 'Price Making and Market Hierarchy in Early Mediaeval South India'. *Indian Economic Social History Review* **14**: 207-230.

Harischandra, B.W., 1908 (reprinted 1985). *The Sacred City of Anuradhapura* 2nd ed.). New Delhi; Asian Educational Services.

Harrison, T., 1965.'"Dunsun" Jars: from Mayfair and Friesland through Cairo to Sabah'.*Sarawak Museum Journal* **13**: 69-74

Harvey, P., 1990. 'Venerated Objects and Symbols of Early Buddhism'.In K.Werner (ed.) *Symbols in Art and Religion: The Indian and the Comparative Perspectives*: 68-102.London; Curzon.

Haug, G.H., Gunther, D., Peterson, L.C., Sigman, D.M., Hughen, K.A., & Aeschliman, B., 2003. 'Climate and the collapse of the Maya Civilisation.' *Science* **299**: 1731-1735.

Heitzman, J., 1987. 'State Formation in South India, 850-1280'. *Indian Economic Social History Review* **24**: 35-61.

Hettiaratchi, S.B., 1990. 'Procolamation, Clearing, Maintenance and Landscaping of Sites and Monuments 1910-1930'.In N.Wijesekera (ed.)*Archaeological Department Centenary (1890-1990), Commemorative Series Volume One: History of the Department of Archaeology*: 43-74. Colombo; Department of Archaeology.

Higham, C., 2004.'Mainland Southeast Asia from the Neolithic to the Iron Age'.In I.Glover & P.Bellwood (eds.) *Southeast Asia: From Prehistory to History*: 41-67.London; Routledge.

Hocart, A.M. (ed.), 1924. *Anuradhapura*. Colombo; Archaeological Survey Department.

Hocart, A.M. (ed.), 1926. *Memoirs of the Archaeological Survey of Ceylon, Volume II: Three Temples at Polonnaruva*. Colombo; Ceylon Government Press.

Hocart, A.M., 1928a. 'Town Planning'. *Ceylon Journal of Science G* **1**(4): 150-156.

Hocart, A.M. (ed.), 1928b. *Archaeological Survey of Ceylon, Annual Report 1927-1928*. Colombo; Ceylon Government Press.

Hocart, A.M., 1930. 'Archaeological Summary'. *Ceylon Journal of Science* **2**(2): 73-98.

Horton, M.C., 1986. 'Asiatic Colonization of the East African Coast: The Manda Evidence'.*Journal of the Royal Asiatic Society* **2**: 201-212.

Houtart, F., 1977. 'Theravada Buddhism and Political Power-Construction and Destruction of its Ideological Function'.*Social Compass* **24**: 207-246.

Hughes, M.K. & Diaz, H.F., 1994. 'Was there a "Medieval Warm Period", and if so, where and when?' *Climatic Change* **26**: 109-142.

Hughes, S. (ed.), 1996. *The International Canal Monuments List*. Paris; ICOMOS.

Hulagalle, H.A.J., 2000. *Ceylon of the Early Travellers 5th ed*. Colombo; Arjuna Hulagalle Dictionaries.

Hunt, R.C. & Hunt, E., 1976. 'Canal Irrigation and Local Social Organisation'. *Current Anthropology* **17**(3): 389-411.

Indrapala, K. (ed.), 1971a.*Collapse of the Rajarata Civilization in Ceylon and the Drift to the South-West*. Peradeniya; University of Ceylon.

Indrapala, K., 1971b. 'Two Inscriptions from the 'Hindu Ruins', Anuradhapura'. *Epigraphia Tamilica*: 01-05. Jaffna; Jaffna Archaeological Society.

Indrapala,K., 2005. *The Evolution of an Ethnic Identity: The Tamils in Sri Lanka c. 300 BCE to c. 1200 CE*. Sydney; MV Publications.

Indrawooth, P., 2004. 'The Early Buddhist Kingdoms of Thailand'.In I.Glover & P.Bellwood(eds.) *Southeast Asia from Prehistory to History*: 120-148. London; Routledge.

Jayatilika, C.J., Sakthivadivel, R., Shinogi, Y., Makin, I.W. & Witharana, P., 2001. 'Predicting Water Availability in Irrigation Tank Cascade Systems: The Cascade Water Balance Model'. IWMI Research Report 48. Colombo; International Water Management Institute.

REFERENCES

Jayatilika, C.J., Sakthivadivel, R., Shinogi, Y., Makin, I.W. & Witharana, P., 2003.'A simple water balance modelling approach for determining water availability in an irrigation tank cascade system'.*Journal of Hydrology* **273**: 81-102.

Jobin, W., 1999. 'Dams and Disease: Ecological Design and Health Impacts of Large Dams, Canals and Irrigation Systems'. London; E&FN Spon.

Johnson, K., 2008., Personal communication, e-mail 21.04.2008.

Jones, P.D., Osborn, T.J. & Briffa, K.R., 2001. 'The evolution of climate over the last millennium'. *Science* **292**: 662-667.

Kane, P.V., 1955. 'The Supposed Carnage of the City People by the Aryans'. In the: *Presidential Address, Indian History Congress: Proceeding of the 16th Session, Waltair 1953.* Pp: 12-17. Calcutta; Indian History Congress Association.

Karashima, N., 2008.'Temple land in Chola and Pandyan inscriptions: The legal meaning and historical implications of *Kuḍinīṅgā-dēvadāna*.*The Indian Economic and Social History Review* **45**(2): 175-199.

Karashima, N. & Subbarayalu, Y., 2007. 'Kaniyalar old and new: Landholding policy of the Chola state in the twelfth and thirteenth centuries'.*The Indian Economic and Social History Review* **44**: 1-17.

Karlén, W., Fastook, J.L., Holmgren, K., Malmström, M., Matthews, J.A., Odada, E., Risberg, J., Rosqvist, G., Sandgren, P., Shemesh, A. & Westerberg, L.A., 1999a. 'Glacier Fluctuations on Mount Kenya since 6000 cal. years BP: Implication for Holocene climate change in Africa.' *Ambio* **28**(5): 409-417.

Karlén, W., Källén, E., Rodhe, H. & Backman, J., 1999b. 'Man-made versus natural climate change.' *Ambio* **28**(4): 376-377.

Karunananda, U.B., 2006. *Nuwarakalawiya and the North Central Province under British Administration 1833 – 1900.* Kelaniya; Research Centre for Social Sciences, University of Kelaniya.

Karunaratne, W.S., 1990. 'History of Department 1890-1910'.In N.Wijesekera (ed.)*Archaeological Department Centenary (1890-1990), Commemorative Series Volume One: History of the Department of Archaeology*: 3-41. Colombo; Department of Archaeology.

Kennedy, K.A.R., 1995. 'Have Aryans been identified in the prehistoric skeletal record from South Asia Biological anthropology and concepts of ancient races'. In G.Erdosy (ed.) *The Indo-Aryans of Ancient South Asia*: 32-66. Berlin; Walter de Gruyter.

Kenoyer, J.M. 1998., *Ancient Cities of the Indus Valley Civilisation.* Oxford; Oxford University Press.

Khan, F.A., 1963.*Banbhore; a preliminary report on the recent archaeological excavations at Banbhore.* Karachi; Department of Archaeology & Museums.

Khan, F.A., 1964.'Excavations at Banbhore'.*Pakistan Archaeology* **1**: 49-55.

Klejn, L.S., 2001. 'Meta-archaeology'. *Acta Archaeologica* **72**(1): Suppl.3. Copenhagen; Blackwell-Munksgaard.

Klinkenberg, E. (ed.), 2001. *Malaria risk mapping in Sri Lanka – results from the Uda Wela area.*Working Paper 21. Colombo; International Water Management Institute.

Klinkenberg, E., van der Hoek, W. & Amerasinghe, F.P., 2004. 'A Malaria Risk Analysis in an Irrigated Area of Sri Lanka'. *Acta Tropica* **89**: 215-225.

Knight, J., 1999. 'Monkeys on the Move: The Natural Symbolism of People-Macaque Conflict in Japan'. *The Journal of Asian Studies* **58**(3): 622-647.

Knighton, W., 1845. *The History of Ceylon from the Earliest Period to the Present Time.* London; Brown, Green & Longmans.

Knighton, W., 1854. *Forest Life in Ceylon.* London; Hurst & Blackett.

Knox, R., 1681. *An Historical Relation of the Island Ceylon, in the East Indies.* London; Richard Chiswell.

Knusel, C., Coningham, R.A.E. & Mann, S., 2006.'Human Remains'.In R.A.E.Coningham (ed.), *Anuradhapura: The British-Sri Lankan Excavations at Anuradhapura Salgaha Watta 2. Vol. 2: The Artefacts*: 619-627.Oxford; Archaeopress.

Kodagoda, N., 1992. 'Report on the bones collection'.In C.Wikramagamage *Abhayagiri Vihara Project, Anuradhapura: Second Report of the Archaeological Excavation at the Abhayagiri Vihara Complex*: 160-168. Colombo; Central Cultural Fund.

Kolb, C., 1985. 'Demographic Estimates in Archaeology: Contributions from Ethnoarchaeology on Mesoamerican Peasants'. *Current Anthropology* **26**(5): 581-599.

Kopp, H. (ed.), 1977. *The Samantapasadika (8 Vols)*. London; Pali Text Society.

Kosambi, D.D., 1955. 'Dhenukakata'. *Journal of the Asiatic Society of Bombay* **30**: 50-71.

Kramer, C., 1980. 'Estimating prehistoric populations: An ethnoarchaeological approach'. In M.T.Barrelet (ed.) *L'archeologie de l'Iraq*: 315-34. Paris; Centre National de la Recherche Scientifique.

Kramer, C., 1982. *Village Ethnoarchaeology: Rural Iran in Archaeological Perspective*. New York; Academic Press.

Krishna, B., 2000. *Foreign Trade in Early Medieval India*.New Delhi; Harman.

Krishnamurthy, R. & Wickramasinghe, S., (eds.) 2005. *A Catalogue of the Sangam Age Pandya and Chola Coins in the National Museum, Colombo, Sri Lanka*.Colombo; Department of the National Museums.

Kroger, J., 1995.*Nishapur: Glass of the Early Islamic Period*.New York; The Metropolitan Museum of Art.

Lahiri, N., 1992.*The Archaeology of Indian Trade Routes up to c.200 BC: Resource Use, Resource Access and Lines of Communication*.Delhi; OUP.

Lahiri, N., 1998. 'South Asian demographic archaeology and Harappan population estimates: A brief reassessment'.*Indian Economic SocialHistory Review* **35**: 01-22.

Lal, B.B., 1997. *The Earliest Civilisation of South Asia: Rise, Maturity and Decline*. New Delhi; Aryan Books International.

Lamb, A., 1965. 'Some observations on stone and glass beads in early Southeast Asia'. *Journal of the Malaysian Branch of the Royal Archaeological Society* **38**: 87-124.

Lambrick, H.T. 1967. 'The Indus Flood Plain and the 'Indus' Civilisation'. *Geographical Journal* **133**(4): 483-495.

Leach, E.R., 1959. 'Hydraulic Society in Ceylon'. *Past and Present* **15**: 02-26.

Leach, E.R., 1961.*Pul Eliya, a Village in Ceylon*.Cambridge; Cambridge University Press.

Leach, E., 1995. Aryan Invasions over Four Millennia. In E.Ohnuki-Tierney (ed.) *Culture Through Time: anthropological approaches*: 227-245. Stanford; Stanford University Press.

Lee, L.F., 1871. 'Notes on a Sannas'. *Journal of the Royal Asiatic Society of Ceylon* **5**(16): 08-11.

Lemercinier, G., 1981. 'Relationships between Means of Production, Caste and Religion: The case of Kerala between the 13th and the 19th Century'. *Social Compass* **28**: 163-199.

Lewis, B., 1958. 'Some Reflections on the Decline of the Ottoman Empire'. *Studia Islamica* **9**: 111-127.

Lewis, J.P., 1895 (reprint 1993). *A Manual of the Vanni Districts of Ceylon*. New Delhi; Navrang.

Liebeschuetz, J.H.W.G., 2001. *The Decline and Fall of the Roman City*. Oxford; Oxford University Press.

Liesching, L., 1869. *Annual Administration Report for North Central Province, 1869*. Colombo; Ceylon Government Press.

Liu, Z., Harrison., S.P., Kutzbach, J. & Otto-Bliesner, B., 2004. 'Global monsoons in the mid-Holocene and oceanic feedback'. *Climate Dynamics* **22**: 157-182.

Liyanarachchi, G.A., 2009. 'Accounting in ancient Sri Lanka: some evidence of the accounting and auditing practices of Buddhist monasteries during 815 1017 AD'. *Accounting History* **14**:101-120.

Lucero, L., 2002. 'The Collapse of the Classic Maya: a case for the role of water control'. *American Anthropologist* **104**: 814-826.

REFERENCES

McIntosh, J.R., 2002. *A Peaceful Realm: The Rise and Fall of the Indus Civilisation*. Pp: 185-216. New York; Nevraumont.

Mackay, E.J.H., 1937. 'Chanhu-daro Excavations'. *Journal of the Royal Society of Arts* **85**: 528-529.

Maher, B.A. & Hu, M., 2006. 'A high-resolution record of Holocene rainfall variations from the western Chinese Loess Plateau: antiphase behaviour of the African/Indian and East Asian summer monsoons.' *The Holocene* **16**(3): 309-319.

Maisels, C.K., 1999. *Early Civilisations of the Old World: The Formative Histories of Egypt, The Levant, Mesopotamia, India and China*. London; Routledge.

Manguin, P-Y., 2004. 'The archaeology of early maritime polities of Southeast Asia'.In I.Glover & P.Bellwood (eds.) *Southeast Asia: From Prehistory to History*: 282-313.London; Routledge.

Mann, M.E., Bradley, R.S. & Hughes, M.K., 1999. 'Northern hemisphere temperatures during the past millennium: Inferences, uncertainties, and limitations.' *Geophysical Research Letters* **26**: 759-762.

Mansfield, H.C. Jnr., 1979. *Machiavelli's New Modes and Orders: A Study of the 'Discourse on Livy'*. Ithaca; Cornell University Press.

Manuel, M.J., Young, R.L., Coningham, R.A.E., Gunawardhana, P., Adikari, G., Katugampola, M., Senanayake, J. & Rammungoda, U.R. 2013. 'Chapter 5: Survey Data'. Pp. 49-96 in R.A.E. Coningham & P. Gunawardhana (eds.) *Anuradhapura Volume III: The Hinterland* 2568. BAR International Series. Oxford; Archaeopress.

Marcus Fernando, W.B., 1990. 'Section III: History of the Department of Archaeology, Sri Lanka 1930-1950. In N.Wijesekera (ed.), *Archaeological Department Centenary (1890-1990), Commemorative Series Volume One: History of the Department of Archaeology*: 75-116. Colombo; Department of Archaeology.

Marshall, J.H., 1951.*Taxila, an Illustrated Account of Archaeological Excavations*.Cambridge; Cambridge University Press.

Mazzarino, S. 1966. *The End of the Ancient World* (translated by G.Holmes). London; Faber and Faber.

de Menocal,P., Ortiz, J., Guilderson, T., Adkins, J., Sarnthein, M., Baker, L. & Yarusinsky, M., 2000. 'Abrupt onset and termination of the African Huid Period.Rapid climate responses to gradual insolation forcing.'*Quaternary Science Reviews* **19**: 347-361.

Miksic, J.N., 2004. 'The Classical Cultures of Indonesia'. In I.Glover & P.Bellwood(eds.) *Southeast Asia from Prehistory to History*: 234-256. London; Routledge.

Miller, D., 1985.*Artefacts as categories: A study of ceramic variability in Central India*. Cambridge;Cambridge University Press.

Mills, L.A., 1943. 'Government and Social Services in Ceylon'.*Far Eastern Survey* **12** (17): 171-175.

Misra, V.N., 1984. 'Climate, a Factor in the Rise and Fall of the Indus Civilisation: Evidence from Rajasthan and Beyond'. In B.B.Lal & S.P.Gupta (eds.) *Frontiers of the Indus Civilisation*. New Delhi; Books & Books. Reprinted in: N.Lahiri (ed.) 2000. *The Decline and Fall of the Indus Civilisation*: 239-250. Delhi; Permanent Black.

Mittre, V. & Robert, R.D., 1965. 'Pollen Analysis of middle Pleistocene samples from the gempits in Ceylon.' *Spolia Zeylanica* **30**(2): 1-8.

Morrill, C., Overpeck, J.T. & Cole, J.E., 2003. 'A synthesis of abrupt changes in the Asian summer monsoon since the last deglaciation.' *The Holocene* **13**: 465-476.

Mortazavi, M., 2004. *Systems Collapse: A Comparative Study of the Collapse of the Urban Communities of Southeast Iran in the Second Millennium BC*. Unpublished PhD thesis; Department of Archaeological Sciences, University of Bradford.

Muller, E.B., 1880. 'Text and translations of the Inscription of Mahindo III at Mihintale'. *Journal of the Royal Asiatic Society of Ceylon* **6**(21): 05-36.

Muller, E.B., 1883. *Ancient Inscriptions in Ceylon (2 vols.)*. London; Trubner & Co.

Muller, M. (ed.), 1967.*Manudharmasastra*.New Delhi; New Delhi Press.

Murphey, R.,1957. 'The Ruins of Ancient Ceylon'. *The Journal of Asian Studies* **16**(2): 181-200.

Narain, A.K. & Roy, T.N., 1978.*Excavations at Rajghat.*Varanasi; Benares Hindu University Press.

Nicholas, C.W., 1960. 'A short account of the history of irrigation works up to the 11th century'. *Journal of the Royal Asiatic Society of Ceylon* **7**(1): 43-69.

Nicholls, L., 1921. 'Malaria and the Lost Cities of Ceylon'. *The Indian Medical Gazette* **56**(4): 1-13.

Nilsson, M., Klarqvist, M., Bohlin, E. & Possnert, G., 2001. 'Variation in 14C age of macrofossils and different fractions of minute peat samples dated by AMS.' *The Holocene* **11**(5): 579-586.

Oertel, F.O., 1903. *Report on the Restoration of Ancient Monuments at Anuradhapura, Ceylon.* Colombo; Ceylon Government Press.

Oldenberg, H. (ed.), 2006. *The Dipavamsa: An Ancient Buddhist Historical Record.* New Delhi; AES.

Olivelle, P., 1974. *The Origin and the Early Development of Buddhist Monachism.*Colombo; Gunasena.

Olsson, I.U., 1974. 'Some problems in connection with the evaluation of 14C dates.' *Geologiska Föreningens i Stockholm Förhandlingar* **96**: 311-320.

Oomen, J.M.V., de Wolf, J. & de Jobin, W.R., 1990. 'Health and Irrigation'. Publication 45.Wageningen;International Institute for Land Reclamation and Improvement.

Page, J., 2010. 'Archaeology sparks new conflict between Sri Lankan Tamils and Sinhalese'. *The Times* 06.04.2010.

Panabokke, C.R., 1992. 'Rainfed Farming in the Dry Zone of Sri Lanka – Key Note Address'.In R.B.Mapa (ed.) *Rainfed Farming in the Dry Zone of Sri Lanka*: 01-12.Peradeniya; University of Peradeniya.

Panabokke, C.R., 1999.*The small tank cascade systems of the Rajarata: Their setting, distribution patterns and hydrography.* Colombo; Mahaweli Authority of Sri Lanka.

Paranavitana , S., 1936. *Excavations in the Citadel of Anuradhapura.* Colombo; Archaeological Survey Department.

Paranavitana, S. (ed.), 1950. *Archaeological Survey of Ceylon, Annual Report 1950.*Colombo; Ceylon Government Press.

Paranavitana, S. (ed.), 1953. *Archaeological Survey of Ceylon, Annual Report 1953.*Colombo; Ceylon Government Press.

Paranavitana, S., 1958. 'Some Regulations Concerning Village Irrigation Works in Ancient Ceylon'. *The Ceylon Journal of Historical and Social Studies* **1**: 01-07.

Parker, H., 1909. *Ancient Ceylon.* London; Luzac.

Parpola, A., 1994. *Deciphering the Indus Script.* Cambridge; Cambridge University Press.

Patmanatan, C., 2002a. 'Tamil Inscription from the Apaikiri Site, Anuradhapura.'.In P.Schalk & A.Veluppillai (eds.) *Buddhism Among Tamils in Pre-Colonial Tamilakam and Ilam. Vol.2: The Period of the Imperial Cola, Tamilikam and Ilam*: 683-690.Uppsala; AUU.

Patmanatan, C., 2002b. 'The Makkotaippalli of Anuradhapura'.In P.Schalk & A.Veluppillai (eds.) *Buddhism Among Tamils in Pre-Colonial Tamilakam and Ilam. Vol.2: The Period of the Imperial Cola, Tamilikam and Ilam*: 694-698.Uppsala; AUU.

Patmanatan, C., 2002c. 'The Rajarajapperumpalli at Periyakulam'.In P.Schalk & A.Veluppillai (eds.) *Buddhism Among Tamils in Pre-Colonial Tamilakam and Ilam. Vol.2: The Period of the Imperial Cola, Tamilikam and Ilam*: 767-776.Uppsala; AUU.

Pearse, V., Pearse, J., Buchsbaum, M. & Buchsbaum, R., 1987.*Living Invertebrates.*Oxford; Blackwell Scientific Publications.

Perera, L.S., 2003. *The Institutions of Ancient Ceylon from Inscriptions, Volume II, Part 1 (from 813 to 1016 AD) : Political Institutions.*Kandy ; International Centre for Ethnic Studies.

Peiris, G., 1977. 'The Physical Environment' in K.M.de Silva (ed.) *Sri Lanka: A Survey*: 03-30. Honolulu; University Press of Hawaii.

REFERENCES

Phillips, D.A., 1979. 'The Growth and Decline of States in Mesoamerica'. *Journal of the Steward Anthropological Society* **10**: 137-159.

Piggot, S., 1961. *Prehistoric India*. Pp: 238-239, 285-288. Middlesex. Reprinted in: N.Lahiri (ed.) 2000. *The Decline and Fall of the Indus Civilisation*: 282-285. Delhi; Permanent Black.

Pirta, R.S., Gadgil, M. & Kharshikar, A.V., 1997. 'Management of the Rhesus Monkey *Macaca mulatta* and Hanuman Langur *Presbytis entellus* in Himachal Pradesh, India.' *Biological Conservation* **79**: 97-106.

Plato., 1926. *Laws* (translated by R.G.Bury). Cambridge, Mass.; Harvard University Press.

Polybius., 1979. *The Rise of the Roman Empire* (translation by Ian Scott-Kilvert). Harmondsworth; Penguin.

Porter, V., 1998. 'Islamic coins found in Sri Lanka'. In O.Bopearachchi & D.P.M.Weerakkody (eds.) *Origin, Evolution and Circulation of Foreign Coins in the Indian Ocean*: 225-272. New Delhi; Manohar.

Possnert, G., 1990. 'Radiocarbon dating by accelerator technique.' *Norwegian Archaeological Review* **23**: 30-37.

Possehl, G.L., 2002. *The Indus Civilisation: A Contemporary Perspective*. Walnut Creek; Alta Mira Press.

Premathilake, T. R., 2006. 'Relationship of environmental changes in central Sri Lanka to possible prehistoric land-use and climate changes'. *Paleogeography, Paleoclimatology, Paleoecology* **240**: 468-496.

Premathilake, T. R. & Caratini, C., 1994. *Pollen-analytical study of sediments from Sigiriya, Sri Lanka - A Preliminary Report for the French Institute of Pondicherry, India.*

Premathilake, T. R. & Risberg, J., 2003. 'Late Quaternary Climate history of the Horton Plain, Central Sri Lanka'. *Quaternary Science Review* **22:** 1525-1541.

Prematilleke, L. & Silva, R., 1968. 'A Buddhist Monastery Type of Ancient Ceylon Showing Mahayanist Influences'. *Artibus Asiae* **30**(1): 61-84.

Prematilleke, P.L., 1982a. *Alahana Parivena, Polonnaruva: First Archaeological Excavation Report*. Colombo; Ministry of Cultural Affairs.

Prematilleke, P.L., 1982b. *Alahana Parivena, Polonnaruva: Second Archaeological Excavation Report*. Colombo; Ministry of Cultural Affairs.

Prematilleke, P.L., 1982c. *Alahana Parivena, Polonnaruva: Third Archaeological Excavation Report*. Colombo; Ministry of Cultural Affairs.

Prematilleke, P.L., 1985. *Alahana Parivena, Polonnaruva: Fourth Archaeological Excavation Report*. Colombo; Ministry of Cultural Affairs.

Prematilleke, P.L., 1987. *Alahana Parivena, Polonnaruva: FifthArchaeological Excavation Report*. Colombo; Ministry of Cultural Affairs.

Prematilleke, P.L., 1989. *Alahana Parivena, Polonnaruva: FifthArchaeological Excavation Report*. Colombo; Ministry of Cultural Affairs.

Pushparatnam, P., 2002. *Ancient Coins of Sri Lankan Tamil Rulers*. Jaffna; Bavani Patippakam.

Rafique Mughal, M., 1992. 'The Consequences of River Changes for the Harappan Settlements in Cholistan'. *Eastern Anthropologist* **45**. Reprinted in: N.Lahiri (ed.) 2000. *The Decline and Fall of the Indus Civilisation*: 188-200. Delhi; Permanent Black.

Ragupathy, P., 1987. *Early Settlementsin Jaffna: An Archaeological Survey*. Madras; Author.

Rahula, W., 1993. *A History of Buddhism in Ceylon*. Dehiwala; the Buddhist Cultural Centre.

Raikes, R.L., 1964 (Reprinted 1979). 'The End of the Ancient Cities of the Indus'. In G.L.Possehl (ed.), 1979, *Ancient Cities of the Indus*: 297-306. New Delhi; Vikas.

Raikes, R.L., 1965. 'The Mohenjo-daro Floods'. *Antiquity* **39**: 196-203.

Raikes, R.L., 1967. *Water, Weather and Prehistory*. London; Humanities Press.

Raikes, R.L., 1968. 'Kalibangan: Death from Natural Causes'. *Antiquity* **42**: 286-293.

Rao, S.R., 1979. 'Lothal: A Harappan Port Town (1955-1962)'. *Memoirs of the Archaeological Survey of India* **1** (78).

Rao, G.V. & Rao, N.L. (eds.) 1987. *South Indian Inscriptions. Vol. XIII: Chola Inscriptions*.Mysore; Archaeological Survey of India.

Ratnayake, H., 1984. *Jetavanaramaya Project Anuradhapura; First Archaeological Excavation and Research Report.* Colombo; Central Cultural Fund.

Ratnayake, H., 2008. 'Ancient Anuradhapura.' In N.Chutiwongs & N.de Silva (eds.) *Roland Silva: Felicitation Volume*: 158-169. Colombo; Postgraduate Institute of Archaeology.

Ratnayake, H., 2010. 'Hindu Bronzes from Jetavanaramaya, Anuradhapura: Bronzes from Jetavana 1984 – Circumstances of the Discovery', in P.Gunawardhana, G.Adikaria & R.A.E.Coningham (eds.) *Sirinimal Lakdusinghe : felicitation volume*: 263-281. Battaramulla; Neptune.

Ray, H.P., 1987. 'China and the "Western ocean" in the Fifteenth Century'.In C.Satish (ed.) *The Indian Ocean – Explorations in History, Commerce and Politics*: 109-124.New Delhi; Chandra Sage.

Ray, H.P., 1989. 'Early historical trade: An overview'. *The Indian Economic & Social History Review* **26**: 437-457.

Ray, H.P., 1996. 'Early trans-oceanic contacts between South and Southeast Asia'. In A.Srisuchat (ed.) *Ancient Trades and Cultural Contacts in Southeast Asia*: 43-56.Bangkok; The Office of the National Culture Commission.

Reimers, E., 1929. *Constantine da Sa's Maps and Plans of Ceylon.* Colombo; Ceylon Government Press.

Renfrew, C. 1984. *Social Approaches In Archaeology.* Edinburgh; Edinburgh University Press.

Rhys Davids, T.W., 1871. 'Inscription at Wæligama Wihare: Text, Translation and Notes'. *Journal of the Royal Asiatic Society of Ceylon* **5**(16): 21-24.A

Ricalton, J., 1891. 'The City of the Sacred Bo-Tree – Anuradhapura'. *Scribner's Magazine* **10** (3): 319-335.

Richard, A.F., Goldstein, S.J. & Dewar, R.E., 1989. 'Weed Macaques: The Evolutionary Implications of Macaques Feeding Ecology.' *International Journal of Primatology* **10**(6): 569-594.

Roberts, C.R., 2005. 'Book review of C.Greenblatt & M.Spigelman (eds.) 2003 *Emerging Pathogens: archaeology, ecology and evolution of infectious disease*' Oxford; Oxford University Press'. *American Journal of Archaeology* **109**: 572-573.

Robinson, F. (ed.), 1989. *The Cambridge Encyclopaedia of India, Pakistan, Bangladesh, Sri Lanka, Nepal, Bhutan and the Maldives.* Cambridge University Press; Cambridge.

Rosen, F.A., 1830. *Rigvedae Specimen.* London; Taylor.

Sabloff, J.A. 1973. 'Major Themes in the Past Hypotheses of the Maya Collapse'. In T.P.Culbert (ed.) *The Classic Maya Collapse*: 35-40. Albuquerque; University of New Mexico Press.

Sahni, M.R. 1956. Bio-geological Evidence Bearing on the Decline of the Indus Valley Civilisation. *Journal of the Paleontological Society of India* **1**(1). Reprinted in: N.Lahiri (ed.) 2000. *The Decline and Fall of the Indus Civilisation*: 155-166. Delhi; Permanent Black.

Sallares, R. & Gomzi, S., 2000. 'Biomolecular archaeology of malaria'. *Ancient Biomolecules* **3**: 195-213.

Santiago, J.R., 1999a. *Sacred Symbols of Buddhism*.New Delhi; Book Faith India.

Santiago, J.R., 1999b. *Sacred Symbols of Hinduism*.New Delhi; Book Faith India.

Sauer, E.W., 2004. 'The Disunited Subject'.In E.W.Sauer (ed.) *Archaeology and Ancient History: Breaking Down the Boundaries*: 17-45. London; Routledge.

Schalk, P., 2002. 'Introduction to the Study of Buddhism among Tamils in Ilam during the Period of the Colas'.In P.Schalk & A. Veluppillai (eds.) *Buddhism Among Tamils in Pre-Colonial Tamilakam and Ilam. Vol.2: The Period of the Imperial Cola, Tamilikam and Ilam*: 672-681.Uppsala; AUU.

Schalk, P. & Veluppillai, A. (eds.), 2002. *Buddhism Among Tamils in Pre-Colonial Tamilakam and Ilam. Vol.2: The Period of the Imperial Cola, Tamilikam and Ilam*.Uppsala; AUU.

REFERENCES

Schmidt, A., 2005. 'The Geophysics'. In R.A.E.Coningham & P.Gunawardhana (eds.) *Upper Malwattu Oya Exploration Project: Preliminary Report of the 2nd Season 2005*: 13-22. Colombo; Office of the Director General of Archaeology.

von Schroeder, U., 1990. *Buddhist Sculptures of Sri Lanka*. Hong Kong; Visual Dharma.

Seely, P., Canby, S. & Coningham, R.A.E., 2006. 'Glazed Ceramics'.In R.A.E.Coningham (ed.) *Anuradhapura: The British-Sri Lankan Excavations at Anuradhapura Salgaha Watta 2, Vol. 2: The Artefacts*: 91-126. Oxford; Archaeopress.

Seneviratna, A., 1989. *The Springs of Sinhala Civilization: An Illustrated Survey of the Ancient Irrigation System of Sri Lanka*. New Delhi; Navrang.

Seneviratna, A., 1994. *Ancient Anuradhapura: The Monastic City*. Colombo; Archaeological Survey Department.

Seneviratna, A., 1998. *Polonnaruva: Medieval Capital of Sri Lanka*. Colombo; Archaeological Survey Department.

Shaffer, J.G., 1992. *Chronologies in Old World Archaeology: Indus Valley, Baluchistan and the Helmand. (Third Edition)*. Chicago; University of Chicago Press.

Shaw, J. & Sutcliffe, J., 2003.'Water management, patronage networks and religious change: new evidence from the Sanchi dam complex and counterparts in Gujarat and Sri Lanka'.*South Asian Studies* **19**: 73-104.

de Silva, G.P.S.H., 2000.*History of Coins and Currency in Sri Lanka*.Colombo; Central Bank of Sri Lanka.

de Silva, K.M. (ed.), 1977. *Sri Lanka: A Survey*. Honolulu; University Press of Hawaii.

de Silva, K.M., 1981. *A History of Sri Lanka*. Berkeley; University of California Press.

de Silva, K.M., 1999. 'Ceylon (Sri Lanka)'.In R.W.Winks (ed.) *The Oxford History of the British Empire: Volume V - Historiography*: 243-253.

de Silva, K.M., 2005. *A History of Sri Lanka*. Colombo; Vijitha Yapa Publications.

Silva, R., 1988. *Religious Architecture in Early & Medieval Sri Lanka*. Amsterdam; Krips Repro Meppel.

Simpson, I.A., Burbidge, C.I., Sanderson, D.C.W. & Adderley, W.P., 2008a. *Luminescence dating of sediments from ancient irrigation features, and associated with occupation of the hinterland around Anuradhapura, Sri Lanka*.Glasgow; Scottish Universities Environmental Research Center.

Simpson, I.A., Adderley, W.P., McKenzie, J.T., Gilliland, K., Young, R., Batt, C.M., Adikari, G., Madhushanka, G. & Algiriya, P., 2008b. *Arts and Humanities Research Council: The Anuradhapura Hinterland Project. Geoarchaeology Working Paper 1: Field Observations*. Unpublished working paper.

Singh, G. 1971. 'The Indus Valley Culture: Seen in the Context of Post-Glacial Climate and Ecological Studies in North-West India'. *Archaeology and Physical Anthropology in Oceania* **6**(2): 177-189.

Singh, G., Joshi, R.D., Chopra, S.K. & Singh, A.B., 1974. 'Late Quaternary History of Vegetation and Climate in the Rajasthan Desert, India'. *Philosophical Transactions of the Royal Society of London* **267**(889): 467-501.

Sinha, A.,Cannariato, K.G., Stott, L.G., Li, H-C., You, C-F., Cheng, H., Edwards, R.L. & Singh, I.B., 2005. 'Variability of Southwest Indian summer monsoon precipitation duringthe Bølling-¯Ållerød'. *Geology* **33**(10): 813-816.

Sinopoli, C.M., 1999.'Levels of Complexity: ceramic variability at Vijayanagara'. In J.M.Skibo & G.M.Feinman (eds.), *Pottery and People: a dynamic interaction*: 115-136. Salt Lake City; University of Utah Press.

Siriweera, W.I., 2004. *A History of Sri Lanka*. Colombo; Dayawansa Jayakodi.

Sjoberg, G., 1960. *The Pre-Industrial City: Past and Present*. Glencoe; Free press.

Skibo, J.M. 1999. 'Pottery and people'. In J.M..Skibo & G.M.Feinman (eds.) *Pottery and People: a dynamic interaction*: 1-8. Salt Lake City; University of Utah Press.

Smither, J.G., 1894. *Architectural Remains, Anuradhapura, Ceylon*.Colombo;Government of Ceylon Press.

Somasekaram, T. (ed.), 1988. *The National Atlas of Sri Lanka.* Colombo; Survey Department.

Soren, D., 2003. 'Can archaeologists excavate evidence of malaria?'. *World Archaeology* **35**(2): 193-209.

Sorokin, P.A., 1950. *Social Philosophies of an Age in Crisis.* Boston; Beacon Press.

Sorokin, P.A., 1957. *Social and Cultural Dynamics.* Boston; Porter Sargent.

Southworth, W.A.., 2004. 'The Coastal States of Champa'.In I.Glover & P.Bellwood(eds.) *Southeast Asia from Prehistory to History*: 209-233. London; Routledge.

Spencer, G.W., 1976. 'The Politics of Plunder; The Cholas in Eleventh-Century Ceylon' *Journal of Asian Studies* **35**(3): 405-419.

Spencer, G.W. 1983. *The Politics of Expansion: The Chola Invasion of Sri Lanka and Sri Vijaya.* Madras; New Era Publications.

Spencer, G.W. & Hall, K.R. 1974. 'Towards an analysis of dynastic hinterlands: The Imperial Cholas of 11th century South India'. *Asian Profile* **2**(1): 51-62.

Spengler, O., 1926. *The Decline of the West, Volume 1: Form & Actuality* (translated by C.F.Atkinson). London; George Allen & Unwin.

Srivastava, K.M. 1984. The Myth of Aryan invasion of Harappan Towns. In B.B.Lal & S.P.Gupta (eds.) *Frontiers of the Indus Civilisation:* 437-443. New Delhi: Books & Books.

Stein, A., 1931. An Archaeological Tour of Gedrosia. *Memoir of the Archaeological Survey of India* **43**. Calcutta; Government of India Central Publications Branch.

Stein, B., 1980. *Peasant State and Society in Medieval South India.* Oxford; Oxford University Press.

Still, J., 1907. 'Roman coins found in Ceylon'. *Journal of the Royal Asiatic Society of Ceylon* **19**(58): 161-190.

Still, J., 1909. 'Northern Province, East Wanni: Archaeological Tour'. In H.C.P. Bell (ed.) *Archaeological Survey of Ceylon, Annual Report 1905*: 24-38. Colombo; Ceylon Government Press.

Still, J., 1911. 'Northern Province, West Wanni: Archaeological Tour'. In H.C.P. Bell (ed.) *Archaeological Survey of Ceylon, Annual Report 1907*: 26-29. Colombo; Ceylon Government Press.

Still, J., 1930. *The Jungle Tide.* Edinburgh; William Blackwood & Sons.

Strickland, K.M., 2011. *Testing Collapse Theory: A Comparative Study of the Archaeolgical Characteristics of Societal Collapse.* Saarbrücken, Germany; VDM..

Subbarayalu, Y., 1973. *Political Geography of the Cholas Country.* Chennai; Tamilnadu State Department of Archaeology.

Tainter, J.A., 1988. *The Collapse of Complex Societies.* Cambridge; Cambridge University Press.

Tambiah, S., 1986. *Sri Lanka: ethnic fratricide and the dismantling of democracy.* New Delhi; Oxford University Press.

Tampoe, M., 1989.*Maritime Trade between China and the West: An Archaeological Study of the Ceramics from Siraf (Persian Gulf) between the 8th and 15th centuries AD.*Oxford; Archaeopress.

Tampoe, M., 1995. 'The Spice Island Route: Sri Lanka's Participation in Maritime Trade and the Archaeological Evidence from Mantai and Galle Harbour'.In G.P.S.H. De Silva & C.G.Uragoda (eds.) *Sesquicentennial Commemorative Volume of the Royal Asiatic Society of Sri Lanka 1845-1995*: 159 – 210.Colombo; Royal Asiatic Society of Sri Lanka.

Tennakoon, M.U.A., 1980. 'Desertification in the dry zone of Sri Lanka.' in R.L.Heathcoate (ed.) *Perception of Desertification.* Tokyo; United Nations University Press.

Tennent, J.E., 1860. *Ceylon(2 vols.)* London; Longman.

Thanikaomoni, G., 1985. *Mangrove palynology - A Preliminary Report for the French Institute of Pondicherry, India.*

Thantilage, A., 2010. 'Anuradhapura period bronzes of Sri Lanka: Schools and Resource-Utilisation'. http://www.archaeology.lk/uncategorize/anuradhapura-period-bronzes-of-sri-lanka-schools-and-resource-utilization Published 02/01/2010.Accessed 04.03.2010.

REFERENCES

Thapar, R.,1957.'Maski, a Chalcolithic site of the southern Deccan'.*Ancient India* **13**: 04-142.

Thapar, R., 1993. *Interpreting Early India*. Oxford; Oxford University Press.

Thapar, R., 2002. *Early India: From the Origins to AD 1300*. London; Allen Lane.

Thero, R.C., 2007: *The Impact of the Abhayagiri Practices on the Development of Theravada Buddhism in Sri Lanka*. University of Hong Kong; Unpublished PhD thesis.

Theunissen, R., Grave, P. & Bailey, G., 2000.'Doubts on Diffusion: Challenging the Assumed Indian Origin of Iron Age Agate and Carnelian Beads in Southeast Asia'.*World Archaeology* **32**(1): 84-105.

Thierry, F., 1998. 'Chinese coins from the Yapahuwa site in the collection at the Anuradhapura Museum'. In O.Bopearachchi & D.P.M.Weerakkody (eds.) *Origin, Evolution and Circulation of Foreign Coins in the Indian Ocean*: 191-223. New Delhi; Manohar.

Thirunavukkarasu, K.D., 1985. 'Rajaraja – The Great (985 – 1014 AD)'. In S.Venkatasubramaniyam (ed.) *Raja Raja Chola: The high Point in History*: 01-14. Madras; Authors Guild of India.

Thompson, J.E.S., 1970. *Maya History and Religion*. Norman; University of Oklahoma Press.

Tiffen, M., 1991. 'Guidelines for the Incorporation of Health Safeguards into Irrigation Projects through Intersectoral Cooperation'. PEEM Guidelines Series no. 1.Geneva; World Health Organisation.

Toynbee, A.J.1939-1961. *A Study of History (12 vols.)*. London; Oxford University Press.

Trigger, B.G. 2003. *Understanding Early Civilisations*. Cambridge; Cambridge University Press.

Turchin, P., 2003. *Historical Dynamics: Why States Rise and Fall*. Princeton; Princeton University Press.

Turnour, G., 1837. *The Mahavamsa: Part 1, with Translation Subjoined*. Colombo; Turnour.

Uduwara, J., 1990. 'Section V: History of the Department of Archaeology, 1970-1990'.In N.Wijesekera (ed.) *Archaeological Department Centenary (1890-1990), Commemorative Series Volume One: History of the Department of Archaeology*: 153-188. Colombo; Department of Archaeology.

Ueyama, Y. & Nosaki, S., 1993. *The Excavation Report of JOCV Project in the Citadel of Anuradhapura (1991-1992)*. Colombo; Archaeological Survey Department.

Uziel, J., 2010. 'Middle Bronze Ramparts: Functional and Symbolic Structures'.*Palestine Exploration Quarterly* **142: 24-30.**

Velde, B. & Druc, I.C., 1999. *Archaeological Ceramic Materials*.Berlin; Springer.

Vidanpatirana, P., 2008. 'The road network: within the city of Anuradhapura and the suburbs'. In N.Chutiwongs & N.de Silva (eds.) *Roland Silva: Felicitation Volume*: 220-229. Colombo; Postgraduate Institute of Archaeology.

Vignarajah, N., 1992. 'Rainfed farming in the Dry Zone of Sri Lanka – An overview'.In R.B.Mapa (ed.) *Rainfed Farming in the Dry Zone of Sri Lanka: Proceedings of a Symposium*: 01-12.Peradeniya; University of Peradeniya.

Veluppillai, A., 2002. 'A Critical Study of the Makkotaippalli Inscription from Anuradhapura'.In P.Schalk & A.Veluppillai (eds.) *Buddhism Among Tamils in Pre-Colonial Tamilakam and Ilam. Vol.2: The Period of the Imperial Cola, Tamilakam and Ilam*: 690-694.Uppsala; AUU.

Walimbe, S.R., 1993. 'The Aryans: the physical anthropological approach'. In S.B.Deo & S.Kamath (eds.) *The Aryan Problem*: 108-115. Bangalore; Maharashtra.

Webb, J.L.A., 2009. *Humanity's Burden: A Global History of Malaria*. Cambridge; Cambridge University Press.

Webster, D., 2002. *The Fall of the Ancient Maya*. New York; Thames & Hudson.

Weisshaar, H.-J. & Wijeyapala, W., 1993. 'Ancient Ruhuna (Sri Lanka). The Tissamaharama Project: Excavations at Akurugoda 1992-1993'. *Beiträge zur Allgemeinen und Vergleichenden Archäologie* **13**: 127-166.

Wenke, R.J., 2006. *Patterns in Prehistory: Humankind's first three million years*. 5th ed. London; Oxford University Press.

Wheeler, R.E.M., 1946. 'Arikamdeu: An Indo-Roman trading-station on the east coast of India'.*Ancient India* **2**: 17-24.

Wheeler, R.E.M., 1947. 'Harappan Chronology and the *Rgveda*'. *Ancient India: Bulletin of the Archaeological Survey of India* **3**: 58-130.

Wheeler, R.E.M., 1950. *Five Thousand Years of Pakistan*. Pp. 24-34. London; Christopher Johnson.

Wheeler, R.E.M., 1959. *Early India and Pakistan: To Asoka*. New York; Praeger.

Whitehouse, D., 1968.'Excavations at Siraf: first interim report'.*Iran* **6**: 1-22.

WHO (World Health Organisation)., 1999. *WHO Expert Committee on Malaria. Twentieth Report*. Technical Report Series, No. 892. Geneva; WHO.

Wickremasinghe, D.M.de Z., 1912. *Epigraphia Zeylanica Vol.I 1904-1912*. Oxford; Oxford University Press.

Wickremasinghe, D.M.de Z., 1928. *Epigraphia Zeylanica Vol.II 1912-1927*. Oxford; Oxford University Press

Wickremasinghe, D.M.de Z. & Codrington, H.W., 1933. *Epigraphia Zeylanica Vol.III 1928-1933*. Oxford; Oxford University Press.

Wikkramatileke, R., 1957. 'Hambegamuwa Village: An Example of Rural Settlement in Ceylon's Dry Zone'.*Economic Geography* **33**(4): 362-373.

Wisseman-Christie, J., 1990. 'Trade and state formation in the Malay peninsula and Sumatra, 300BC - AD700'. In J.Kathirithamby-Wells & J.Villiers (eds.) *The Southeast Asian Port and Polity: Rise and Demise*: 39-60.Singapore; Singapore University Press.

Wijayapala, W.H., 1990. 'Section IV: History of the Department of Archaeology, Sri Lanka: 1950-1970' in N.Wijesekera (ed.) *Archaeological Department Centenary (1890-1990), Commemorative Series Volume One: History of the Department of Archaeology*: 117-150. Colombo; Department of Archaeology.

Wijeyapala, W. & Prickett, M., 1986.*Sri Lanka and the International Trade: An Exhibition of Ancient Imported Ceramics found in Sri Lanka's Archaeological Sites*.Colombo; Department of Archaeology.

Wijesekera, N. (ed.), 1990. *Archaeological Department Centenary (1890-1990), Commemorative Series Volume One: History of the Department of Archaeology*. Colombo; Department of Archaeology.

Wijesuriya, G. 1998., *Buddhist Meditation Monasteries of Ancient Sri Lanka*. Colombo: Department of Archaeology.

Wikramagamage, C., 1984. *Abhayagiri Vihara Project, Anuradhapura: First Report of the Archaeological Excavation at the Abhayagiri Vihara Complex*. Colombo; Central Cultural Fund.

Wikramagamage, C., 1990. 'Section II: 500 – 1000 AD'. In N.Wijesekera (ed.) *Archaeological Department Centenary (1890-1990) Commemorative Series Volume Four: Sculpture*: 45-94. Colombo; Department of Archaeology.

Wikramagamage, C., 1992. *Abhayagiri Vihara Project, Anuradhapura: Second Report of the Archaeological Excavation at the Abhayagiri Vihara Complex*. Colombo; Central Cultural Fund.

Wikramagamage, C., 1998. *Entrances to the Ancient Buildings in Sri Lanka*. Colombo; Academy of Sri Lankan Culture.

Wikramagamage, C., Hettiarachchi, S., Bouzek, J.,Břeň. J., and Charvát, P., 1983. 'Excavations at Abhayagiri Vihara (Anuradhapura, Sri Lanka) in 1982'. *Archív Orientální* **51**: 337-371.

Wikramagamage, C., Hettiarachchi, S., Bouzek, J., Břeň, J., and Charvát, P., 1984. 'Excavations at Abhayagiri Vihara (Anuradhapura, Sri Lanka) in 1983'. *Archív Orientální* **52**: 42-74.

Wilkinson, C. K., 1973.*Nishapur: Pottery of the Early Islamic Period*.New York; Metropolitan Museum of Art.

Williamson, A., 1974.'Harvard Archaeological Survey in Oman, 1973: III Sohar and the Sea Trade of Oman in the Tenth Century AD'.*Proceedings of the Seminar for Arabian Studies* **4**: 78-96.

Wilson, J.A., 1960. 'Egypt through the New Kingdom: Civilisation without Cities'. In C.H.Kraeling & R.McC.Adams (eds.) *City Invincible: A Symposium on Urbanisation and Cultural Development in the Ancient Near East*: 124-164. Chicago; University of Chicago Press.

Wittfogel, K., 1957. *Oriental Despotism: A Comparative Study of Total Power.* New Haven; Yale University Press.

Wood, N., 1999.*Chinese Glazes: Their Origins, Chemistry and Recreation.* Philadelphia; University of Pennsylvania Press.

Wright, A., 1999 (reprint). *Twentieth Century Impressions of Ceylon.* New Delhi; Asian Educational Services.

Wypyski, M., 1992.'Technical analysis of Gandhara glass medallions'.In E.Errington & J.Cribb (eds.) *The Crossroads of Asia: Transformation in Image and Symbol*: 281-283.Cambridge; Ancient India and Iran Trust.

Yadava, M.G. & Ramesh, R., 2005. 'Monsoon reconstruction from radiocarbon dated tropical Indian speleothems.' *The Holocene* **15**: 48-59.

Yadava, M.G., Ramesh, R. & Pant, G.B., 2004. 'Past monsoon rainfall variations in peninsular India recorded in a 331-year-old speleothem'.*The Holocene* **14**: 517-524.

Young, R.L., Coningham, R.A.E., Nalinda, K., Perera, J., & Khan, H., 2006. 'Faunal Remains'. In R.A.E.Coningham (ed.) *Anuradhapura: The British-Sri Lankan Excavations at Anuradhapura Salgaha Watta 2, Vol. 2: The Artefacts*: 501-618. Oxford; Archaeopress.

Zarins, J. & Zahrani, A., 1985.'Recent Archaeological Investigations in the Southern Tihama Plain (The sites of Athar and Sihi, 1404/1984).*Journal of South Arabian Archaeology* 9: 65-107.

de Zoysa, L., 1873. 'Transcript and Translation of an ancient Copper-plate Sannas'.*Journal of the Royal Asiatic Society of Ceylon* 5(18): 75-79.

Websites Accessed:

http://lankapura.com/2009/11/ancient-hindu-goddess-durga-at-anuradhapura
(accessed 05.06.10)

http://www.mahaweli.gov.lk/Other Pages/DSWRPP_WEB_new/
(accessed 10.04.2010)

http://www.statistics.gov.lk/pophousat/index.asp
(accessed 20.01.2008